Classroom Assessment

Issues and Practices

Steven R. Banks
Marshall University

WAVELAND

PRESS, INC.

Long Grove, Illinois

For information about this book, contact:
Waveland Press, Inc.
4180 IL Route 83, Suite 101
Long Grove, IL 60047-9580
(847) 634-0081
info@waveland.com
www.waveland.com

CONTENTS

3   Planning for Instruction and Assessments   45

6   Constructing Formal Classroom Assessments   122

10 Using Standardized Assessments   215

11   Assessments, At-Risk Students, and Special Education   237

PREFACE

Issues and Practices

One advantage of a new textbook is the fresh look it can provide about contemporary issues and practices. This is especially important in the classroom assessment field. In recent years, few areas in education have changed so dramatically as classroom assessment. First and foremost, the No Child Left Behind Act has transformed the role of assessments in schools by mandating annual assessments as part of a federal system of educational accountability. Second, national accreditation organizations, such as National Council for Accreditation of Teacher Education (NCATE), have mandated standards-based performance and emphasized specific assessment benchmarks in meeting these standards. Third, the inclusion movement has brought about a change in many classroom assessment practices in order to accommodate the inclusion of special students in the regular education classroom.

Classroom Assessment: Issues and Practices addresses these topics as major themes of the book. The impact of No Child Left Behind is examined in Chapters 1 and 10 with a detailed summary of this legislation provided in an appendix. Standards-based performance is examined in Chapters 1 and 14. A full chapter, Chapter 11, is devoted to the issues of special education and assessment.

Other topical features of this textbook are separate chapters on informal assessment practices, performance assessment, and the assessment of teachers. Some additional unique highlights of this textbook include a review of Anderson and Krathwohl's revision of Bloom's Taxonomy (Chapter 3); a full chapter on diversity and gender issues (Chapter 4); and a full chapter on assessment and student motivation (Chapter 12).

Organization of the Book

The overall organization of the book falls into three basic sections. The first section (Chapters 1–4) examines some of the basic aspects of assessment practices, including state standards, instructional objectives, and assessments; taxonomies and assessments; and gender and diversity issues. The second section (Chapters 5–9) examines the actual construction of various types of classroom assessments. The third section (Chapters 10–14) examines a variety of other classroom assessment issues and practices, such as standardized testing, motivation and assessments, special education and assessments, and the assessment of teachers.

Chapter Features

The organization of each chapter follows the same basic sequence. Each chapter begins with the case study of a practicing teacher. The sequence continues with an introduction, a sectioned discussion of assessment practices and issues, a series of point/counterpoint debates, a set of teacher applications, a case study epilogue, a chapter summary, and a series of end-of-chapter activities. The activities include opportunities for students to construct their own portfolios as well as websites and activities for websites; to confirm their understanding of key concepts; and to answer self-assessment questions and chapter review questions. There are 14 case studies, 32 teacher application exercises, 42 websites, and over 200 multiple-choice and review questions in the book. The end-of-chapter activities provide the basis for a series of directed learning activities for your students. Additional instructor's resources can be accessed electronically by contacting your local representative.

Acknowledgments

I express my deep appreciation to the editorial staff at Allyn and Bacon. Their patience and perseverance are a central part of this book. In particular, I thank Arnis E. Burvikovs, senior editor; Megan Smallidge, editorial assistant; Tara Whorf, marketing manager; Andrew Turso, manufacturing buyer; and Joel Gendron, cover designer. Also thank you to freelancer Lynda Griffiths for her editorial-production services.

My appreciation goes to the following reviewers for their helpful comments on the manuscript: Jane Benjamin, Mansfield University; Susan M. Brookhart, Dusquesne University; Beth E. Gridley, Ball State University; Courtney Johnson, University of South Carolina; Audrey Kleinsasser, University of Wyoming; Anuradhaa Shastri, SUNY Oneonta; Brian G. Smith, Minnesota State University of Moorhead; Cindy M. Walker, University of Wisconsin-Milwaukee; and Dale Whittington, John Carroll University.

I thank David Holliway for writing Chapter 5 and Jane McKee and Karen Lucas for cowriting Chapter 8. I also express my appreciation to Jane McKee for her continued editorial help, support, and good counsel with this book.

Finally, it is important to give many thanks to family. To my beautiful wife, Anna, and to my wonderful daughter, Cathleen, I owe so much. They suffered through this book project just as I did. It is good for them to see it finally come to fruition. To my brothers and sisters, Marilyn, John, Anne, and Tom, I appreciate your keen wit and constructive critiques over these many years. To my parents, on your far distant shore, I give thanks and hope that you remain forever together.

1 Instruction and Assessment

CASE STUDY

Ms. Dupree was hired to teach chemistry in a large urban school district in the New England region. The school district had chronic teacher shortages in recent years. The school system actively recruited people in industry for the district's growing shortages in the physical sciences and mathematics. One recent hire was Ms. Dupree, who formerly was a chemist for eight years at a Fortune 500 company. She decided to teach for a number of reasons, including a long time interest in teaching and a desire to help young people.

Since Ms. Dupree had no education courses, she agreed to an alternative certification program that has two parts: a Master's of Art in Teaching (MAT program) and an intensive four-week in-service program before the start of the fall term. During her first week of the in-service program, Ms. Dupree was handed a bulletin that listed the 47 state-mandated objectives and 22 school district objectives for high school chemistry courses. A school administrator spent three hours explaining that these objectives are directly linked to the statewide accountability plan required by federal legislation under the No Child Left Behind Act. These objectives must be aligned with the curriculum, and Ms. Dupree must demonstrate this alignment in her lesson plans. The administrator stated that a good part of Ms. Dupree's teaching evaluation was dependent on how well she met these objectives and aligned her curriculum with them.

A school psychologist came to speak about assessments. Ms. Dupree listened intently, remembering the two-hour exams she took in her college chemistry classes. The school psychologist did not address classroom assessments; rather, he spent two hours discussing the importance of the statewide assessments and of increasing the school system's test scores. As part of the statewide accountability plan required by the No Child Left Behind Act, progress must be made on these statewide assessments. The school psychologist explained that a good part of Ms. Dupree's teaching evaluation was dependent on how well her students did on these test scores.

Ms. Dupree believed that she knew the chemistry field very well. In fact, she was certain that she could hold her own with most experts. She also is motivated to teach students at the high school level. But Ms. Dupree was left with a number of questions:

What do all these objectives mean?

How can any teacher actually meet every single objective?

What is a lesson plan and how do these objectives fit in a lesson plan?

Where do classroom assessments fit with lesson plans?

What are the current issues and problems with classroom assessments?

What should a new teacher know about assessment policies?

What is the relationship between accountability, instructional standards, and assessments?

Introduction

The first time I entered my own classroom was unlike any other that I experienced as a teacher. I cannot remember a more exhilarating or a more lonely moment. The exhilaration came from the feeling that finally I had made it on my own and this was what I should be doing. The loneliness was from knowing that it was all my responsibility now. I would either sink or swim from here on out. The only time that can compare with such aloneness was the first time I handed back a midterm exam and faced a class of unhappy teenagers.

The first moments in your own classroom will probably be the same. It is a time filled with anxiety, exhilaration, and a churning stomach. There is so much going on when you close that door. You are trying to deal with all the stress that a new job entails. You are full of hope and expectations about your career. You are face to face with the intense excitement and commotion of students at the start of a school year. In addition, you are about to take on a thousand and one new decisions.

These decisions vary from seating arrangements to homework assignments. You have to make choices about managing student behavior, developing your lesson plans, and determining the academic level of your students. Although it is not quite triage in a trauma center, it is difficult to prioritize all the different tasks.

Speaking of stress, many educators I know have the same recurrent nightmares at the start of each fall semester. I have had my own version of it for over 20 years. I walk in the classroom and I am incredibly late—by 30 to 40 minutes. Sometimes, I walk in and everyone starts laughing at me. Sometimes, I walk in the classroom and I am half-dressed. I always have these nightmares the week before classes start. After the first class, I somehow mentally sort things out and I never have the dreams again—until the next fall semester.

I think that whenever people enter a new situation, they invariably try to make sense of what is happening. For example, when you first begin your classes, you inevitably try to make sense out of all the chaos in your classroom. Either consciously or unconsciously, you also begin constructing a mental portfolio of each student's actions and achievements.

The best way to understand your students is to collect valid and reliable information about them. This is the fundamental role of positive assessment practices: to provide a framework that will allow you to collect quality information about your students. By using a variety of methods to collect this information, you will have an effective counterpoint to any unconscious or subjective impressions of your students.

Spinning off from this basic role is another important aspect about classroom assessments: to provide appropriate feedback to students and parents. If you collect quality information, then you can provide quality feedback to students about their performance. This will help them (and you) target areas for improvement.

Speaking of feedback to parents, portfolio assessments are excellent to use. Portfolios offer feedback about student performance, but they go way beyond that with parents. Parents often see a portfolio like a family album that displays their child's growth and development. Bring out a child's portfolio first whenever you have a parent-teacher conference. (You will thank me; it is a great icebreaker.)

Another related, but often overlooked, aspect about good assessment practices is the feedback it gives us about our teaching. Assessments can indicate what part of our instruction needs rethinking and reworking. Comparing our classroom assessments with certain standardized tests also may indicate areas that we need to concentrate on with our instruction.

Appropriately used, assessments have the potential to help both students and teachers to improve their classroom performance. A major theme of this book is to encourage you to integrate a variety of assessments into your everyday instructional practices. Teachers need to go beyond the more traditional forms of assessments. By using different types of assessments, you generate different types of information about your students. The greater the amount and variety of information collected, the more informed your decisions will be. *This constitutes the first law of assessment practices: A variety of assessments is the best policy.*

As part of the preceding themes, the first section of this chapter concentrates on the link between assessment and instruction. The second section focuses on some key policy issues that involve instruction and assessment practices. Among the policy issues reviewed in the second part of this chapter are educational accountability, student privacy rights, individual differences based on gender and cultural diversity, and inclusion for students with disabilities. The first two issues have recently been influenced by national events: the No Child Left Behind Act and the recent Supreme Court case on the Buckley Amendment. The issues of individual differences and inclusion are among the most critical questions in contemporary public education. Diversity and inclusion issues form a central and recurrent theme in this book. Separate chapters are devoted to reviewing diversity and special education issues.

Linking Assessment with Instruction

The Missing Link

When thinking about assessment and instruction, educators probably concentrate too much on using tests to determine grades. It is important to remember that grades are only one aspect of assessment practices. One change in this area involves the nature of assessment itself. **Assessment** currently is viewed as the collection and interpretation of all information gathered about a student. Thus, assessments can include everything from informal classroom observations to statewide achievement tests. When we make judgments and decisions about assessments, such as assigning grades, we are making evaluations.

I think that this viewpoint is critical for beginning teachers to understand. You need to move beyond just the traditional evaluator-student role. Assessments can be an informational tool that can help your students and your teaching. In developing the role of assessments in your classroom, try to view instruction and assessment as two sides of the same coin. Just as good instructional plans can enhance teaching, good assessment plans can enhance instruction. By making assessments an integral part of your instruction, you may provide "the missing link" between your instructional methods and your assessment practices.

Other aspects of classroom assessments also have changed. For example, informal assessments offer teachers another way to link instruction with assessment. By using probes and other structured questions, teachers can find out during instruction about the knowledge levels of their students. Informal assessments also can provide immediate instructional feedback. Since they are not used as part of classroom grades, the focus of informal assessments is solely on providing feedback. Therefore, informal assessments can be given immediately after instruction and can provide a quick gauge of the instruction and its effect on student performance.

Another part of this change in assessments practices is an increase in the use of peer assessments and self-assessments for aiding instruction. These assessments can elicit a variety of different viewpoints that may help students improve their class work. Appropriate feedback from peers can offer guidance and suggestions that sometimes may be missed by the teacher. Many educators increasingly use nonthreatening, ungraded assessments that concentrate both on finding out where students are coming from and on providing feedback about classroom activities. Here is an example of one type of peer assessment activity that teachers might use.

Teacher Application

Good Student Game

One example of using peer assessment techniques is exemplified by the Good Student Game (Landrum & Tankersley, 1997; Babyak, Luze, & Kamps, 2000). With this activity, teachers assign students to teams. Each team also is assigned an independent peer evaluator. The goal is to use cooperative learning and peer assessments to encourage appropriate classroom behaviors. The reward for appropriate activity may be extra free time or recess. This game is generally appropriate for elementary classrooms.

Team size should be three to six students. After dividing students into teams, the teacher assigns a student peer evaluator to assess each separate team. The peer evaluator assesses and monitors the points that each team is rewarded during classroom activities. For example, a team might receive 10 points for completing an academic task, remaining in seat, or remaining on task during the activity.

The amount of time to play the game and to be evaluated by the peer should be in relatively small increments in the beginning. For instance, the peer evaluator initially may make an assessment every 1 to 3 minutes, with the game being played 15 to 20 minutes. It is important to ensure that everyone understands the rules of the game and that there is a specific time limit from start to finish. It is also necessary to have a point penalty in place for arguing with the teacher, the evaluators, or team members. Before the game begins, the teacher needs to determine the reward or reinforcer for the team who wins the game.

A recent idea is that assessments can serve as a method of focusing students on certain aspects of instruction. This idea is sometimes called *using assessments as instructional magnets.* Classroom assessments are used to direct students to particular parts of the curriculum or to specific skills in a course. For example, a beginning teacher may want to emphasize class participation and discussion in her fifth-grade language arts unit. The teacher could design an assessment rubric that measures the amount of participation during class discussions. This can attract students to discussing material in the unit.

Not only can assessments serve as instructional guides, but different types of assessments can generate different ways of thinking in students. For instance, a portfolio assessment can stimulate ways of thinking that are different from thinking elicited by a traditional exam. Peer assessments can elicit unique perspectives that give feedback to students that goes beyond what the teacher can provide.

By providing a variety of assessment practices in your classroom, you may be able to increase the variety of cognitive skills in your students. Appropriately used, assessments have the potential to help students improve their classroom achievement. By the same token, integrating a variety of assessments into your everyday instructional practices can enhance your teaching performance.

Types of Objectives

The traditional role ascribed by the U.S. Constitution is that educational decisions are made at the state level, but now this has changed somewhat. The federal government has sharply increased its role in recent years with its requirements for statewide performance goals. Nevertheless, most curriculum decisions are generally decided by each individual state. This includes creating overall objectives for each specific grade level or academic program. Krathwohl and Payne (1971) state that there are three types of objectives in education: global, educational, and instructional. These objectives range from overall (global) objectives to specific classroom (instructional) objectives. A flowchart of these objectives along with their relationship to lesson plans and assessments is provided in Figure 1.1.

Global objectives generally are made at the state level. These types of objectives are usually determined by state school boards or curriculum committees of practicing educators. Global objectives, also known as *state standards and objectives,* are the most encompassing curriculum guidelines for each grade level. An example of a global objective is:

> Students will learn the concepts of responsible citizenship and will learn ways to participate in the democratic process.

The decision-making process for creating these objectives may be based on a variety of factors, including political and social considerations. Regardless of who determines global objectives, teachers generally are held accountable for addressing these objectives.

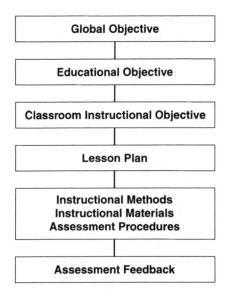

FIGURE 1.1 Instruction to Assessment

Although states differ in the degree of centralized authority concerning the creation of these overall instructional mandates, states now must formally submit a plan with explicit standards, objectives, and performance goals. They also must provide an assessment system to evaluate whether they achieve these goals. The standards, curriculum, and assessments must match. This is what is meant by *alignment of the standards with instruction,* which is part of the federal mandates under the No Child Left Behind Act. The standards and goals may still vary from state to state, but each state must submit a plan and will be held accountable to that plan.

After receiving the global objectives for instruction, most states or school districts further specify their objectives into what Krathwohl and Payne (1971) call **educational objectives**. This type of objective serves as an intermediate level of specification for curriculum and instructional decisions. In general, these types of objectives provide a common link among the schools in a given state or district. The following is an example of an educational objective for fifth grade:

> "In 5th grade students will list and explain the functions of the executive, legislative and judicial branches of government" (Marockie, 1996, p. 89).

Curriculum supervisors and teachers further develop global and educational objectives into classroom instructional objectives and lesson plans. Classroom **instructional objectives** are specific in nature and address a particular classroom activity. For instance, an example of an instructional objective for a fifth-grade social studies class is:

> Students will analyze and describe the concept of "separation of powers" as indicated in the United States Constitution.

Classroom instructional objectives also directly relate to the purpose, goals, and outcomes for a particular course. This level of objectives is the link to your lesson plans. **Lesson plans** are the teaching methods, classroom materials, and assessment procedures used in a classroom. The process of translating state mandates into local instructional objectives and lesson plans may occur in a number of different ways. For instance, school district curriculum committees may decide the basic plans for translating state standards into actual classroom instruction. Teachers who teach the same grades or subjects may meet and develop plans for their classes. Nevertheless, most school systems expect teachers to meet the state and local objectives by creating their own explicitly detailed set of lesson plans.

Many school districts base their annual reviews and tenure decisions of teachers on these lesson plans, observed classroom teaching performance, or student achievement on state standardized exams. In most states, performance assessments also are conducted on local school systems. School district performance assessments are a method of evaluating the overall performance of the school system. Generally, these are based on how well the school system meets state standards. Student achievement on standardized exams may be an important factor in the performance assessment of the school system.

Teacher Application

Instructional Decisions: Who Decides What?
When my grandmother began teaching in 1910, she worked in a one-room schoolhouse. It was so far up in the Appalachian Mountains that visits from the central office were as common as Christmas. Other than basic reading, spelling, and math books, she was pretty much left to her own devices about curriculum. Even during my own time in public schools in the 1970s, curriculum and instruction decisions generally were a matter between the teacher and the principal. That has changed quite a bit. Both federal and state involvement in instructional decisions has increased dramatically in the last 25 years.

A study completed by the Carnegie Foundation for the Advancement of Teaching (1988) illustrates some of these changes. Teachers from each of the 50 states were surveyed about instructional decisions. The survey measured teachers' own sense of involvement and control over three major professional areas: *curriculum decisions, textbooks/instructional materials,* and *student promotion/retention decisions.* Overall, teachers felt that they had less involvement in issues related to student promotion/retention (34 percent involvement) than in the issues of curriculum (63 percent involvement) and textbook/instructional issues (79 percent involvement). In fact, teachers in all 50 states generally had more involvement in curriculum and instructional issues than they did in student retention issues.

Many educators now believe that classroom teachers have even less involvement in instructional decisions than they did in the 1980s (Manzo & Hoff, 2003). This is a big concern among elementary school teachers, who appear to be more affected by the No Child Left Behind Act than are secondary school teachers. In particular, the emphasis on uniform reading and assessment practices in elementary schools appears to further limit teacher involvement in instructional decisions.

Objectives, Lesson Plans, and Assessments

As shown in Figure 1.1, there are a series of steps in moving from global objectives to specific lesson plans using this format. Let's return to Ms. Dupree, the new chemistry teacher in the Case Study. She needs to detail the steps involved in moving from global objectives to lesson plans. Ms. Dupree receives a set of global objectives and educational objectives. One global objective is:

> Students will demonstrate the ability to apply statistical formulas to different aspects of the physical sciences.

An educational objective for Ms. Dupree's course is:

> Students in tenth-grade chemistry courses will be able to complete the following statistical calculations: mass-mass, mass-volume, volume-volume to determine percent yield and heat of reaction.

This educational objective is further developed into specific instructional objectives. Ms. Dupree applies these instructional objectives to several lessons. One lesson may include the specific objective:

> The student will perform mass-mass calculations for various reactants and products of chemical reactions.

An instructional objective for another lesson may include:

The student will calculate the theoretical percent yield and the actual percent yield for various chemical reactions.

For the next step, most school systems expect teachers like Ms. Dupree to devise lesson plans that are aligned with the instructional objectives. These lesson plans are then used in classroom instruction. As previously noted, lesson plans contain three basic components: instructional methods, instructional materials, and assessment procedures. **Instructional methods** are the different types of teaching methods used to provide the information. Instructional methods may include the following practices:

- Lecture, discussion, or independent learning
- Cooperative learning groups or whole class instruction
- Computer-assisted instruction or traditional instruction
- Constructivist instruction or basic skills instruction

Ms. Dupree's instructional methods include teaching the mathematical basis for these formulas by lecture during whole class instruction. She also uses computer-assisted instruction.

Instructional materials are the actual format or materials used to present the information. These materials can range from simple flash cards to computer software programs. Ms. Dupree's instructional materials are worksheets with the basic formulas on them that supplement her lecture. She also assigns students to work on a computer software program that takes them through the steps needed in calculating these formulas.

The final step in Ms. Dupree's lesson plan is her assessment. **Assessments** are the total set of information gathered about students in the classroom. As mentioned previously, assessments may range from informal classroom quizzes to final exams. Ms. Dupree decides to use a weekly quiz to assess her students on the above objectives.

Another example of the transition from global objectives to lesson plans is provided here. The first step is the development of a global objective:

Students will demonstrate a level of proficiency in mathematical concepts and operations appropriate to their grade level.

The second step involves an educational objective for fourth grade:

"Students in 4th grade will add and subtract decimals to tenths, hundredths, thousandths" (Marockie, 1996, p. 71).

The third step is completed at the local level. This step takes the educational objective and translates it into an instructional objective that forms a logical instructional sequence. For instance, at the start of the school year an initial local instructional objective for decimals would be:

Students will be able to add the decimal .1 with .1.

For the next step, the individual teacher devises lesson plans that apply these objectives to specific classroom instruction. For example, one instructional method involves cooperative learning groups to teach the concepts involved in calculating basic

FIGURE 1.2   Assessment of Learning Outcomes

Tammy lives .6 mile from school. How many miles does she travel in one week, both to and from school?

List your answer first in decimals and whole numbers.

Then list the answer in fractions: _____

Which of the following is the correct answer for converting the fraction ¾ into a decimal number?
a. .070
b. .075
c. .75
d. .25
e. .05

Which of the following is the correct answer for converting the decimal .60 into a fraction?
a. 3/4
b. 3/7
c. 3/6
d. 3/5
e. 6/7

decimals. These cooperative groups then work in teams at the computer center using computer-assisted instruction.

The instructional materials include student workbooks that provide math problems using decimals. The teacher also includes hands-on manipulatives, such as wood blocks, that indicate different decimal units. A sample assessment for this lesson plan might include word problems and multiple-choice questions, such as the examples provided in Figure 1.2.

The integration of good assessment practices into your lesson plans can enhance your instruction. Included among the positive aspects are providing appropriate feedback to increase student achievement, focusing students on key aspects of the instruction, and ensuring that students use a variety of cognitive skills. The next section examines yet another reason for linking assessment with instruction: educational accountability.

Policy and Practice

The No Child Left Behind Act, Assessment, and Accountability

Accountability is currently one of the major policy issues in public education. It is a central theme in the federal legislation commonly called the No Child Left Behind Act. In this context, **educational accountability** means that educators are held accountable for ensuring certain activities and skills in schools. For example, school superintendents are accountable for ensuring fair and equal education for all students in the school district. Principals may be held accountable for administering a schoolwide discipline policy. School personnel may be accountable for ensuring a safe school environment.

For teachers, **teacher accountability** means that teachers are accountable for teaching children a certain skill in a certain grade or at a certain age. For instance, state global objectives might require students to develop a mastery of basic multiplication concepts by the end of the third grade. Teachers are accountable for providing the instructional basis for children's mastery of multiplication in that grade. Two of the changes in recent years with this issue are (1) the shift in focus to performance-based standards of accountability and (2) increasing involvement at the federal level in ensuring accountability.

Performance-based standards mandate a specific level of performance for students on a given assessment. Therefore, to satisfy accountability requirements teachers must have students who attain a specific level of proficiency. This is met through a variety of assessments. For example, some performance standards are determined by percentile ranks on state tests, such as a student who reaches the 50th or 60th percentile will have met the performance standard.

In conjunction with performance-based standards, there is an increasing effort at the federal level to ensure greater educational accountability. New federal laws and guidelines now mandate assessment and accountability practices that reach to the local level. These are incorporated in the No Child Left Behind Act, which specifies that all states will be required to set standards and assess these standards in most grade levels. Schools and school districts will publish the results of these assessments. According to the act, there will be real consequences for districts and schools that fail to make progress. Some of the major aspects of No Child Left Behind are given on page 12.

The No Child Left Behind Act has produced considerable change in how public schools operate. This is particularly true in the areas of accountability and assessment. Further information and application of this legislation is provided in later chapters.

Clearly, there is an increase in the relationship between accountability and assessment practices. In addition to student feedback and guidance, assessments are used to validate how well a teacher or a school system meets instructional standards. Educational accountability often is determined through using either standardized state exams or locally determined assessment methods. You may aid in this process by aligning your lesson plans and classroom assessments with the appropriate objectives. By linking objectives with lesson plans, you can facilitate student performance on the assessments required to demonstrate accountability.

Privacy Issues in Providing Assessment Feedback

In providing feedback about assessments, another important policy consideration is the privacy issue. The Family Educational Rights and Privacy Act of 1974, commonly known as the **Buckley Amendment,** is a federal law that restricts the disclosure of academic records. This law requires prior permission of the student, parent, or legal guard-

No Child Left Behind Act

Accountability and Assessment

The **No Child Left Behind Act** of 2001, signed into law by President Bush in January 2002, requires states to implement accountability systems covering public schools and students. These systems must be based on specific performance standards in reading and mathematics. Annual testing is required for all students in grades 3 through 8. Annual statewide progress goals must be documented to ensure that all groups of students reach proficiency on these standards within 12 years. Assessment results and state progress objectives must be broken down by poverty, race, ethnicity, disability, and limited English proficiency.

School Choice

The No Child Left Behind (NCLB) Act increases school choices available to the parents of students attending schools that fail to meet statewide standards. School systems must give students at those schools identified for improvement the opportunity to attend a better public school within the school district. The school district must pay for and provide transportation for students who transfer from a failing school to a new school.

Educational Flexibility for States, School Districts, and Schools

Another aspect of No Child Left Behind gives states and school districts greater flexibility in the use of federal education funds in exchange for strong accountability for results. New flexibility provisions in the NCLB Act include authority for states and school districts to transfer up to 50 percent of the funding they receive under four major state grant programs to any one of the following: Title I programs, Teacher Quality State Grants, Educational Technology, Innovative Programs, and Safe and Drug-Free Schools.

Emphasis on Basic Reading Skills

The No Child Left Behind Act also mandates that every child should be able to read by the end of third grade. To accomplish this goal, the new Reading First initiative significantly increases the federal investment in reading instruction programs for the primary grades. One major benefit of this approach would be to reduce the number of children identified for special education services due to a lack of appropriate reading instruction in their early years.

Other Major Provisions: Teacher Quality and School Safety

Another focus of NCLB is on using practices grounded in research to prepare, train, and recruit high-quality teachers. The new program gives states and school districts flexibility in selecting the strategies that best meet their particular needs for improved teaching that will help them raise student achievement in the core academic subjects.

Other changes support state and local efforts to keep schools safe and drug free, while at the same time ensuring that students—particularly those who have been victims of violent crimes on school grounds—are not trapped in persistently dangerous schools. As proposed in No Child Left Behind, states must allow students who attend a persistently dangerous school, or who are victims of violent crime at school, to transfer to a safe school.

Source: Adapted from U.S. Department of Education (2003).

Point/Counterpoint: Teacher Accountability

Point

Supporters of teacher accountability state that it is reasonable for the taxpaying public to require students to demonstrate a certain achievement level by a given grade. These supporters also state that it is reasonable to require that tenure and job performance ratings of teachers should be based on the progress of their students. This policy ensures that the public gets a viable return on the tax money spent on education.

For example, students should demonstrate a specified level of achievement in understanding multiplication principles by the end of third grade. Teachers should be held accountable for student progress in reaching a certain level of understanding of multiplication. By using specific standards for accountability, teachers will emphasize the type of instruction that will guarantee appropriate student achievement.

Counterpoint

Critics of teacher accountability policies point out that state instructional standards and objectives often are subject to a variety of external social pressures unrelated to actual classroom teaching and assessment. These external demands may not take into account the internal classroom pressures produced by large variations in students' backgrounds or achievement levels. Thus, the pressure for teacher accountability may not take into consideration individual differences due to cultural diversity, socioeconomic status, or disability status.

The result may be that teachers are held accountable for instructional objectives that do not match the backgrounds of students in their classroom. For instance, teachers with numerous ESL students or students with disabilities may be required to meet the same accountability standards as teachers who do not have at-risk students. Critics of accountability ask: When classrooms are not equal in ability at the outset, how can teachers be held accountable to a uniform standard?

ian before academic records can be made public. (Parental permission is required until students are 18 years old.) The law limits the communication of school records to the student, their parents, or educators who have direct educational contact with the students. Therefore, when meeting with parents of one student, the teacher should never discuss the performance of other students.

One feature of the Buckley Amendment is that, by restricting such communications, this law could limit some unwanted comparisons and competitions between students. In general, a cooperative rather than a competitive classroom atmosphere tends to foster student achievement. Cooperative classroom practices include developing assessments that minimize academic competition among students.

Another role of assessment is that of communication. Although linked to feedback, communication also includes the transfer of information about student achievement to other teachers, administrators, and institutions such as colleges. For instance, a student successfully passes second grade and is placed in third grade. The third-grade teacher does not need parental permission to view this child's permanent record. The school principal or school counselor does not need permission to view a child's permanent record. However, any member of an external agency, such as a human services agency, must seek parental permission to view the child's record.

There are questions and problems concerning how far the Buckley Amendment goes in restricting graded activities. For example, can a teacher display the artwork of first-grade students in the classroom? What about a visible checklist where second-graders can see who receives a gold star or a check mark? Should high school class rankings of the top 10 percent of students be published? A recent U.S. Supreme Court decision addressed some of these aspects of the Buckley Amendment.

This Supreme Court case (*Owasso Independent School District* vs. *Falvo*) reviewed the issue of peer grading practices (Lane, 2002). The case involved a child with a diagnosed learning disability who was mainstreamed in a regular classroom. The teacher had a policy of allowing for peer grading of classroom assignments. In effect, children were grading each other's work and thus were able to see the grades of the child with a learning disability. The parents of the child with the learning disability sued the school system on the basis of the Buckley Amendment. The parents also claimed that the child was subjected to taunts from other children because of low grades due to his disability.

The Supreme Court ruled that peer grading does not violate the Buckley Amendment. In the legal opinion produced by the Court, it was noted that the correction of student work by classmates can be as much a part of the classroom activities as taking the test itself. The Court also noted that it was not the intent of Congress in creating the Buckley Amendment to limit teachers to the extent that no other student could see whether a teacher put "a happy face, a gold star or a disapproving remark on a classroom assignment" (Lane, 2002, p. AO6). The Court did affirm that there was a distinction between permanent records kept by the school and the individual teacher's grade book. The permanent records are fully protected by the Buckley Amendment, whereas the grade book is not fully protected.

Many teachers zealously guard student grades from unwanted eyes. This Supreme Court case does somewhat redefine what many took to be a strict interpretation of the Buckley Amendment to protect the confidentiality of student grades. I still believe that the best practice is to continue to restrict access to student grades, if for no other reason than to decrease unwanted competition between students. On the other hand, this ruling does affirm the right of the teacher to use peer assessments and evaluations as part of the grading process.

Individual Differences: Gender and Diversity Issues

Individual differences, due to socioeconomic status, ethnicity, or gender, comprise another major issue in educational assessment. Included are the topics of gender bias in assessment scores and ethnic differences in grade-level retention rates.

A number of research studies have examined the basis for gender bias both in the classroom and in assessment scores (Feingold, 1992; Sadker, Sadker, & Klein, 1991).

For example, the study completed by Sadker, Sadker, and Klein (1991) indicated that teachers were more likely to call on and respond to males in the classroom. If a teacher preferentially calls on male students, even if she is unaware of what she is doing, she is signaling to the female students that their contributions to the class are not as valued as contributions by male students. This behavior can have a very negative effect on female students' academic self-esteem.

Reviews of research studies by Schaeffer (1998) and the American Association of University Women (1992) reported a number of gender disparities in college entrance exams. A summary of the 2002 college test scores is provided in Table 1.1. The table indicates some evidence of gender disparities on college entrance exams. The difference between males and females on the SAT total score was 39 points. Gender differences on the SAT Math portion accounted for most of this discrepancy. The actual magnitude of gender differences has fluctuated by only a couple of points since the SAT was revised in 1995. The 2002 test year showed a slight narrowing of gender differences on the Math section.

Overall, gender differences on the ACT composite score have narrowed considerably. The ACT composite score in 1990 for males was 21.0 and for females the composite score was 20.3. The composite scores for 2002 were 20.9 for males and 20.7 for

TABLE 1.1   Gender Differences in College Entrance Exams: 2002

Scholastic Assessment Test (SAT)

	Verbal	Math	Total
Males	507	534	1041
Females	502	500	1002
All Examinees	505	512	1017

Note: Total Number of Examinees: 1.3 million
54% of examinees were female; 46% were male

Source: College Board (2002).

American College Test (ACT)

	Composite Scores
Males	20.9
Females	20.7
All Examinees	20.8

Note: Total Number of Examinees: 1.1 million
56% of examinees were female; 44% were male

Source: American College Test (2002).

Point/Counterpoint: Gender Differences and Assessments

Point

Perhaps the best known case for pronounced gender differences on assessments was presented by the American Association of University Women (AAUW) (1992). The AAUW published a report on gender differences entitled, "How Schools Shortchange Girls," which claimed a number of gender disparities that negatively influenced educational outcomes. In regard to classroom assessments, the AAUW report reviewed research indicating that girls were still less likely to do as well in the sciences than were boys. On nearly every index of science achievement, girls scored considerably lower than boys.

In the AAUW report, the above findings in science achievement were contrasted with the considerable gains by girls in mathematics performance. Thus, the once noted gender gap in math achievement no longer occurred at the elementary school level. However, at the high school level considerable gender differences in math remained. As previously noted, the AAUW report also found that boys outscored girls on college entrance exams, particularly on the SAT.

Counterpoint

Critics of the AAUW viewpoint state that, except for the specific exceptions listed in the AAUW report, girls do better than boys on overall classroom grades in public schools. In fact, the research on teacher-constructed assessments shows that girls outperform boys at nearly every level and in nearly every category. Critics of the AAUW report point out that, even on state standardized exams for public schools, girls outperform boys in most areas except math and science.

Critics give two reasons for the "gender paradox" between classroom assessments and SAT scores. Boys drop out from high school at a higher rate than girls and girls are more likely to go to college than boys. Thus, there are now considerably more females than males who are taking college entrance exams. This may make for a larger pool of girls with a wider variety of backgrounds competing against a smaller, more selective group of boys. Therefore, the score disparities on college entrance exams may be due to demographics rather than gender inequities.

females. Currently, the ratio of gender differences (female to male overall scores) is considerably larger on the SAT than it is on the ACT.

A number of factors interact in any examination of gender or ethnicity. One part of the previously mentioned AAUW report (1992) analyzed the effects of gender, ethnicity, and socioeconomic status on retention rates in public schools. This report reviewed the percentage of eighth-grade students who had been retained at least one time prior to eighth grade. These results are provided in Table 1.2. The table shows that boys were consistently more likely to be retained, regardless of their socioeconomic status (SES) or ethnicity. There were no significant differences found among low SES African American, Hispanic American, or white boys in retention rates. However, low SES Native

TABLE 1.2   **Retention Rates among Eighth-Grade Students: Percentage Retained at Least One Grade**

	Low SES		High SES	
	Girls	*Boys*	*Girls*	*Boys*
Native American	27	41	3	17
Asian American	15	26	5	5
African American	29	34	7	10
Hispanic American	23	34	9	13
White	24	33	5	10

Source: AAUW (1992).

American boys were retained at a higher rate than any other low SES group. Low SES Asian American boys were retained at a lower rate than any other low SES, male group. Within the high SES groups, the AAUW report indicated that the gender gap in retention rates narrowed a great deal. In the high SES groups there were two major gender gaps: Native Americans and whites. High SES Native American boys and white boys were much more likely to be retained than Native American girls or white girls.

As with other studies of academic achievement, the AAUW report showed the predominant effect of socioeconomic status on school achievement. This variable appeared to account for more differences than did gender or ethnicity. Certainly, gender and ethnic differences still remain, but educational and social programs dealing with socieconomic problems seem most needed.

The key issue for beginning teachers is how to use these data. Teachers need to be proactive in reducing the negative effects of low socioeconomic status on school achievement. They also need to remain aware of their own biases in regard to gender and ethnicity and to avoid unconsciously stereotyping children because of their backgrounds. It is sometimes difficult to avoid creating expectations about achievement based on background. However, teachers must strive to avoid such expectations and to make a conscious effort to have the same expectations for all their students.

Inclusion Policies and Assessment Practices

Another issue in assessment practices is inclusion. Inclusion policies differ from the previous practice of mainstreaming. **Mainstreaming** focused on placing children with disabilities in the least restrictive environment. The determination of least restrictive environment was based on an individualized educational plan that provided a range of placements from special schools to special education classes to regular education classes.

Inclusion focuses first on placing children with disabilities in the general classroom and then offering special services. Inclusion also mandates that the percentage of children with disabilities be uniform across schools within a school district. This policy increases the amount of interaction between children with disabilities and their regular classroom peers. This policy also avoids designating certain schools as special education schools. Inclusion requires that instruction and assessment be provided to individuals with disabilities in the regular classroom. With inclusion, children with disabilities enter a program designed to meet their needs. Mainstreaming implied that children with disabilities were outsiders who entered the regular classroom primarily for socialization.

The increasing emphasis on inclusion practices has raised a series of questions about assessment policies in public schools. Among the more difficult questions regarding inclusion and assessment is the issue of *reasonable accommodations* for individuals with disabilities during assessments. Since the Rehabilitation Act of 1973, reasonable accommodations for assessments have been mandated for individuals with disabilities by federal law (Public Law 94–142, 1975; Public Law, 101–476, 1990).

The most recent legislation, called the **Individuals with Disabilities Education Act (IDEA),** was enacted in 1990 and reauthorized with amendments in 1997. **Reasonable accommodations** for individuals with disabilities during assessments range from providing appropriate test materials for the visually impaired (Braille, large print, oral, or audiotape materials) to extended time accommodations for individuals with learning disabilities.

Very few educators appear to oppose reasonable accommodations for individuals with sensory or physical disabilities. On the other hand, there are many questions about what is a "reasonable accommodation" for individuals with learning disabilities. Learning disabilities often involve difficulties in reading, writing, or spelling. For instance, individuals with reading disorders may have very low word-per-minute reading rates. Because of these difficulties, some educators believe that such individuals may need special time accommodations or other assistance on assessments.

Other educators have challenged the practice of giving time accommodations for individuals with learning disabilities on both classroom assessments and standardized exams. Some instructors believe that extra time on tests is essentially unfair, whereas others believe that extra time is necessary only when large amounts of reading are required on the test (Runyan, 1991).

However, the testing organizations that administer college entrance exams, such as the SAT, the ACT, and even the Medical College Admissions Test, do allow time extensions for students with diagnosed learning disabilities (Banks, Guyer, & Guyer, 1995). Similar accommodations appear to be warranted for individuals with disabilities on classroom assessments. In addition to extra time, these individuals may need a distraction-free alternative test room or the use of adaptive equipment such as a computer.

With the growing emphasis on inclusion by school systems, the need for appropriate instruction and assessment practices for children with disabilities in the regular classroom also appears to be increasing. Regular education classrooms are being transformed by these changes in inclusion practices. Teachers in these classrooms will have to accommodate both the changing instructional and assessment environment brought about by these new inclusion policies.

Chapter Summary

Linking Assessment and Instruction

Global objectives and standards are now mandated by the federal government but determined by each individual state. Educators receive mandated instructional standards and translate these standards into instructional objectives and lesson plans. Assessment procedures should be viewed as an integral part of instructional objectives and lesson plans. The fundamental relationship between good instruction and good assessment practices is emphasized.

Policy and Practice

Classroom assessment practices play a central role in determining instructional accountability. Part of the impetus for using standardized assessments of students is an increasing public demand for accountability. Various social issues also have an effect on assessment practices.

The Buckley Amendment protects students' privacy rights. Teachers generally cannot release grades to anyone other than the student or the parents of the student. Diversity and gender issues are becoming an increasing concern in classroom assessments. Although gender and ethnic differences appear to be narrowing, women still do not achieve as well as men in science disciplines. The interaction of complex socioeconomic, gender, and ethnic factors appear to affect dropout rates and retention rates.

Reasonable accommodations for individuals with disabilities during assessments is another important social and educational issue. It is noted that individuals with learning disabilities still do not always receive reasonable accommodations during classroom assessments. Adjustments in assessment practices by teachers are needed to fully establish reasonable accommodations as required by federal law.

CASE STUDY EPILOGUE

Ms. Dupree is coming to understand the complexities involved with teacher accountability. She realizes that performance standards and educational objectives are now mandated by the federal government. Each state designs and implements a performance plan with stated goals that must be met. This plan is translated into global objectives and educational objectives at the state level. These are then developed into instructional objectives at the school-district level.

For Ms. Dupree, this means that her instruction and assessments must be aligned with the state performance plan. Her individual professional choices about the curriculum are somewhat restricted. She is troubled about the effects of these standards on her students. Because the standards and objectives will be assessed by statewide assessments, she is concerned that her instruction may be limited to only those specified standards. She is worried that she may simply end up teaching to the test.

A good deal of Ms. Dupree's first year of teaching has been devoted to writing lesson plans that address the issue of curriculum alignment. As part of these lesson plans, she has devised a number of assessments to measure her instruction. She still likes her subject area and working with students, but she is a bit overwhelmed by all the paperwork.

CHAPTER ACTIVITIES

Websites

Relevant websites are provided at the end of each chapter as an informational resource. Some chapter activities include certain websites as part of the instructional process.

www.ablongman.com   This site features Allyn and Bacon resources, student study guides, concept maps, homework help, and test banks.

www.collegeboard.org   This site is created by the College Entrance Exam Board. It provides research and information on a variety of issues related to standardized assessments.

http://putnamvalleyschools.org/Standards.html   This site contains an index about instructional standards and curriculum frameworks throughout the United States. It includes links with all state education departments.

www.cgocable.net/~rayser/index.html   This award-winning site, created by English teacher Ray Saitz, features classroom lesson plans, handouts, and ideas.

Portfolio Activities

A portfolio is a repository of a student's work in a particular academic discipline or course. In an art class, a portfolio is the accumulated artwork that a student has created. In other academic areas, a portfolio may contain written work, such as essays, lesson plans, or publications.

The following exercises are designed to encourage you to keep a portfolio as an accompaniment with this text. Each activity will include material to be used in the portfolio. A separate binder notebook is useful as a container for these portfolio activities.

1. Review this chapter's Case Study. Write the answers in your portfolio to the following questions:
   - What are the different types of objectives in education?
   - How can teachers meet these objectives?
   - What is a lesson plan and how do these objectives fit in a lesson plan?
   - Where do classroom assessments fit with lesson plans?
   - What are the current issues and problems with classroom assessments?
   - What should a new teacher know about assessment policies?
   - What is the relationship between accountability and assessment?

2. Find this website: http://putnamvalleyschools.org/Standards.html. Then use the index to find the state in which you are presently planning to teach. Switch to the State Department of Education website for your state. Go to the section that lists standards

and objectives. Find the appropriate subject and grade level for which you are planning to teach. List three state standards for your subject and grade level. Detail the instructional methods, materials, outcomes, and assessments for each of these standards.

3. Since the 1980s, the issue of developing a set of national instructional standards has been debated. In 1994, Goals 2000, the Educate America Act, was enacted at the federal level. As noted previously, the No Child Left Behind Act also sets specific instructional and assessment standards, such as reading proficiency in all children by third grade. Among some of the national education goals created by these federal acts are the following two educational standards:

   - The high school graduation rate will increase to at least 90 percent.
   - U.S. students will be first in the world in mathematics and science achievement.

   Write an essay for your portfolio that addresses the following questions:

   - As a prospective teacher, what position would you take on the debate over developing national instructional standards?
   - What position would you take on the issue of a national standardized assessment for all school children?
   - What kind of impact would such national standards have on local curriculum?
   - How would it affect the type of lesson plans that a beginning teacher might develop?
   - Should a teacher in California and a teacher in South Carolina write the same lesson plans? Why or why not? Should they be held to the same standards? Support your answer.

KEY CONCEPTS

Assessment	Instructional objectives
Buckley Amendment	Lesson plans
Educational accountability	Mainstreaming
Educational objectives	No Child Left Behind Act
Global objectives	Reasonable accommodations
Inclusion	Teacher accountability
Individuals with Disabilities Education Act	

REVIEW QUESTIONS

1. What is the specific definition of assessment?

2. What is meant by "using assessments as instructional magnets"?

3. What is the relationship between global objectives, educational objectives, and instructional objectives?

4. With lesson plans, describe what is involved with methods, materials, and assessments.

5. What are the basic provisions of the No Child Left Behind Act?

6. List the major aspects of the Buckley Amendment.

7. What are some of the major gender differences in assessment performance?

8. What is meant by "reasonable accommodations" with assessments?

SELF-ASSESSMENT

1. Lesson plans include all of the following:
   a. Methods, materials, assessments
   b. Methods, treatments, assessments
   c. Materials, programs, outcomes, assessments
   d. Objectives, outcomes, treatments, evaluations

2. Which of the following is a type of instructional method listed in this chapter?
   a. Phoenician phonics reasoning
   b. Reading reactivity
   c. Whole class instruction
   d. Whole language phoneticism

3. Providing appropriate test materials such as Braille, audiotapes, or extra time to complete exams is called:
   a. Phonics
   b. Reasonable accommodations
   c. Inclusion
   d. Instructional objectives

4. According to a survey of teachers in all 50 states, which issue did teachers feel they had the *least* amount of involvement?
   a. Curriculum
   b. Textbooks
   c. Instruction
   d. Retention

5. The purpose, the goals, and the outcomes of a particular course are termed:
   a. Retention standards
   b. Instructional objectives
   c. Instructional materials
   d. Teacher in-service performance standards

6. Privacy rights of students are protected by:
   a. *Brown* vs. *Board of Education*
   b. Public Law 94–142
   c. Buckley Amendment
   d. Brevard Amendment

7. The most recent federal amendment to provide special education to qualified children is:
   a. Individuals with Disabilities Education Act
   b. The Physically Challenged Special Education Act

Answers to Self-Assessment: 1. a, 2. c, 3. b, 4. d, 5. b, 6. c, 7. a, 8. c

    c. Buckley Amendment
    d. Brevard Amendment

8. Performance goals, statewide assessments, and state accountability are mandated by:
    a. National Education Association Act
    b. Individuals with Disabilities Education Act
    c. No Child Left Behind Act
    d. Public Law 97–152

REFERENCES

American Association of University Women. (1992). *How schools shortchange girls.* Washington, DC: American Association of University Women Educational Foundation.

American College Test. (2002). *2002 national score report.* Iowa City, IA: ACT Inc.

Babyak, A.E., Luze, G.J., & Kamps, D.M. (2000). The good student game: Behavior management for diverse classrooms. *Intervention in School and Clinic,* 35, 216–224.

Banks, S.R., Guyer, B.P., & Guyer, K.E. (1995). A study of medical students and physicians referred for learning disabilities. *Annals of Dyslexia,* 45, 233–245.

Carnegie Foundation for the Advancement of Teaching. (1988). *Teacher involvement in decision making: A state by state profile.* Princeton, NJ: Author. (ERIC Document Service No. ED 299 690).

College Board. (2002). *College board seniors' national report, 2002.* Princeton, NJ: Author.

Feingold, A. (1992). Sex differences in variability in intellectual abilities: A new look at an old controversy. *Review of Educational Research,* 62 (1), 61–84.

Goertz, M.E., Floden, R.E., & O'Day, J. (1996). *The bumpy road to education reform.* Philadelphia, PA: Consortium for Policy Research in Education. (ERIC Document Service No. ED 398 653).

Krathwohl, D.R., & Payne, D.A. (1971). Defining and assessing educational objectives. In R.L. Thorndike (Ed.), *Educational measurement* (pp. 17–45). Washington, DC: American Council of Education.

Landrum, T., & Tankersley, M. (1997). *Implementing effective self-management for students with behavioral disorders.* Paper presented at the Midwest Symposium for Leadership in Behavior Disorders, Kansas City, MO.

Lane, C. (2002, February 20). Student grading by peers passes high court test. *The Washington Post,* p. A06.

Manzo, K.K., & Hoff, D.J. (2003, February) Federal influence over curriculum exhibits growth. *Education Week.* Retrieved September 22, 2003, from http://www.edweek.org/ew/ewstory.cfm?slug=21curric.h22.

Marockie, H.R. (1996). *Instructional goals and objectives for West Virginia schools.* Charleston, WV: Department of Education.

Runyan, M.K. (1991). The effect of extra time on reading comprehension scores for university students with and without learning disabilities. *Journal of Learning Disabilities,* 24, 104–108.

Sadker, M., Sadker, D., & Klein, S. (1991). The issue of gender in elementary and secondary education. *Review of Research in Education,* 17, 269–334.

Schaeffer, B. (1998). College board hides growing SAT gender gap. Fair Test Press Release. [On-line]. Available: www.fairtest.orgprsatact98.htm.

U.S. Department of Education. (2003, September). No Child Left Behind Act. Retrieved September 19, 2003, from http://www.ed.gov/nclb/.

CHAPTER

2   Types of Assessments

CASE STUDY

Two weeks before the start of the fall term, Mr. Strickland was hired as a middle school social studies teacher. It is his first teaching job. Like other teacher education majors, Mr. Strickland completed some assessment and grading activities during his student teaching. Nevertheless, he evaluated students only with his supervising teacher's guidance. Also, Mr. Strickland used only the grading policies developed by his supervising teacher.

Now, Mr. Strickland must develop his own system in a very short time. His school district requires a written classroom assessment policy to be ready by the first day of school. It has to be reviewed by both the principal and the curriculum supervisor. Mr. Strickland has to choose among a wide array of assessment practices. He wants answers to the following questions:

What different types of assessments are available?

What types of assessments are appropriate for teaching social studies?

What types of assessments will provide positive feedback to his students?

What types of assessments will satisfy state and school district criteria for educational accountability?

How does a teacher determine what is a good assessment and what is not a good assessment?

Introduction

In the last decade teachers have seen an expansion in their assessment practices. Performance-based assessments, such as portfolios, have become more common. Other assessments, including formative assessments, peer assessments, and self-assessments, also have become integrated into instructional practices. These developments offer you a greater variety of assessment choices.

The array of choices is almost bewildering. To help you through these choices, a classification system for assessments is presented in this chapter. This system includes recently developed assessment procedures, as well as more traditional assessments. The classification scheme provides an advanced organizer for more detailed presentations of each assessment procedure in later chapters. Accompanying this assessment typology is an examination of the quality control procedures that you could use with your assessments. These procedures include a discussion of reliability and validity. The contribution of an item analysis to increase the quality of assessments also is provided.

Assessment Definitions and Distinctions

As mentioned in Chapter 1, *assessment* is the total set of information gathered about students in the classroom. It is the most all-encompassing concept in the field. Other categories are subsumed under assessment. A flowchart indicating the relationship among the various concepts used in assessment practices is provided in Figure 2.1. As you can see, classroom assessment practices are divided into two basic types. One type is developed to make judgments about students. This category is used to determine grades and make placement decisions. The second type of assessments includes nonjudgmental assessments, which are used for instructional feedback, student growth, and development.

In reviewing the terms in Figure 2.1, the first distinction refers to evaluations. **Evaluations** are the specific process of describing and making judgments about assessments. It is important to reemphasize that not all assessments are evaluative. Some assessments, such as informal assessments, are used simply as an aid in instruction. Evaluations of formal assessments, such as classroom tests and papers, are used to determine student outcomes and assign grades.

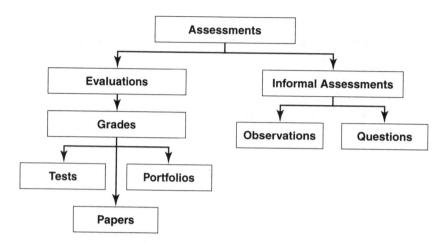

FIGURE 2.1   Assessment Concepts

Grades are the measurement of student progress in a way that can be communicated to others. Grades are the aggregate of the formal assessments and evaluations used in the classroom. Since grading is partly a communicative process, it should be as interactive as possible. In effect, grades should be used as an opportunity for the kind of feedback that enables students to increase their classroom achievement. Thus, grading should be seen as a chance for growth and development, not just as a judgmental activity at the end of the semester.

Tests are a type of assessment procedure that provides an estimation, often with a quantitative aspect, of student achievement or ability. Classroom tests, constructed by the teacher, are one way of measuring student achievement. When used with other assessment procedures, such as performance-based assessments or research papers, these tests may form the basis for determining classroom grades.

The other part of Figure 2.1 presents assessments that are generally nonevaluative. These assessments include informal assessments and sometimes formative assessments. Since these assessments may not be used for evaluation purposes such as grades, they offer a nonthreatening way to provide feedback to your students about their classroom performance. They also offer a way for you to get feedback about the effectiveness of your instruction. Informal assessments might include informal classroom observations about students during classroom activities. They also may involve questions or probes during classroom discussions.

Categorizing Assessment Procedures

Perhaps the biggest distinction among the various assessment procedures is in terms of who is responsible for developing the assessments. In effect, as the classroom teacher, do you develop your own assessments or are they developed for you? Although many standardized assessments are available, these usually are too general to use for your own classroom assessments. Certain programmed instructional packages for reading and arithmetic also offer assessment items. But these tend to be limited in scope. They measure only those areas that are specific to the part of the programmed instruction for which the student is studying.

For instance, some of the phonics-based programs, such as the Open Court reading series, provide detailed instructional methods and assessments. However, the assessments are explicitly tailored to the program. In assessing the ability to decode a sound such as *th* or *oi*, the teacher uses oral dictation of various sounds. Students then copy into an instructional workbook the correct letters or words. The assessment is based on specific parts of the instructional module.

For the most part, standardized assessments are not applicable to other areas. Thus, as with other parts of your lesson plans, you develop your own assessment materials just as you develop your own instructional methods. Assessment instruments constructed by the classroom teacher usually best address the particular needs of each instructional module.

When properly designed, quality assessments can increase student motivation. Appropriate assessment practices also can be a good defense against possible grade challenges. The front-end time you spend in making good assessments will save you some time later (or at least save you a lot of grief and headaches).

There are six types of assessment procedures summarized in Figure 2.2. There is some overlap among the categories in any system of making assessment classifications. Educators have proposed a number of alternative assessments in the last decade in an attempt to develop more realistic or effective assessments. One result of this trend is to increase the variety of assessments available in public schools (Hambleton, 1996).

FIGURE 2.2   Categorizing Assessments

By Method of Development:
Teacher-Constructed or Standardized

By Level of Formality:
Informal or Formal

By Instructional Purpose:
Formative or Summative

By Type of Grading Standard:
Criterion-Referenced or Norm-Referenced

By Item Format:
Objective or Constructed-Response

By Degree of Authenticity:
Performance or Traditional

By Method of Development: Teacher-Constructed or Standardized Assessments

One category of assessments is by method of development, such as teacher-constructed or standardized assessments. As the name indicates, **teacher-constructed assessments** are created by the classroom teacher for a specific instructional purpose. These assessments may involve a variety of activities, such as a spelling quiz, an art class portfolio, or a performance assessment in physical education. As previously stated, teacher-constructed assessments should be directly tied into the individual lesson plans created for a specific classroom. Therefore, they are tailored for a particular classroom and may not be useful beyond that given classroom.

In contrast, **standardized assessments** are used across any number of different classrooms. The use of the term *standardized assessment* means that all students answer the same questions, complete the assessment under similar conditions, are scored the same way, and are compared with a uniform reference group. It is with this comparison group that individual scores are compared. Standardized assessments are distinguished from teacher-constructed assessments by at least two other features:

1. Standardized assessments use extensive pretesting on sample groups to provide statistical norms.
2. Standardized assessments purport to assess a much larger, more general knowledge base.

For instance, a standardized achievement test for third-grade students attempts to assess the knowledge base acquired by third-grade students. In this sense, the test measures relatively global aspects of what would typically be expected of a third-grade student. The result is that a standardized measure provides a fair amount of comparative data. But by increasing the domain to be assessed, a standardized assessment may sacrifice the ability to assess specific instructional needs of an individual classroom.

One method of using teacher-constructed and standardized assessments together is to cross-check student problems. For instance, a second-grade teacher notices that a student has a reading problem. On the student's classroom reading assessments, the child was scoring well below the expected scores for students at that age level. However, in all other academic areas, the student scored above age level. A cross-check of scores on the state standardized exam indicates the same score pattern: above-average scores in all areas except for reading. This type of pattern may indicate a reading problem or even a reading learning disability, such as dyslexia. Possible referrals for a medical exam, a visual exam, or a psychoeducational assessment for a possible special education placement could be warranted.

By Level of Formality: Informal or Formal Assessments

A second assessment category is the continuum formed by informal and formal assessments. Teachers begin making informal assessments of students from the first day of

Point/Counterpoint: Standardized Assessments

Point

Supporters of standardized assessments state that these tests offer an external, objective view of student achievement. Since these assessments are not influenced by teacher, classroom, or school factors, they provide an unbiased outside view of student performance. Supporters also note that standardized assessments generally are able to offer a more valid and reliable measure of achievement than classroom assessments.

Although supporters of standardized assessments note that aligning these tests with the curriculum can be a challenge, this problem tends to be true about specific tests but not standardized assessments in general. In effect, standardized assessments can easily be devised that are aligned with specific curriculum. In terms of measuring curriculum, appropriate standardized assessments can be just as effective as teacher-constructed assessments. The problem is that states and school systems simply make bad choices about which tests are appropriate to use.

Supporters of standardized assessments also note that these types of tests should be used in conjunction with other assessments. By using these assessments with teacher-constructed measures, teachers have the benefit of another viewpoint about their children. Supporters claim that, if correctly used, standardized assessments can offer an important piece of information about a classroom. It is the misuse or misinterpretation of the assessment that is the problem, not the fact that it is standardized.

Counterpoint

Critics of standardized assessments point out that teacher-constructed tests ensure a more direct connection between instruction and assessment. The classroom teacher constructs these assessments and is accountable for aligning them with the instructional objectives and the curriculum. Critics state that these teacher-constructed tests have served public schools quite well and there is no good reason to change the policy.

According to critics of standardized assessments, the change from teacher-constructed tests to high-stakes standardized testing was *not* completed for sound educational reasons; instead, the reasons were political and social. As part of this change, the public became convinced that teachers could not appropriately assess their students. When the public became convinced that teachers could not assess their students, public stakeholders demanded that other methods of assessment be used to evaluate students. Therefore, externally created standardized assessments were developed to ensure teacher accountability.

Critics of standardized assessments state that these assessments often are not aligned with the mandated curriculum. They claim that such tests simply measure a somewhat nebulous, general level of achievement that is typically expected of a specific grade level. Since these tests are not directly connected with the curriculum, they cannot actually gauge student performance on that curriculum. Critics also note that these tests also do not measure teaching performance. Teaching performance is dependent on a specified curriculum and these tests do not measure that curriculum.

class. **Informal assessments** consist of finding out the developmental level of students: where they are coming from and where they presently are in their subject mastery. Informal assessments are based on a variety of unofficial activities.

For example, Mr. Strickland, the new teacher in introduced in the case study might include informal observations of class performance or student interactions during group discussion as part of his informal assessments. Mr. Strickland also might use a series of diagnostic questions or probes when he first meets with his social studies class. He might ask: What did the Founding Fathers mean by a Constitutional balance of power between the executive, legislative, and judicial branches of government? What is meant by the separation of church and state? These types of questions give Mr. Strickland an idea of the level of knowledge and thinking in his students. By using these types of informal assessments, he can tailor his instruction to the level of his students.

Formal assessments are preplanned, structured assessments developed for evaluative purposes. Formal assessments can range from a weekly quiz in a second-grade reading group to a standardized state exam. Formal assessments generally are used to make judgments about student achievement. Formal assessments are used as the basis for student grades.

Another distinction between informal and formal assessments is that informal assessments are used just as an aid in the teacher's instructional process. Formal assessments are constructed to measure learning outcomes and student achievement. Based on informal assessments many teachers adjust their presentation level to adapt to the cognitive level of their students. While such adjustments also may be made after formal assessments, only formal assessments are used to measure student outcomes and to determine grades.

By Instructional Purpose: Formative or Summative Assessments

A major categorization of assessment procedures is the distinction between formative and summative assessments. **Formative assessments** are planned assessments that provide a guide and a direction for both teacher and student. Formative assessments may or may not be used as part of course grades. An example of a formative assessment that might be graded is a checklist of completed steps in a chemistry lab assignment. A self-assessment, such as those used with computer-assisted instructional programs, is an example of a formative assessment that might not be used to determine grades.

Summative assessments are a type of formal assessment used to measure student outcomes at the end of the instructional program or course. They may be used to determine if the student achieved mastery of an instructional segment or an academic program. Summative assessments can be used in a number of other ways, such as to determine whether a student should pass a course or whether a student should receive a high school diploma. A final exam and a minimum competency test are examples of summative assessments.

By Type of Grading Standard: Criterion-Referenced or Norm-Referenced Assessments

Among the major issues regarding classroom assessments are two questions concerning overall standards for assessments and grades: Should teachers grade students on the basis of how they perform on a specific standard? Or should teachers grade students on the basis of how they compare with other students?

When students are graded on the basis of a specific performance standard, it is called a **criterion-referenced assessment** (Hambleton, 1990). For example, Mr. Strickland sets the performance criterion for an assessment at 40 correct responses out of 50 items. Regardless of how many students reach or surpass the criterion of 40 correct responses, all such students will have met the performance standard on that measure. Therefore, all the students who meet or surpass this standard will have completed the activity.

A similar system can be applied to Mr. Strickland's letter grades. All students who achieve 90 out of 100 possible correct responses receive a grade of A. All students who achieve 80 to 89 of possible correct responses receive a B. Other cutoff scores may be used for C, D, and F. Regardless of how many students achieve a certain level, they still receive the same letter grade.

In contrast, a **norm-referenced assessment** is based on how well students do only in comparison to each other. The top scorers receive the highest grades and the lowest scorers receive the lowest grades. For instance, in Mr. Strickland's social studies class a student achieved a 90 out of 100 correct response rate on an exam. However, many other students had even higher scores. The student with a 90 might be given a B or even a C, since so many other students did better.

Norm-referenced assessments are sometimes called *grading on the curve*. In effect, the assignment of grades is based on certain reference points on the normal curve. But in the typical classroom this term is frequently a misnomer. There should be the same number of Fs as As and the same number of Ds as Bs when a teacher grades strictly on the normal curve. (This is hardly what my students want when they ask if test grades will be curved. With my students, "curving the grades" means to raise the low scores— never to lower those "inflated" high scores.)

Norm-referenced assessments usually require some sort of transformation procedure to change the actual test scores to grades. Teachers can use normal curve statistics or some other type of scoring system to transform student scores. In using norm-referenced assessment procedures, teachers compare students' scores and then transform them into grades. This can be used to ensure a given number of A, B, C, and even D and F grades.

By Item Format: Objective or Constructed-Response Assessments

Assessments also can be divided into objective assessments and constructed-response assessments. **Objective assessments** are based on structured items that require the student to choose an answer from among a number of alternatives or to fill in words that will correctly complete a statement. Multiple-choice items, true/false items, and matching items are used in objective assessments.

It is generally agreed that multiple-choice items are both the most popular and most appropriate type of objective item (Popham, 1990; Banks & Thompson, 1995). Nearly all standardized tests predominantly use the multiple-choice format. In judging the quality of objective assessments, most researchers in the field maintain that multiple-choice items offer better quality control than any other objective item.

Constructed-response assessments use items that require the student to make a detailed written or oral narrative. In general, constructed-response assessments use written essay items. A possible alternative is to use an oral exam format.

Constructed-response assessments have certain positive benefits. If presented in a written essay format, they may increase writing skills by requiring the student to write in an organized and coherent manner. They also may increase higher-level cognitive skills by encouraging students to synthesize and defend their ideas. When the structure of the essay item is appropriate, the ability to apply and integrate ideas into a coherent whole can be increased.

Some critics of constructed-response assessments note that certain problems may be present. The grade assigned to such assessments is often dependent on who is doing the grading. There may be little consistency from one person to another person in determining essay grades.

By Degree of Authenticity: Performance or Traditional Assessments

A number of alternatives to traditional assessment procedures have been proposed in recent years. The focus of these alternatives has been on the development of more realistic assessments—that is, more directly related to the performance of activities they assess than are traditional assessments. These alternative assessments led to a trend in teacher education called the **Authentic Assessment Movement** (Wiggins, 1989). This movement emphasizes the use of performance measures, including portfolios, exhibitions, and simulations as alternatives to the more traditional assessments of classroom tests and research papers.

Performance-based assessments often measure skills that involve some type of observable activity. In many teacher education programs, performance-based assessments are used to evaluate student teachers during field experiences and student teaching. Performance-based assessments may include the evaluation of skills used in a science lab or a special project. They are also frequently used in areas such as assessing public speaking. In his review of performance assessments, Carey (1988) states, "They enable teachers to analyze students' performances and to comment on such aspects as timing, speed, precision, sequence, and appearance" (pp. 220–221).

Another example of a performance test is the driver's test required by each state for a driver's license. The typing speed test, required by many companies for hiring employees in word-processing positions, is another example. Physical education teach-

Point/Counterpoint: Performance or
Traditional Assessments

Point

Proponents of performance-based assessments claim that these assessments can be more effectively aligned with instruction than traditional assessments. In effect, performance assessments may be more directly related to instruction than traditional assessments. This claim is made because of the apparently more realistic nature of performance assessments as compared to traditional assessments. For example, in a physical education class or a driver's training class, performance assessments can directly involve observations of specific skills linked to instruction. In the physical education class, completing a particular skill, such as rope climbing, can be easily documented. In a driver's training class, the ability to parallel park also can be easily observed and documented.

Even with typically academic subject areas, supporters of performance assessments state that they can be more authentic than traditional assessments. For example, with performance-based curriculum and assessment, students complete a science project on amphibians. This project includes a portfolio that illustrates a sequence of skills that were completed during the project. Using a performance rubric that evaluates each skill, the teacher then completes a performance-based assessment of the project that is directly linked to each skill.

According to supporters of performance-based assessments, this measurement can be more closely aligned with standards-based instruction. This is because the student must display work and be assessed on work that is tied to a specific standard for learning. Not only is the activity linked to a standard, but it is tied to an idea or an experience. The activity and the assessment of the activity allow the student to plan and implement a solution to an authentic problem. This type of performance-based assessment may provide a better way of measuring performance abilities, higher-level cognitive skills, and creative abilities than more traditional assessments.

Counterpoint

Critics of performance-based assessments state that the degree of subjective judgment involved in grading some forms of performance assessments may produce a number of problems. Because some performance assessments require a high degree of judgment, grading problems may be similar to those found with grading essays. In effect, the reliability or consistency of grading performance-based assessments may be questionable. Critics point out that objective assessment with quantifiable numbers are much more reliable. They are easier to explain and defend to parents and students. It also does not require the teacher to make subjective judgments, since the answers are generally clear-cut.

In addition, critics of performance assessments state that such assessments take time and planning. For example, devising a portfolio assignment, creating a grading rubric, and then grading the portfolio are very time consuming. Teachers' time may be better spent in creating more efficient traditional assessments. Critics also point out that the trend at the federal and state levels is to emphasize traditional standardized assessments. Teachers need to create assessments that focus on the same skills and tests required by the federal and state regulations.

ers increasingly use performance-based assessments in measuring physical performance activities.

Portfolios are an accumulated record of a student's performances or performance-based assessments in a particular academic discipline. They usually contain the "best work" of the student. In journalism, a portfolio is the repository for the best articles that a student has written for the school newspaper or for journalism classes. The portfolio may contain items for just a semester or it may contain material needed to complete graduation requirements. Wiggins (1989) provides the following example of a general portfolio developed for graduation requirements: "The requirements include a written autobiography, a reflection on work (including a resume), an essay on ethics, a written summary of coursework in science, an artistic product or a written report on art (including an essay on artistic standards used in judging artwork)" (p. 42).

Exhibitions tend to be a more summative type of performance-based assessment that indicates the mastery of a subject area (Wiggins, 1989). In this sense, exhibitions are like a performance test. However, exhibitions also are used to determine whether the course of study is now completed. Some examples of exhibitions are the oral defense of a doctoral dissertation and the final recital performance at a music school.

In summary, there is an increasing variety of assessment practices available to teachers. There also is considerable debate about what types of assessments are best to use. As previously stated, the first law of assessments applies: *A variety of assessments is the best practice.*

Because of the variety of assessments available now, there is some degree of overlap among the categories of assessment practices. For instance, a multiple-choice, final exam in a math class could be classified as teacher constructed, summative, objective, and criterion referenced. Thus, categorizing assessments into a single category may not always be appropriate.

Quality Control with Assessments

To judge the quality of assessments, two basic methods are used: reliability and validity. These methods apply both to standardized assessments and to teacher-constructed assessments. In general, these measures of quality control are applied to performance-based assessments as well as to traditional assessments. In addition, item analysis of individual test questions is used to assist in increasing the quality of an assessment. By analyzing each individual test question, the overall reliability and validity of an assessment may be increased. This section examines reliability and validity, as well as reviewing the role of item analysis.

Reliability

Reliability measures the consistency of an assessment. In understanding reliability, think of measuring the quality of a classroom assessment as similar to judging the quality of any other measurement instrument. For instance, in measuring the reliability of a thermometer, the consistency of the temperature readings are determined by multiple examinations of the instrument under similar conditions. A similar procedure is completed with the bathroom weight scales. When you get on the bathroom scales in the morning, you weigh yourself two or three times to see if the readings are consistent. (Maybe five times if you don't like what you see.)

The same basic principle is used with assessments. One of the most common forms of reliability is test-retest reliability. This type of reliability addresses the following question: When the same students take an assessment and then retake this same assessment after an appropriate interval, do they score approximately the same?

If students score approximately the same in comparison to each other, the assessment scores are consistent. For example, the students who had the higher test scores and those who had the lower scores on the first test administration maintained their relative class rankings on the subsequent test administration. If rankings are relatively maintained across test administrations, the assessment is judged to have appropriate test-retest reliability.

There are many types of reliability. Alternate forms reliability, for example, is a commonly used way to measure reliability. It uses two equivalent forms of the same assessment. The same students take the two alternate forms. If students score approximately the same in comparison to each other on the two forms of the test, then the test is considered to have reliability. In effect, if student rankings are generally the same when the alternate forms are compared, the assessment is judged to have acceptable alternate forms reliability.

In contrast, internal consistency reliability examines one single administration of an assessment. In this case, the consistency of students' scores across items is measured within that one assessment. This type of reliability addresses the question: Are students' scores consistent across the different sections of a single assessment? If students' scores are consistent across the different sections, then the assessment is considered to be reliable.

Validity

Validity is used to determine whether the test measures what it claims to measure. The analogy with a thermometer or a weight scale also applies with the concept of validity. To determine if a thermometer or a weight scale measures what it claims to measure, the instrument is calibrated with another similar instrument. In effect, a new thermometer is compared with an established thermometer under similar conditions. If their readings are the same, then the new thermometer has established its validity. A new weight scale is compared with an established weight scale. If the weights are the same, then the new scale has established its validity. (If the weights are different, of course, you go with the lowest reading.)

A common form of assessment validity is called *criterion-related validity*. With this type of validity an assessment is given to a group of students. Their assessment scores are then compared to their scores on an external criterion appropriately related to what the test claims to measure.

With a new standardized achievement test, criterion-related validity may be measured by comparing the students' scores on the achievement test with an older, already established achievement test. If the new test scores are closely related to the established test, then the new test is considered valid. As with reliability, the key statistical aspect is in terms of student rankings. Likewise, students who had higher scores on the new test also should have higher scores on the older test. Students with lower scores on the new test should also have lower scores on the old test. If this pattern holds true when the tests are compared, then the new test has good validity.

A second type of validity is called *content validity*. This type of validity usually is based on whether the assessment appropriately measures or samples the domain of instructional material presented to the student. For instance, given the state instructional standards and objectives for a seventh-grade history class, does the assessment fully assess the range of objectives and knowledge included in these standards? The measurement of content validity may involve a degree of subjective opinion. To minimize possible subjective biases, some researchers use a panel of expert judges to review the test content and then compare it with the instructional content.

Construct validity is another form of validity. This type of validity is used when a new assessment is developed that attempts to measure some type of educational or psychological construct or ability. Construct validity is the process of analyzing and relating the assessment to a particular construct. For example, let's say you want to create an assessment that measures the construct of job stress. The scores on the job stress assessment should relate to various predictions indicated by theories about job stress. For example, job stress test theories indicate a relationship between job stress and the variables of absenteeism, job turnover, or peer ratings of job stress. If the job stress test is able to predict these variables, then the test is considered to have construct validity.

Validity is the most important type of quality control procedure for measuring assessments (Thorndike, 1997). If a test is not valid, if it does not measure what it claims to measure, then the test has no meaningful use. Procedures similar to those discussed here can be used to determine validity with teacher-constructed assessments. Student scores on a classroom assessment can be related directly to their scores on standardized achievement tests. Scores on different exams can be compared with each other.

Item Analysis

Item analysis is an in-depth examination of individual assessment items after an assessment has been given. Item analysis reviews the pattern of scores and answers to the assessment items. By reviewing these items, the teacher may want to discard certain items and modify other items. By doing so, the teacher will increase the reliability and validity of the assessment.

According to Hopkins, Stanley, and Hopkins (1990), there are two fundamental aspects involved in conducting an item analysis for classroom assessments: item difficulty and item discrimination. (For classroom assessment practices, classic test theory and item analysis is presented rather than the technically more complicated item response theory.)

Item difficulty is the percentage of individuals who correctly answered a given item. When reviewing the results of a classroom assessment, this is one of the first questions that should be answered. Although there is no hard and fast rule for item difficulty on classroom assessments, there are some general guidelines. Hopkins, Stanley, and Hopkins (1990) note two aspects about item difficulty on objective assessments:

1. An item, correctly answered by fewer than 25 percent of students, may be a questionable item.
2. An item, correctly answered by more than 75 percent of students, may be a questionable item.

On criterion-referenced assessments or performance tests, the level of item difficulty may be set in a different manner. In effect, a teacher would expect students to correctly answer more items on these types of assessments. Therefore, the number of items that are answered correctly (item difficulty level) could be substantially different for criterion-referenced than for other types of assessments. Clearly, item difficulty must take into account the type of assessment procedure.

Another reason for conducting an analysis of item difficulty is for instructional decisions and student feedback. If certain items are missed by nearly everyone, then an instructional change may be in order. It may be that the classroom instruction did not appropriately cover the information. Or it may be that the item was incorrectly worded or inappropriate for the developmental level of the students. Another way of determining the efficacy of the item is to compare those who missed very few items on the assessment with those who missed many items.

Item discrimination is the ability of each separate item to differentiate between the high scorers on the assessment and the low scorers on the assessment. An item that successfully discriminates is an item where students who have high scores on the assessment answer it correctly, whereas students who have low scores answer it incorrectly. The better an item differentiates between the high scorers and the low scorers, the better the level of item discrimination.

Who is a high-scoring student and who is a low-scoring student? A review of this question is provided by Hopkins, Stanley, and Hopkins (1990). They state that the optimum division is the top-scoring 27 percent versus the lowest-scoring 27 percent. They also state that for classroom assessments, it makes little difference if the teacher uses a figure as low as 21 percent or as high as 33 percent. Therefore, depending on the classroom circumstances, a teacher may want to compare the top 25 percent versus the lowest 25 percent on each item to determine the item discrimination. Figure 2.3 provides an application for using item discrimination with classroom tests.

Using Reliability, Validity, and Item Analysis

Reliability, validity, and item analysis offer methods for a classroom teacher to examine different aspects of his or her own assessments. Effectively used, these techniques can increase the quality of your classroom assessments. For instance, one frequently asked question is: How many test items should one have on a formal classroom assessment? Although there is no specific right answer to this question, the general answer is: the more the merrier. In effect, as long as the items are good questions, the longer a test is, the more it will meet the reliability, validity, and item analysis standards. Think of it this

FIGURE 2.3   Applying Item Discrimination

Mr. Strickland's middle school social studies class of 32 students just completed a midterm exam. He wants to use item discrimination to analyze the results of the multiple-choice part of the exam. He decides to examine the top 25 percent of students on the test versus the lowest scoring 25 percent.

Question 9	Item Alternatives			
	A	B	C	D
Top Group	0	8	0	0
Low Group	0	0	4	4

The correct answer for Question 9 was B. As shown, all eight members of the top group answered this item correctly. None of the eight members of the low group answered the item correctly. Thus, this item perfectly discriminated between the top group and the low group.

Question 12	Item Alternatives			
	A	B	C	D
Top Group	4	0	4	0
Low Group	0	2	4	2

The correct answer for Question 12 was C. Equal numbers of the top group and the low group answered this item correctly. This question has zero item discrimination and would be considered inappropriate. Mr. Strickland decides to review and change item alternative A. This item was answered by a large number of the top group. When a significant number of the top group lists the same incorrect answer, careful scrutiny should be given to that item alternative.

Question 17	Item Alternatives			
	A	B	C	D
Top Group	1	1	0	6
Low Group	2	2	2	2

The correct answer for Question 17 is D. Six members of the top group answered this item correctly, and two members of the low group answered this item successfully. This item successfully discriminated between the two groups, and therefore should be retained.

way: The more samples or measurements that one takes of any phenomenon, the more reliable and valid is one's final evaluation of the phenomenon. This is true of earthquakes; it also is true of middle school boys.

This section presents two ways of using these measures of quality control:

1. *Formal Analysis.* Many statistical programs are available that will examine and report reliability, validity, and item analysis. Although these programs require training for individual use, some school systems may offer assistance through their technology specialists or their research bureau. Other computer programs offer much easier to learn applications. For instance, some machine scoring programs that use bubble sheets (computer-scored answer sheets) will also offer reliability and item analysis. Some spreadsheet programs, such as Excel, also provide the ability to complete some types of reliability and validity analysis.

2. *Informal Analysis.* It is relatively easy to complete an informal analysis of quality control procedures. However, you sacrifice some accuracy and precision by an informal analysis. The first thing is to transform test scores into class rankings. You can then compare students' class rankings and get an approximation of reliability and validity scores. For instance, with reliability, the questions are: Do the same students have the same or similar rankings on different sections of the same test? Are the top-scoring students still the top-scoring students? Are the lower-scoring students still the lower-scoring students?

With validity, it is essentially the same procedure. You want to determine the validity of a new chemistry exam. You obtain the test scores on the new exam and the overall chemistry grades. You rank both the exam scores and the grades. You then compare the rankings on both measures to see if the students have approximately the same rankings on both the test and the grades.

An informal item analysis can be easily completed by examining the test scores of your top 21 to 33 percent students. If the test items are appropriate, your top students should be missing different items. If they miss different items, this would indicate that the items are not the problem. If the top group consistently misses the same items, then these are the items that need to be closely reviewed. This indicates a problem and these items may need to be discarded.

By carefully applying reliability, validity, and item analysis procedures, you can discard inappropriate assessment items (or even entire assessments). You then retain those items that are appropriate. This increases the quality of your assessments. You will be a happier teacher and your students will reinforce that happiness.

Chapter Summary

Assessment Definitions and Distinctions

The variety of assessments has markedly increased in the last two decades. One aspect of this change is to create a number of alternatives to traditional assessments. A second aspect is to distinguish between assessments and evaluations. Assessments may be evaluative in nature and lead to formal grades or academic judgments. However, certain assessments, such as informal assessments, are nonevaluative and are used simply to provide feedback.

Categorizing Assessment Procedures

To help conceptualize assessment practices, a classification system for assessments is presented. The different classifications of assessments are based on the following aspects: who constructs the tests, the degree of formality, how they are graded, how they are used, and how authentic they are. Assessments range from informal observations to standardized state exams.

Quality Control with Assessments

Reliability, validity, and item analysis are used to measure quality control with assessments. Reliability measures the consistency of an assessment. Validity measures the degree to which the assessment measures what it claims to measure. Item analysis reviews individual items after the assessment has been administered in order the examine the quality of the items.

CASE STUDY EPILOGUE

Mr. Strickland has decided to use a variety of assessments as part of his assessment policy in his social studies classes. He begins his first fall term with a series of informal assessments. These informal assessments use question-and-answer discussion sessions with the whole class. Mr. Strickland begins these sessions by asking a series of questions that initiate the discussion. He then informally observes the knowledge and ability level of his students.

After two weeks of informal assessments, Mr. Strickland gives bi-monthly formal assessments that use both objective and essay items. After these assessments, he reviews each of his new formal assessments. He completes an item analysis of each assessment. He then examines and discards a number of items that appear to have problems. Next he checks the internal consistency reliability of his new assessments. Along with two other teachers, Mr. Strickland reviews the construct validity of his formal assessments.

In addition to these assessments, Mr. Strickland also requires that his students complete a journal that documents and analyzes current news stories. At least twice a week each student must document a news story by describing it. Then he or she must analyze the different aspects of the news story and analyze the relationship of the news story to the social studies course. At the end of the term, each student is required to write a research paper on one of these news stories.

CHAPTER ACTIVITIES

Websites

www.unl.edu:80/buros   This is the online version of the *Mental Measurements Yearbook* developed by the Buros Institute. The website has perhaps the most complete index on published tests. It also includes an index for test reviews.

Cresst96.cse.ucla.edu/index.htm   Funded by the National Center for Research on Evaluation, Standards, and Student Testing, this website is created by UCLA. The site includes a variety of information and research on assessment practices.

www.edusource.com   This general site for educational resources and issues features a number of recommended educational links.

www.nytimes.com   This website for the *New York Times* provides some of the most current information on educational issues. The site also provides an archive for previous newspaper articles on educational issues.

Portfolio Activities

1. Review Mr. Strickland's situation as listed in the chapter Case Study. In your portfolio try to answer the questions that Mr. Strickland has about his teaching. Here are some of the questions:
   - What type of assessments are appropriate for teaching social studies and history?
   - What type of assessments will provide appropriate feedback to students?
   - What type of assessments will satisfy state and school district criteria for educational accountability?
   - How does a teacher determine what is good assessment and what is not good assessment?

2. Find this website: www.unl.edu:80/buros. (As indicated above, this website features nearly all published standardized assessments.) Go to this website and the search engine involved with this site. Find a test that you have taken at some point. This might include the ACT, the SAT, a state standardized assessment for your state such as the Comprehensive Test of Basic Skills (CTBS), or the Stanford-9 Achievement Test. In two paragraphs summarize the basic aspects of this test. Include statements about the test's validity and reliability.

3. Using the examples provided in this chapter on item analysis, complete an examination of both item difficulty and item discrimination with material from your own class. (If you do not have your own students, borrow some test data. There are plenty of teachers who need to make their assessments better.) With item difficulty, review items that were correctly answered by fewer than 25 percent of students or items that were correctly answered by more than 75 percent of students. These are items that may need to be changed or discarded. With item discrimination first determine which students were in the top 25 percent on the assessment and which students were in the bottom 25 percent. Then for each question devise a grid like the one provided below.

Question_____	Item Alternatives			
	A	B	C	D
Top Group				
Low Group				

Review each item on the test to see which questions effectively discriminate between the top and low groups. (The top group answers them correctly and the low group does not answer them correctly.) Again, those items that produce the greatest response difference between the two groups are generally the best items.

KEY CONCEPTS

Authentic assessment movement
Constructed-response assessments
Criterion-referenced assessments
Evaluation
Exhibitions
Formal assessments
Formative assessments
Informal assessments
Item analysis
Item difficulty

Item discrimination
Norm-referenced assessment
Objective assessments
Performance-based assessments
Portfolios
Reliability
Standardized assessment
Summative assessments
Teacher-constructed assessment
Validity

REVIEW QUESTIONS

1. What are the basic differences between assessment and evaluation?

2. Compare and contrast informal assessment with formal assessment.

3. Describe when a formative assessment would be used and when a summative assessment would be used.

4. What are the positive features of a criterion-referenced assessment?

5. What are the major types of reliability?

6. List and describe the major types of validity.

7. Explain the basic features of item analysis.

8. What are the advantages of a performance-based assessment?

SELF-ASSESSMENT

1. A statistical index of the extent to which an assessment measures what it claims to measure is termed:
   a. Reliability
   b. Item analysis
   c. Standard deviation
   d. Validity

Answers to Self-Assessment: 1. d, 2. c, 3. d, 4. a, 5. c, 6. b, 7. c, 8. b

2. Which of the following is a type of performance-based assessment?
   a. Multiple-choice exam
   b. IQ test
   c. Portfolio
   d. Survey

3. A type of item analysis that examines differences between the highest-scoring students and the lowest-scoring students is called:
   a. Item difficulty
   b. Reliability
   c. Item reactivity analysis
   d. Item discrimination

4. On a general science exam the students must correctly answer 90 out of 100 items to pass the test. This type of assessment is called:
   a. Criterion-referenced
   b. Norm-referenced
   c. Extended response reaction
   d. Validity

5. The consistency of an assessment is termed:
   a. Validity
   b. Item difficulty
   c. Reliability
   d. Criterion-referenced

6. "Grading on the curve" where students scores are comparatively ranked against each other is known as:
   a. Criterion-referenced
   b. Norm-referenced
   c. Inter-rater reliability
   d. Content validity

7. The most commonly used type of objective assessment item is:
   a. Matching
   b. True/False
   c. Multiple choice
   d. Fill-in-the-blank

8. What type of assessment is a final exam in a history class?
   a. Formative
   b. Summative
   c. Informal
   d. Authentic

REFERENCES

Banks, S.R., & Thompson, C.L. (1995). *Educational psychology for teachers in training.* Minneapolis: West Publishing.
Carey, L.M. (1988). *Measuring and evaluating school learning.* Boston: Allyn and Bacon.

Hambleton, R.K. (1990). Criterion-referenced testing methods and practices. In T.B. Gutkin & C.R. Reynolds (Eds.), *The handbook of school psychology* (pp. 388–415). New York: Wiley.

Hambleton, R.K. (1996). Advances in assessment models, methods, and practices. In D.C. Berliner & R.C. Caffee (Eds.), *The handbook of educational psychology* (pp. 899–925). New York: Macmillan.

Hopkins, K.D., Stanley, J.C., & Hopkins, B.R. (1990). *Educational and psychological measurement and evaluation* (7th ed.). Englewood Cliffs, NJ: Prentice Hall.

Mosenthal, J.H., & Ball, D.L. (1992). Constructing new forms of teaching: Subject matter knowledge in inservice teacher education. *Journal of Teacher Education, 43*(5), 347–356.

Popham, W.J. (1990). *Modern educational measurement: A practitioner's perspective.* Englewood Cliffs, NJ: Prentice Hall.

Thorndike, R.M. (1997). *Measurement and evaluation psychology and education* (6th ed.). Columbus, OH: Merrill.

Wiggins, G. (1989). Teaching to the (authentic) test. *Educational Leadership, 46*(7), 41–47.

CHAPTER

3 Planning for Instruction and Assessments

CASE STUDY

Mrs. Martinez teaches advanced high school algebra. It is the start of the fall semester and she just transferred to a new consolidated high school. She begins her first day with what she believes is a basic review of algebraic models and equations. After 20 minutes of instruction, Mrs. Martinez notices that two students in the back row are staring out the window. Some of the students on the other side of the room appear confused and unable to follow her review. Three students at the front of the class are furiously writing down notes about her lecture. One of these students raises his hand and says, "Mrs. Martinez, I don't remember any of this stuff from Algebra I. I can't speak for anyone else but I am already lost. Could you repeat everything you just said?"

Mrs. Martinez faces the same problem as any other teacher: how to initially determine and then teach to her students' level. Mrs. Martinez also has the same questions about her students as other teachers:

What is the students' knowledge base?

What is their cognitive level?

What is the best way to help students learn about highly abstract subjects?

What type of assessment might be appropriate at the start of a fall term to help find the students' level?

Introduction

As a teacher, you will need to ensure that your level of teaching matches your students' level of knowledge and thinking. This connection between teacher and student is critical for effective instruction. Problems occur when your teaching does not match your students' level. If your presentation is too far above the students, they may be unable to follow your instruction and they may simply give up. If your presentation is too far below the students' level, they may become bored with the presentation and tune out what you are saying.

A lack of compatibility between instructional level and student level also may cause problems with assessments and grades. Students often equate effort with grades. If instruction is too far above the students' level, their effort may not result in an anticipated grade. Students may believe that they did not receive the grades they deserved and their hard work was wasted.

On the other hand, if a teacher's instructional level is too far below the students' knowledge level, students may perceive that the teacher is an easy A. They may believe that everyone gets a good grade, so why make any extra effort. These reactions can negatively affect both instruction and assessment. Therefore, for all teachers, just as for Mrs. Martinez, there are three critical aspects in planning for instruction and assessments:

1. Finding out students' baseline knowledge in a particular subject area
2. Finding out students' cognitive ability level
3. Aligning instructional objectives with actual instruction and assessments

Two comprehensive models address these aspects. These models are Bloom's Taxonomy and Anderson and Krathwohl's Revision of Bloom's Taxonomy. In addition, two other models address certain of these aspects and offer some alternative ideas about this area: Hunter's Model of Planning and Constructivism.

This is a heavy load of models. But there is no denying the importance placed on these models by school systems, curriculum supervisors, and principals. Many school districts emphasize some sort of framework for planning, writing, and implementing instructional activities. That is what these models try to do. And that leads us to the purpose of this chapter: to review these models, their educational approaches, and their assessment methods.

Bloom's Taxonomy

I would be very surprised if you have not heard of Bloom's Taxonomy. It may be the most widely known model in this book; indeed, Bloom's Taxonomy is regarded as one of the most influential curriculum writings of the twentieth century (Anderson & Krathwohl, 2001; Shane, 1981). This model integrates cognitive levels, instructional objectives, and assessments. Bloom's original work developed a framework for just the cognitive domain. This cognitive framework is usually what is referred to when speaking of **Bloom's Taxonomy** (Bloom, Engelhart, Furst, Hill, & Krathwohl, 1956). However, a framework for the affective domain was subsequently provided (Krathwohl, Bloom, & Masia, 1964). A separate group of writers (Simpson, 1966; Harrow, 1972) created a model for the psychomotor domain.

Bloom's Taxonomy includes six separate cognitive domains or levels. These cognitive levels progress from less complex cognitive abilities to more complex abilities. Each level is cumulative and is intended to serve as a building block for the higher levels. A summary of each cognitive domain follows (Bloom et al., 1956):

Bloom's Taxonomy

1. *Knowledge.* The student is able to recognize specific information, such as the ability to recognize words, definitions, numbers, and formulas.
2. *Comprehension.* The student is able to understand and interpret information through translating knowledge-level information into his or her own words and concepts. For example, the student can translate a statistical graph into words.
3. *Application.* The student is able to apply comprehended information to solve a particular problem. For instance, the student can apply the Pythagorean theorem to solve the length of the hypotenuse in a triangle.
4. *Analysis.* The student is able to break down and analyze each separate component in order to derive a conclusion about the whole. For example, the student can analyze the separate contributions of dominant and recessive genes in determining genetic inheritance and physical characteristics.
5. *Synthesis.* The student is able to combine disparate ideas to create a new understanding. For instance, the student can make a connection between the loss of tropical rain forests and global climate changes.
6. *Evaluation.* The student is able to understand a set of criteria and then use the criteria to make judgments about an activity or idea. For instance, the student can understand criteria for judging student newspaper articles and then use those criteria to award students who are judged the best writers.

Constructing Instructional Objectives and Assessments for Bloom's Taxonomy

As mentioned in Chapter 1, instructional objectives are a key connection between state-mandated standards and your classroom instruction. Bloom's Taxonomy provides a framework for translating different cognitive levels into instructional objectives and assessments. Appropriately used, this taxonomy can provide a guide for both instruction and assessment. Nevertheless, Bloom provided certain cautions about using his taxonomy to construct instructional objectives. As noted by Bloom and colleagues (1956), this taxonomy was *not* developed to classify a teacher's instructional methods, academic subjects, classroom materials, or any other teacher activities. It was constructed to define and categorize students' responses. "What we are classifying is the intended behavior of students—the ways in which individuals are to act or think as the result of participating in some unit of instruction" (p. 12).

Lower-Level Cognitive Domains

Knowledge Level.   The *Knowledge* level calls for the student to demonstrate a basic recall and recognition of information. Bloom, Hastings, and Madaus (1971) note that this level of cognitive ability is frequently disparaged by educators as a form of rote learning. The authors also emphasize that the Knowledge level was the foundation for other types of cognitive domains.

Bloom and colleagues (1956) indicate that certain key terms may be used to construct instructional objectives for each level. These key terms serve to guide both instruction and assessment. For instance, at the Knowledge level some of the key terms include *define*, *identify*, *recall*, and *recognize*. An example of an instructional objective for the Knowledge level of Bloom's Taxonomy is:

> Students will recognize the correct use of antonyms in reading and writing sentences.

An item that assesses this objective at the Knowledge level of the taxonomy is:

> Which of the following is an antonym of difficult?
> a. Hard
> b. Generous
> c. Soft
> d. Easy

Comprehension Level.   The *Comprehension* level involves an adaptation or an elaboration of a new concept into one's own words. This level may involve a restatement or rephrasing of the new concept that goes beyond the recognition of the Knowledge level. Writing instructional objectives at the Comprehension level may include the following key terms: *elaborate*, *extrapolate*, *interpret*, and *translate*. An instructional objective for the Comprehension level of Bloom's Taxonomy is:

Students will interpret the changes in the main characters of novels and plays.

An item that assesses this objective at the Comprehension level of the taxonomy is:

Interpret the changes in a sense of conscience that Macbeth and Lady Macbeth demonstrate during the course of the play.

Application Level. At the *Application* level students take a principle or a concept then apply it to solve a particular problem. Some of the key terms associated with instructional objectives at the Application level are *apply*, *generalize*, and *predict*. An instructional objective for the Application level is:

Students will predict outcomes of events using the principles of probability.

An item that assesses this objective at the Application level of the taxonomy is:

Using probability principles, which of the following would be most likely to occur?
a. Drawing an ace from a full deck of cards
b. Drawing either the King or Queen of hearts from a full deck
c. First drawing the 10 of spades and then the 9 of spades from a full deck
d. Drawing the Jack of hearts from a full deck

Higher-Level Cognitive Domains

Analysis Level. The next three levels, *Analysis*, *Synthesis*, and *Evaluation*, progressively increase in terms of cognitive complexity and critical thinking skills. At the *Analysis* level a problem or a communication is broken down into its separate elements in order to derive a conclusion. Among the key terms associated with objectives at this level are *analyze*, *break down*, *differentiate*, and *distinguish*. An instructional objective for the Analysis level is:

Students will analyze the effects of technology on economics in the twentieth century.

An assessment item that addresses this objective is:

Analyze the effects of new technologies on worker productivity since World War II. List a general principle or conclusion that supports your analysis.

Synthesis Level. At the *Synthesis* level the student is able to generate a unique response to a problem, activity, or situation. Bloom, Hastings, and Madaus (1971) state that synthesis is most closely related to divergent thinking—a type of thinking often associated with creative activities. Some of the key terms used in constructing Synthesis-level objectives are *construct*, *create*, *design*, *devise*, *generate*, and *produce*. An example of an instructional objective at the Synthesis level is:

Students will construct an original essay, short story, or poem.

An item that assesses this objective is:

Imagine that you are able to visit the United States 100 years into the future. Write an original essay about this future time. Generate a number of unique aspects that would distinguish this time from the present time. List the new types of technological inventions, artistic trends, and political changes that would occur.

Evaluation Level.   The *Evaluation* level involves making judgments about an activity or concept based on an explicit set of criteria. Some of the key terms used in constructing Evaluation-level objectives are *appraise*, *critique*, *evaluate*, and *judge*. An instructional objective for the Evaluation level is:

Students will complete a peer evaluation using a specified set of guidelines.

An item that assesses the Evaluation level is:

During class presentations, complete a peer evaluation on each peer presenter in your class. (Use the rating form listed in Figure 3.1.)

FIGURE 3.1   Peer Evaluation Rating Form

Rate each peer presenter on the following 5-point scale:

1	2	3	4	5
|	|	|	|	|
Strongly Disagree	Disagree	Neutral	Agree	Strongly Agree

The peer presenter demonstrated:

1. _____ Clarity of main idea
2. _____ Originality of thought
3. _____ Use of research
4. _____ Use of examples
5. _____ Development of ideas
6. _____ Effective introduction
7. _____ Effective organization
8. _____ Appropriate voice pitch
9. _____ Good eye contact
10. _____ Appropriate speed of speaking
11. _____ Clear speaking voice
12. _____ Response to questions

Teacher Application

Mandating the Revised Taxonomy

For the last 20 years, Ms. Kennedy has taught fifth grade at a large urban elementary school. This year, the city school superintendent just returned from a national workshop about the new revision of Bloom's Taxonomy. The superintendent is excited about the new revision and thinks that it is an excellent format for basing systemwide instructional changes in the school district. By mandating the use of Anderson and Krathwohl's revision of Bloom's Taxonomy, the superintendent believes that it will enable teachers to increase critical thinking skills and higher-level cognitive abilities in all students.

Therefore, the school district has decided to require teachers to document that they are using this revised taxonomy in writing their instructional objectives. Faculty must list the objectives in their lesson plans and assessments.

Ms. Kennedy wants to know just what the revised taxonomy involves and how she can effectively implement it. However, the superintendent has issued only the most general guidelines about the revised taxonomy. Ms. Kennedy's colleagues have little idea about what the superintendent's intention is regarding the new policy. She has a number of questions about how exactly to implement this mandate:

How does the revised taxonomy compare with Bloom's Taxonomy?

How does one write instructional objectives with the revised taxonomy?

In the revised taxonomy what is the difference between higher-level thinking skills and lower-level thinking skills?

Where do critical thinking skills fit in with other types of cognitive abilities?

How does one write instructional objectives that will effectively increase higher-level thinking and critical thinking?

What are the ways to assess students to increase these thinking skills?

The Anderson and Krathwohl Revision of Bloom's Taxonomy

Anderson and Krathwohl (2001), with a team of contributors, recently published a major revision of Bloom's Taxonomy. (Krathwohl was one of the coauthors of the original version of Bloom's Taxonomy.) According to the authors, this current revision is in response to a number of changes in psychology and education since Bloom's original taxonomy. Among these changes are the increasing emphasis on cognitive psychology in the United States and the growing emphasis on standards-based accountability in U.S. education.

In contrast to Bloom's original taxonomy, **Anderson and Krathwohl's Revision of Bloom's Taxonomy** includes t a 4 × 6 matrix consisting of two separate dimensions. One dimension is called the *Knowledge Dimension* and contains four separate categories. The second dimension is termed the *Cognitive Process Dimension* and has six separate processes. These two dimensions interact in designing objectives and assessments. Therefore, an instructional objective or assessment procedure would fit in one of the 24 cells or sections created by this 4 × 6 matrix.

Wait a minute! I know what you are thinking: This is an overly complicated model with 24 separate components to understand. Your eyes may be glazing over or your head may be spinning. But, as explained in detail in the next section, there is a relatively easy way to understand this revision. The six Cognitive Process Dimensions are all verbs, like the verbs *to understand* and *to apply*. In using the model, these six verbs always refer to different types of knowledge, such as "understanding factual knowledge." As a teacher, you will mostly use the six Cognitive Process Dimensions in describing the desired activity of students in your objectives. Another thing about the Cognitive Process Dimension is that it is not very different from Bloom's original taxonomy.

Knowledge Dimension

As part of their revision to Bloom's Taxonomy, Anderson and Krathwohl (2001) transformed the Knowledge level from Bloom's Taxonomy into one separate dimension of the matrix. This transformed **Knowledge Dimension** has four categories: factual, conceptual, procedural, and metacognitive. Within these four sections there are a total of 11 subtypes. (Space does not permit a full coverage of each subtype.) The following description focuses on the four main categories.

Factual Knowledge.   This is knowledge of the basic facts, terms, or details of an area of study or of an academic discipline. This can range from knowledge of the alphabet to basic facts about a foreign country or culture. There are two subcategories in this aspect: knowledge of terminology and knowledge of details and elements.

Conceptual Knowledge.   This is knowledge of the ways that ideas or objects can be classified, categorized, or developed into principles, models, or theories. Essentially, it is knowledge of the relationships among objects or concepts. Conceptual knowledge may encompass classifying different objects in the solar system into planets, moons, asteroids, and comets. It can include knowledge of scientific principles, such as the effects of the moon's gravity on ocean tides. It also may comprise knowledge of theories, such as the theory of relativity. Conceptual knowledge includes three subcategories: classifications and categories; principles and generalizations; and theories, models, and structures.

Procedural Knowledge.   This is knowledge of the process or procedure in performing an activity. As noted by Anderson and Krathwohl (2001), "Procedural knowledge is the knowledge of how to do something" (p. 52). This can include knowledge of specific skills, such as the knowledge of how to read a map. It also may comprise knowledge of how to conduct a chemistry experiment or how to write a dissertation. There are three subcategories of procedural knowledge: subject-specific skills; subject-specific techniques; and knowledge of when to use appropriate procedures.

Metacognitive Knowledge. This is knowledge about cognitive processes and self-awareness about one's own thinking processes. Some aspects of metacognitive knowledge are knowledge about mnemonic strategies, knowledge about in-depth processing and elaboration strategies that can increase learning, and knowledge about self-monitoring activities (such as self-awareness of one's own goals, capabilities, and interests) that can aid in learning. There are three subcategories of this aspect: strategic knowledge, cognitive task knowledge, and self-knowledge.

Cognitive Process Dimension

The second dimension of the matrix is the **Cognitive Process Dimension,** which consists of six separate cognitive processes. These processes are remember, understand, apply, analyze, evaluate, and create. A number of changes from Bloom's Taxonomy also occurred with this dimension of the matrix. Each cognitive process is presented as a verb in order to facilitate the writing of objectives and assessments (Anderson & Krathwohl, 2001). In writing instructional objectives, a cognitive process, such as *apply,* will be used as a verb, whereas a knowledge aspect, such as *procedural knowledge,* will be used as an object noun.

Description of the Cognitive Process Dimension

In addition to the six listed cognitive processes, there are a number of subcategories within each Cognitive Process Dimension. For instance, *remember* has 2 subcategories, whereas *understand* has 7 subcategories. Overall, there are 19 subcategories within the total Cognitive Process Dimension. (As with the Knowledge Dimension, space does not permit a full coverage of each subcategory.) The following description presents each of the main categories of the Cognitive Process Dimension.

Remember. This cognitive process involves retrieving relevant knowledge from long-term memory. Anderson and Krathwohl divide this process into two separate aspects: recognizing and recalling. *Recognizing* is the process involved in identifying an action or an event with a prompt. For instance, the student is asked to recognize the synonym of a word from a list of words. *Recalling* is a step beyond recognizing in that there is no external stimulus or list to help prompt memory retrieval. If the student is asked to name the first three presidents of the United States just from memory (without a list of all U.S. presidents), then it is a pure recall task.

Understand. This process includes the ability to derive meaning from varying types of instructional activities. There are seven subcategories: interpreting, exemplifying, classifying, summarizing, inferring, comparing, and explaining. In general, these subcategories refer to a transformation of knowledge that show some type of new comprehension of the information. For example, the student will be able to provide an explanation of a road map.

Apply.   This is the cognitive process involved in using a procedure to perform a task. This category is divided into executing and implementing. *Executing* is when the task is familiar to the student, such as executing a task in a chemistry lab. *Implementing* is when the task is new to the student—for instance, the student will determine the best way to pay for a new home. (Should a variable mortgage rate or a locked-in mortgage rate be used? Should the average monthly house payments be based on a 15- or 30-year mortgage? How much should be allowed for a down payment?) With implementing, the student must select among various options that have no immediate, clear-cut, right answer.

Analyze.   This process includes breaking down a problem or structure into separate components and deriving a conclusion about how the parts fit together or reaching a conclusion about the total structure. The three subcategories are differentiating, organizing, and attributing. These three aspects each contribute in separate ways to the overall process involved in analyzing a structure. *Differentiating* distinguishes among separate parts of a structure, such as discriminating between the central characters in a play and the secondary characters. *Organizing* determines how the parts fit together as a whole. *Attributing* is deconstructing or discovering the underlying intention in a communication.

Evaluate.   This process requires the student to make judgments from a standard set of criteria. There are two subcategories: checking and critiquing. *Checking* requires the student to detect inconsistent or illogical conclusions from a set of data, such as checking the conclusions about global warming to determine if they logically follow from the data. *Critiquing* involves judging a product or procedure based on established criteria and listing its positive and negative features.

Create.   This process includes developing a unique product or idea, as well as making a new synthesis of existing information. As noted by Anderson and Krathwohl (2001), "Educators must define what is original or unique. . . . It is important to note, however, that many objectives in the Create category do not rely on originality or uniqueness" (p. 85). Therefore, the criteria for the Create process ranges from devising new perspectives on existing material to actual creative products. The three subcategories are generating, planning, and producing. *Generating* is producing divergent solutions to the problem. *Planning* is developing a plan of action to carry out the divergent solution. *Producing* is the fulfillment of the plan by demonstrating a finished solution to the problem.

Using the Revised Taxonomy

In terms of practical use by teachers, the revised taxonomy has certain positive features. After mastering the 4×6 matrix, the use of the verb (Cognitive Process Dimension) with the object noun (Knowledge Dimension) may facilitate the writing of objectives and assessment items. Therefore, as previously noted, the development of appropriate objectives should list one Cognitive Process and one Knowledge Category in a sentence. Anderson and Krathwahl (2001, p. 23) recommend the following format for writing instructional objectives: "The student will be able to, or learn to, verb/noun." For example, an instructional objective for a world history class would be stated:

The student will be able to recall three events that caused World War II.

This objective fits into the *remember* aspect of the Cognitive Process Dimension and the *factual knowledge* of the Knowledge Dimension. In Figure 3.2, the full revised taxonomy is presented. The X marks the spot in the matrix where the above objective should be listed.

Anderson and Krathwohl (2001) state that this matrix can be used to align objectives with both instruction and assessments. They provide the following example of aligning objectives, instruction, and assessments. The instructional objective is:

"The student will be able to understand the theory of plate tectonics as an explanation for volcanoes" (Anderson & Krathwohl, 2001, p. 191).

The verb *understand* indicates that this belongs to the understand category of the Cognitive Process Dimension. Since the object noun is *theory*, this places the noun in the *knowledge* category of conceptual knowledge.

An instructional activity listed for this objective is: "I then talked to them about the theory of plate tectonics, using three-dimensional models and a filmstrip to convey

FIGURE 3.2   The Revision of Bloom's Taxonomy

	The Cognitive Process Dimension					
The Knowledge Dimension	*1. Remember*	*2. Understand*	*3. Apply*	*4. Analyze*	*5. Evaluate*	*6. Create*
A. Factual Knowledge	×					
B. Conceptual Knowledge						
C. Procedural Knowledge						
D. Metacognitive Knowledge						

its major elements. I asked questions throughout the presentation, honing in on the utility of the information for the overall task" (Anderson & Krathwohl, 2001, p. 196).

This instructional activity involves explaining theories. *Explaining* is listed as a subcategory of *understand*. *Theories* are listed as a type of *conceptual knowledge*. Therefore, in this case, the authors state that there is an alignment (agreement) between the type of objective and the type of instructional activity. The preceding activity also provides assessments partly linked to the original objective: "I engaged in two 'assessment conversations' during the unit. The first took place on Day 8 following the assignment in which students answered four questions about rock types and volcanism. The second took place on Day 13 and involved a class discussion of the students' base map projects" (Anderson & Krathwohl, 2001, p. 203).

The authors indicate that the above informal assessments include a number of different aspects of the taxonomy. In addition to *understand/conceptual knowledge*, these parts are *remember/factual knowledge* and *apply/procedural knowledge*. As before, the part that dealt with understanding the theory of plate tectonics was *understand/conceptual knowledge*.

Anderson and Krathwohl (2001) also indicate that the matrix can be used to generate critical thinking skills. In using the taxonomy for critical thinking skills, the authors state that these skills cut across many different parts of the matrix. A number of different Cognitive Processes can be involved in critical thinking. Nevertheless, they note that *critiquing*, a subcategory of *evaluate*, is most closely linked to critical thinking. Critiquing uses an external set of criteria to make a judgment about an event or product. For example, the student is asked to critique, using criteria from the physical sciences, the various proposals to limit global warming made by the European Union.

Anderson and Krathwohl (2001) provide other examples of how other parts of the revised taxonomy may be used with critical thinking skills. For instance, critical thinking about a particular issue would involve *analyze/conceptual knowledge*. If critical thinking was used to develop a unique viewpoint about a situation or problem, then *create* would be used.

The following information provides a series of examples of instructional objectives for the revised taxonomy.

Teacher Application

Writing Objectives for the Revised Taxonomy

Teachers, such as Ms. Kennedy in the previous Teacher Application, are often required to write specific instructional objectives as part of their lesson plans. The following instructional objectives are presented for each of the six Cognitive Processes in the Anderson and Krathwohl's Revision of Bloom's Taxonomy. Examples of each of the four aspects of the Knowledge Dimension are included.

1. An example for *remember* is:

   Students will be able to correctly recognize the names of the first three presidents of the United States from a list of all U.S. presidents.

The Knowledge Dimension for this objective is *factual knowledge*.

2. An example of *understand* is:

Students will be able to interpret a population graph and verbally explain the underlying concepts displayed in the graph.

With this example, the Knowledge aspect is *conceptual knowledge*.

3. An example of *apply* is:

Students will be able to apply knowledge of procedures from plane geometry in order to calculate each angle in a parallelogram.

With this example, the Knowledge aspect is *procedural knowledge*.

4. An example of *analyze* is:

The student will be able to analyze the different proposals for reducing greenhouse emissions then select and defend one of these proposals.

With this example, the Knowledge aspect is *conceptual knowledge*.

5. An example of *evaluate* is:

The student will be able to evaluate various mnemonic strategies, such as the key word and peg word methods, and effectively use the best strategy in studying Spanish.

With this example, using mnemonic strategies is part of the Knowledge aspect of *metacognitive knowledge*.

6. An example of *create* is:

The student will be able to generate appropriate procedures for reducing bullying at school.

With this example, *generate* is a subcategory of *create*, while the Knowledge aspect is *procedural knowledge*.

Assessment Practices with the Revised Taxonomy

Anderson and Krathwohl (2001) generally recommend that assessments be aligned with or agree with the instructional objective for a particular instructional activity. This means that each assessment should fit in the same cell or block of the 4 × 6 matrix that is addressed by the instructional objective. For instance, the instructional objective is:

Students will be able to recall knowledge of five basic geometric forms.

This objective fits into the cell formed by *remember (Cognitive Process)* and *factual knowledge (Knowledge Dimension)*. The assessment for this instructional objective should also fit into the *remember* and *factual knowledge* block in the matrix. An assessment item for this type of objective would be:

List and describe five basic types of geometric forms.

The difficulty in constructing objective assessment items, such as multiple-choice questions, for the higher-order cognitive processes of *analyze, evaluate,* and *create* is acknowledged by Anderson and Krathwohl (2001): "Forty-four years after the publication of the Handbook (Bloom's Taxonomy), we could add little that would show any advance in item writing. Educators should not forget the usefulness of portfolios and other performance assessments" (p. 298).

Anderson and Krathwohl (2001) still have a certain number of suggestions that may be used in constructing assessments with their revised taxonomy. For example, they recommend varying the types of assessment items so that both constructed-response items (essay items) and objective items be used to assess instructional objectives. They also note, "If assessment tasks are to tap higher-order cognitive processes, they must require that students cannot answer them correctly by relying on memory alone" (p. 71).

The authors offer some individual examples. Within the Cognitive Process, *understand,* they propose an assessment technique for the subcategory *comparing.* This assessment technique, called *mapping,* requires the student to show how two separate objects, events, or ideas correspond to or compare with each other. For example, on an assessment, the student is asked to detail how the human memory system (neurons, memory centers, short-term and long-term memory processes) corresponds to the parts of a computer (circuitry, files, RAM memory, and hard drive memory).

Using the Cognitive Process, *create,* Anderson and Krathwohl (2001) offer a brainstorming type of assessment activity for the subcategory, *generating.* With this activity, students are given a problem situation and asked to generate as many solutions as possible to the problem. The teacher uses a scoring rubric that scores the solutions on such factors as number of solutions, appropriateness of solutions, and practicality of solutions.

Comparing the Revised Taxonomy with Bloom's Original Taxonomy

In reviewing these two taxonomies, there are a number of similarities as well as differences. In certain respects, the Cognitive Process Dimension from the revised taxonomy is acknowledged as somewhat similar to Bloom's original work (Anderson & Krathwohl, 2001), as shown here:

Revised Taxonomy	*Original Taxonomy*
Remember	Knowledge
Understand	Comprehension
Apply	Application
Analyze	Analysis
Evaluate	Synthesis
Create	Evaluation

As previously mentioned, the revised taxonomy uses verbs, whereas Bloom's original taxonomy used nouns. The order of the taxonomies also has slightly changed, with *evaluate* listed as the fifth cognitive process in the revision. Both *understand* and *create* appear to be more comprehensive than their counterparts from the original taxonomy.

There are other noticeable differences between the two taxonomies. Bloom and colleagues (1956) considered their taxonomy as a cumulative hierarchy. This meant that each subsequent level required mastery of the lower levels. For instance, to use *comprehension* also required mastery of using *knowledge*. *Evaluation* required mastering all five of the lower levels. Anderson and Krathwohl (2001) reject the strict cumulative hierarchy concept with their taxonomy. Their viewpoint is that certain cognitive processes will overlap. For example, they note that *understand* and *apply* contain some degree of overlap. Therefore, it is not possible to claim that mastery of *understand* is always necessary for mastery of *apply*. The authors do recognize that there is a general increase in cognitive complexity when the lower levels (*remember*, *understand*, and *apply*) are compared with the higher levels (*analyze*, *evaluate*, and *create*.) They also state that there is more research support for a cumulative hierarchy at the lower levels of the taxonomy than at the higher levels.

Hunter's Model of Planning

Hunter's Model of Planning was created to provide a link among instructional objectives, instruction, and assessment (Hunter, 1982). Hunter's model is part of a group of instructional models often called *direct instruction.* The focus of these models is to lock in all instructional and assessment steps so that they directly refer back to the original instructional objective. In general, these models appear to use similar ideas about instructional objectives to those originally provided by Bloom's Taxonomy.

Hunter (1982) also offers some unique tips on how to better integrate assessments with instruction. Her viewpoints on using modeling and guided practice may be particularly useful for beginning teachers. The seven steps or elements of Hunter's approach are listed here:

Hunter's Model of Planning
Focus Set
Objective
Instructional Input
Modeling
Checking for Understanding
Guided Practice
Independent Practice

Description

The following is a detailed description of Hunter's seven-step approach to linking instruction with assessments.

1. *Focus Set.* This provides an advanced organizer for the day's instructional activity. It includes a brief review of previous material, a discussion with students about their knowledge of previous material, and an overview of the day's instruction.

2. *Objective.* This is the specific instructional objective for the day's lesson. Hunter apparently agrees with the writing objectives in Bloom's Taxonomy. She does include an extra aspect, however. In addition to describing what is expected of the student, Hunter states that the teacher also needs to explain the purpose and the rationale for the instruction.

3. *Instructional Input.* This is the content and materials of the instruction. It is both the instructional information presented to the students and the format in which the information is presented.

4. *Modeling.* This is where the teacher demonstrates part or all of the instructional activity, such as completing a computer program in math. In some cases, the teacher may provide a visual display or a graph of the concept. The teacher needs to show students the appropriate process for the activity or the correct outcome.

5. *Checking for Understanding.* This is a type of nonevaluative assessment procedure. The teacher may use informal assessments, such as observation or probes (questions) about the instruction. The teacher also may employ some type of formative assessment, such as a skill checklist. The key with this element is that the teacher is checking in a nonevaluative, ungraded way for student understanding.

6. *Guided Practice.* This is an instructional situation where students attempt to practice the activity on their own, but the teacher or student mentors are available for immediate assistance and feedback. This is similar to Vygotsky's zone of proximal distance. When working on a new concept or activity, Vygotsky noted the difference between working with the guidance of someone and working on one's own. In a sense, both Vygotsky and Hunter offer a rather unique type of assessment: a sort of informal joint student-mentor or student-teacher cooperative assessment.

7. *Independent Practice.* This is where the student works the problem or demonstrates understanding of a concept on his or her own. This may range from informal to formative to formal types of assessments. It may involve graded homework assignments or simply checking the student's work in the classroom.

Here is an example of how to use Hunter's Model in developing your instruction.

Teacher Application

Hunter's Model of Planning: Understanding Tornados in Fifth Grade
As a teacher, you may want to consider this type of direct instruction model. One of the positive features of this model is that it provides a very precise format for integrating an instructional module with a variety of informal and formal assessments.

1. *Focus Set.* You start with a series of informal assessment questions about tornados to focus attention on the subject and to find out exactly what students know about the topic. For example, you might ask:
   - What is a tornado?
   - How do tornados form?
   - Have you seen pictures of tornados on television?

   You also should provide a handout with more questions and problems about tornados.

2. *Objective.* There are two things you need to do at this level. First, develop some objectives for the topic. Here are some examples:

   Students will be able to explain the basic processes involved in causing tornados.

   Students will be able to differentiate the type of atmospheric conditions that cause tornados from other weather conditions.

   Students will be able to identify the safest places in their house or environment in case of a tornado warning.

   Then you need to explain the purpose for the subject to the class. You might start by explaining that tornados do a lot of damage each year to property and people's lives. They are one of nature's most devastating forces. The better people understand them and what to do about them, the better off people will be.

3. *Instructional Input.* The types of instructional materials and methods you might need include:
   - A vocabulary word list of the terms and concepts associated with tornados
   - Verbal explanations with pictures of cloud formations and weather patterns associated with producing tornados
   - The time of year and season associated with most tornado outbreaks
   - An explanation of the Fujita scale for rating tornados

4. *Modeling.* These activities should involve some types of physical demonstration or visual demonstration. Examples include:
   - A short video of a tornado
   - An explanation and a demonstration of what to do if a tornado warning is given in your town or area
   - Civil defense officials coming to the classroom and demonstrating what to do in the school during a tornado alert

5. *Checking for Understanding.* During classroom instruction you might ask your students a series of informal assessment questions to ensure that they understand tornados. For example, you might ask:
   - What is the difference between a hurricane and a tornado?
   - What is the most destructive level on the Fujita scale for rating tornados?
   - What month of the year are tornados most likely?
   - Where in the United States are tornados most likely to occur?

6. *Guided Practice.* With this activity, try cooperative learning groups, while circulating among the groups to ensure understanding. You might assign different aspects about understanding tornados to each group. For example, one group might review and discuss how tornados form, another group might review and discuss how tornados move, and a third group might review and discuss how to prepare for a tornado strike. At the

(continued)

end of this activity, you need to bring the whole class together and review each group's discussion. This will ensure that everyone has a chance at understanding all aspects of tornados.

7. *Independent Practice.* With this aspect of the model, you probably will want to try a formal assessment with each student. Aligning your assessment items from the objectives and instruction, you might want to try a combination of objective and constructed-response items about tornados.

The Constructivist Approach

Constructivism focuses on creating conditions that enable students to construct their own ideas and models about their world. As part of this viewpoint, the approach to planning tends to be student centered and process oriented. *Student-centered instruction* means that instructional activities are planned with student participation and input. *Process-oriented instruction* means that the process of completing the instructional activity is usually more important than the end product or outcome.

Mosenthal and Ball (1992) perhaps best capture the idea of process learning with their discussion of mathematics education:

> The primary criterion for understanding is no longer correctness, but the ability to show the coherence or logic of the problem, a solution path, and a solution. For example, a child who, in computing 32 + 19, makes 32 little slashes and 19 little slashes and then circles groups of 10 likely understands place value better than the one who uses the standard carrying procedure. A child who can use blocks to model 32 / 7 understands division better than one who can simply compute the answer. (p. 350)

The student-centered and process-oriented aspects of constructivism are somewhat different from the models previously listed in this chapter. The emphasis by many constructivists is *not* on what to teach but how to teach. Therefore, constructivist teachers emphasize the development of thinking processes and problem-solving skills that can facilitate higher-order thinking. For example, whole language instruction is one example of the type of instructional approach often associated with constructivism (Swicegood & Linehan, 1995). Cooperative learning is another type of approach frequently used by constructivists.

Constructivists typically use a democratic and thematic approach to planning for instruction and assessments. A constructivist approach often emphasizes an ongoing dialog between teachers and students in classroom activities. This dialog may enhance the active thinking skills of students. The emphasis is on the involvement of students in the planning process of instructional activities. Planning often focuses on developing a theme for each instructional unit (Perrone, 1994). For instance, a theme for the primary grades could be "trains." For planning purposes, the teacher and the students work together to develop a Train Topic Map, such as the one seen in the following Teacher Application.

Teacher Application Train Topic Map

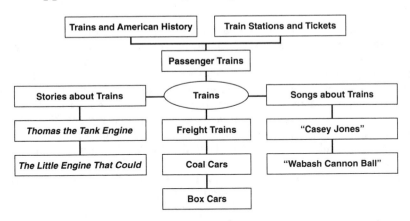

In exploring these themes, a constructivist teacher would ask questions and provide situations for student self-discovery. The teacher might question primary-grade students in this way:

Why does a train blow its whistle?

Why does a train need train tracks?

How quickly can a train stop?

What role did trains play in settling the American West?

What are some differences among the types of cars in a freight train?

Other aspects of the theme "trains" might include reading stories and singing songs about trains. A constructivist teacher also might encourage a cooperative learning activity, such as having students build their own model train from cardboard and other classroom materials. All of these hands-on activities increase student involvement in the instruction. They also are oriented toward the process of thinking about trains rather than achieving an end product.

For assessments, constructivists tend to use performance-based assessments rather than traditional approaches (Swicegood & Linehan, 1995). Therefore, the assessment focus is on portfolios, simulations, journals, projects, peer assessments, and self-assessments. An example of a constructivist assessment might include having students work in cooperative groups with each group submitting a journal. For instance, groups might write a journal together that details their work on the train theme.

Swicegood and Linehan (1995) also discuss the use of constructivist instruction and assessment procedures with literacy education. They note that a constructivist approach to literacy is based on providing meaningful, authentic learning experiences through communicating across a variety of settings and contexts. In terms of learning outcomes, the focus is on the development of thinking processes and strategies, as well as the metacognitive awareness of language constructs. Some of the instructional strategies include story maps, journal writing, literature-based reading, and a writing folder. Assessment strategies involve informal reading assessment inventories, retelling of stories, writing checklists, and student-teacher conferences.

Point/Counterpoint: Using Taxonomies

Point

Supporters of Bloom's Taxonomy (and the recent revision of this taxonomy) state that such a taxonomy provides a well-known blueprint for teachers to apply in devising instructional objectives and assessments. Bloom's Taxonomy is widely used and endorsed by many school systems. In terms of teaching, this model offers a good deal of direction for teachers to use in determining exactly where students should be in a given instructional activity. This taxonomy provides a means for relating state standards to classroom instructional objectives. Formal assessments then can be directly linked to these instructional objectives and classroom activities.

At the federal level, the No Child Left Behind Act appears to agree with this direct approach to standards, objectives, and assessments. Curriculum and classroom activities are to be tied directly to standardized assessments. The focus of this approach is strictly on academic content and student outcomes.

Counterpoint

There is considerable question among some educators about the kind of lockstep instruction produced by strictly defined instructional objectives, including those associated with taxonomies. For example, constructivists endorse a process-oriented instruction to stimulate higher-level thinking as opposed to a content and outcome orientation that may diminish such thinking. Constructivists also emphasize active student involvement in many instructional activities. By including students in instructional decisions, constructivists believe that students will become more active learners.

Kohn (1996) provides part of the constructivist interpretation, stating that educators frequently believe that an effective teacher is one who "retain[s] control over just about everything, closely directing and monitoring students and providing tasks that were highly structured. Again, these results are perfectly logical if we accept the premises; the techniques follow naturally from the objective" (p. 55). However, Kohn further notes that highly directive instruction does not promote any depth to learning or any motivation to continue to learn. It simply promotes task orientation and conformity. Kohn asks the simple question: Is this really the goal of education?

In the end, teachers must make their own decisions about being directive or not with their instructional techniques. What is your comfort level in allowing students a major voice in determining certain types of classroom decisions? Can you combine Bloom's Taxonomy in some way with a constructivist viewpoint? Can a process-oriented instruction somehow be integrated in today's standards-based instruction?

Making Sense of It All

This chapter presents a number of different ways to plan for instruction and assessment. One question in this area is the issue of developmentally appropriate practices and taxonomies. Developmentally appropriate practices are based on providing instruction and assessment to the actual cognitive, social, and behavioral levels of each individual child. The individual child's developmental level may be unrelated to his or her age or grade level. However, a number of factors may relate to developmental level: health history, gender, ethnicity, socioeconomic level, disability status, type of native language, and so on. All of these factors might result in a child being developmentally different from the classroom norm. If these taxonomies and their highly specific instructional objectives are used, will some children be left behind? Can teachers use very directive instructional objectives and still address the individual developmental level of each child?

These questions are of particular concern when we examine diversity and inclusion practices. For example, children with English as a second language may fall behind academically as they progress from elementary school to secondary school. Clearly, these children will need extra assistance in mastering certain language-related objectives. Inclusion policies also present a daunting task for regular classroom teachers in adapting instruction. Not only will some children with disabilities need classroom accommodations, but inclusion policies almost certainly will increase the overall range of student abilities in the classroom. Instructional objectives may need some type of adaptation to accommodate children with special needs.

Therefore, it seems evident from recent research that any framework linking an exact age or grade level to specific cognitive abilities may be questioned. There is considerable variation within a given age group, at least in terms of using higher-level cognitive abilities. Even when applying the most general models, such as Piaget's model of cognitive development, there seems to be a great deal of variation within and across age groups. Flavell, Miller, and Miller (1993) note this problem in their review of the stages in Piaget's model: "The problem is that children often do not act as though they belong in that stage. Conservers do not always conserve; formal operations thinkers often think very concretely. The particular materials, tasks, social contexts, and instructions appear to influence the children's performance" (pp. 11–12).

A related developmental issue is that students of different age groups and in different academic subjects may use different levels of Bloom's Taxonomy or the revision of this taxonomy. For instance, at what age will children be able to use *analyze, evaluate,* and *create* (or *analysis, synthesis,* and *evaluation*)? Can teachers reasonably expect primary-grade children to use higher-level cognitive skills? This question also was discussed by Bloom, Hastings, and Madaus (1971): "Analysis is not frequently found in elementary school objectives; it is more common at the secondary and higher education levels. Some justification of this may be found in Piaget's work, which questions how far preadolescents can pursue the kind of reasoning and the analytic processes which are so central in what we have termed analysis" (p. 177).

Mathematical understanding by students in the primary grades often appears to operate at the *remember (knowledge)* and *understand (comprehension)* levels. Regardless of age, many entry-level courses such as basic college chemistry often focus mostly on the *remember (knowledge)* and *understand (comprehension)* levels. On the other hand, academic subjects such as English Literature may concentrate on *analyze (analysis)* and *create (synthesis)*. Deriving the underlying meaning of a sonnet or connecting two disparate themes in a novel are important aspects of studying literature. Therefore, a number of factors can be involved in planning for instruction, including developmental age, educational background, and type of academic course.

There also seems to be a relationship between the type of assessment and the type of cognitive level. *Remember (knowledge)* and related basic skills appear to be more effectively measured by criterion-referenced techniques and objective items. Formative assessments also may be useful in adjusting instruction with basic skills learning.

Higher-level cognitive skills appear to be more appropriately measured with constructed-response (essay items) and with performance-based assessments. Anderson and Krathwohl (2001) also note a similar relationship between these types of assessments and these types of cognitive level. With *create (synthesis)*, there is a clear need for performance-based assessments. With *create*, the need to allow the student to diverge and generate his or her own responses seem to require alternative assessment items.

Chapter Summary

Bloom's Taxonomy

Bloom's Taxonomy remains one of the most frequently used frameworks describing the relationship among instructional objectives, cognitive levels, and assessments. This taxonomy has six levels that are cumulative in how they are mastered. For example, to appropriately use *evaluation*, the highest level, the student must master all five lower levels. Bloom also stated that the essential focus of his taxonomy is on how students respond to instruction. In effect, do they respond by attempting a *synthesis*, do they respond by *comprehension*, or do they respond at some other cognitive level? Bloom provided a number of examples of how to link instructional objectives to assessments.

The Anderson and Krathwohl Revision

A team of educators recently revised Bloom's Taxonomy. This latest revision of the taxonomy forms a 4 × 6 matrix that consists of two separate dimensions: the *Knowledge Dimension* and the *Cognitive Process Dimension*. In order to facilitate the writing of objectives, the Knowledge Dimension has four categories and the titles are listed as nouns. The Cognitive Process Dimension has six levels and each level is listed as a verb. These two dimensions are interactive and are used together to construct both objectives and assessments. A variety of examples are provided with the revised taxonomy that illustrate how to align objectives with assessments.

Alternative Approaches

Two other approaches to instructional planning and assessments were offered in this chapter. *Hunter's Model of Planning* provides a detailed seven-step approach to planning for instruction. Hunter's model also distinguishes between assessment activities that are completed as a group activity, as a guided activity, or as an independent activity. The *Constructivist* approach takes a much different orientation to instructional planning. Constructivist educators generally reject the more rigid planning approaches that are exemplified by the other models. Constructivism emphasizes a student-centered approach to planning that actively involves students in the decisions about instruction.

Constructivist educators also are more likely to use performance-based assessments in their classrooms.

CASE STUDY EPILOGUE

Mrs. Martinez has decided to try a number of strategies to find out where her students are academically and where they should be headed. She first decides to incorporate two informal assessments at the start of her next class. One assessment is an informal (ungraded) written assessment, and the other assessment uses questioning techniques. She gives the written assessment first. This assessment is based on a number of simple basic concepts involved in basic mathematics and beginning algebra. After completing this assessment, Mrs. Martinez uses the review of the assessment to begin her questioning technique.

Mrs. Martinez uses a series of questions to probe her students' comprehension of basic math and algebra concepts. She addresses the entire class throughout this discussion of basic concepts. By using a nonevaluative approach that encourages student involvement, her students become active in discussing these concepts. She quickly finds out from this assessment about her students' ability levels and their understanding of the subject. Mrs. Martinez then explains to them that the written informal assessment that they previously took is very similar to their future formal (graded) assessments.

CHAPTER ACTIVITIES

Websites

http://illinois.online.uillinois.edu/model/bloomtaxonomy.htm   Created by the University of Illinois, this site has a nice overview of Bloom's Taxonomy with some interesting links to other sites.

http://www.stedwards.edu/cte/bwheel.htm   This site is developed by educators at St. Edward's University. It has a unique diagram on Bloom's Taxonomy that provides a number of verbs for constructing objectives as well as a number of activities to use with each level of the taxonomy.

www.oise.utoronto.ca   Created by the University of Toronto, this is one of many websites that provide information on Hunter's Model of Planning.

Portfolio Activities

1. Examine the Chapter Case Study and Mrs. Martinez's difficulties with her class. Answer the following questions about her class:
   - What are some ways to determine the students' knowledge base?
   - What types of cognitive level or domains are necessary for this class?
   - What is the best way to help students learn about highly abstract subjects?

■ What type of assessment might be appropriate at the start of a fall term to help find the students' cognitive levels?

2. Review the Teacher Application section on pages 56–57 and Ms. Kennedy's questions about the superintendent's new policy on writing objectives and assessments. Answer her questions about the new policy:
   ■ How does the revised taxonomy compare with Bloom's Taxonomy?
   ■ How does one write instructional objectives with the revised taxonomy?
   ■ In the revised taxonomy, what is the difference between higher-level thinking skills and lower-level thinking skills?
   ■ Where do critical thinking skills fit in with other types of cognitive abilities?
   ■ How does one write instructional objectives that will effectively increase higher-level thinking and critical thinking?
   ■ What are the ways to assess students to increase these thinking skills?

3. Design your own theme for a class based on the constructivist planning and assessment model as indicated by the section on constructivism in this chapter. List the type of theme, the type of activities to go along with the theme, and how you would assess the theme. Also discuss what types of cognitive domains might occur in your instruction.

KEY CONCEPTS

Anderson and Krathwohl's Revision of
  Bloom's Taxonomy
Bloom's Taxonomy
Cognitive Process Dimension

Constructivism
Hunter's Model of Planning
Knowledge Dimension

REVIEW QUESTIONS

1. What are the differences between lower-level and higher-level cognitive domains in Bloom's (original) Taxonomy?

2. What are the four Cognitive Process Dimensions listed in the revision of Bloom's Taxonomy?

3. In the revision of Bloom's Taxonomy, what is the relationship between the Knowledge Dimension and the Cognitive Process Dimension?

4. How can a taxonomy be used to write assessment questions?

5. How is a focus set used in Hunter's model of planning?

6. What are the major components of a constructivist approach to instruction and assessment?

7. What are some challenges to the use of taxonomies in instruction?

8. What is the relationship between type of assessment and cognitive level?

SELF-ASSESSMENT

1. Billy wants to use a mathematical formula to predict flight times for airplanes. Which level of Bloom's Taxonomy is most likely to be involved in this problem?
   a. Knowledge
   b. Comprehension
   c. Synthesis
   d. Analysis
   e. Application

2. Coach McNairy is using a physical performance skill test to rate his soccer team players. Which level of Bloom's Taxonomy is most likely to be involved in this situation?
   a. Comprehension
   b. Application
   c. Analysis
   d. Synthesis
   e. Evaluation

3. In Anderson and Krathwohl's revision of Bloom's Taxonomy one aspect of their matrix focuses on the different mental procedures that are used in responding to information. This aspect of the matrix is termed:
   a. Knowledge Dimension
   b. Metamemory Dimension
   c. Cognitive Process Dimension
   d. Comparative Dimension
   e. Factual Dimension

4. One of the distinctions that Anderson and Krathwohl make about lower-level and higher-level assessment items is:
   a. Higher-level items require only comprehension.
   b. Lower-level items require some type of creative ability.
   c. Higher-level items require just memory alone.
   d. Higher-level items require more than just memory alone.
   e. Lower-level items require the ability to both analyze and synthesize.

5. The first three levels of Bloom's Taxonomy generally focus on:
   a. Behavioral objectives
   b. Affective objectives
   c. Lower-level thinking skills
   d. Abstract skills
   e. Language ability

6. According to Hunter's Model of Planning, the type of informal assessment situation where the teacher can help the student is termed:
   a. Independent practice
   b. Inner zone of proximal distance
   c. Guided practice
   d. Self-discovery
   e. Focus set

Answers to Self-Assessment: 1. e, 2. e, 3. c, 4. d, 5. c, 6. c, 7. e, 8. b

7. Which of the following models deemphasizes the use of instructional objectives as part of the planning process?
   a. Bloom's Taxonomy
   b. Anderson and Krathwohl's revision
   c. Gagne's Hierarchy
   d. Hunter's Model of Planning
   e. Constructivism

8. In the Anderson and Krathwohl revision of Bloom's Taxonomy, the writers note that the *create* level is best assessed by the following type of assessment:
   a. Multiple choice
   b. Performance-based
   c. Informal questions
   d. True/False
   e. Zone of proximal development

REFERENCES

Anderson, L.W., & Krathwohl, D.R. (Eds.). (2001). *A taxonomy for learning, teaching, and assessing: A revision of Bloom's taxonomy*. New York: Longman.

Bloom, B.S., Engelhart, M.D., Furst, E.J., Hill, W.H., & Krathwohl, D.R. (1956). *Taxonomy of educational objectives: Handbook I: Cognitive domain*. New York: David McKay.

Bloom, B.S., Hastings, J.T., & Madaus, G.F. (1971). *Handbook on formative and summative evaluation of student learning*. New York: McGraw-Hill.

Flavell, J.H., Miller, P.A., & Miller, S.A. (1993). *Cognitive development* (3rd. ed.). Englewood Cliffs, NJ: Prentice Hall.

Harrow, A. (1972). *A taxonomy of the psychomotor domain: A guide for developing behavioral objectives*. New York: David McKay.

Hunter, M. (1982). *Mastery teaching*. El Segundo, CA: TIP Publications.

Kohn, A. (1996). *Beyond discipline: From compliance to community*. Alexandria, VA: Association for Supervision, Curriculum, and Development.

Krathwohl, D.R., Bloom B.S., & Masia, B.B. (1964). *Taxonomy of educational objectives: Handbook II: The affective domain*. New York: David McKay.

Mosenthal, J.H., & Ball, D.L. (1992). Constructing new forms of teaching: Subject matter knowledge in inservice teacher education. *Journal of Teacher Education*, 43(5), 347–356.

Perrone, V. (1994). How to engage students in learning. *Educational Leadership*, 51, 11–13.

Shane, H.G. (1981). Significant writings that influenced the curriculum: 1906–1981. *Phi Delta Kappan*, 63, 311-314.

Simpson, B.J. (1966). The classification of educational objectives: Psychomotor domain. *Illinois Journal of Home Economics*, 10(4), 110–114.

Swicegood, P.R., & Linehan, S.L. (1995). Literacy and academic learning for students with behavioral disorders: A constructivist view. *Education and Treatment of Children*, 18(3), 335–348.

4

Diversity, Gender, and Assessments

CASE STUDY

A site team of federal evaluators arrives at a large city on the West Coast. They are assigned to complete a program evaluation of an inner-city school. The school was originally awarded a federal education grant for a special reading program to help increase reading achievement test scores. Even though a substantial amount of money has been awarded to the program at this school, the test scores have not markedly improved. The site team is there to make evaluations and recommendations about the program.

The evaluators first meet with Mr. Jenkins, the principal of the school. Mr. Jenkins has a a set of papers in his hands. He gives each member of the team a copy of the paper.

"This handout addresses the basic nature of our problem," Mr. Jenkins says without any prompting from the team.

The paper presents the following information:

- There are 611 students in a school originally designed for 400 students.

- Sixty-four percent of the students are designated as low-income students by the federal guidelines.
- Of the 611 students, 118 are ESL students. Among these 118 ESL students, there are nine different first languages, including Korean, Hmong (a Laotian dialect), Spanish, and Arabic.
- The percentage of ethnic minority students in the school is 47 percent.

"We have a three-year bilingual transitional program for entering ESL children. That is what the state mandates and all they will fund," Mr. Jenkins explains. "With some children it works okay and they can pick up enough English in three years to make it in the classroom. Unfortunately, it is not enough for many of the children. They are pretty much sent 'cold turkey' into the regular classroom.

"Our biggest problem is finding enough ESL teachers and tutors," Mr. Jenkins continues. "You can't imagine how hard it is to find qualified people who speak Hmong or even Arabic. Parent-teacher meetings have to be planned weeks in advance in order to find capable translators. The district office does provide some extra money for our school just because of our ESL needs. But we have a perpetual lack of money to fund the ESL program.

"To address your questions about our reading scores before you ask," Mr. Jenkins states, "We are lucky to get many of our students to a basic communication level in English. If we could get them at a basic proficiency level in English, then we could work on raising our reading scores. But just getting to that point is an incredible challenge. And as you probably know, we are now required to have all the students take the state tests. Our ESL students are no longer excused from these state tests. Since our funding formulas are partly based on the test scores, we are now facing an additional problem with getting enough money.

"We would more than welcome any ideas or suggestions that the site team might have," Mr. Jenkins concludes.

What would you do if you were on the evaluation team?

Do you have any recommendations for Mr. Jenkins and his school?

Would you vote to continue funding the grant for the reading program?

Are we putting the cart before the horse in expecting students at this school to take a standardized reading test in English before they know English?

Do you think Mr. Jenkins's school is that different from other schools?

What is in the best interests of all the children at this school?

Introduction

For most teachers, classroom diversity is an everyday fact of life. Teachers hardly need census reports stating that at least 25 percent of U.S. school children have ethnic minority status or that millions of school children have English as a second language (ESL) status. For teachers, the issue is how to transform their classrooms to meet the needs of these students. Two things are clear about diversity education: Some successes have occurred and a number of problems remain.

For example, the efforts of compensatory programs with large minority populations have produced mixed results. Head Start children tend to show early academic gains in the primary grades. But these academic gains fade out by the end of third grade, showing little long-term academic gains for these children. Chapter 1 reading programs have increased reading achievement in minority children, but these students still have higher functional illiteracy rates than mainstream students. The number of minority students entering college has increased substantially since the 1960s. However, many minorities still have lower scores on college entrance tests than mainstream students.

These problems indicate that, where diversity issues are concerned, there remains a formal agenda and a hidden agenda in the classroom. The formal agenda is distinguished by the court cases and legislative reforms that transformed civil rights in the United States. These changes began with *Brown* vs. *Board of Education* (1954), continued with the Civil Rights Act (1965), and were sustained by other federal programs, such as Head Start, Affirmative Action, and Title programs. The hidden agenda is perhaps best characterized by the following tongue-in-cheek description provided by Cushner, McClelland, and Safford (1989):

> Real Americans are white and they are adult; they are middle-class (or trying very hard to be); they go to church (often Protestant, but sometimes Catholic as well, although that is a bit suspicious); they are married (or aim to be) and they live in single-family houses (which they own, or are trying to); they work hard and stand on "their own two feet;" they wash themselves a good deal, and generally try to "smell good" (p. 216).

If you are white, middle class, and "smell good," then you will probably do well in the U.S. version of meritocracy that are our schools. Regardless of ethnicity, religious creed, or national origin, this country's classrooms tend to be a central mechanism for socialization in U.S. society. In this sense, public schools often help define what it means to be American for each new generation of children. Those who fit the mold are ready for college and their place in U.S. society. Those who do not fit the mold may be increasingly alienated from this society. Their future may be alternative schools, underemployment, or the criminal justice system.

Some writers refer to parts of this hidden agenda as the *informal curriculum* or the *hidden curriculum* (McCaslin & Good, 1996). This informal curriculum can drive classroom instruction in much the same manner as the more recognized formal curriculum. It is the discrepancy between what is preached (equal educational opportunity) and what is practiced (socialization to an almost unconscious cultural standard) that causes some of the diversity and gender differences with assessments.

For example, several critics of current standardized tests state that these types of assessments force many at-risk students into an academic double bind. Because students at risk often have a different language, a low socioeconomic background, or an ethnic minority status, they may be excluded from much of the mainstream culture. Yet they are being asked to demonstrate on standardized assessments knowledge of the very culture from which they are excluded. It is hardly surprising that they display an attitude of increasing alienation.

Whatever the student's background or personality, there is a social expectation that one role of teachers and of public schools is the remediation of student problems. This role can comprise the remediation of problems such as learning disabilities or behavior disorders. It also can include the remediation of difficulties created by cultural, ethnic, or gender differences.

The focus of this chapter is on exploring the issues and problems of assessing individuals from diverse cultural, ethnic, and gender backgrounds. In order to understand these assessment problems, we first need to examine the underlying aspects of diversity and gender differences.

Ethnic Issues and Assessments

Culture and Identity

Ask yourself: What is your identity? What comes to mind?

You might answer: I am an American. I am a teacher or a student teacher (or a future teacher or a present student). You also might answer: I am a woman or I am a man. You might list your religious affiliation or your political party. And you might list your ethnic background, whether it is Irish American, Mexican American, or Japanese American. These are all aspects of how we identify ourselves and they are all dependent on our culture. It also might surprise you to know that racial and ethnic classifications are culturally determined and vary from culture to culture.

In examining the relationship between ethnicity and education, writers often address the effects of culture on personal identity. One of the questions about culture is the issue of cultural assimilation versus cultural pluralism. **Assimilation** is a sociocultural process where a group adopts or adapts to a particular culture (Gollnick & Chinn, 2002). For example, many of the European immigrants of the nineteenth and twentieth centuries assimilated into the dominant culture of the United States. **Cultural pluralism** is the process where two or more distinct cultural groups coexist separately without any requirement to assimilate (Gollnick & Chinn, 2002). Nieto (1992) more explicitly states a view of the cultural divide between assimilation and pluralism:

> There is an inherent and natural tension between Americanization, with its commonly accepted meaning of assimilation, and keeping one's culture and language. As we approach the beginning of the twenty-first century, however, the question shifts a bit. No longer a choice of whether one should assimilate or not, the question now becomes, how far can society, and the institutions of society such as schools, be pushed to accommodate the changing definition of America? (pp. 271–272)

Ogbu (1988) points out that many disadvantaged ethnic minorities view education and related intellectual activities as another facet of control by a dominant white culture. Many of these minority members believe "that in order for a minority person to succeed, academically, in school, he or she must learn to think and act white" (p. 177). The result is that many individuals rebel against this perceived form of cultural control by developing an **oppositional identity** (Ogbu, 1988). Individuals and groups displaying an oppositional identity may have a negative attitude toward academic work, have a large amount of peer reinforcement for breaking school rules and norms, and value physical over intellectual activities (Gollnick & Chinn, 2002).

The problems caused by an oppositional identity may be amplified when minority students are assessed and evaluated. After all, formal assessments require students to be measured. Minority students may see such assessments as an overt form of academic judgment and white control. This may be one reason for their level of resentment about tests and grades.

In addition, the oppositional identity appears to be greater among those ethnic groups who are considered **involuntary minorities**—that is, those ethnic groups whose historical circumstances forced them into minority status against their will. This would include African Americans, Native Americans, and certain other ethnic minority groups. On the other hand, many recent immigrants from Asia are not involuntary minorities. They are considered voluntary minorities because they chose to immigrate to the United States. This explanation is sometimes offered as to why Asian Americans appear to have fewer academic problems than some minorities.

A number of proposals have been made to counteract the problems of oppositional identity and school alienation. Some proposals specify the following: diversity education programs that focus on self-esteem building; specialized ethnic studies as part of the curriculum; heterogeneous groupings for small group instruction and assessments; and special schools, such as the Young Women's Leadership Academy in Harlem. Many of these proposals attempt either to make instruction more relevant for a particular culture or to address particular challenges that ethnic minorities encounter. To this end, some educators emphasize the placement of teachers who can demonstrate familiarity with the cultural background of their students.

Some believe that it takes more than just the efforts of individual classroom teachers to change these behaviors and attitudes. Ogbu (1992) recommends collective action by ethnic minority communities in order to change attitudes about education. But he notes that it must be completed without giving up ethnic cultural values and identities. This action includes active minority community participation to reward academic success on a level with success in nonacademic areas. Ogbu also states that minority communities and schools need to concentrate on trust-building strategies and mutual collaboration about the curriculum.

Learning Style Differences

A related educational issue is the question of differences in learning styles between ethnic groups. **Learning styles** are a person's preferred method of processing and recalling information. If there are major ethnic differences in learning styles, these variations could affect your classroom instruction. For example, differences in learning styles could produce differences in performance on certain types of assessments.

Vasquez (1990) reviewed a series of studies on learning styles among Latino American, African American, and Native American students. In this review Vasquez claimed that some learning style differences did occur when different ethnic groups are compared. For instance, some research studies (Avellar & Kagan, 1976; Kagan & Mad-

Point/Counterpoint: Diversity Education

Suggestions for diversity education are not without controversy. Nearly everyone acknowledges the need for diversity education, but there are questions about the effectiveness of some programs. In general, these critiques are on practical grounds, such as curriculum and instructional issues.

Point

Some educators endorse using heterogeneous groups (placing students with differing achievement levels in the same group) for cooperative learning and assessments. The idea is that the higher-achieving students in the cooperative group can aid the lower-achieving students. This practice also may reduce the possibility of negative academic attitudes, since assessment performance is determined by group performance rather than individual performance.

Counterpoint

On the other hand, there are some practical considerations about teaching and assessing individuals with differing academic levels in heterogeneous groups. In small group instruction, many teachers prefer students who have similar achievement levels. In terms of assignments and instructional materials, the teaching process may be facilitated if students start an instructional task at approximately the same level.

There also are concerns about assessments that evaluate group performance. Ungraded assessments, used with informal assessments, generally are not a problem with cooperative learning groups. In effect, the accountability issues involved in the assignment of grades are not involved in assessments that are done only for student feedback. It is a somewhat different case in cooperative learning groups where actual group grades are determined by group performance. It may be difficult for the teacher to determine who is responsible for the work (and the good grades or not so good grades) in cooperative learning groups. Therefore, the issue of grading is still questionable with these cooperative groups.

Point

Other diversity issues address the need for special instruction in self-esteem and in ethnic minority studies. As noted earlier, some educators emphasize special courses in order to raise self-esteem in minority students. It is believed that raising student self-esteem will, in turn, increase academic achievement. In regard to ethnic studies, a number of educators support the use of ethnic studies to increase a sense of personal identity within a minority culture. It is believed that these types of programs will enable students to be more successful in school and to avoid a sense of school alienation.

Counterpoint

Critics of these approaches state that there is no clear research evidence that such courses actually increase self-esteem or decrease school alienation in the long term. They also point out that these courses may end up taking away instructional time from core academic subjects needed by students to be successful in the workplace. Other critics of ethnic studies programs claim that they "Balkanize" the curriculum (Will, 1992). This means that if each ethnic group teaches its own separate view of culture and history, the end result may be to further exacerbate the existing cultural divisions in U.S. society.

sen, 1971) showed that Latino American children achieved better in cooperative rather than competitive learning environments. These studies indicated that some types of assessment activities appeared more appropriate for certain ethnic minority children. Therefore, teachers may want to consider cooperative assessment strategies with Latino American children. Teachers also may want to minimize public displays of assessment performance, such as singling out students for special recognition of their performance. Vasquez provides his own anecdote about this situation: "The author remembers well his refusal to participate in a school activity in which he excelled simply because the teacher put him in a competitive position vis-à-vis his classmates. The experience is not uncommon among Hispanic students as many will testify" (p. 299).

According to Vasquez (1990), the extended family environment of Latino American children could be the main reason for this attitude. This is the typical developmental context of life for most Latino American students. Socialization in Latino culture is completed with a primary sense of loyalty toward extended family. Vasquez recommends that, instead of directly reinforcing Latino American students for classroom achievement, teachers have a system whereby students' families are informed of their academic achievement. Vasquez also recommends cooperative learning activities as more appropriate for the needs of Latino American students.

In regard to African Americans, Vasquez (1990) reviewed research suggesting that children from this ethnic group were more person-centered than were mainstream children. According to Shade (1982), the cognitive style and interests of African American children are in interpersonal areas rather than objective-centered approaches that characterize the responses of the mainstream child. As noted by Vasquez, "This distinction between black and white children takes on considerable importance when we become aware of the requirement in typical classrooms to focus on objects (mathematics, natural phenomena, letters of the alphabet, rules, etc.), not people for extended periods of time in order to learn well" (p. 300). Sanders and Wiseman (1990) found somewhat similar results. Their study showed that African American students preferred teachers who used interpersonal examples during instruction, humor, and a relaxed body language.

In regard to Native American children, Vasquez (1990) reviewed research indicating that they are more field dependent than field independent in their learning styles. *Field independent* means that individuals learn better without contextual cues. It is a learning style that is analytical—one that develops first from details and then puts together the whole picture. *Field dependent* means a learning style that is holistically oriented. This style looks at the big picture first and then focuses on the details. To some extent, this again indicates the degree to which mainstream students are more familiar with objects and abstracting abilities than are some minority students.

These differences raise some concerns about appropriate assessment activities for students from diverse ethnic backgrounds. Therefore, in addition to possible language differences that may occur, some minority students also may face learning style differences that could affect their ability to process information in a mainstream classroom. According to Sanders and Wiseman (1990) and Vasquez (1990), two types of assessment activities may cause problems for some minorities. One type is assessment activities that call for abstracting detailed information from a general knowledge base. The second type is assessments that require analysis without reference to an interpersonal context. In order to counteract these problems, some experts believe that cooperative learning activities and appropriate cooperative assessments should be emphasized.

A certain amount of caution must be taken with research on learning styles. Some educators point out that the overall differences between ethnic groups may be less than differences within ethnic groups. For example, the variations in learning styles *within* Latino American groups may be as great or greater than the differences *between* Latino Americans and African Americans. Other writers express concern that, by claiming learning style differences between ethnic groups, educators may end up stereotyping ethnic groups. Latino American students, for example, may be labeled as not wanting to be singled out for leadership roles in the classroom or in extracurricular activities. Such stereotypes could produce negative expectations for ethnic minorities and end up doing more harm than good.

Ethnicity and Student Achievement

A number of studies have examined the relationship of ethnicity with student performance. Although language, identity, and learning style have an impact on student achievement, the major influence remains socioeconomic in nature. For instance, income appears to be the prime predictor of scores on the Scholastic Assessment Test (SAT), which is the oldest and most frequently used college entrance exam (College Board, 2002). Since many ethnic minority groups make up a larger proportion of the lower socioeconomic levels, their test scores on the SAT tend to reflect the disparities caused by income.

Critics of the SAT (and similar standardized tests) also claim that there is an inherent test bias in measuring ethnic minorities with these assessments. This test bias is purportedly due to the vocabulary and general knowledge items used in the tests. These are the types of test items that appear to be most affected by culture. For instance, certain words may have different definitions or connotations within certain ethnic groups. Idiomatic expressions used by mainstream students may not be used at all by minority ethnic groups. These language differences could have an effect on assessment scores for some minority groups. Table 4.1 indicates some of these disparities.

The table indicates that there is some evidence to support these claims. In 1992, African Americans had an average score of 737 on their combined SAT scores, Mexican Americans' average score was 797, and the average score for white students was 933 (College Board, 1995). These disparities also continued to be a problem in recent test scores as well. In 2002, the scores for African Americans were 857; for Mexican Americans scores were 903; and for whites they were 1,058 (College Board, 2002).

These differences in test scores recently led to a federal court ruling on discriminatory practices. In *Cureton et al.* vs. *NCAA*, a federal judge ruled that the present policy of using SAT and ACT test scores in determining athletic scholarships constituted a discriminatory practice. Five times as many African American athletes were denied scholarships when compared with white athletes (Suggs, 1999). This ruling is presently being appealed.

TABLE 4.1   SAT Score Comparisons

	1992*			2002		
	Verbal	*Math*	*Total*	*Verbal*	*Math*	*Total*
African American	352	385	737	430	427	857
Mexican American	372	425	797	446	457	903
White	442	491	933	527	533	1058

*These scores are prior to the current revisions in the scoring system for the SAT.

Source: College Board, 1995; College Board, 2002.

On the other hand, some defenders of the SAT note that the disparities between some minorities and mainstream students on the Mathematics section of the SAT tend to be as large or larger than the Verbal scores. For example, African Americans scored 97 points lower than whites on the Verbal section of the SAT in 2002. On the Math section, African Americans scored 106 points lower than whites (College Board, 2002). It is difficult to claim that vocabulary or general cultural knowledge would impact the types of mathematics items used on the SAT. Therefore, an inherent test bias due to vocabulary differences is more difficult to claim on the Math section.

It should be emphasized again, however, that most researchers agree that the effect of socioeconomic status clearly plays a major role in test scores when minority students are compared to mainstream students. Therefore, assessments such as the SAT reflect an inherent income bias among social groups in the United States. Changing these economic circumstances may be necessary in order to change the standardized assessment scores.

One associated problem related to the preceding findings is the issue of expectations. Teacher, student, and parental expectations can be influenced by a variety of events, including some of the factors previously listed in this chapter. For example, teacher expectations may be influenced by students' socioeconomic backgrounds. Of perhaps greater concern is the research indicating teachers' expectations and classroom behaviors may be influenced by the ethnicities of their students.

Lipman (1997) found that teachers had differing expectations for students related to the ethnicity of the students. Teachers tended to have stereotypically biased perceptions of students based on ethnicity, which, in turn, affected instructional practices. Lipman noted that teachers tended to be less innovative and more traditional when the classroom composition was ethnically diverse. Other research has also noted that the expectations of educators are affected by ethnicity (McCabe, 1996). These educator expectations may lead to either negative expectations (Simpson & Erickson, 1983) or lowered expectations (Crosby & Owens, 1991) for students from ethnic minorities.

Negative expectations by teachers can have serious effects on student assessments and student achievement. If students and their parents internalize expectations for ethnic minorities, these expectations simply become a self-fulfilling prophecy perpetuating a lowered sense of expectations on the part of the students and their parents. In the end, these attitudes may adversely affect the students' academic self-efficacy and self-esteem. This will, in turn, produce lower student achievement on classroom assessments.

Ethnicity, Language, and Appropriate Assessments

Creating appropriate assessments for students from diverse backgrounds is a major concern for teachers. Students with an oppositional identity present a number of challenges when it comes to classroom assessments. Student alienation, resentment, and other negative attitudes can limit a teacher's ability to assess students. These emotions and attitudes may cause assessments to be less reliable and valid measures of actual student abilities. The result of such assessments could be to further increase school alienation. When this alienation occurs, it may cause a downward spiral in academic attitudes and performance as children move from elementary school into middle school and high school.

These problems may be compounded when students have an English as a second language (ESL) background. The typical ESL program involves what is commonly called *transitional bilingual education*. These programs may involve as much as six years of bilingual education. During this time, children are taught in their native language and in English. However, many language transition programs fail to help ESL children reach an appropriate level of English proficiency before they enter the mainstream classroom (Schulte, 2002).

Some evidence on long-term multilingual transition programs (five to six years of education in both languages) or short-term rapid immersion programs (one to two years) indicate that these programs may work only when parents are actively involved in ESL programs (Schulte, 2002). The end result of many ESL programs is that students increasingly fall behind their mainstream peers on classroom assessments. Because of these results, the No Child Left Behind Act proposes limiting transitional bilingual education programs to no more than three years. The following Point/ Counterpoint provides a further discussion of the two most common types of ESL programs.

The problems of ESL students with assessments are noted in other areas. A recent report (Medina, 2002) indicated that ESL students are having problems with high school graduation exams. The Regents Exam, now required by New York for all high school students, is causing massive increases in high school dropout rates among ESL students. The report indicated that almost one-third of ESL students dropped out of high school in the 2000–2001 school year. The chief reason given was their inability to pass the Regents Exam.

Because of the problems with developing assessments for students from diverse backgrounds, a number of proposals have been made to create appropriate guidelines in this area. Page 82 shows a list of ideas adapted from some generally acknowledged standards for assessing diverse student populations. These standards were created by some of the major professional organizations involved in developing and reviewing

Point/Counterpoint: Transitional Bilingual Education or Language Immersion

Point

Supporters of transitional bilingual education programs state that these programs offer a long-term educational solution for students who speak English as a second language. For example, students in a six-year language transition program receive some instruction in English each day. But they receive content instruction in science, math, and other academic areas in their native language. This allows ESL students to maintain pace with native English-speaking students in academic areas, while they are gradually acquiring English at a normal pace. It also allows them to learn academic subjects with other students who speak the same native language. Another positive aspect of transitional programs is that they teach many basic skills in the native language, particularly reading and writing skills. Proponents believe that this increases general literacy skills and that these skills will transfer to English. Supporters also note that long-term transitional programs reinforce native languages and that these children will become fully bilingual in adulthood.

Counterpoint

Opponents of long-term transitional programs point out that rapid immersion programs are generally supported by the research and have a number of advantages. Rapid immersion programs break what many people believe is a long-term dependency on native language use among ESL students. Immersion programs force ESL students to deal with the reality of U.S. society by using English as soon as possible. Opponents of long-term transition programs point out that transition programs simply reinforce the use of native language and that students in transition programs rarely appear to catch up with native English speakers. They simply fall further and further behind on standardized and teacher-constructed assessments. Immersion programs have better results for students and are more cost effective.

---

assessments (American Educational Research Association, American Psychological Association, & National Council on Measurement in Education, 1999). These guidelines also should be useful in reviewing your content and procedures for your own classroom assessments.

Just as increasing the number of minority role models and story lines has transformed textbooks, the same changes are possible with your assessments. Make your assessments relevant for your students by including examples and questions that are specifically geared to their culture. The relevancy of assessment appears to be the focus of many recommendations for change in dealing with culture and identity. As noted by Gollnick and Chinn (2002), assessments should focus on applications, knowledge, and skills that are specific to the students' cultural background. A variety of assessments should be used to allow students to demonstrate their knowledge in various ways.

Standards for Educational and Psychological Testing

1. Assessments should be conducted in a manner that is as fair as possible for individuals from diverse backgrounds, including gender, race, and ethnicity. This involves avoiding insensitive content or language. Such language might involve slang expressions that could be construed as offensive to a particular group. It also might include items that involve stereotypes or historical viewpoints of particular groups that could be considered derogatory. For instance, some people may be offended by certain Eurocentric views of history. Native Americans, in particular, might take exception to claims that Columbus "discovered America."

2. Assessments should relate only to instruction and not include other aspects that might unfairly penalize students from diverse backgrounds. In effect, assessments should not require special knowledge that might be available to mainstream students but not available to students from diverse backgrounds. These might include certain idioms or, in some cases, political or social ideas. Teachers should carefully review assessment scores of individuals from diverse backgrounds to determine if some questions might require knowledge that is available to one group of students but not to another group of students. Teachers should also carefully review questions that might indicate bias about a certain social or political viewpoint.

3. Assessments for ESL students may be a special problem. If a student does not adequately know the language in which an assessment is given, then the test becomes a test of language proficiency as well as a test of a particular subject area. There are some valid concerns regarding whether a test can be accurate when given to students who are not proficient in the language of the test. Teachers may need to provide special accommodations for students with ESL backgrounds, such as allowing the use of language dictionaries and special time accommodations on assessments.

Teachers also may want to offer additional help on academic tasks, particularly the use of ungraded, informal assessments that will enhance cognitive development and achievement. By providing practice tests or informal assessments with extra tutoring, a teacher may facilitate the acquisition of test-taking skills as well as increase the familiarity with course content. Informal group assessments, where students are encouraged to help each other, also may help in the development of these skills.

Teacher Application

Students from Diverse Backgrounds

Some educators have suggested using specific instructional and assessment procedures for students from diverse backgrounds (Gersten, 1996; Goldenberg, 1996). One suggested approach is to use **scaffolding.** Scaffolding is a concept taken from the idea of building a house. The builders construct a scaffold that provides a framework for completing the house. In education, the idea behind scaffolding is for the teacher to construct a framework to guide the student in accomplishing a task. The teacher gradually reduces the scaffolding or guidance until the student is able to complete the task without outside help. Gersten (1996) suggests combining this framework with frequent informal assessments. These assessments provide feedback without grades so that the student can develop appropriate skills in a positive atmosphere prior to actually taking formal assessments.

Vygotsky's **zone of proximal development** may be another way to enhance achievement from ethnically diverse populations. The zone of proximal development is the developmental "grey area" where a student is unable to solve a problem alone but can solve the problem with adult or peer help (Wertsch, 1991). In effect, students are able to complete a task with adult or peer help that they are unable to complete on their own. For example, in teaching a new computer program you might want to provide very exact, detailed information about each step of the new program. You would then walk through each step with your students. The next time, you would provide less information and help. Gradually, you would wean students away from any instruction and encourage them to complete each step on their own. After this process is completed, you would provide a formal assessment. Again, this approach may help students from diverse backgrounds unfamiliar with the language, content, or skills for a given task.

Other educators have suggested using what is termed the **dynamic assessment procedure** for students from diverse backgrounds (Dixon-Krauss, 1996). This approach combines some of the preceding ideas with other procedures, such as those developed by Feuerstein (Feuerstein et al., 1987). The basic idea is to move away from a formal evaluator-examinee (teacher-student) relationship to an interactive, dynamic assessment relationship. The hope is that this approach will reduce student anxiety and increase collaboration between teacher and student.

The dynamic assessment procedure includes other recommendations. For instance, the teacher should begin by establishing a baseline level of student functioning through formative assessments on a particular task. The teacher then instructs and assists the child to work on a comparable task. After the instruction, the teacher will posttest the student on the task. Another idea with this procedure is to review the student's performance on the posttest through both quantitative and qualitative procedures. This means that the review should be more than just a number. It should focus on such things as the type of information-processing skills that will optimize improvement by the student. It should also include a plan for the next steps that the student needs to take in learning the course content.

The suggestions in this Teacher Application provide procedures to merge instruction with assessment. In fact, some of these approaches often are called an *assessment-instruction-assessment approach*. Another aspect of these viewpoints is that they may reduce some of the anxiety and frustration that many students from diverse backgrounds encounter with assessments.

Gender Differences and Assessments

The issue of gender differences on assessments includes a number of different areas that range from historical questions about differences on intelligence tests to present controversies about standardized assessments. In terms of scores on general intelligence tests, nearly all researchers agree that there are no gender differences on overall intelligence test scores. Some recent questions still remain about specific subtest scores on standardized assessments, such as vocabulary scores favoring women and science scores favoring men. The research findings in this area remain mixed. Nevertheless, most researchers now agree that gender differences on subtest scores are due to social and cultural factors rather than innate gender differences.

This latter finding is supported by research in the 1980s that indicated a considerable narrowing of gender differences on some of the major standardized assessments (Feingold, 1988; Hyde & Linn, 1988). A narrowing of gender differences points to environmental factors that originally produced such differences. Another related finding is that, as a group, males are more variable in their academic performance. In effect, there is a greater spread or variation of scores in males than in females.

Achievement and Aptitude

As noted in Chapter 1, a major research finding about gender differences and achievement is that girls tend to have better grades on classroom assessments in elementary and secondary education but boys have higher scores on the Scholastic Assessment Test (AAUW, 1992). A related finding is that girls generally outperform boys on standardized state achievement tests, from the primary grades through at least middle school. In regard to scores on state tests during these years, Sax (1989) noted the following:

> The average female outperforms the average male on vocabulary, reading, language, work-study skills, and mathematics; the boys, in contrast, show higher scores in the use of maps, graphs, and in mathematics only for those students who are in the upper ten percent of the achievement distribution. The average and below-average male obtains lower scores on virtually every subtest of the Iowa Tests of Basic Skills. On tests having science or social studies subtests, however, the tendency is for the boys to do somewhat better than the girls. (p. 453)

It is clear that the relationship of gender with achievement changes in the high school years in the mathematics and science areas. Gender differences on standardized assessments in math and especially in science increasingly favor boys during secondary school. There are a number of factors apparently involved in the gender differences during the high school years in math and science. Included as contributing factors that appear to favor males are the amount of advanced placement or higher-level math and science courses, extracurricular interests, self-selection processes, and self-esteem and self-efficacy.

Males tend to be more likely to take higher-level and advanced placement classes in mathematics and physical sciences. Extracurricular activities, such as membership in science clubs or participation in science projects, also may be influenced by gender. Again, the evidence indicates that males are more likely to participate in science clubs and science projects. All the preceding factors point to possible gender-related attitudes about science and math that appear to produce a greater likelihood of males being interested in and rewarded for math and science participation.

As mentioned in Chapter 1, self-selection appears to be a major variable in explaining gender differences on some assessments such as standardized tests like the SAT. Males are more likely to be retained in each grade level and to drop out at a much higher rate. These two factors make the population of high school students considerably different from elementary and middle school populations. This particularly appears to be the case with students who are in "college prep" tracks and who take the SAT. For instance, in the academic year 2002, the population of students taking the SAT was approximately 54 percent women versus 46 percent men. This means that a more select group of men are competing against a more diverse group of women.

Self-esteem and self-efficacy also are frequently cited factors that may have a relationship with gender differences in the high school years. These factors are examined in the next section.

Academic Performance, Self-Esteem, and Self-Efficacy

Self-esteem is a person's sense of self-worth. In effect, it is one's own self-evaluation. Self-esteem is largely formed by parents, significant others, society, and teachers. Because of a possible relationship between self-esteem and school achievement, some educators have raised questions about possible gender differences in self-esteem. Such differences could have an effect on academic performance.

There are a number of separate aspects to a person's sense of self-esteem, including physical, social, and academic dimensions. Academic self-esteem and academic self-efficacy are intertwined concepts that reflect how a person views his or her own academic capability and how that person perceives his or her potential in a particular subject area. For example, academic self-esteem is a general self-evaluation about one's ability in school. **Academic self-efficacy** is a prediction about how successful one will be in a particular subject area, such as biology, or on a particular academic task, such as multiplying fractions. As noted by Bandura (1982, 1997), if an individual has a positive self-efficacy about a task, he or she sets higher goals and has greater motivation to achieve the task. Negative self-efficacy results in low motivation or avoidance of the task. In terms of academic self-efficacy and assessments, every student faces two essential questions: Can I pass this course? Can I pass this test?

Figure 4.1 represents the relationships among the types of self-esteem and academic self-efficacy. Notice in the figure that a student's academic self-esteem tends to have a positive relationship with his or her overall self-esteem. However, academic self-esteem may have little or no relationship with either social or physical self-esteem (Byrne, 1984). Therefore, a student may do quite well in the classroom but still have low social self-esteem and poor social skills. A student also may have good academic self-esteem but have a low sense of physical self-esteem and a poor body image.

Some research indicates that there is a general downward trend in students' overall self-esteem from late elementary school to the sophomore year in high school (AAUW, 1992). Although there is some variation in these declines (Berk, 1999), this negative trend appears to affect girls more than boys. This finding parallels a number

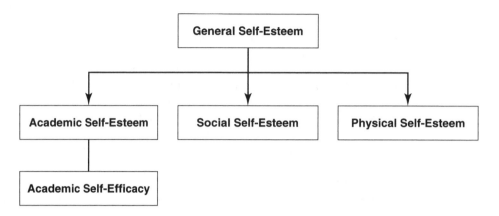

FIGURE 4.1   Types of Self-Esteem

of other developments, such as an overall decline in academic achievement motivation as children move from elementary school into middle school and then into high school (Stipek, 1984).

A number of reasons are offered as to why self-esteem declines from late elementary school into high school and why the declines are more dramatic in girls than boys. The effects of the biological changes that accompany puberty may explain some of these factors. Girls appear to have more difficulty in adjusting to the physical changes of puberty than do boys. Some research also indicates that the educational transitions from elementary school to middle school to high school may have a more negative impact on girls than boys (Berk, 1999).

Another important aspect is that, in general, boys are more likely to rate themselves higher than are girls. In fact, boys may consistently overrate themselves in many areas, especially in academic and social functioning. These findings are consistent on a variety of other self-report tasks and also appear true when boys are asked to rate their overall success in either school or career. This sense of inflated self-report may have a relationship with self-esteem and self-efficacy.

Self-efficacy affects more than just how students view their possibilities of achievement in a particular subject area. It also may affect how they view their successes and failures. Self-efficacy may play a key role in understanding the link between gender and assessment. An example of this role is found in the self-efficacy research on achievement in high school classes.

Several research studies have found a positive relationship between academic self-efficacy and classroom achievement (Zimmerman, Bandura, & Martinez-Pons, 1992; Zimmerman, 1995). Not surprisingly, students who make positive predictions about their performance tend to have higher achievement. However, a subtle gender bias may remain concerning certain academic subjects, particularly science and mathematics (favoring males) as well as English and foreign languages (favoring females.)

These biases point to a complex relationship between gender and academic achievement. For instance, in high school, self-efficacy for girls in science classes may be influenced by incorrect attitudes and beliefs that science is for boys or that boys have some sort of special inherent advantage in these classes. The reverse may be true for language and vocabulary skills. These latter areas may be viewed as being areas where girls have distinct advantages because of inborn language skills. There may be a tendency for these factors to be associated with possible stereotypical cognitions and behaviors about what is "appropriate" for each gender. For example, math and science may still be seen as academic subjects that are "masculine," whereas English and foreign languages may be viewed as "feminine" areas.

These findings become very important in examining the complexity of the relationship between self-efficacy, gender, and achievement. The process of identifying gender-related cognitions starts in the preschool years. For example, gender-related cognitions produce such attitudes as Hot Wheels are for boys and Barbie dolls are for girls. It continues with gender-related cognitions such as chemistry sets are for boys and tea sets are for girls. It may culminate in academic attitudes in high school and college that physics and computer science are for males, whereas social science and education are for females.

Type of Assessment Format

A number of claims have been made that assessment formats may produce differential results when women are compared with men. There are two assessment areas where gender and type of format are often believed to interact to produce disparate outcomes. These areas are the type of assessment item and the type of assessment conditions. Much of the controversy about test-item format centers on whether there are gender differences with multiple-choice items or constructed-response items. In terms of testing conditions, the debate focuses on the question of timed versus untimed assessments.

Some educators attribute gender differences on the SAT to the test's multiple-choice format and timed conditions. These assessment features are presumed to have adverse effects on girls. In classroom assessments, girls outperform boys supposedly because these assessments are more likely to use constructed-response items, such as essays, and because time constraints are less of a consideration.

There is no question that girls generally outperform boys on K–12 classroom assessments and boys do better on the Scholastic Assessment Test, but the research often does not support the statements about multiple-choice items or time constraints. Cole (1997) completed a research review of standardized assessments including the SAT. Her findings indicated that neither the multiple-choice format or time constraints produced gender differences. However, there were some gender differences on certain constructed-response items (essay items) that sometimes favored females, though this difference was not always consistent. Hunter and Schmidt (2000) also reviewed standardized assessments for gender bias. They, too, found no substantive gender differences based on type of test item.

Other research has focused on assessments in public schools. Again, as previously noted by Sax (1989), the research on standardized assessments indicates that girls, rather than boys, will have higher average scores from the primary grades at least through middle school. With few exceptions, these findings appear consistent. The research on teacher-constructed assessments found similar results: Item format did not result in significant gender differences (Takei, Clark, & Johnson, 1998).

Therefore, gender differences on timed, standardized assessments, using multiple-choice formats, tend to be the same as what is found on teacher-constructed assessments. Girls generally do better on both of these tests, with the exception of science and mathematics in high school.

As with related diversity issues, gender differences present a series of intertwined educational questions. The questions of gender stereotyping, assessment options, and curriculum decisions may affect the development of girls. These questions could have long-term consequences for women in the areas of self-esteem and career choices.

The current view of gender differences in academic and intellectual areas is that these differences are relatively minor and are caused by social and cultural development. These differences narrowed considerably in the past two decades, presumably because of the women's movement. Yet it is still important for teachers to understand the needs of both girls and boys as individual students.

Chapter Summary

The issues of diversity, gender, and assessment represent key elements of an ongoing debate about U.S. education. This debate has social and economic implications that extend well beyond just classroom assessments in public schools. For example, standardized test scores can have a long-term impact on both schools and individuals. Funding formulas for schools may be based on state test scores. College aptitude tests determine whether an individual will get a scholarship. Students from diverse backgrounds may be penalized by these assessment policies.

Problems such as school alienation and oppositional identity are sometimes blamed on a public school system that appears to be disconnected from the culture of many minority students. Low standardized assessment scores remain a problem for many minorities. Literacy levels and college aptitude scores also remain a problem for many minorities, particularly those who speak English as a second language.

Somewhat similar problems are echoed in the writings about girls in public schools. Some educators view the nation's public school system as a male-oriented institution with negative effects on both the self-esteem and career development of women. Nevertheless, recent scholarship in the area of gender differences appears to indicate that both teacher-made and standardized assessment scores favor girls from elementary school through middle school. Assessment scores in high school and college in the math and science areas still favor males.

As noted in the introduction to this chapter, certain progress has been made in the areas of diversity and gender issues. Nevertheless, 50 years after *Brown* vs. *Board of Education*, there remains a formal agenda and a hidden agenda in U.S. schools. It is clear that in a number of cases, minorities and women are not accorded a fair shake in the public schools. Rather than separate but equal, today's schools appear more equal but still separate.

CASE STUDY EPILOGUE

At the conclusion of their visit, the site team of federal evaluators have a four-hour exit interview with Mr. Jenkins and members of his staff. Their evaluation statement is very positive about the efforts of Mr. Jenkins and his staff. As the evaluators state, "Mr. Jenkins and his staff have made the best of a difficult situation." Nevertheless, the evaluators are critical about the state and school district policies regarding diversity, second language programs, and assessments.

The evaluators note that no real attempt has been made by the school district to accommodate the excess amount of students at the school. One evaluator speculates, "If this were a suburban school, would the parents stand for having such an overcrowded school?" The state and the school district are cited by the team for not providing more support for tutors and translators. As the team notes, most ESL children are chronically underserved. With the exception of Spanish transition programs, there are no genuinely effective language programs provided by the school district.

In terms of assessments, the evaluators recommend that some of the grant money for the reading program be used for a test-taking skills program. This program also can involve some funds for tutoring ESL students in their native language about how to take standardized assessments. Therefore, both children from minority backgrounds and from ESL backgrounds can receive a certain amount of training in simply how to read and take tests.

CHAPTER ACTIVITIES

Websites

www.aauw.org   This is the website for the American Association of University Women. This organization publishes and interprets a variety of research on women's issues. Their reports on public schools and assessments practices are well worth taking a look.

www.ahanabusiness.org   This is an up and coming minority coalition organization. AHANA is an acronym for African, Hispanic, Asian, and Native American ethnic groups. Although the focus of the site is on helping entrepreneurs, it is has a number of interesting articles on diversity issues. There is a special review of affirmative action policies.

www.blackwebportal.com   This is an independently owned and operated site and search engine for African American news and issues. It provides a number of links to various sites related to the African American community. Go to the Education section for information on assessment and instruction.

Portfolio Activities

1. Review the Case Study and answer the following questions about Mr. Jenkins and his school:
   - What are your recommendations for Mr. Jenkins and his school?

- Would you agree to continue funding the grant for the reading program? Why or why not?
- Are we expecting too much from students to have them complete a standardized reading test in English before they know English? Support your answer.
- Would it be better to have long-term multilingual programs for these students? Why or why not?
- Is it really fair to expect Mr. Jenkins's school to have test scores comparable to wealthy suburban schools? Explain.
- When legislators and stakeholders design assessment regulations on state tests, do you think that they understand that there are situations like Mr. Jenkins's school? Why or why not?
- What is in the best interests of all the children at this school? Support you answer.

2. Write an essay for your portfolio that addresses the following questions:
- As a prospective teacher, what position would you take on the debate over developing ESL courses?
- What position would you take on the issue of endorsing a rapid one-year language immersion program for ESL students?
- What kind of impact would such an immersion program have on children?
- How would it affect the type of instruction that a beginning teacher might develop with ESL students?
- What type of assessment practices or test preparation methods could you use with ESL students?

KEY CONCEPTS

Academic self-efficacy

Assimilation

Cultural pluralism

Dynamic assessment procedure

Involuntary minorities

Learning styles

Oppositional identity

Self-esteem

Scaffolding

Zone of proximal development

REVIEW QUESTIONS

1. What are the differences between assimilation and cultural pluralism?

2. What factors are associated with producing an oppositional identity?

3. Describe the relationship between ethnicity and learning styles.

4. List and describe the proposals used to overcome oppositional identity and school alienation.

5. Compare and contrast the proposals made about ESL programs.

6. Describe the relationship between gender, self-esteem, and self-efficacy.

7. What are the major gender differences in academic performance?

8. Describe the relationship between age, gender, and achievement as students move from elementary school to high school.

SELF-ASSESSMENT

1. Which ethnic group appears to achieve better in cooperative rather than competitive learning environments?
   a. African Americans
   b. Hispanic Americans
   c. Native Americans
   d. Asian Americans

2. Which ethnic group appears to be more person-centered than mainstream children?
   a. African Americans
   b. Hispanic Americans
   c. Native Americans
   d. Asian Americans

3. Which ethnic group appears to be most field dependent?
   a. African Americans
   b. Hispanic Americans
   c. Native Americans
   d. Asian Americans

4. Recent research indicates that science achievement is:
   a. Better in females than males from elementary school to college
   b. Better in males than females only in high school and college
   c. Better in females after adolescence
   d. The same for both genders

5. Which of the following appears to be a prime predictor of scores on the SAT?
   a. Ethnicity
   b. Mother's education level
   c. Income
   d. Geographic region of the country
   e. Type of high school

6. One of the major reasons for gender differences on science scores in high school and college appears to be:
   a. Self-satisfaction
   b. Self-efficacy
   c. Self-awareness
   d. Social maturation
   e. Psychosocial developmental processes in becoming adults

7. Students who have a negative attitude toward academic work, break school rules, and devalue intellectual activities may be displaying:
   a. Conduct assimilation
   b. Cultural pluralism
   c. Reactive identity formation
   d. Oppositional identity
   e. Academic self-efficacy

Answers to Self-Assessment: 1. b, 2. a, 3. c, 4. b, 5. c, 6. b, 7. d, 8. b

8. Which gender is more likely to overrate themselves on self-report measures?
   a. Females
   b. Males
   c. No gender differences
   d. Females until puberty

REFERENCES

American Association of University Women. (1992). *How schools shortchange girls.* Washington, DC: American Association of University Women Educational Foundation.

American Educational Research Association, American Psychological Association, & National Council on Measurement in Education. (1999). *Standards for educational and psychological testing.* Washington, DC: Author.

Avellar, J., & Kagan, S. (1976). Development of competitive behaviors in Anglo-American and Mexican-American children. *Psychological Reports, 39*(1), 191–198.

Bandura, A. (1982). Self-efficacy mechanisms in human agency. *American Psychologist, 37,* 122–147.

Bandura, A. (1997). *Self-efficacy: The exercise of control.* New York: Freeman.

Berk, L.E. (1999). *Infants, children and adolescents* (3rd ed.). Boston: Allyn and Bacon.

Byrne, B.A. (1984). The general/academic self-concept nomological network: A review of construct validation research. *Review of Educational Research, 54,* 427–456.

Cole, N.S. (1997). *The ETS gender study: How females and males perform in educational settings.* Princeton, NJ: Educational Testing Service.

College Board. (1995). *National report: College bound seniors 1972–1995.* Princeton, NJ: Author.

College Board. (2002). *College Board seniors' national report, 2002.* Princeton, NJ: Author.

Crosby, M.S., & Owens, E.M. (1991). *An assessment of principal attitudes toward ability grouping in the public schools of South Carolina.* Clemson University, SC: Houston Center for the Study of the Black Experience in Higher Education. (ERIC Document Reproduction Service No. ED 364 634).

Cushner, K., McClelland, A., & Safford, P. (1989). *Human diversity in education.* New York: McGraw-Hill.

Dixon-Krauss, L. (1996). *Vygotsky in the classroom: Mediated literacy instruction and Assessment.* White Plains, NY: Longman.

Feingold, A. (1988). Cognitive gender differences are disappearing. *American Psychologist, 43*(2), 95–103.

Feuerstein, R., Rand, Y., Jensen, M.R., Kaniel, S., & Tzuriel, D. (1987). Prerequisites for assessment of learning potential: The LPAD model. In C.S. Lidz (Ed.), *Dynamic assessment: An interactional approach to evaluating learning potential* (pp. 35–51). New York: Guilford Press.

Gersten, R. (1996). Literacy instruction for language-minority students: The transition years. *The Elementary School Journal, 96,* 217–220.

Goldenberg, C. (1996). The education of language-minority students: Where are we, and where do we need to go? *The Elementary School Journal, 96,* 353–361.

Gollnick, D.M., & Chinn, P.C. (2002). *Multicultural education in a pluralistic society* (6th ed.). Upper Saddle River, NJ: Merrill.

Hunter, J.E., & Schmidt, F.L. (2000). Racial and gender bias in ability and achievement tests: Resolving the apparent paradox. *Psychology, Public Policy & Law, 6*(1), 151–158.

Hyde, J.S., & Linn, M.C. (1988). Gender differences in verbal ability: A meta-analysis. *Psychological Bulletin, 104,* 53–69.

Kagan, S., & Madsen, M.C. (1971). Cooperation and competition of Mexican, Mexican-American, and Anglo-American children of two ages under four instructional sets. *Developmental Psychology, 5*(1), 32–39.

Lipman, P. (1997). Restructuring in context: A case study of teacher participation and the dynamics of ideology, race and power. *American Educational Research Journal, 34*(1), 3–38.

McCabe, J. (1996). Afro-American and Latino teenagers in New York City: Race and language development. *Community Review*, 14, 13–26.

McCaslin, M., & Good, T.L. (1996). The informal curriculum. In D. Berliner & R. Calfee (Eds.), *Handbook of educational psychology*. New York: Simon and Schuster Macmillan.

Medina, J. (2002, June 23) Groups say Regents exams push immigrants to drop out. *The New York Times*, p. A28.

Nieto, S. (1992). *Affirming diversity*. New York: Longman.

Ogbu, J. (1988). Class stratification, racial stratification, and schooling. In L. Weis (Ed.), *Class, race, and gender in American education* (pp. 163–183). Albany: State University of New York Press.

Ogbu, J. (1992). Understanding cultural diversity and learning. *Educational Researcher*, 21, 8, 5–14.

Sanders, J.A., & Wiseman, R.L. (1990). The effects of verbal and nonverbal teacher immediacy on perceived cognitive, affective, and behavioral learning in the multicultural classroom. *Communication Education*, 39, 341–353.

Sax, G. (1989). *Principles of educational and psychological measurement and evaluation* (3rd ed.). Belmont CA: Wadsworth.

Schulte, B. (2002, June 9). Trapped between two languages. *The Washington Post*, p. A01.

Shade, B.J. (1982). Afro-American cognitive style: A variable in school success? *Review of Educational Research*, 52, 219–244.

Simpson, A.W., & Erickson, M.T. (1983). Teacher's verbal and nonverbal communication patterns as a function of teacher race, student gender, and student race. *American Educational Research Journal*, 20(2), 183–198.

Stipek, D. (1984). The development of achievement motivation. In C. Ames & R. Ames (Eds.), *Research on motivation in education: Student motivation* (Vol. 1, pp. 145–170). Orlando, FL: Academic Press.

Suggs, W. (1999, April 9). Fight over NCAA standards reflects long-standing dilemma. *The Chronicle of Higher Education*, pp. A48–A49.

Takei, Y., Clark, M.E., & Johnson, M.P. (1998). Academic achievement and impression management as factors in the grading of white junior high school pupils. *Sociological Perspectives*, 41(1), 27–48.

Vasquez, J.A. (1990). Teaching to the distinctive traits of minority students. *The Clearing House*, 63(7), 299–304.

Wertsch, J.V. (1991). *Voices of the mind: A sociocultural approach to mediated action*. Cambridge, MA: Harvard University Press.

Will, G.F. (1992, December 29). Clinton's promise of quotas returns to bedevil him. *The Washington Post*, p. 7A.

Zimmerman, B.J. (1995). Self-efficacy and educational development. In A. Bandura (Ed.), *Self-efficacy in changing societies* (pp. 202–231). New York: Cambridge University Press.

Zimmerman, B.J., Bandura, A., & Martinez-Pons, M. (1992). Self-motivation for academic attainment: The role of self-efficacy, beliefs and goal-setting. *American Educational Research Journal*, 29, 663–676.

5

Informal Assessments

DAVID HOLLIWAY
Marshall University

CASE STUDY

Today is the first day of the statewide tests. Seth, a precocious fourth-grader, asks his teacher, "Do we have to take another test today?"

This testing ritual is a week-long period of avoidance, emotional struggle, and resistance for Seth. If we were to observe Seth for the first time as he struggles with the test, we might conclude that he is a candidate for special education. He has a hard time focusing on such tests and periodically disrupts other test-takers in class. While taking the test, Seth often gets up, fidgets in his chair, and otherwise seems attracted to every other aspect of the environment but the test before him. He squirms and wiggles the entire test-taking time. On past tests, he has been the last student to finish.

Like Seth, many students have a developmental history of test-taking aversion that ultimately affects their self-perceptions, motivation, and strategies about tests. For these students, the arrival of standardized testing may bring insomnia, stomach aches, and even depression. In Seth's case, his personal struggle with testing leads him to make responses that undermine his ability to take the test.

Fortunately, Mr. O'Brian, Seth's teacher, is not only sympathetic about Seth's predicament but respects his potential and his needs as a student. Mr. O'Brian realizes that some student learning is difficult to quantify. He understands the unanticipated consequences of standardized tests and seeks other ways to support his students' intellectual and emotional strengths and weaknesses. Mr. O'Brian has watched Seth demonstrate his intelligence in other ways besides standardized tests, and wants to help Seth succeed on assessments and to demonstrate his potential beyond the restrictions of state tests. He is interested in informal assessments as a way to help Seth develop his potential.

In this regard, Mr. O'Brian has a number of questions about informal assessments:

What are informal assessments?

What types of informal assessments are available?

How does one construct informal assessments?

How can informal assessments help students?

How can informal assessments help a student like Seth?

What are some challenges to informal assessments?

Introduction

Informal assessments are nonevaluative (ungraded) assessments that focus on students as unique learners. The purpose of informal assessments is to gather information from multiple sources to assist in teaching, learning, and educational decision making. Depending on the teacher's intention, informal assessments can be included in a portfolio as one source of evidence about student learning and may supplement other more traditional forms of assessment. Informal assessments can provide teachers, students, principals, and parents with an alternative view on student learning, classroom instruction, and ultimately the quality of education.

High-stakes testing or standardized testing typically is formal, "objective," and centrally controlled. High-stakes testing sometimes is criticized as being used solely for making judgments rather than improving instruction. Too often, standardized assessments have unintended consequences that leave many children fearing tests rather than loving learning.

Informal assessments, however, allow a teacher to gather classroom information in a variety of ways, yielding very different perspectives on classroom instruction and student learning. Students see informal assessments as nonthreatening because no grade, judgment, or evaluation stems from them. In contrast to the evaluative stance that summative and standardized testing takes, an informal assessment is a nonjudgmental ongoing observation process that can provide feedback to guide and encourage learning and development. Informal assessments are usually teacher initiated, modified to the content of the specific classroom, and conducted by both students and teachers. It can be meaningful to both students and teachers and may create a classroom culture that fosters self-esteem, trust, respect, and, most important, learning. Informal assessment is one important attribute in designing a student-centered classroom (National Research Council, 2000).

A wide variety of information-gathering techniques and activities are included in informal assessments. Some of these techniques are similar to the field techniques of an anthropologist studying culture (observation checklists, participant observation, interviews, video portraits). Some techniques allow a teacher to find out what their students know, what they want to know, or what they don't know about a particular topic (questioning strategies, surveys). Other techniques challenge students to question their own learning through self-assessment techniques, such as self-assessment checklists. Still other informal assessment techniques assist teachers who are interested in learning about their own teaching (i.e., daily journal keeping). As you will see, informal assessments take many different forms, depending on the teacher and his or her intentions, as well as the content of the assessment.

As you might have already surmised, informal assessments are not "official," nor are they institutionalized. Informal assessments enable the teacher to tailor his or her instruction as students' needs arise throughout the course of a day, throughout the course of a unit, or throughout the course of the school year. Informal assessments are teacher dependent; they are eclectic and idiosyncratic. Each teacher creates a unique classroom environment requiring assessment procedures that mirror the needs of the students and the instruction. If you will refer back to Chapter 1, you will see that informal assessments can assist in meeting educational and classroom instructional goals.

Informal assessments can be a powerful tool for teachers in gathering evidence about instruction and student learning. Shepard (1989) notes, "Assessments designed to support instruction are informal, teacher-mandated, adapted to local context, locally scored, sensitive to short-term changes in students' knowledge, and meaningful to students. They provide immediate, detailed, and complex feedback; and they incorporate tasks that have instructional value in themselves" (p. 7). In general, an informal assessment is an information-gathering procedure that is teacher created, unique to specific circumstances, and intended to improve instruction and assist student learning.

The informal assessment techniques discussed here are embedded within specific teaching approaches within specific content areas. Some of the techniques include questioning strategies, checklists, and the creation of performance profiles through systematic observations, informal journal writing for students and teachers, and student self-assessment questionnaires.

Informal Assessment and Reflective Teaching

One of the necessary ingredients for any informal assessment is to be reflective. That is, a teacher who reflects is thoughtful and inventive. "Reflective teachers think back over situations to analyze what they did and why and to consider how they might improve learning for their students" (Woolfolk, 2001, p. 7). Most reflective teachers already use some form of informal assessment without conscious recognition.

One example of how such self-reflection may apply is with the case study at the beginning of the chapter. The following information provides an example of Seth and Mr. O'Brian from this case study.

Teacher Application

Using Informal Assessments

Mr. O'Brian tried a number of ways to more effectively instruct and assess Seth. One day he noticed that Seth often would spend any free time that he had drawing pictures. Not only would he draw pictures, but he seemed to have some talent for drawing. Mrs. O'Brian observed that Seth drew as a way to express his personal history, to give his perspective on the classroom, and to "anchor" and cope with new classroom activities.

Mr. O'Brian began to praise Seth's drawings and started to use them as a way of informally observing him. The teacher was able to use Seth's drawings and the activity of drawing to understand his ideas and the struggles he faced as a learner. Through discussing Seth's drawings with him, observing when and what he drew, Mr. O'Brian was able to informally assess and understand Seth's strengths and weaknesses. Then he was able to tailor his instruction to meet Seth's needs as a learner.

The teacher did not use drawing as an assessment for each of his students. He observed that Seth was unique in the way he used drawing to interpret his world. This observation gave Mr. O'Brian an entry into Seth's world—an open door that ultimately assisted Mr. O'Brian in helping Seth become a more self-confident and competent classroom learner.

Teachers like Mr. O'Brian make hundreds of decisions daily. Many decisions are made without written records, explicitly articulated reasons, or traditional assessments. As you will see, informal assessment is an ongoing information-gathering process that can offer a powerful tool to assist you in linking your instructional methods with your students' learning. Informal assessments will assist you in making the numerous decisions that you will make as a classroom teacher.

Student-Centered Basis of Informal Assessments

One of the defining elements of informal assessments is their nonjudgmental nature. Informal assessments allow a teacher to understand the unique qualities of each student. Students are not "normalized" so that they can be compared with other students; rather, informal assessments assume that variation is the norm in student learning. In short, informal assessments make learning, thinking, and feeling "visible."

As you read in Chapter 4, diversity and gender differences are a major issue underlying educational assessment. One of the strengths of informal assessment is that individual differences in student talent can be highlighted. Informal assessments can assist you in gaining information about your students' experiences outside of the classroom so that you can better meet their needs inside the classroom. Individual differences exist on several interwoven planes, including gender, age, ethnicity, culture, cognition, metacognition, and temperament.

Traditional standardized testing sometimes appears to assume that all students learn in the same way at the same pace. All students are seen as having learning "traits" that can be measured in a fashion similar to their height, weight, and head circumference. Traditional education with behaviorist assumptions suggested that all students learn the same way at the same rate and that they need to learn the same things. This "universal child model" assumed that students are empty vessels to be filled by the knowledge authority of the teacher. Yet within the last 25 to 30 years, there has been an impressive accumulation of experimental and field research indicating that there are many paths to learning and many paths to instruction (National Research Council, 2000).

Informal assessments reveal that students are unique. Four assumptions made with student-centered approaches to informal assessment are:

1. Each student has a distinct learning history, including a unique combination of emotional, cognitive, and social strengths and weaknesses.
2. Students can constructively engage their past experiences in new learning situations if they are meaningful.
3. Learning occurs best in environments where the students are respected and where positive interpersonal interactions are fostered.
4. Learning is not a fixed procedural script that all teachers and students follow everywhere at all times. On the contrary, learning is a natural outgrowth and emerges in contexts where personal relevance and meaning are highlighted.

Lambert and McCombs (1998) summarize the APA's learner-centered principles that serve as the basis for an extensive research-based establishment of instructional and assessment approaches to reforming education. Although the principles apply to all learners in all situations, they are realized through each particular learner in specific learning contexts. The principles include metacognitive and cognitive domains, affective domains, developmental domains, personal and social domains, and individual differences that influence student learning and instruction. Following are brief descriptions of the 12 principles.

Metacognitive and Cognitive Principles

1. Learning is a "natural" process emergent through discovery and constructed through each individual's worldview.
2. Learners strive to make learning personally meaningful and coherent, independent of the amount and quality of information available to them.
3. Learners connect their present understandings to past experiences while questioning possible future knowledge and information.

4. Learners are capable of "thinking about their own thinking," and thus become aware of their strengths and weaknesses as they struggle in creating new understandings.

Affective Principles

5. Learners have varying degrees of self-awareness, personal values clarification, and expectations for success that ultimately influence their motivation to learn.
6. Learners have a natural intrinsic motivation to understand their world.
7. Learners are highly motivated in environments that are novel and unexpected, challenge critical thinking, foster personal relevant information, and offer freedom to explore and make personally meaningful insights.

Developmental Principles

8. Learners are genetically unique and progress through developmental transitions that require developmentally sensitive curriculum.

Personal and Social Principles

9. Learners make meaningful contributions to learning environments and new personal connections when their unique social and cultural backgrounds are adapted to the learning setting.
10. Learners' self-esteem and social acceptance are strengthened when the learning environment fosters respectful, caring, and positive relationships among peers and teachers.

Individual Principles

11. Learners can be characterized with basic principles of learning, motivation, and development, yet each individual is born with unique capabilities and talents that can be optimized to highlight individual differences.
12. Learners have personal worldviews based on prior experiences that inevitably filter their cognitions, their emotions, and their social expectations for learning.

Informal assessment procedures can help teachers better understand these integrated complex principles as they are expressed uniquely by each student. Research reviews have concluded that prior knowledge, in-depth subject matter, metacognitive skills, regular formative assessments, and a sense of belonging to a community of learners are crucial educational practices that can assist students in becoming self-motivated, life-long learners (National Research Council, 2000). Indeed, many teachers have found that student-centered assessments reveal much about student learning and instruction that was otherwise hidden to them prior to using alternative forms of assessment (Bauer & Garcia, 2002).

Informal assessments are one way to approach the variability that you observe in your individual student learning. As one assessment specialist has pointed out, student performance varies greatly depending on the task: "The students who perform well on one task may well not be the same students who perform best on the second" (Herman, 1997, p. 200). Informal assessments will allow you to gather multiple points of information that can clarify student variability, thus assisting you in tailoring your instruction to assist each student in reaching his or her learning potential.

Constructing Informal Assessments

Now that you have a general understanding of the purpose of informal assessments, we will take a close look at several examples of informal assessments in various learning settings. The multiple layers of your educational and instructional goals will determine what you choose to assess, how you assess, when you assess, and how you actually use the assessment information. As you will see, creating informal assessments is a complex process that does not follow any strict decision rules. Some assessment scholars refer to the assessment construction process as WYGWYA ("what you get is what you assess"). In short, your informal assessments can serve several purposes simultaneously (Herman, 1997).

For example, you may wish to assess how closely students are approaching state-mandated goals, district-related goals, specific lesson goals, or goals related to a particular student's individualized education plan (IEP). Your goal may be simply to get a sense of how your students are feeling after they have completed a challenging classroom activity. In short, what and how you informally assess will depend on your teaching context. Butler and Stevens (1997) suggest three basic questions that you need to ask yourself before constructing an informal assessment:

1. What information do you want to collect from your assessment?
2. How will that information be collected?
3. How will that information ultimately be used and who will use it?

In the next sections of this chapter, you will read examples of informal assessments that are unique to specific contexts, content, teachers, and students. Each example attempts to answer these three questions directly and indirectly. You will read examples that demonstrate the multiple possibilities and strategies of using informal assessment in your classroom practice. We will discuss how *journaling, questioning, performance profiles, checklists*, and student *self-assessment* techniques are used to conduct informal assessments in classrooms. Although these examples are context specific, each example has as its focal point successful student learning. These are informal assessment strategies that you may wish to use in constructing your own informal assessments.

Journaling and Collecting Informal Writing Samples

Journaling

At the beginning and throughout the school year you may find yourself asking:

Who are my students?

What do they know about my classroom?

How are they feeling today?

How are my students connecting the contents of our lessons with their life outside the classroom?

These are questions to ask yourself as you begin a new school year, a new school week, and a new unit lesson, or at the completion of a unit. One of the most important uses of informal assessment leads to an expanded understanding of the diversity of your students. As you know, current educational theories emphasize that all students are unique and bring with them unique past learning experiences that they use in different ways.

Journals are one of the most widely used informal assessments and they can be used in numerous ways. Pressley, Allington, Wharton-McDonald, Block, and Morrow (2001) found that "exemplary" first-grade literacy teachers use the **journaling** technique for three interrelated purposes:

1. Offering students *an outlet for expression and fluency* in language usage
2. Offering students an outlet *to apply what they have learned*
3. Providing students *a tool of communication* to express their own personal narratives and ideas

Although journals can be used in numerous ways (Wharton-McDonald, 2001), writing can give students the freedom and power to express experiences that they may not be comfortable speaking about in the presence of other students.

One of the most common forms of communication that younger students use in their journals is the narrative. At this young age, most children are primarily focused on themselves and their experiences in the world. Therefore, it is not surprising that personal expression through narrative appears regularly in student writing (Pressley et al., 2001). Teachers can periodically read student journals to learn about their students' recent experiences and to gather information to relate class content to students' lives. As you can see, this is not an official requirement, but rather a process of reflective teaching that assists in filling the gap between instruction and learning. By giving your students a chance to express in writing their personal experiences, you are gaining insight into their worldview; equally important, you are also assisting students in exploring and expressing their personal lives through writing.

Teachers also can use journals to learn how students interpret the teachers' instructional intentions. For example, I know a high school science teacher who discovered that journaling gave him an insight into his teaching that he was unaware of until he participated in written dialogs with his students. In traditional science classrooms, there is very little writing used as a learning tool or as a way of assessing student learning. One of the challenges that this science teacher faced in using journals was constructing questions and/or issues that motivated students to write. Each week prompts were used to assist the students in focusing on the specific content of physics. For example, the students were asked to respond to these questions in their journals:

1. How can you determine the coefficient of friction if you know only the angle of the inclined plane?
2. Compare and contrast some of the similarities and the differences between magnetic, electronic, and gravitational fields.
3. If you were to describe the physical concept of sound to your best friend, what music would you use to demonstrate this concept? Why?

These prompts gave students the space in which they could respond to the specific information of physics, yet the writing allows students to respond using their own understanding, their own language. Responding to one student's written response, this science teacher commented that many students made fundamental assumptions about friction, acceleration, and velocity that were based on personal experiences and not scientific reasoning. The teacher further reflected that other examples and other approaches would be needed if he were to reach his students. This teacher clearly appreciates his students' attempts to make sense of the class content; he too realizes a need to modify his own instruction to meet his students' needs.

Another challenge this science teacher faced (as would any teacher who uses writing tasks for informal assessments) is finding the time to respond to all of his students individually. Although collecting writing samples from student journals may be a time-consuming activity, the benefits outweigh the challenges. Reading and responding to 25 students writing about a class activity may be seen as an added burden by some teachers. However, you may find that journals enable you to create assessments in your classroom that fit with the ongoing learning process, that support an open dialog between students and yourself, that provide immediate feedback, and that encourage individual discovery and growth.

Journaling is clearly one strategy you can develop to informally assess your students' learning, assist in student self-learning, and to improve your own learning as well! Two other examples of journaling include:

1. *Dialogic Journaling* (Hughes & Woodrow 1997). Students and teachers converse with one another in either a paper journal or in an electronic format.
2. *Double-Entry Journals* (Ross, 1998). Students divide their journal pages in two sides. They write quotes from their texts on one side and their personal reactions to those quotes on the other side.

The Reflection Log.   Another way to use journals is to collect student reflections of their own learning in order to create a *reflection log*. For example, after you have held a discussion in class, you can ask students to respond to the following prompts:

- What were the main points in our discussion?
- What connections can you make to other classes that you have?

- What connections can you make in your own life with the issues raised in our discussions?
- What questions do you still have after today's discussion?
- What are several additional points you would add if we were to continue our discussion at a later date?

You can collect the responses to study them for the next lesson and address some of the issues at that time. Another possibility is to have students independently read aloud their response to the prompts. This process will often lead to further discussion and further student learning.

Reflection logs can give students an opportunity to think more deeply about the content of classroom discussions. They will allow you to keep an ongoing record of student responses to a variety of classroom discussions and thereby gain an understanding of how each student is learning. Reflection logs also provide another insight into the unique world of each of your students.

Some teachers use *self-journals.* These self-journals enable students to analyze their perceptions, feelings, and thoughts that motivate certain behaviors. They can assist students in tracking the origins of negative beliefs and emotions. By using the journal as a context for self-reflection, students may realize certain inconsistent reasoning patterns that have led an inappropriate frame of reference. Students may learn that there are other ways to approach and represent current problems (Marzano, 1998). Here, journaling informally assists students and teachers in understanding problems and in changing these problems.

The Wrap-Around. *Wrap-around* is another writing activity that helps you informally assess your classroom. Again, this activity will allow you to check in informally with your students to see how they are feeling about specific issues related either to the classroom or to their own lives. To construct a wrap-around you can write several stem sentences on the board, give the students a chance to respond reflectively in writing to the questions, then go around the room and have students read aloud their responses to the stem questions. This process not only gives the students a chance to think before they respond but it also gives you a chance to hear their responses. Here are a few examples of wrap-around you may want to consider:

The most important thing about myself that I learned today is _____ _____.

I was really surprised by today's discussion when _____.

When I am a parent I'm sure I will tell my children about _____.

Given today's debate, I would have changed _____ .

An additional way to bring your students into the informal assessment would be to have them create their own stems. Have each student write one stem question on a slip of paper, collect them all, read them aloud, have the students write down their responses, then have the class as a whole volunteer their responses.

The KWL Response Chart.   *What do you know?* is yet another way to use journaling as an informal assessment procedure. The common KWL chart (Know, Want, Learn) is the most usable format here and can be kept in students' journals so that they can respond to it as time passes in your lesson. This procedure can be used prior to a lesson to engage students about pertinent background information as well as helping students predict what they might learn. A possible chart might look like the following teacher application:

Teacher Application

Using a KWL Chart

What do you **know** about _____?	What do you **want** to know about _____?	What have you **learned** about _____?
1.	1.	1.
2.	2.	2.
3.	3.	3.

The KWL chart requires students to divide a piece of paper into three sections. In one column students write what they already *know* about a specific topic. This is the *K* column. In a second column students write what they *want* to find out about the current lesson. This is the *W* column. In the third column students write what they *learned* after the lesson or unit has been completed. This is the *L* column. The chart provides a record of students' own perceptions of what they knew and what they learned. Again, this gives you an insight into their learning that you might not otherwise get if you stuck to traditional testing at the end of each unit. This form of informal writing also assists students in recognizing their own learning pathways by revealing to them what they already knew, what they were interested in learning, and what they actually did learn.

Reflection logs, the wrap-around, and the KWL chart are but a few ways that you can use journaling and writing to informally assess and assist your students in learning. The informality of journaling allows you to be flexible in your use. Yet through the students' written responses, it gives you an insight into student perspectives on the classroom instruction, the content of classroom lessons, and the specific topic. Writing can be used in a variety of forms as a very powerful informal assessment tool.

Questioning as an Informal Assessment

Another technique for informal assessment is **questioning**. The joint construction of questions can lead teachers and students to uncover unpredicted complexities that ultimately lead to deeper understanding of content matter (Duckworth, 1991.) Informal assessment of your students through the asking of questions is probably the most basic way you can determine your students' understanding and assist in their learning.

Students of all ages are natural questioners. However, not all questions are created equal. Different teaching strategies will influence the *level* of questioning (Sternberg & Spear-Swerling, 1996). This, in turn, influences the level of thought and response students are likely to offer. These factors influence the type of assessment information you can gather.

Remember that your assessment and teaching strategy will influence to what extent you are interested in collecting informal assessments. A **didactic-based teaching strategy** is typically demonstrated when a teacher lectures. There is usually no interaction between the teacher and the students or between the students themselves. There is an assumption here that the students are passive receptacles waiting to be filled with the teacher's wisdom and knowledge. Most likely, a didactic teacher is not interested in collecting informal assessments about their students' learning.

A **fact-based teaching strategy** is demonstrated when a teacher is focused on eliciting particular information that may be deemed "right" or "wrong." Here, too, there is very little social interaction in the classroom. An example might be the mathematics teacher who asks, "How do you compute the square root of 16?" Upon hearing "8" from a student, the fact-based teacher would respond, "No, let me tell you how it's done." The teacher then proceeds to show the students on the board the process of finding square roots. This teacher strategy is primarily teacher centered and would be unlikely to use informal assessments.

With a **dialogic-based teaching strategy** students are central. The teacher encourages, models, and participates in discussion with students. Questioning is used as a part of both learning and instruction. Answers to questions are seen as raising possibilities and considering alternative perspectives. Questioning is the basis for teaching for understanding. An example would be a first-grade literacy teacher who asks a student, "Can you tell me, Ariel, before we even start, why you chose this story to read to me?" Clearly the focus is on Ariel and her interests. The teacher is a co-constructor in learning.

With these three contrasting approaches to classroom questioning, the use of questions (or the lack thereof) is considerably different. These basic teaching approaches lead to two basic types of questions: Convergent questions and divergent questions. **Convergent questions** seek a single response, an answer that converges to the question. A fact-based teaching strategy would include such convergent questioning. For example, a history teacher might ask, "Class, what is the date of the Norman Conquest?" Convergent questions seek one single response—there is a "correct" answer to this type of questioning.

Divergent questions, on the other hand, encourage multiple responses that often lead to raising other questions. Divergent questions would be used in a dialogic approach to teaching where conversation is crucial to learning. In the context of discussing the Emancipation Proclamation, a history teacher might ask, "How would you describe 'freedom' to a space alien? Give us several personal examples to demonstrate this abstraction to your new alien friend." Divergent questioning leads to the consideration of numerous perspectives and possibilities. There are no "correct" answers here.

As you can see, divergent and convergent questions serve different purposes and require different thought processes. Convergent questions often rely on rote memorization with very little critical or reflective thought; either you know the answer or you don't. Divergent questions, however, require "mindful learning" (Langer, 1997). They allow for several possibilities, promote openness to new information, invite the construction of divergent representations of the issue under question, and allow for consideration of multiple perspectives to issues. Divergent questioning is consistent with student-centered theories of education.

Divergent Questions and Mathematics

Using divergent questions with math instruction can emphasize problem solving in everyday life. The focus here is on math that is relevant and meaningful to your students. One aspect of this type of math instruction is to challenge students to clarify problems, create possible solutions, and then interpret and explain how they arrived at their findings. As you might anticipate, divergent "open-ended" questioning is one type of informal assessment that is consistent with a student-centered approach to mathematics instruction.

A California State Department of Education report (1989) recommends a number of ways that questioning could be used for mathematical thinking. The report suggests that questions serve multiple aims in mathematics education in the following ways:

1. Questions give students the opportunity to think for themselves and express mathematical ideas that are within their developmental understanding.
2. Questions challenge students to construct responses in their own words rather than choosing from a predetermined list of single responses.
3. Questions allow students to explore and demonstrate the depth of their mathematical understanding rather than being forced to choose from a multiple-choice item.
4. Questions challenge students to approach problems from several perspectives.
5. Questions model divergent thinking to mathematical concepts rather than force convergent thinking.

Here are some sample questions representative of this type of math instruction:

There are 27 children in Mr. Norton's class. Twelve of the students have dogs at home. Five children have no pets at home. Six children have cats at home. Four children have fish at home. How many of the students in the class do not have dogs at home?

The Smiths want to put a new 5-foot fence around their property. The property is a rectangle 70 feet wide and 80 feet long. How many feet of fencing do the Smiths need to purchase?

A horse is tied up by a 10-foot rope and its hay is 15 feet away. How does the horse reach the hay?

As you can see, divergent open-ended questioning can play a vital role in mathematics. It can be a crucial part of informally assessing your students' understanding and ability in mathematical problem solving. Indeed, questioning as an assessment method may be used at all levels of math instruction.

Levels of Questioning and Response

Your teaching strategy will influence the types of questions you ask and the types of responses you will receive. Questioning can be organized on six levels dependent on "characteristic ways of responding" (Sternberg & Spear-Swerling, 1996, pp. 56–59). Table 5.1 clarifies general response types with question types.

At the lowest of the **six levels of questions** is *rejection of questions.* These are questions that an adult or teacher may assume are inappropriate or out of reach of students. Interaction with the students and the question is denied. A teacher using a didactic

TABLE 5.1   Seven Levels of Questioning and Response

	Question Types	
Levels of Question Response	*Convergent Questioning*	*Divergent Questioning*
Question Rejection	I can't believe you would ask a silly question like that!	Hmm . . . interesting question, John, but I don't think that question connects with today's discussion.
Question Restatement	So, Jason, you are asking "What is the definition of oblique sunlight?"	So are you asking "How does sunlight create the seasons?"
Question Ignorance	I don't know. Only an expert would know such a thing.	Sara, that's a great question! I don't know—does anybody else have an answer to the question?
Appeal to Authority	Of course only a doctor would know the correct answer to that one!	That's a great issue! Where might we go, who might we ask to clarify the issues involved here?
Appeal to Alternatives	There are no alternatives—it's a fact we all must accept.	That's clearly one way we can think about it. Can we think of another way to see this issue?
Follow-Through Evaluation	I know this is too complex for you, so you don't need to ask me any more questions.	If that's the case, are there other explanations we might also consider when we discuss climate variability?

approach might respond this way. A teacher may be so close-minded to student-centered learning that he or she acts as if students are only to be seen and not heard. Such a teacher responds only to teacher-generated discussion questions. In this case a possible rejection question might be, "I can't believe you would ask a silly question like that!"

At the next level of questioning and responding, the teacher would restate the question as her response. *Restating questions* is one way to assess informally just what it is a student may be asking. Restating may be the surest way to clarify a student's question and to reframe student knowledge. A middle school science teacher might respond, "So, Jason, you are asking 'What is the definition of oblique sunlight?'"

Of course, it may also be the case that a teacher will not know the answer to a student's question. In this case, *admitting ignorance* or *giving a direct response* with what one knows is yet another way to assess student knowledge and teacher knowledge. Some teachers would not feel comfortable responding that they did not know the answer. Yet when a teacher admits openly that he or she does not have a ready-made answer for a question, it is a clear signal to the students that the teacher is in on the learning and that the teacher values learning and honesty.

Another level of question and response, students are encouraged to seek *authoritative responses* to student-initiated inquiries. This allows a teacher to inquire whether students know of direct information that may assist their learning and how they discover a source of potential information that would help them learn.

Another level of questioning is to see if students can create *alternative explanations* or seek alternative answers to questions. By asking for alternative explanations, a teacher can assess whether a student can take another perspective and will encourage students to seek other possible explanations to certain issues. To probe further, teachers can assess whether students are considering the soundness of other explanations. By considering other explanations and then asking evaluative questions, teachers can informally assess whether students can evaluate the adequacy of alternative explanations. Finally, the highest level of question includes *follow-through evaluation questions*. Here, the teacher can assess to what degree students have considered alternatives and ultimately how those alternatives may affect them personally. Follow-through questions allow elaboration on the issue under discussion.

The level of the questions asked, answered, and addressed will determine the quality of the informal assessment you will do. In general, "the levels go from rejecting children's questions, at one extreme, to encouraging hypothesis formation and testing, at the other. The levels go from no learning, to passive rote learning, to analytic and creative learning, as well as practical learning" (Sternberg & Spear-Swerling, 1996, p. 59). A good example of where dialogic teaching, divergent follow-through questioning, and informal assessment would be useful is in the learning and teaching of history.

Questions in Action: Questioning History

If you were to ask students about their experiences in learning history, they might inform you that they learned important dates, important people, important places, important facts, and important wars. In short, many students would summarize by saying that history is a boring subject that has no relevance to their everyday lives.

Thinking historically, however, encourages students into a conversation about the effects of history in their own lives. By inviting students into an ongoing classroom discussion, the teacher can demonstrate mindfulness. *Mindfulness* assumes the following: Historical knowledge is laden with values and choices, authentic materials promote critical thinking, and students know much more than we give them credit for (Holt, 1990). Thinking historically is clearly consistent with a student-centered approach to education. Although Holt does not define his teaching practice with assessment language, he informally assesses student understanding by encouraging students to ask questions like a historian.

By using dialogical questions about primary historical documents, Holt (1990) demonstrates that students learn that they, too, can be historians. Equally important, students learn about their own learning: "A question is formulated and gains meaning only in the context of the experience of a questioner living in the present, albeit a present that includes that accumulated experience of time past" (p. 14). Instead of asking students fact-based questions, such as "What effect did the war have on the plantation system?" Holt asks his students "What does freedom mean to you?" By basing his questions about certain documents not in the cut-and-dried formula of a fact-base mission but rather in the terms of a thought-provoking reflection, Holt encourages his students to define history "in terms of their own lives" (p. 21). Here, we see in the informal assessment of dialogic questions a strategy that not only informs the instructor about his or her students' understandings about history but also encourages the students to think historically.

There are other ways to think about questions. For example, some scholars have suggested that questions be categorized into inference questions, interpretation questions, transfer questions, hypothesis questions, and reflective questions. Some even suggest that questioning is an art to be acquired (Wolf, 1987): "Teachers keep questions alive through long stretches of time, coming back to them days, even weeks after they have been asked" (p. 3). Clearly, questions can serve as a vital informal assessment.

A Performance Profile

Clear communication is a desired standard common to many disciplines. How can you informally assess the oral language competence of your students? One way is to collect examples of students' demonstrations of oral behavior in the ongoing flow of the classroom. This can be done by keeping a journal or daily notes that describe students' language performances (Butler & Stevens, 1997).

These spontaneous language performances can range from classroom discussions to joke telling. Although telling a joke may at first seem irrelevant to understanding student learning, joke telling can offer a great deal of information about students' personalities, their abilities, and their willingness to use language in unique ways. "Oral language profiles kept informally can provide information about student's language skills that can supplement test scores" (Butler & Stevens, 1997, p. 215). Spontaneous uses of language may be hard to capture regularly; nevertheless, by structuring "book talks and group discussions," a teacher can create an open environment where students are free to use their oral language skills.

Although information for the profile may be collected informally, there can be systematic ways to assess oral language performance. For our purposes here, we will focus on *book talks* as an informal assessment that can offer opportunities for you to collect oral language information about your students. The book talk is an oral book report that challenges students to present their interpretations of books they chose to read. Book talks allow students to bring in pictures, objects, costumes, and even multimedia productions that can support their presentation. Butler and Stevens (1997) suggest that for content, students might include the following: (1) title and author of the book, (2) descriptions of the characters, (3) description of the setting(s), (4) a brief retelling of the plot, and (5) recommendations for reading the book. To rate the delivery of the book talk, students can use the following rating criteria:

S = secure in delivery

D = developing a good delivery

B = beginning of a good delivery

N = no evidence of a prepared delivery

To assess the delivery of the book talk, additional points can be considered for eye contact with the audience, good posture while talking, use of appropriate "formal" language, and use of appropriate voice level. The ratings of the content and the delivery can help students understand what they need to work on before their next book talks. This informal assessment process also gives some useful information about student effort and performance, competence, and comfort that the teacher can use in working with each student.

Observational Checklists

Observational checklists are widely used to assess informally a wide range of student knowledge, including specific content knowledge, performances within specific content, and the emotional temperament of your students. Checklists are rather quick and easy to conduct, but they can also be developed as a thorough process in which to collect information about student knowledge. Teachers can assess student learning prior to, during, and after lessons by using checklists. They can also be used to assess student readiness for formal assessments. "Checklists show teachers and students the areas that need work early enough to be able to help the student before he or she fails the test or the unit" (Burke, 1993, p. 106).

For example, one teacher uses an informal checklist on a weekly basis in her introductory literature classes. For each student, she uses either a 0 (indicating the behavior was not observed), a check (if the student demonstrates a minimal level of the behavior), or a check plus (if the student demonstrates a maximal amount of the behavior).

	Comes to class with summaries prepared	Comes to class with book and shows signs of "reading engagement"	Contributes to small group discussions	Asks relevant questions in larger class discussions	Makes connections between the story and personal life
Student # 1					
Student # 2					
etc.					

Checklists are based on teacher observations and therefore allow for systematic collection of information about the students that is not available from other traditional forms of testing. They help teachers keep an ongoing record of student work, whether it is in the content areas of reading, writing, math, science, and social studies, or in the numerous other activities that make up a student's school day. For example, checklists may assess student behavior as the students move across the various settings at school, such as the playground, the hallways, the classroom, and at the computer; as they work individually; and as they work with other students in groups.

Self-Assessment

One way to enable your students to conduct a **self-assessment** about their own sense of achievement is with a *graphing sheet*. Using a scale that ranges from "Never," "Sometimes," "Usually," and "Always," you can ask your students to self-assess their learning skills and work habits, their literacy learning, their mathematics performance, their understanding in science and health, or what they have learned in social studies. As noted by one teacher, "If children really have learned to assess what they understand, they may have the confidence to use their skills to figure out something they haven't seen before" (Poynter, 2000, p. 28). A self-assessment graphing sheet is shown in Figure 5.1.

Along with the self-assessment (Figure 5.1), you can have the students take the graphing sheet home for review with parents. The students can explain to their parents several specific things that they have learned the past semester and a few things that they need to work on; and the parents can comment on their progress.

Another form of self-assessment can be used for a daily homework assessment. You can create a form that lists questions that your students can ask themselves about success in completing their homework. For example, a common self-assessment list encourages students to take a close look at their homework process, as shown in Figure 5.2.

The basic purpose behind self-assessment is to support your students' independence as learners. By asking them regularly to consider their own strengths and weaknesses in various academic content and social areas, they can begin to take responsibility

FIGURE 5.1   Self-Assessment Graphing Sheet

	Never	Sometimes	Usually	Always
Academic Skills and Work Habits				
I listen closely.				
I contribute to class discussions.				
Reading and Writing				
I read to understand.				
Before I begin writing I think about my audience.				
Mathematics				
I try to use various strategies to solve problems.				
I know basic number facts.				
Science				
I create questions that I am interested in researching.				
I bring in additional information from home.				
Social Studies				
I understand concepts.				

for their own learning. In short, they can begin to master their metacognitive system that may assist learners in "reframing" their personal perspectives on certain issues (Marzano, 1998). The semester self-assessment and the daily homework forms are just two ways that teachers have used self-assessment to encourage students to reflect on their own learning. Self-assessment is another path that you can use to become familiar with students' perceptions of their own learning, and you, in turn, can check what you know with their perceptions to determine what instructional steps you may need to take in the future.

Summing up the Construction of Informal Assessments

We have reviewed only a few ways that you can use informal assessments in your teaching practice. Other forms of informal assessment that may assist you in getting to know your students are:

FIGURE 5.2   Homework Self-Assessment

Self-Questions	Yes	No	Comments
Did I turn in my homework this morning?			
Did I write all my assignments in my notebook that goes home?			
Do I have all my homework organized in my homework file?			
Do I have all the materials I am going to need tonight?			
Has somebody else checked my homework before I turn it in?			
After it was checked, did I put it back in my folder?			
Did I give the homework to my teacher?			

Holding informal interviews and conferences

Asking students to bring something of importance with them to share with the class

Videotaping classroom interactions

Using student surveys that ask various questions about students' background experiences

Keeping informal observations of student behavior in a teacher journal

Challenges to Informal Assessments

As noted in Chapter 2, there are two basic measures of quality control with assessments: *reliability,* which refers to the consistency and repeatability of a test, and *validity,* which refers to whether the test measures what it claims to measure. Because informal assessments tend to be unique to the individual, without standardization procedures or objective items, they are often challenged in regard to reliability and validity. In particular, the ability to consistently and accurately measure student activities with informal assessments is questioned.

Point/Counterpoint: Informal Assessments

Point

Informal assessments provide unique information and support for student-centered learning and instruction. By using informal assessments, teachers can gather information about their students that is not otherwise available in standardized and formal testing situations. Informal assessments allow a teacher to focus on the unique behaviors of each student that may offer information to aid instruction. For example, the *wrap-around* (described earlier) is a useful tool to gather student impressions about the progress of instruction, to gather impressions of student sentiments about a certain circumstance, and to collect feedback for the instructor that may assist him or her in modifying a lesson. Some teachers use wrap-arounds as a midlesson, a midunit, or a midterm assessment, which allows them to make any changes that students may need as they progress through the term.

Counterpoint

Informal assessments are unreliable and too subjective. Informal assessments are usually created by a single teacher and are thus prone to individual interpretations and biases. Without the public jurying that accompanies more formal and standardized assessments, informal assessments are arbitrary. The information gathered is difficult to use beyond specific contexts and thus are highly unreliable. Because of their eclectic creation, the information gathered is challenging to communicate to students, other teachers, parents, and administrators. Finally, beyond gathering information of limited use to the teacher, informal assessments do not assess state or federal learning standards.

In general, standardized assessments, such as the SAT or the ACT, have considerably higher reliability and validity than do teacher-constructed assessments. On the other hand, objective, teacher-constructed assessments tend to have better reliability than do essay or portfolio assessments. Informal assessments tend to have less reliability than these latter forms of assessments.

When using informal assessments, reliability in the traditional sense may be difficult to calculate because of the individualized and ongoing nature of the information gathering. You may find a particular technique that consistently gathers the kind of information you are trying to find. For example, perhaps a questioning strategy helps you find out where students are in a particular subject area. The technique itself may be reliable, but the specific information may be impossible to replicate. Therefore, some traditional methods of determining reliability may not be used with informal assessments.

In terms of accountability, legal issues, or assessment policies, this might not be as big a problem as it may appear. By definition, informal assessments are used for instructional purposes and not for formal student evaluation. Therefore, they are not subject to the types of legal or grade challenges that are involved with formal assessments. In effect, since students are not given grades with informal assessments, these assessments are not going to be challenged based on the usual criteria for test quality.

Much of what was said about reliability also applies to validity. Basically, the ongoing, student-centered nature of informal assessment creates problems with measuring validity. Nevertheless, a better case can be made for the validity of informal assessments than for the reliability of informal assessments.

With validity, the question is: Does the assessment measure what it claims to measure? With informal assessments, the purpose or claim is to collect useful information about students' learning and teachers' instruction. Therefore, with informal assessments validity is determined by the collection of this useful information. Usefulness can be multidimensional: useful to the particular student, useful to the particular group of students, useful to the particular setting, or useful to the particular unit. In the sense of collecting useful information, a valid informal assessment is similar to the kind of judgments made with content validity. For example, with content validity a judgment is made that there is a relationship between the assessment and the instruction. With informal assessments, a judgment also is made by the teacher that the informal assessment provided useful information about the student or the instruction.

If the information is useful, then in one sense of the word the informal assessment is valid. However, it is a subjective judgment, not an objective measurement. In this sense, informal assessments by their very nature are impossible to formally determine validity. However, in an informal sense, validity can be determined by the usefulness of the assessment.

Closely related to issues of reliability and validity is test bias. As noted in Chapter 4, any type of assessment may be challenged by issues of **test bias** in their test construction (National Evaluation Systems, 1991). Because informal assessments can cover a range of subjects for a range of students, similar problems of test bias may occur with these assessments as are found with formal assessments. Language usage, stereotyping, fairness, and content are issues in the construction of informal assessments. Following is a description of four basic areas of bias that may affect the usefulness of your informal assessments.

Basic Bias Categories

Language Usage. Our language use is often transparent; we unconsciously assume others understand what we mean, when in reality, the words we use may evoke very different responses from those with whom we are attempting to communicate.

Stereotypes. With stereotypes we make assumptions about general qualities based on limited specific exposure. When we assume that "Aborigines are primitive and backward" it may be the case that we have never even met an Aborigine but we have seen some television show or read a *National Geographic* magazine article.

Representational Fairness. Often in educational materials (i.e., textbooks, standardized tests) there is an underrepresentation of girls and women, minorities, elders, and people with disabilities. In the same materials there may be an overrepresentation of middle-class, white males.

Content Inclusiveness. For an assessment to be useful, the content of that assessment needs to be relevant, especially with issues of culture, gender, and historical information.

By keeping in mind these four factors in developing your informal assessments, you can achieve assessments that may be relatively free from test bias.

Chapter Summary

A famous psychologist once wrote "Generalizations decay" (Cronbach, 1975, p. 122). With informal assessments, we don't *generalize*, rather we *particularize*. Informal assessments challenge teachers to see their students in unique ways, beyond universal generalizations. Informal assessment allows teachers to collect information in an ongoing process that enables them to see the unique characteristics of their students. Because informal assessments are student centered, teachers can gather multiple sources of information about each individual student. That data can be complied into a more telling picture of student learning than if a single test were used to measure students' accomplishments.

We have discussed several examples of informal assessments that have given you some ideas of the range and the possibilities of creating your own informal assessments. We considered journaling and informal writing examples as one way to collect evidence of student learning. We took a detailed look at the multiple dimensions of questioning and how you can use open-ended questions to gather information about your students' understanding while at the same time encouraging them to consider multiple points of view. We considered how checklists could be used to collect information about student behavior. We saw how one teacher created profiles of student oral language usage that would not have been captured with traditional testing. Finally, we saw how one teacher created a self-evaluation summary that challenged students to personally assess their learning across literacy, mathematics, science, and social studies. Of course there are other options, including regular informal interviews, videotaping, and assessing student drawing as evidence of student learning. Informal assessments are an effective way to collect information about your students that ultimately will influence how you, as their teacher, create the missing link between your instructional approach and student learning.

CASE STUDY EPILOGUE

Seth is now an active, self-confident, fifth-grader. Although he still struggles with the structures of standardized testing, his teacher has assisted him in developing learning strategies that he successfully uses to learn in class and, yes, even to accomplish finishing the dreaded spring-time tests. Mr. O'Brian was able to learn more about Seth's interpretations of the classroom environment, his home life, and the nuances that make up his emotional and intellectual perspective by using Seth's drawings and other artwork as informal assessments. Seth's teacher discovered that Seth was an articulate artist who expressed complex personal and social needs through his in-class artwork. Mr. O'Brian was an open, "mindful" teacher concerned with the success of each of his students. He sought numerous ways to better understand Seth's unique and individual learning approach. He not only appreciated Seth's drawings but he also recognized Seth's artwork as a window into Seth's world, as a meeting point where he could assist Seth in becoming a successful, motivated learner. By collecting various pieces of Seth's artwork throughout the year, Seth's teacher demonstrated the potential that informal assessments can have in helping teachers acknowledge that students often have their own goals and their own paths to meaning-making in the classroom. Informal assessments are powerful tools that help explain and honor the individuality of both students and teachers.

CHAPTER ACTIVITIES

Websites

www.ericae.net/pare   This site, entitled Practical Assessment, Research and Evaluation, offers professionally reviewed articles for all types of educational assessments and decisions.

www.NCTM.org   This site is an invaluable resource for all mathematics teachers. The National Council of Teachers of Mathematics offers numerous sources for informal assessment in your mathematics classrooms.

www.angelfire.com/wi/writingprocess/specificgos.html   This page will link you to numerous writing process activities. If you are in need of the ABCs of writing, this is a great connection.

www.inspiringteachers.com/tips/journaling/index.html   This page focuses specifically on issues of journaling, which has numerous uses and is extremely effective as an informal assessment tool.

Portfolio Activities

1. Review the Case Study at the beginning of the chapter. Write the answer to Mr. O'Brian's questions in your portfolio:
   - What are informal assessments?
   - What types of informal assessments are available?
   - How does one construct informal assessments?
   - How can informal assessments help students?
   - How can informal assessments help a student like Seth?
   - What are some challenges to informal assessments?

2. You are a fourth-grade language arts teacher beginning a school year with new students. You want to know a little bit about their backgrounds, how they spent their summer vacation, and their levels of writing proficiency. Create an informal assessment for your portfolio whereby you can learn of all three.

3. Develop your own informal assessment by using questioning techniques from this chapter to determine the cognitive abilities of your students. Earlier we discussed the revision of Bloom's Taxonomy, which included Knowledge Dimensions and Processing Dimensions. As we learned in this chapter, questioning is a very effective way to assess these dimensions informally. To refresh your memory, there is factual knowledge, conceptual knowledge, procedural knowledge, and metacognitive knowledge. The cognitive processes that can operate on these types of knowledge include remembering, understanding, applying, analyzing, evaluating, and creating. Using this chart as an example, construct some sample questions that you might use to assess your students' cognitive knowledge informally through the use of questioning. Create a question for each cell of this matrix.

	Remembering	Understanding	Applying	Analyzing	Evaluating	Creating
Knowledge Dimension						
Factual knowledge						
Conceptual knowledge						
Procedural knowledge						
Metacognitive knowledge						

KEY CONCEPTS

Checklists
Convergent questions
Dialogic-based teaching strategy
Didactic-based teaching strategy
Divergent questions
Fact-based teaching strategy
Informal assessment

Journaling
Oral language profile
Questioning
Self-assessment
Six levels of questioning
Test bias

REVIEW QUESTIONS

1. In your own words how would you describe informal assessments?

2. Create examples of divergent and convergent questions that are specific to your area of content specialization.

3. Explain in your own words the four underlying assumptions of a student-centered approach to teaching.

4. Describe a learner-centered classroom by giving examples of the five key principles.

5. Focus on one of the key principles underlying learner-centered instruction (for example, metacognition) and discuss how you might use informal assessments to assess that particular principle.

6. Explain how you might use checklists in your classroom.

7. How can writing be used as an informal assessment?

8. Explain the differences between dialogic-based and didactic-based teaching strategies by using content-specific examples.

9. What are some uses of student self-assessments?

10. Describe some of the strengths and the weaknesses of informal assessments.

SELF-ASSESSMENT

1. Which is a characteristic of informal assessment?
   a. Parent initiated
   b. State mandated
   c. Objective and summative
   d. Student centered

2. A recommended teaching approach is:
   a. Fact based
   b. Dialogic based
   c. Authoritarian based
   d. Didactic based

3. What is a general questioning strategy that encourages multiple points of view?
   a. An alternative question
   b. An authoritative question
   c. A follow-through question
   d. A divergent question

4. Which item is a principle included in a student-centered approach to informal assessment?
   a. Group principles
   b. Administrator principles
   c. Teacher principles
   d. Affective principles

5. Which of the following is an example of an informal assessment?
   a. A 20-item multiple-choice test
   b. An essay final exam
   c. A statewide test
   d. A wrap-around

Answers to Self-Assessment   1. d, 2. b, 3. d, 4. d, 5. d

REFERENCES

Bauer, E., & Garcia, G.E. (2002). Lessons from a classroom teacher's use of alternative literacy assessment. *Research in the Teaching of English*, 36, 462–494.

Burke, K. (1993). *The mindful school: How to access authentic learning*. Arlington Heights, IL: Skylight Training and Publishing.

Butler, F., & Stevens, R. (1997). Oral language assessment in the classroom. *Theory into Practice*, 36(4), 214–219.

California Department of Education. (1989). *A question of thinking: A first look at students' performance on open-ended questions in mathematics*. Sacramento: Author.

Cazden, C. (1988). *Classroom discourse: The language of teaching and instruction*. Portsmouth, NH: Heinemann.

Cronbach, L. (1975). Beyond the two disciplines of scientific psychology. *American Psychologist*, 30, 116–127.

Duckworth, E. (1991). Twenty-four, forty-two, and I love you: Keeping it complex. *Harvard Educational Review*, 61(1), 1–22.

Dyson, A.H. (1988, March). Appreciate the drawing and dictating of young children. *Young Children*, 25–32.

Falk, B. (1998). Testing the way children learn: Principles for valid literacy assessments. *Language Arts*, 76(1), 57–66.

Heinmiller, B. (2000). Assessing student learning—and my teaching—through student journals. *ENC Focus: A Magazine for Classroom Innovators*, 7(2), 31–33.

Herman, J. (1997). Assessing new assessments: How do they measure up? *Theory into Practice*, 36(4), 196–204.

Holt, T. (1990). *Thinking historically: Narrative, imagination, and understanding*. New York: College Entrance Examination Board.

Hughes, H., & Woodrow, M. (1997). Dialogic reflection and journaling. *Clearing House*, 70(4), 187–191.

Lambert, N.M., & McCombs, B.L. (Eds.). (1998). *How students learn. Reforming schools through learner-centered education*. Washington, DC: American Psychological Association.

Langer, E.J. (1997). *The power of mindful learning*. Reading, MA: Addison-Wesley.

Marzano, R. (1998). Cognitive and metacognitive considerations in classroom assessment. In N.M. Lambert & B.L. McCombs (Eds.), *How students learn: Reforming schools through learner-centered education* (pp. 241–246). Washington, DC: American Psychological Association.

McDevitt, T., & Ormrod, J. (2002). *Child development: Educating and working with children and adolescents* (2nd ed.). Upper Saddle River, NJ: Merrill Prentice Hall.

Messick, S.J. (1989, April). High stakes testing in kindergarten. *Educational Leadership*, 16–22.

Moss, P.A. (1994). Can there be validity without reliability? *Educational Researcher*, 23(2), 5–12.

National Evaluation Systems. (1991). *Bias issues in test development*. Amherst, MA: National Evaluation Systems, Inc.

National Research Council. (2000). *How people learn: Brain, mind, experience, and school*. Washington, DC: National Academy Press.

Pandey, T. (1990). Authentic mathematics assessment. *Practical Assessment, Research & Evaluation*, 2(1), http://ericae.net/pare/getvn.asp?v=2&n=1.

Paris, S.G., Lawton, T.A., Turner, J.C., & Roth, J.L. (1991). A developmental perspective on standardized achievement testing. *Educational Researcher*, 20(5), 12–19.

Poynter, L. (2000). Using self evaluation with fourth graders. *ENC Focus: A Magazine for Classroom Innovators*, 7(2), 28–30.

Pressley, M., Allington, R. L., Wharton-McDonald, R., Block, C. C., & Morrow, L. M. (2001). *Learning to read: Lessons from exemplary first-grade classrooms*. New York: Guilford Press.

Ross, C. (1998). Journaling across the curriculum. *Clearing House*, 71(3), 189–191.

Shepard, L. A. (1989, April). Why we need better assessments. *Educational Leadership*, 4–9.

Shulman, J.H., Whittaker, A., & Lew, M. (2002). *Using assessments to teach for understanding: A casebook for educators.* New York: Teachers College.

Sternberg, R.J., & Spear-Swerling, L. (1996). *Teaching for thinking.* Washington, DC: American Psychological Association.

Washor, E. (1993). Show, don't tell: Video and accountability. *Coalition of Essential Schools Fieldbook.* http://www.essentialschools.org/pubs/exib_schdes/showvid.html.

Wharton-Mc Donald, R. (2001). Teaching writing in the first grade: Instruction, scaffolds, and expectations. In M. Pressley, R.L. Allington, R. Wharton-McDonald, C.C. Block, & L.M. Morrow (Eds.), *Learning to read: Lessons from exemplary first-grade classrooms* (pp. 70–91). New York: Guilford Press.

Wolf, D. (1987, Winter). The art of questioning. *Academic Connections,* 1–7.

Woolfolk, A. (2001). *Educational psychology* (8th ed.). Boston: Allyn and Bacon.

6 Constructing Formal Classroom Assessments

CASE STUDY

Ms. Lopez has taught second grade for 11 years. She teaches in a wealthy suburb outside a large midwestern city. Her school district is known for its educational excellence. The district has a high degree of parental involvement as well as a large amount of instructional resources.

    For years, Ms. Lopez used homogeneous groups for reading instruction. She found it easier to teach and assess students who read at similar levels. She never had any problems until now. But this year, her principal received two complaints from parents about Ms. Lopez.

    Both parents stated that Ms. Lopez showed bias in placing their children in the lowest-level reading groups. The complaints filed by the parents specified that Ms. Lopez based her selection criteria solely on her own personal subjective opinion. There was no other basis for her selection process. The parents also claimed that Ms. Lopez placed some children in higher reading groups because she knew their families.

Before responding to the parents, Ms. Lopez met with her principal. The principal asked her the following questions:

How do you want to respond to these parents?

Is there any basis to the complaints that you use personal reasons to select children for the different reading groups?

Do you have a documented policy about how you select children for reading groups?

Do you have any documentation about how you select children for reading groups?

Do you use any type of assessments to place children in reading groups?

Do you use any objective assessments to place children in reading groups?

Introduction

As I write these words, in the back of my mind there is a nagging thought that I have not yet finished writing the formal assessment due this coming week for my new course. Even though I know it must be finished (or else I am finished with my student teachers), it is a beautiful spring day and the outdoors are calling me. Part of me wishes that some nice testing company would just hand me a pre-made exam, but I know it won't work. My own assessment is best for my own instruction.

Few tasks in education are more important than creating a good test. The effect of assessments goes well beyond just grades. Assessments affect placement decisions, high school academic tracks, and college selections. Students and their parents can have strong emotional reactions to assessment decisions. Therefore, creating a good assessment will save a lot of trouble and pain in the long run. A bad assessment is like a bad penny: The problems created by it just never seem to go away.

Like me, you will spend a lot of time and effort constructing formal classroom assessments. There are a number of choices to make about what kind of formal assessments you want for your students. This chapter, as well as this section of this book, examines the different ways of constructing formal classroom assessments. The first part of this chapter reviews the different options that you need to consider before you make the plunge. Like a newspaper story, there are five questions that you need to answer about your formal assessment story: Who? What? Where? When, and How?

Making Choices

The Who Question

The Who Question looks at who will receive a formal assessment. On the surface, this seems like a simple question with a simple answer: Everyone gets assessed at the same time in the same way on the same assessment. But it is not quite so simple. There are a number of situations that may call for different formal assessments of students in the same classroom. For example, teachers who use homogeneous reading groups in elementary school may provide different assessments based on the group's reading level. As noted in Chapter 1, there are times when children with disabilities may be assessed in different ways in order to meet the guidelines of what is a reasonable accommodation. To determine certain disabilities, such as learning disabilities or mental retardation, children need to be assessed on an individual basis rather than in groups.

The What Question

The What Question examines exactly what will be the content of the formal assessments that you devise for your classroom. As noted in previous chapters, there are two aspects that determine assessment content: your instructional objectives and your actual classroom instruction. As we all know, what you plan to teach and what you actually teach may be two different things. In fairness to your students, the most important aspect of your assessments should reflect what you actually teach in class. To a lesser extent, your assessments should cover what is assigned, such as outside readings or computer activities.

Besides your instruction and objectives, there are many ways to determine what to measure on your formal classroom assessments. As mentioned in Chapter 2, content validity is really what we are doing with the What Question. **Content validity** determines whether the assessment appropriately samples the full range of instructional material presented to the student. For example, given the instruction, and the standards and objectives for your classroom, does the assessment fully measure the range of these criteria? One possible way of approximating the content validity of your own assessments is to develop a diagram or checklist of your assessments.

For instance, Ms. Cook is creating a new formal classroom assessment for her tenth-grade World History class. She wants to check to what extent the major topics of a particular module (years 1919–1945) are measured by her formal assessment. A checklist of her classroom instructional activities by her assessment activities is shown in shown in Table 6.1.

This checklist provides a quick overview of whether Ms. Cook's assessment matches her instruction. Ms. Cook can then determine if the amount of instruction on a given topic (such as the Great Depression) matches the weight given to this topic on her assessment. Generally speaking, the more instructional activity means the more assessment questions. By increasing or decreasing the questions on each topic, Ms. Cook can then match the assessment to the instruction. Ms. Cook allots each objective question a 2-point value for a total of 60 points, whereas each of the five essay questions is worth 8 points for a total value of 40 points.

The other question about formal assessment content concerns cognitive domains. In effect, at what level of cognitive skill do you want to assess your students? Like the previous issues, let your instruction be your guide. To some extent, cognitive domain issues are directly tied to the developmental level of students. As mentioned in Chapter 3, Bloom noted that some of the higher levels of his taxonomy may be difficult

TABLE 6.1   Assessment Checklist

Instruction: The Years 1919 to 1945	Assessment	
	Objective Items	*Essay Items*
The Treaty of Versailles	3	0
Colonialism and the Great Powers	2	0
The Rise of Totalitarian Regimes	4	1
The Great Depression	7	2
Political Causes of World War II	4	1
Economic Causes of World War II	2	0
World War II—European Theater	5	1
World War II—Pacific Theater	3	0
Item Total	30	5
Point Total	60 points	40 points

to use with younger children. Therefore, you need to consider the students' developmental level when constructing assessments. For example, questions for first-grade students that require extensive synthesis or evaluation may not be appropriate. Questions that focus just on knowledge would not be appropriate for high school students.

The Where Question

This question also appears to be a simple question with a simple answer. Where we test is in our regular classroom. However, not all assessments are conducted in the classroom. Some teachers use take-home assessments. Take-home formal assessments have both good and bad features to them. On the plus side, if they have constructed-response or essay formats, they can tap into higher-level cognitive skills. They can allow the student considerable time to research and synthesize information about a topic. On the down side, if take-home exams are poorly constructed, they can be widely misused. They can end up being a research paper rather than a formal classroom test and thus become open invitations for cheating. It can be difficult to determine who is actually responsible for the work on the exam when it comes to a take-home test.

Other aspects of the Where Question include the contextual features of learning and assessment and the issue of special accommodations. The context aspects of the assessment situation are the physical and social context of the original learning environment and how well it duplicates the environment of the assessment. For a number of decades research has shown the effects of context or state dependent learning. **State dependent learning** is when information learned under one condition is best recalled under the same condition. This is true of students, classrooms, and tests. Students who learned information in a particular room performed better on tests taken in a similar room than they did on tests taken in a different room (Smith, Glenberg, & Bjork, 1978).

There is some indication that even the emotional and sensory aspects of the original learning affect student recall during an assessment. (Further discussion of classroom environment issues with assessments are presented in Chapter 13.)

Special assessment accommodations also can be a factor to consider in your classroom. These can include children with sensory and physical disabilities who need assisted learning devices and assisted assessments. Another important consideration concerns children who have attention-deficit/hyperactivity disorder (ADHD). These children, by the very nature of their disability, can be highly affected by environmental stimuli and outside distractions. Separate private assessment facilities may be warranted for ADHD children in order to provide them with reasonable accommodations. Some students with learning disabilities, particularly reading or writing disabilities, also may need special accommodations. These students may need a teacher to read aloud certain questions (reading disability) or have computer access (writing disabilities) to meet their needs for reasonable accommodations.

The When Question

The When Question addresses the issue of when to schedule an exam. A variety of timing and sequence decisions must be made about your formal classroom assessments. For instance, during your instructional term when is the best time to give an assessment? Is it better to give many assessments or is it better to give only one or two assessments per term? Another aspect of the When Question is: When do you give an assessment in terms of a particular time of day?

Here is one question that every teacher asks: Is it better to give multiple formal assessments during a semester or just one or two formal assessments? Generally speaking, it is better to give multiple assessments instead of just one or two. There are a several reasons for this viewpoint. First, research indicates that recall of material is better when there are multiple assessments appropriately spaced over time. Second, in providing feedback to students about their achievement, multiple assessments also provide more feedback over a longer time period. Third, when multiple assessments are used, a low grade on one assessment will not affect an overall grade nearly as much as when only one or two assessments are used. Therefore, multiple assessments may slightly reduce student test anxiety since an entire grade for a course is not riding on one or two tests.

Multiple assessments almost certainly provide a more reliable and valid way of measuring student achievement. As stated in Chapter 2 about the number of test items, the same generally could be said for the number of assessments—that is, the more the merrier. As long as the tests are quality assessments, more is better than less. Nevertheless, you can reach a saturation point on giving too many tests (anything more than once a week or once every two weeks is probably too much). Another consideration is that too many formal assessments can ultimately cut into your instructional time. Other than these considerations, though, multiple assessments are the way to go.

Related to the issue of multiple assessments is another question: Should you give a comprehensive exam at the end of the term? Usually, I recommend against comprehensive exams. But the research on this issue is somewhat different from the multiple assessment research. What little research there is on this topic appears pretty much mixed. My own view is that there are a few courses where comprehensive exams may be justified, with the caveat that you give other formal assessments that lead up to the comprehensive exam. Some physical sciences and math courses use a cumulative set of laws, principles, or theorems to construct a framework for understanding the subject. For example, geometry is almost like staircase, where theorems are built one on another. With this type of class, comprehensive exams may have limited applicability.

Another part of the When Question concerns some practical instructional and timing issues. I generally find that taking a test in the first part of the school day is most beneficial. Most students, especially the younger ones, seem to do best shortly after the class day begins (give them a half hour after the first bell in the morning). You might want a little review period before the exam but I only do it for anxiety reduction. I find that students hardly ever get much from a review right before an assessment. When a person learns content material, he or she needs to sleep on it to assimilate it.

Once students enter middle or secondary school, you generally should create your exams so that they are tailored to a full class period. In effect, the length and time for a formal classroom assessment should match the time of one class period. This avoids a couple of problems. The first problem is one of the worst things that you can do: *Do not give a test right after teaching something new that is not on the test.* Research has shown that this can noticeably interrupt the recall of information for the test. Not only that, but hardly anyone is going to remember the new material. The second thing is: Right after a formal assessment most people need some sort of break or at least a change of pace. Again, it is unlikely that you are going to get a lot of attention from your students if you have instruction immediately after a test. The optimum thing to do after a test is to go over it and provide feedback as soon as possible. Unfortunately, this may not be possible because of time constraints.

There are some other practical considerations to make about formal classroom assessments. With children in the primary grades, there are plenty of bad times to give assessments. Right before and right after lunch seem to be bad times. Very late in the day also seems to be an ineffective time, as is the day of a big field trip. (In fact, there hardly seems to be a good time at all for primary-grade children.) With middle and secondary school students, you have to schedule tests during your class time, regardless of whether it is the first or last period of the day. Still, there are some times to avoid. The day of the big ball game or a day when there is a special event in the school will not be a good time to give a test.

The last aspect of the When Question is the issue of timed versus untimed tests. I generally recommend allowing as much time as practical on formal classroom assessments. I do not think that time should be a factor in determining student test scores. Granted, there are some practical classroom issues that have to be considered. For instance, you cannot allow your assessments to cut too much into your instructional time. On the other hand, by being flexible on the amount of time allowed on your formal assessments, you may reduce some student anxiety. If you must have time limits, be sure that you let students know how much time they have left. Giving a 20-minute or a 10-minute warning is a good practice.

The How Question

The How Question cuts to the heart of what teachers commonly think of with assessments: How do you construct formal classroom assessments? As noted in Chapter 2, you have a variety of options when preparing formal classroom assessments. This chapter and the following chapters consider these options and how to implement them in your classroom.

We will begin with one cliché that everyone uses: Objective tests are harder to make but easier to grade than essay tests. As this cliché indicates, the question of using objective items is a mixed bag. One of the most positive features about them is that they limit any personal bias that may occur in grading an assessment. When dealing with students and parents, this feature can be very important. Objective items can serve as a cross-check with more subjective forms of assessments, such as essays or portfolios. It is hard to argue about unfair assessments when a variety of assessments give the same sort of grade. It is difficult to claim that a teacher is biased against a student when an objective test is used. On the other hand, it is difficult, if not impossible, to measure some of the higher-order thinking skills with multiple-choice questions. Keep in mind the first law of assessment: A variety of assessments is the best policy.

Constructing Objective Assessments

Whatever else you do, keep track of your old assessments. I never cease to be amazed at how many old questions I can recycle. Like old soldiers, old test items never die, though their ink may fade away. Ideally, put your old assessments on a computer and develop your own test bank. You also will find that, over the years, your ability to write assessments will develop just as your ability to teach will develop. If you keep a test bank of your assessment items, you can see the progress in your assessment ability.

This section reviews three major types of objective items: multiple choice, matching, and true/false. Fill-in-the-blank items often are listed as a type of objective item. However, fill-in-the-blank items also can be seen as part of a continuum of constructed-response items that include sentence completion items and cloze items. These types of items will be reviewed in the next chapter.

Constructing Multiple-Choice Items

Most researchers in the assessment area generally endorse **multiple-choice** items as the best format for objective assessments (Gronlund & Linn, 1990). The publishers of standardized assessments clearly agree; the vast majority of objective items on these tests are multiple choice. There are a couple of reasons for the use of this type of item. In terms of reliability and item discrimination, multiple-choice items tend to be superior to other objective formats. Although successful guessing isn't completely eliminated, it usually is more difficult to correctly guess the right answer with multiple-choice items than with other objective formats.

The construction of multiple-choice items involves two separate but linked parts. The question or the statement is called the **stem**. The various answers are known as the **alternatives**. The alternatives consist of the correct answer and the three or four incorrect answers, which are called the **distractors**.

Like other parts of current assessment practices, certain ideas have developed over time that can help you construct quality items. Some information comes from the research on test development and some of it comes from the practical art of constructing good test items. Like teaching, there is both a science and an art to writing good assessment items.

Dealing with the Stem. The first rule is that the *stem* should deliver the major part of the information. My view is that when students read the stem and know the course content, they should be able to select the correct answer. With a good multiple-choice item, the stem should be longer than any of the alternatives. Here are examples of what not to do and what to do.

What not to do:

The Pythagorean theorem is:

a. The diagonal of a rectangle is equal to the square of the sum of the two equal sides from which the diagonal is calculated.
b. The square of the hypotenuse is equal to the square of the sum of two equal sides of an isosceles triangle.
c. The octave is expressed in a repetition of eight intervals based on pitch.
d. For every action there is an opposite but equal reaction.

What to do:

The square of the hypotenuse is equal to the square of the sum of two equal sides of an isosceles triangle expresses what well-known concept?

a. Newton's second law of thermodynamics
b. Archimedes law
c. The Pythagorean theorem
d. The Euclidean principle

The stem should be a meaningful statement in and of itself. It should not be an incomplete sentence or an incomplete question. The stem should be concise but contain as much of the content as possible. A long-winded stem only serves to confuse the anxious.

Here is the wrong way to write a stem:

A record number of fallacies and trends characterize the twenty-first century world economy. Most macro economic viewpoints state that there are only two essential features with which economists and businesses need to be concerned. These are:

a. Robotics and automation

b. Robotics and electronics
c. Globalization and robotics
d. Globalization and privatization

Here is a better way:

What are the two essential features of macro economics in the twenty-first century?

a. Robotics and automation
b. Robotics and electronics
c. Globalization and robotics
d. Globalization and privatization

Another aspect of the stem is that it should be a positive question or statement rather than a negative one. Again, the possibility of student confusion is much greater with a negative stem.

The following question is an example of a negative statement:

Which one of the following is not guaranteed by the First Amendment?

a. Freedom of the press
b. Freedom of religion
c. Freedom of movement
d. Freedom of assembly

Not only can students sometimes miss seeing the *not*, but even the slightest possibility of an exception to one of the distractors can confuse students.

A better alternative is this question:

Which one of the following amendments guarantees freedom of the press?

a. Fifth Amendment
b. Third Amendment
c. Articles of Confederation
d. First Amendment
e. Twenty-First Amendment

This item avoids any potential confusion and it should increase the reliability of your assessment.

When writing stems, beginning teachers may provide grammatical clues that give away the answer. One of the most common mistakes is to give clues in the grammar or sentence structure of the stem that aids the student in correctly guessing the answer. For example, the use of the articles *a*, *an*, and *the* can often provide a clue as to the correct answer on a multiple-choice question.

Here is an example of this problem:

A frog is classified as an:

a. Reptile

b. Mammal
c. Amphibian
d. Crustacean
e. Cetacean

A better alternative is the following item:

A frog is classified as:

a. A Reptile
b. A Mammal
c. An Amphibian
d. A Crustacean
e. An Arachnid

In effect, by adding the appropriate article to each alternative you eliminate the possibility of cueing students about the correct answer.

Other grammatical mistakes involve the use of words in the stem that can identify the correct answer. These may be subject-verb agreements or the use of singular and plural.

The following item gives an unintended clue:

Among the settlers of the American West, one of the chief modes of transportation were wagons nicknamed:

a. Dirt cart
b. Prairie schooners
c. Buster buggy
d. California goldmobile
e. Indiana carriage

A better alternative to this item is:

Among the settlers of the American West, one of the chief modes of transportation were wagons nicknamed:

a. Dirt carts
b. Prairie schooners
c. Buster buggies
d. California goldmobiles
e. Indiana carriages

Again, checking each distractor for singular/plural agreement with the stem will reduce any clues that may give away the correct answer.

Dealing with Alternatives. There are a number of ideas about writing good *alternatives*. First of all, each of the alternatives should be plausible; however, someone who has studied the course content should be able to determine the correct answer. The goal of a test is not to trip up students with trick stems and alternatives. A formal classroom assessment should not be a measure of test-taking skills. What it should be is a method to discriminate between those students who have reached a level of proficiency with the course material and those who have not.

Various studies have shown that students, when unsure of the correct answer, have a tendency to choose the longest answer. So beware. Generally speaking, avoid having the longest answer as the correct answer. Another warning: Students may soon become aware of your tendency to avoid having the longest answer as the correct answer, so you will may need to have a few long answers as the correct answers. Also, there is a tendency for students to select the first answer when they are unsure of the correct answer. You have to make a choice about how many times you want to have A be the correct answer on your tests.

Another thing to watch out for is your own personal tendencies to give away answers on tests. Many teachers have an unconscious bias about selecting too many of the same alternatives as the correct answers on multiple-choice items. In effect, you may unknowingly prefer B as the correct answer. It is easy to check your own correct answers and determine if this is true on your own assessments. In the long run, you probably need to have pretty much the same number of B, C, D, and E alternatives as the correct answers. You probably should have fewer A alternatives as the correct answer but still keep some in there.

Nearly everyone in the assessment field is against having combinations of alternatives as the correct answers. Here is an example of an unclear item:

The theory of relativity is mathematically expressed by the following equation: $E = MC^2$. What do the different symbols in this equation tell us?

a. The relationship of sound with light
b. The relationship of energy with light
c. The relationship of energy with mass
d. B but not A
e. Neither A nor B
f.   Both B and C

Even Einstein might be confused by the above question. The other problem with the item is that a student could rationally pick more than one answer. (And yes, I know you are supposed to pick out the *best* answer. That is always the rejoinder to make after a confusing question.)

A better alternative to the above question is:

The theory of relativity is mathematically expressed by the following equation: $E = MC^2$. What do the different symbols in this equation tell us?

a. The relationship of sound with mass and light
b. The relationship of energy with light
c. The relationship of energy with mass and light
d. The relationship of metric energy to mass and carbon

The above item format avoids the confusion of combination answers with a straightforward set of alternatives. Remember: *The goal of formal assessments is to distin-*

guish between those who know the material and those who do not. The goal is not to measure the logic skills or test-taking skills of the students. Stay away from confusing combination alternatives.

The same problem with confusion applies to "none of the above" and "all of the above" as alternatives. Generally, they compound problems with understanding and responding.

The following example is not recommended:

> Which of the following is a major cognitive development in Piaget's stage of concrete operations?
>
> a. Egocentrism
> b. Metaphorical thinking
> c. Object permanency
> d. None of the above

A better item format is:

> Which of the following is a major cognitive development in Piaget's stage of concrete operations?
>
> a. Egocentrism
> b. Metaphorical thinking
> c. Object permanency
> d. Conservation

Items with "all of the above" may be even more capable of creating confusion than "none of the above."

Here is another example not recommended:

> Which of the following factors is cited in your textbook as a cause of global warming?
>
> a. Globalization
> b. Nationalization
> c. Automation
> d. All of the above

A better item format is:

> Which of the following factors is cited in your textbook as a cause of global warming?
>
> a. Greenhouse gases
> b. Solar energy
> c. Automation
> d. Geopolitics

Higher-Order Thinking and Multiple-Choice Items. As previously indicated, Bloom noted the difficulty in assessing higher-order thinking skills through multiple-choice items. A number of educators have made proposals about possible ways to complete this task. In a recent review on the use of multiple-choice items, Tanner (2003) stated that there are ways that multiple-choice items can be used to measure higher-order thinking skills. The key issue is that the assessment item must require more than rote memorization. It must require the student to transform or apply the content of the item. Here is an example of a multiple-choice item adapted from Tanner:

> Mr. Trotter is a dynamic classroom lecturer who talks full steam during class. However, a few moments before he finishes each lecture, he runs his hand through his receding hairline three times. He then ends his lecture and dismisses his class. His students now stop listening to him and start putting away their class materials as soon as he touches his hair. Analyze the following responses and apply classical conditioning procedures to determine the correct answer:
>
> a. Mr. Trotter's lecture is an unconditioned stimulus and the student behavior is an unconditioned response.
> b. Mr. Trotter's hairline is a conditioned stimulus and student behavior is an unconditioned response.
> c. When Mr. Trotter touches his hairline, it is a conditioned stimulus and the student behavior is a conditioned response.
> d. When Mr. Trotter touches his hairline, it is a conditioned response and the student behavior is an unconditioned response.

As noted by Tanner (2003), this type of question primarily involves analysis. The ability to correctly determine the answer cannot be due to memory alone but involves the ability both to analyze and apply a model. Therefore, Tanner makes a good case that multiple-choice items can involve some type of higher-order thinking. Major testing companies, such as the Educational Testing Service, also attempt to generate multiple-choice items that measure some higher-order thinking skills.

Two other thoughts about multiple-choice items: Never use just multiple-choice items alone on assessments; that would violate the first law of assessment practices. And, your students are your best critics when developing good multiple-choice items. Review both the test content and the items themselves after using multiple-choice assessments (or any other type of assessment item). If students can make a good rationale for challenging items, give them credit for those items. Do a quick item analysis on your assessments, using the procedures listed in Chapter 2.

Constructing Matching Items

Most assessment experts prefer multiple-choice items over matching or true/false items. In general, an objective question is better framed in a multiple-choice format than any other objective format. Nevertheless, there are certain cases when matching can be a useful assessment tool. It seems especially appropriate in the primary grades. There is something about matching and drawing lines from one picture to another picture or from a word to a picture that is inherently appealing to many children in the early grades.

Point/Counterpoint: Standardized Assessments and Multiple-Choice Items

Point

Supporters of the use of multiple-choice item formats on standardized assessments, such as achievement tests and college aptitude tests, state that these formats have a number of advantages. First, they are more reliable to score. Second, they are relatively easy to administer because of the simplicity of the format. Therefore, untrained test administrators, such as teachers or school personnel, can appropriately administer these tests. This is different from the standardized tests used to diagnose special education classifications. These required trained, licensed psychologists. Third, the content and format are uniform enough so that national versions of these tests can be used.

Supporters also note that standardized assessments with multiple-choice formats have survived a number of legal challenges. These legal challenges often are based on the validity of the tests and whether the tests constitute a discriminatory practice. Supporters claim that multiple-choice assessments have survived these legal challenges because they are objective in nature and because of their validity and reliability.

Counterpoint

Opponents of the traditional use of multiple-choice formats on standardized tests point out that the use of this format has a noticeable negative impact on three areas: assessment, instruction, and test preparation. Opponents claim that multiple-choice formats tend to assess only certain types of thinking skills. Other item formats, such as essay or performance-based assessments, can do a more effective job of evaluating a wider range of thinking skills. Using multiple-choice formats on standardized assessments tends to bias instruction in the classroom. Teachers end up teaching to the format and content of the test. Therefore, they focus instruction on skills and content that are measured by multiple-choice formats. Essentially, the same problem occurs with any test preparation activities. These activities focus on how to prepare for a multiple-choice format, but students get little or no test preparation experience with other formats.

Matching items consist of two separate columns: a **stem list** and a **response list**. An example for second grade consists of the following:

Draw a line to match the plant with its usual color:

Stem List	Response List
Carrot	Brown
Potato	Yellow
Tomato	Green
Lettuce	Red
Corn	Orange

With older students you generally have more responses than stems. You may also use numbers and letters instead of drawing lines. The following is an example of a matching item for twentieth-century American History:

Match the correct person with the office. Write the letter of the person beside the number that indicates the office that he held.

_____ 1. President		A.	Robert Rubin
_____ 2. Vice-President		B.	Ernest Hemingway
_____ 3. Secretary of State		C.	Robert McNamara
_____ 4. Secretary of Defense		D.	Thomas Edison
_____ 5. Secretary of Treasury		E.	Hubert Humphrey
		F.	John Foster Dulles
		G.	Warren G. Harding
		H.	Henry Ford

As with multiple choice, there are similar practical recommendations. The stem list should provide most of the information. You need to make sure that there is only one correct response for each stem. Both lists for each item should focus on one single topic.

You also should limit the number of stems in a list to 5 or 6. You can have more options in the response list, though I would recommend limiting the number of responses to a maximum of 10. If you think you need more stems and responses, then you probably need to separate your material into different matching items. In effect, you are better off with two separate matching items that have 6 stems and 10 responses apiece instead of one matching item with 12 stems and 20 responses.

Constructing True/False Items

As with matching items, there is some limited usefulness with true/false questions. **True/false items** may be most useful for children who are in the early grades of elementary school. In terms of assessing lower-level cognitive domains in children with special needs, true/false questions generally can be adapted for most elementary grades. The simplicity of the written format would appear to make true/false especially suited for these students. The format may allow the teacher to assess a large amount of knowledge-level information in a relatively efficient fashion.

The structure of true/false questions consists of a statement and two choices. There are a number of considerations to make. You need to ensure that the statement is unequivocally true or false—get rid of any ambiguity in the statement. As mentioned previously, you are not trying to trick your students. If they know the material, they should be able to get the correct answer.

There often are clues that tend to give away the correct answer with true/false items. For instance, the use of absolutes, such as *always*, *never*, and *all the time*, can be clues that a statement is probably false. Stay away from them. The same can be said for certain qualifiers, such as *usually, generally,* or *most of the time.* These are clues that a statement is probably true.

As with using negatives in multiple-choice items, the use of negatives with true/false items generally will create confusion in the ranks of your students. There have been two interesting studies with the use of negatives with these types of questions (Wason, 1961; Zern, 1967). Both studies found that the time needed to answer a negative statement was greater than that needed for a positive statement. Both studies also found that the overall error rate was greater with negative statements than with similarly worded positive statements. Examples of the types of negative and positive statements used in these studies are shown below:

T__ F__   A kangaroo is not a mammal.

T__ F__   A kangaroo is a mammal.

There are two other cautionary notes about constructing true/false items. First, you need to have the same number of true answers as false answers. (The few times that I have used this format, I found that I had quite a few more true answers than false answers.) Second, avoid the tendency toward writing longer statements when you have a true answer than a false answer (Thorndike, 1997). Teachers tend to use more qualifiers when the statement is true, thus making the statement longer.

Challenges to Objective Items

Objective items have been much maligned in recent years. This is particularly true of multiple-choice items. Some of the reason for these attitudes appear to be due to the overuse of objective items. Some of it is due to the association of these items with standardized assessments. The increasing development of performance-based assessments that attempt to assess simulated or actual activities also has led to changes in attitudes about the use of objective items.

A major challenge for objective items is the ability to assess higher-level cognitive domains. Anderson and Krathwohl (2002) note little positive development in the last 40 years in creating objective items to assess higher-level skills. Many experts agree with the authors. For the most part, objective items do not measure the ability to synthesize or evaluate information.

A related argument is that objective formats reinforce a type of straightjacket thinking on the part of students and possibly teachers. Students are reinforced for studying in a way that will enable them to succeed on objective formats. They often are not encouraged to go beyond a sort of cursory knowledge of the material. Therefore, the ability of students to transfer information to new situations or to generalize it beyond the test situation is limited.

Another challenge to objective items is in terms of developmentally appropriate practices. These practices encourage teachers to find the cognitive developmental level of the student and then instruct as well as assess at that level. It is clear that some written assessment formats will not work effectively with younger children. They are simply not developmentally ready for these assessments. On the other hand, students in high school and college need assessments that will stimulate higher-level cognitive skills. This is something that many objective items seldom do. Poor readers (or children with reading disabilities) also can be penalized by items with written objective formats.

Strengths of Objective Assessments

There are a number of positive reasons to include objective formats. As previously mentioned, Tanner (2003) completed a review of multiple-choice items and listed the following positive aspects about them:

1. Given the relatively short amount of class time to take multiple-choice assessments, the items provide a greater amount of coverage and content validity than most other formats.
2. The reliability of multiple-choice items is generally better than other formats.
3. Careful construction and use of multiple-choice items can offset many of the challenges that are leveled against these items. For example, relevant and challenging multiple-choice items can be designed that will stimulate student thinking and assess some higher-level thinking skills.

Other supporters of objective items point out that these items can provide an effective counterpoint to grade challenges that might occur with more subjective forms of assessments. As previously noted in this chapter, when students have the same grades on subjective and objective items, it tends to limit grade challenges. A criticism of objective assessments is that they cause problems for students with differing developmental levels or with reading problems. Supporters of objective items note that this same criticism could apply to written essays or portfolios.

Given all the good, the bad, and the ugly about objective items, what should a teacher do? The best advice is to remember the first law of assessment practices: A variety of assessments is the best policy. Objective items do provide a measure of protection against claims of bias with grades. Of the different critiques of objective items, the most telling one is the claim that these items have difficulty assessing higher-level thinking skills. You may need to devise other forms of assessments for some of these skills. In fact, that is part of the reason for the next two chapters. I bet you can hardly wait to read them.

Chapter Summary

This chapter began our discussion about the construction of formal classroom assessments. There are a number of considerations to make about your assessments, including choices about who to test, what to test, where to test, when to test, and how to test. Among the decisions you must make are a number of practical considerations. You must decide about the time of day or week of your assessments, the amount and range of assessment content, and the type of assessment items. Each of these options needs to be examined before you construct your own assessments.

The second part of the chapter reviewed the construction of objective items. In general, multiple-choice items are endorsed as the preferred format for objective items. A number of different suggestions are made for the construction of the various objective items. These suggestions include a careful analysis of assessment items to ensure that you do not provide clues about the right answer on your tests. Inadvertent clues, such as your use of the plural or singular, the length of the correct answer, and the use of articles, need to be checked to avoid giving away the correct answer.

Problems with objective items also are noted. Chief among these problems is the question of assessing higher-level cognitive domains with objective items. Another challenge addresses the question of whether written objective items can be developmentally appropriate for certain groups of students. The strengths of objective items also are noted.

CASE STUDY EPILOGUE

Ms. Lopez is going to revise both her classroom assessment procedures and her methods for placing children in reading groups. She has decided to use a number of different assessment formats for her class. In addition to some of the performance-based aspects she previously used, Ms. Lopez has settled on a series of short, objective assessments using both multiple-choice and matching items. Therefore, students' grades will be based on both objective and performance-based criteria.

In placing students in reading groups, Ms. Lopez will now use an approach based on three separate criteria. She will continue to use observed reading-level performance based on her observation of students' reading level. She also will use reading test scores based on her own objective classroom assessments. In addition, she will use standardized test scores in reading from the statewide assessment tests mandated in her state.

Ms. Lopez decides to give approximately equal weight to each of these three criteria in determining who will be in each specific reading group. She compiles this weighted formula and provides it first to her principal for review. After his approval, Ms. Lopez provides a copy of her policy to all parents during the first two weeks of the fall term. She will also carefully document her assessments in order to answer parents' questions about their children.

CHAPTER ACTIVITIES

Websites

www.nwrel.org   This website is created by Northwest Regional Educational Laboratory in Portland, Oregon. It is one of the premier federally funded education centers in the country. The website has quite a bit of research and information sources on objective tests, and it gives both sides of the issue.

www.fairtest.org   This site is run by FairTest, a private organization critical of both standardized and objective assessments. The site provides quite a bit of information about testing controversies.

www.edweek.org   This website is associated with *Education Week*, a major print magazine about educational issues. Go to the assessment section and you will find plenty of current information on school issues and practices about assessments.

Portfolio Activities

1. Review Ms. Lopez's situation in the Case Study. In your portfolio, answer the following questions:
   - How would you respond to these parents?
   - Would you have a documented policy about how you select children for reading groups?
   - How would you select children for reading groups?
   - Would you use assessments to place children in reading groups?
   - Would you use any objective assessments to place to children in reading groups?

2. Design your own objective test of this chapter. Create at least four multiple-choice items, one matching item, and three true/false items. For a really good time, give this assessment to one of your fellow students.

KEY CONCEPTS

Alternatives	Response list
Content validity	State dependent learning
Distractors	Stem list
Matching items	Stems
Multiple-choice items	True/false items

REVIEW QUESTIONS

1. List and describe the reasons given for using multiple assessments rather than one or two assessments during a semester.

2. What are the problems with giving a comprehensive exam?

3. What is meant by state dependent learning and how is this concept related to assessments?

4. List and describe the three major parts of a multiple-choice item.

5. Explain the various problems that can occur with writing the stem for a multiple-choice item.

6. Describe the problems that can occur with writing alternatives for multiple-choice items.

7. Describe the parts of a matching item and list the concerns that may occur with such items.

8. Compare and contrast the challenges and strengths of objective items.

SELF-ASSESSMENT

1. If only one of these factors could be considered in constructing a classroom test, which should be selected?
   a. The instructional objectives
   b. The textbook's lesson plans
   c. The teacher's lesson plans
   d. The actual instruction
   e. The textbook test bank

2. Which part of a multiple-choice item should contain the most information?
   a. Correct answer
   b. Stem
   c. Response list
   d. Alternatives
   e. Distractors

3. The most commonly used type of objective item is:
   a. True/false
   b. Matching
   c. Multiple choice
   d. Essay
   e. Fill-in-the-blank

4. Which of the following is recommended about administering assessments over the course of a semester?
   a. Single comprehensive exams
   b. Multiple assessments over different parts of the unit
   c. Informal assessments then single comprehensive exams
   d. Two comprehensive exams per semester

5. When information learned under one condition is best recalled under the same condition, it is called:
   a. Static learning
   b. Reactive inhibition learning style

Answers to Self-Assessment: 1. d, 2. b, 3. c, 4. b, 5. c, 6. d, 7. c

c. State dependent learning
d. Cognitive learning styles

6. Objective items have been criticized mostly for:
   a. Subjectivity
   b. Personal bias in regard to how students are evaluated
   c. Failure to achieve a higher retention rate
   d. Failure to measure higher-level thinking skills

7. What are the two parts of a matching item?
   a. Stem and distractors
   b. Alternatives and response list
   c. Stem and response list
   d. Root and stem

REFERENCES

Anderson, L.W., & Krathwohl, D.R. (Eds.). (2001). *A taxonomy for learning, teaching, and assessing: A revision of Bloom's Taxonomy.* New York: Longman.

Gronlund, N.E., & Linn, R.L. (1990). *Measurement and evaluation in education.* New York: Macmillan.

Smith, S.M., Glenberg, A.,& Bjork, R.A. (1978). Environmental context and human memory. *Memory and Cognition, 6,* 342–353.

Tanner, D.E. (2003). Multiple-choice items: Pariah, panacea or neither of the above. *American Secondary Education, 31*(2), 27–36.

Thorndike, R.M. (1997). *Measurement and evaluation in psychology and education* (6th ed.). Upper Saddle River, N J: Merrill.

Wason, P. (1961). Response to affirmative and negative binary statements. *British Journal of Psychology, 52,* 133–142.

Zern, D. (1967). Effects of variations in question phrasing on true-false answers by grade-school children. *Psychological Reports, 20,* 527–533.

7 Constructed-Response Assessments

CASE STUDY

Mrs. Whitmore is a high school English teacher. She was selected to serve on a committee of educators, school administrators, and testing specialists to design a new statewide assessment for a southwestern state. Mrs. Whitmore believes that the previous statewide assessment was too oriented toward multiple-choice questions. She wants to see a major portion of the new assessment to be essay questions.

Other members of the committee disagree with her position. They point out that most standardized assessments use multiple-choice items. For large groups, objective assessments usually are more reliable to score.

Mrs. Whitmore remains unconvinced by their arguments. She believes that essays provide a better way to assess many skills, including critical thinking and communication skills. She wants to demonstrate that essay items can be successfully used on state assessments. She needs to know the following:

What are the best types of essay items to use?

Can essay items be used with large groups of students?

What are the different ways that essay items should be scored?

What types of procedures can be established to reliably score the test?

Introduction

In Chapter 2, there was a short discussion of **constructed-response assessments.** Constructed-response assessments ask students to construct their own responses to assessment questions. Student responses involve a detailed written or oral narrative. The most frequently used type of constructed-response items are essay questions.

There is a certain amount of overlap between constructed-response assessments and some types of performance-based assessments. For example, when students write in their portfolios, they are constructing their own responses. Of course, one big difference between constructed-response assessments and portfolios is in assessment administration. Constructed-response assessments generally are given during a formal classroom assessment, sometimes with objective assessment items. Portfolios are more likely to be written as part of an out-of-class assignment.

Constructed-response assessments (and some performance-based assessments) also share certain strengths. Chief among these strengths is the ability to assess higher-order thinking skills. A second strength is in the development of writing skills. Think of writing as simply another form of self-expression. Anytime a person writes and receives appropriate feedback, it helps the person's writing. Generally, the more an individual writes, the better he or she becomes at writing.

This chapter presents various types of constructed-response items. One section examines how to make constructed-response items; another reviews the scoring rubrics that are needed with these items. This chapter also evaluates the challenges involved with constructed-response items.

Constructing Essay Items

In terms of time and cost factors (in this case, time spent plus emotional costs by the teacher), constructing essay questions are relatively cost effective. They are not as labor intensive as creating multiple-choice items, but essays definitely are harder to grade. As a teacher, you want essay assessments that maximize learning as well as feedback about this learning (while minimizing your own stress and eye strain.) There are a number of ways to do all of this with essay items.

The first step is to decide what type of essay items you want to use. As noted in previous chapters, there are certain considerations that apply to essays, just as they do to other types of assessment methods. Here are six questions to consider:

Six Questions about Essay Items
1. What is the relationship between your essay items and your actual classroom instruction?
2. What is the relationship between your essay items and your instructional objectives?
3. Do you want a restricted-response answer from students or an extended-response answer?

4. Do you want to ask a series of interrelated essay questions or completely different questions?
5. How many essay questions do you want to give on an assessment?
6. Do you want to give optional essay items?

Question 1 and Question 2 are pretty straightforward. As indicated in previous chapters, you need to create assessments that match your actual classroom instruction and objectives. This is a critical part of a good assessment, but is *essential* with essays. Because essays are time consuming for students to take, you will be able to sample only a limited amount of the knowledge base with these items. Given this limited amount of essay items that can be used, your essay questions should focus on the most salient and essential parts of your instruction.

So make each question count by assessing only the "big questions" in your instructional unit. And remember: The value of essays goes beyond just the assessment role. Essays can make students think about a topic and take a position. This is an important part of critical thinking skills.

Question 3 deals with **extended-response essay questions** versus **restricted-response essay questions**. These types of items define how much and what type of writing you want from your students. To some extent, the type of question reflects your comfort level as a teacher. Here are your choices:

- Do you want to give open-ended questions that allow a large degree of choice by students in answering the questions? (These can be difficult for you to grade reliably.)
- Do you want to restrict the responses of students by asking very specific questions that require very specific answers? (These limit the creativity and unique responses of your students.)

Another aspect of this question depends somewhat on the type of academic subject that you teach. For example, the need to restrict essays to precise information may be more relevant in science classes than in literature courses. The need to restrict written responses may not be appropriate in expository writing or creative writing classes.

The differences between extended-response and restricted-response essays are determined by the restrictions on the amount of writing you want from your students. The simplest restriction is in terms of length. One commonly used standard is that an extended-response assessment takes more than one page. The following extended-response and restricted-response essay items indicate the actual differences between these two items.

Extended Response

Describe all the factors listed in your textbook and in the classroom instruction about the decision to use the atomic bomb during World War II.

Restricted Response

In two to three paragraphs describe three major factors involved in the decision to use the atomic bomb during World War II. Which factor is the most important one? List this factor and provide a rationale for why it is the most important one.

Extended Response

List and describe all the possible motives of the main conspirators in the assassination of Caesar as indicated in the play *Julius Caesar*.

Restricted Response

Compare and contrast the motives of the main conspirators in the play *Julius Caesar*. Describe the specific reasons of three of the conspirators for the assassination of Caesar.

As you can see with these items, length can be used to restrict the responses of your students. In addition, you also can restrict responses by describing exactly what is required from your students to answer the questions. Rather than ask them to describe everything they know about a topic, restricted-response questions deliberately narrow the focus of answers.

The best way to do this is to pinpoint specific information that each student needs to provide. By making specific requests in your items, you can avoid essay bluffing, or what I call "tap dancing" on the essay. This means that you avoid providing an opportunity for students to tap dance around the essential parts of the question. Another way of pinpointing specific information can be found in the next example:

Restricted Response

Name each of Piaget's four stages of cognitive development and describe one major developmental change that occurs in each stage. Explain the specific importance of each developmental change to overall cognitive development.

This item avoids some of the problems with tap dancing on essays. By pinpointing the information needed, restricted-response essays may enable you to develop more valid and reliable types of grading procedures (discussed later).

Question 4 examines the issue of interrelated versus separate essay items. The most common form of interrelated items is in response to student interpretation of a map, graph, or narrative paragraphs. The following is an example of this type of essay item, which is sometimes called an **interpretive essay.**

Interpretive Essay

Here is a map of the mythical country of Murea. Colonists are faced with six different choices for building new cities. Given what you know about the pattern of city building from this section of geography, where would be the two most likely places for new colonists to build new cities? Provide a rationale for each of the two choices based on the following factors:

1. In terms of transportation, where are the two best possible locations? Provide a detailed rationale of why these are good locations for transportation.
2. In terms of access to natural resources, which two sites are best? List at least two reasons why these sites have the best access to natural resources.
3. What two locations would have the optimum climates for city building? Provide an critical analysis of climate and weather conditions for your selections.
4. What other geographical factors would be optimum for city building? List two other factors that support your choices for city sites. Provide a detailed rationale for your factors.

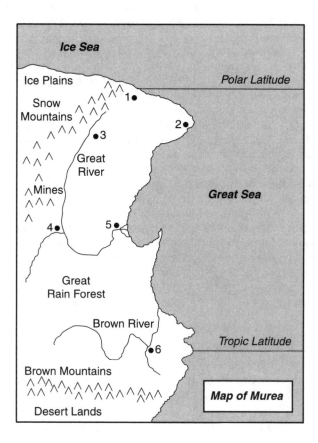

Another use of the interpretive exercise is based on a paragraph or a series of paragraphs. Here is an example of this type of interpretive essay:

Interpretive Essay

In our class activities we have debated and discussed the different methods of parenting and their effects on children's behaviors. Listed below are excerpts from two different child care books of the twentieth century.

A. "There is a sensible way of treating children. Treat them as though they were young adults. Let your behavior always be objective and kindly firm. Never hug and kiss them, never let them sit in your lap. If you must, kiss them once on the forehead when they say good night. Shake hands with them in the morning.

"Won't you remember then, when you are tempted to pet your child, that mother love is a dangerous instrument. . . . An instrument which may wreck your adult son or daughter's vocational future and their chances for marital happiness."

B. "You know more than you think you do. Don't take too seriously what the neighbors say. Don't be overawed by what the experts say. Don't be afraid to trust your common sense.

"In general, remember that what makes your child behave well is not threats or punishments but loving you for your agreeableness and respecting you for knowing your rights and his. Stay in control as a friendly leader rather than battle with him at his level."

1. What type of feelings about affection and physical contact would result in a child raised with the guidelines in the first quote? Provide a rationale for your viewpoint based on a specific set of research.
2. In terms of parenting styles, what type of parenting style (authoritarian, authoritative, permissive) is displayed in the second quote? Provide a detailed explanation for your choice of style.
3. In terms of providing direction to a child for his or her behavior, compare and contrast the two quotes. Which quote appears to focus more on dictating child behavior? Explain your reasons for choosing the quote. Which quote appears to focus more on trusting one's own perceptions about children? Explain your reasons for choosing the quote.
4. Which quote would be more likely to focus on using some type of corporal punishment? Provide a rationale for your choice.

As seen in both of the preceding essay items, interpretive essays involve a series of essay questions about a specific piece of information and allows you to make an in-depth probe of the topic. You could even combine this format with other types of assessment items, such as short answer items (fill-in-the-blank or sentence completion items).

Question 5 from the earlier list of essay items addresses the issue of how many essay questions to give in a single assessment. First, each formal classroom assessment should be tailored to a single class period. Second, as much as possible, students should not be penalized by time constraints. Therefore, you have to gauge the number of essays based on the test-taking time of students who take the longest on the test. In a 50-minute period with high school students you may be able to offer only three to five restricted-response essay questions.

This leads us to Question 6: Do you want to give optional essay items? In other words, should you give four essays and let students choose two or three to write about for their grade? Most experts discourage the use of essay options. One reason is that they actually create a different test based on student choice. Therefore, student grades can vary based on what questions they choose. This problem also can reduce the overall test reliability or test consistency by using different questions on the same assessment.

Grading Decisions with Essay Assessments

Nearly all of us have heard stories or read research about grading essay exams. Imagine that different teachers were asked to grade the same essay exam. The results of the scoring ranged across the grading spectrum. Some teachers gave the exam a good grade; others indicated that the exam was a failure. The key point is that these teachers were grading the exams blindly. In effect, they did not agree on a preset scoring system. If they had been appropriately trained together on a common scoring system, their grading policies on essay items could have reached agreement at an acceptable level.

When essays are used on standardized assessments, there is a team of graders employed to score the essays. The graders spend many hours reviewing items and grading policies. They then train together on essays until they reach a level of agreement known as **interscorer reliability** or inter-rater reliability (Salvia & Ysseldyke, 1998). This type of reliability measures the level of consistency of different raters in rating the essays. Some institutions have a policy of employing two graders on each essay. If they agree on the grade, then that is the given grade. If they disagree on the grade, the essay goes to a third party who then rates the item.

This brings us to an essential point about grading constructed-response items. You need to train your students about your scoring methods. Think of them as colleagues or at least as collaborators in your assessment enterprise. If your students have a good idea of what it takes to make the grade, your mutual suffering may be diminished. But before you can explain it to your students, you need to have a good understanding about your own grading policies.

Developing Grading Policies for Essays

There are a number of separate issues to consider about grading policies for essays. Here are some questions:

- What exactly do you want to assess?
- Do you want to focus just on content when you grade essays?
- Do you want to grade on just style?
- Do you want to strike a balance between grading on content knowledge versus grading on stylistic aspects?
- What kind of scoring system do you want to use?
- Do you want to use a numerical scoring system or some other type of system?

Rubrics for Essay Assessments

Besides assessing for content knowledge, there are a number of separate skills that can be measured by essays (and to some extent by written performance-based assessments). These skills often focus on specific writing abilities. Among these are English composition skills, written communication skills for business, and research report writing skills.

You need to consider exactly what you want to base your grades on besides content knowledge. For instance, you may want to consider grading essays based on a particular stylistic skill and a separate grading system for content knowledge. Another possibility is to split your grading system into two sections—one that deals with style and one that deals with content.

In terms of scoring rubrics for essays, there is a basic division into two types of scoring systems: holistic scoring and analytical scoring. *Holistic scoring* involves giving one single grade for the whole essay. This type of scoring ranges from grading based on a relatively subjective overall impression of the essay to a more defined approach that uses some preset criteria. In either case, there is still just one grade given. There are no subsection or separate areas that are graded. For example, the teacher may develop a relatively small set of global criteria for classroom essays. The following is a set of possible criteria for holistically scoring an English composition essay.

Teacher Application

Holistic Scoring for English Composition Essay

The following areas will be used to determine your overall grade on this essay test:

Vocabulary Usage
Grammatical Rules
Syntax
Organization
Spelling

In contrast to holistic scoring, *analytical scoring* provides a numerical scoring system to grade specific aspects of the essay. In effect, each aspect is assigned a numerical grade based on a point system. The points can then be summarized or transformed to develop one single grade. This procedure may provide a considerable amount of feedback to students about separate areas in their essays. An example follows.

Teacher Application

Analytical Scoring for English Composition Essay

Rate each category on a four-point scale with a 4 being Outstanding, a 3 being Proficient, a 2 being Satisfactory, and a 1 being Unsatisfactory. Add the categories together for the total score.

_____ Vocabulary Usage
_____ Grammatical Rules
_____ Syntax
_____ Organization
_____ Spelling
_____ Total Score

The amount of feedback appears to be crucial in selecting which type of scoring system to use. Analytical scoring procedures offer a more extensive amount of feedback to the student than does the holistic system. In general, this is a clear-cut advantage. Another advantage is that you can more specifically spell out to students in advance of assessment about your grading policy. Holistic scoring, though, may be more appropriate for children in elementary school who are just learning the basics of writing. For them, distinctions between certain scoring systems may result in some confusion about grading policies.

What I do *not* recommend is to have no grading policy. Relying only on subjective opinion is a recipe for problems. Besides the issue of fairness in your grading policies, there are other reasons. If students know what you expect and the basis for your evaluation decisions, they tend to achieve better.

The next section examines some other distinctions among rubrics for scoring essays. In general, the examples provided here will be based on analytical scoring systems. Let's look at an example of a scoring rubric that addresses some common stylistic concerns.

Teacher Application

Scoring Rubric for Style

Rate each category on a four-point scale with a 4 being Outstanding, a 3 being Proficient, a 2 being Satisfactory, and a 1 being Unsatisfactory. Add the eight categories together for the total score.

_____	Introduction	Provides a clear introductory statement that sets the stage for the reader. The statement allows the reader to understand the direction of the essay.
_____	Clarity	Provides a clear and understandable writing style. The writing is concise and avoids jargon.
_____	Grammar	Uses appropriate grammar in writing sentences. The subject/verb agreement is correct and there is an appropriate use of singular and plural forms.
_____	Syntax	Uses words in their correct order in writing complete sentences and avoids run-on or incomplete sentences.
_____	Punctuation	Demonstrates the appropriate use of punctuation rules, such as the correct use of commas, semicolons, and periods.
_____	Spelling	Correctly spells words in the writing task.
_____	Organization	Shows organized and logical continuity of ideas. Each paragraph is stylistically linked with the preceding and subsequent paragraphs.

_____ Conclusion   Contains an appropriate conclusion that restates the thesis of the paper and provides a reflection on the major ideas in the paper.

_____ Total Score

The next scoring rubric is for scoring academic content. This type of scoring focuses just on the knowledge aspects of writing essays.

Teacher Application

Scoring Rubric for Content

Rate each category on a four-point scale with a 4 being Outstanding, a 3 being Proficient, a 2 being Satisfactory, and a 1 being Unsatisfactory. Add the eight categories together for the total score.

_____ Thesis Statement   Presents the basis for the essay by a well-defined statement of the major points.

_____ Theoretical Framework   Clearly articulates a theoretical and philosophical framework in the essay.

_____ Research Citations   Appropriately cites research findings in the essay.

_____ Use of Applications   Applies knowledge and research to specific real-world situations.

_____ Originality of Thinking   Demonstrates an original or "fresh look" at the knowledge and research.

_____ Development of Ideas   Shows a logical progression of ideas in writing the essay.

_____ Critical Analysis   Evaluates and analyzes the knowledge base in writing the essay.

_____ Conclusion   Appropriately synthesizes the major points in the essay. Reflects on the central thesis and provides a conclusion about the essay question.

_____ Total Score

Standardized Assessments and Essays

The issue of how to grade essay questions is a continuing difficulty for many people. Recently, this topic spilled over into the standardized assessment field. In 1999, the

Graduate Management Admissions Test (GMAT) developed an essay for its Analytical Writing Assessment. (The GMAT is the major standardized test taken for admission to graduate work in business colleges.) The use of an essay item on a standardized exam is not, in and of itself, unique. Previous attempts were made to use essays on standardized assessments. What is unique about the GMAT is that a computer program is grading the essay.

According to the Graduate Management Admissions Council (2003), the organization that oversees the content of the GMAT, the Analytical Writing Assessment essay consists of two separate parts: analysis of an issue and analysis of an argument. Scoring is completed either by two humans (actually college professors) or by one human and one e-rater. The e-rater is a computer program that scores essays based on syntax, organization, analysis, and usage of standard English. The Graduate Management Admissions Council states that the e-rater and human raters agree approximately 87 to 94 percent of the time. If there is a major discrepancy in the scoring of an essay, a third human reader will assign the score.

Other organizations and institutions also are developing or mandating the writing of essays on standardized assessments. High school students in Maryland and Virginia are now required to write essays for their standardized high school graduate tests (Matthews, 2003). The Scholastic Assessment Test (SAT) will require an essay on its college aptitude test beginning in 2005.

Critical Thinking Skills, Essays, and Rubrics

In addition to writing skills, another type of skill to assess with essays is critical thinking or reasoning skills. **Critical thinking skills** are cognitive skills that relate to logical, clear-headed thinking as well as problem-solving abilities. A number of models can be used to assess critical thinking skills with essays.

Chapter 3 included a discussion by Anderson and Krathwohl (2001) of their revision of Bloom's Taxonomy. This discussion provided examples of ways that the taxonomy could be used to develop critical thinking skills. Although a number of cognitive processes can be used for critical thinking, Anderson and Krathwohl stated that critiquing, a subcategory of *evaluate,* was most closely linked to critical thinking. Critiquing uses an explicit set of criteria to make judgments about an event or product. For example, the student is asked to critique, using a set of criteria from political science and history, the different proposals to avoid international conflicts.

Paul (1995) also offers a widely used model for critical thinking and reasoning tasks. He makes a number of points about assessing critical thinking. As he points out, we want to evaluate "not just that students are reasoning but how well they are reasoning" (p. 154). In his model, Paul presents the main aspects for assessing critical thinking tasks. They can be summarized as follows:

1. Purpose, goal, or end in view
2. Question at issue or problem to be solved
3. Point of view or frame of reference
4. Reasoning dimensions

Point/Counterpoint: Standardized Assessments and Essay Items

Point

Supporters of essay items on standardized assessments state that these items offer a viable alternative to the traditional use of objective items. They point out that essays on standardized tests can effectively examine students' abilities in terms of grammar, sentence structure, and clarity. Some supporters also claim that the essay assessment will be able to evaluate how well students develop ideas, create supporting examples, and demonstrate their ability to analyze an issue. Proponents also indicate that, by requiring essays, public school teachers will be called on to further develop English writing and composition classes. There is another aspect about the SAT that supporters note. By requiring essays (a task that women generally do better on than men) the long-standing gender difference on the SAT will be diminished.

Counterpoint

Opponents of using essay items on standardized assessments raise a number of objections. They state that essays cannot demonstrate either the reliability or validity of traditional item formats. The time and cost factors involved in the production and scoring of essays is simply not worth any benefit that may accrue from adding the new format. Another critique of essay items on standardized assessments involves the issue of style versus content. Opponents question whether grading essays will simply revolve around the issues of style, such as syntax, grammar, and English usage. There will be no grading on content. An additional concern is that because the SAT will soon include essay items, teachers in high school will teach to the essay format. Students will be taught to write to a carefully prescribed writing format used on the standardized test. This will decrease the time spent on preparing to write as an actual skill.

---

5. Assumptions and implications
6. Conclusions

Paul (1995) defines *purpose or goal* in a broad sense. All reasoning involves some sort of purpose that serves as a catalyst to initiate the task. The purpose for a reasoning task might include a desire to master an academic question or to solve a social dilemma. In terms of assessing purpose, Paul suggests that clarity of purpose, significant of purpose, and consistency of the presented purpose are key areas to evaluate.

The *question or problem* directly relates to purpose. For example, there is an outstanding question or problem that needs resolution and closure. The student is able to clearly state the main question or problem in his or her essay. He or she is able to distinguish the central question or problem from ancillary questions, and is able to focus on the significant questions and avoid trivial questions.

The *point of view or frame of reference* includes the various perspectives on an issue. For example, the student should be able to write about the different sides of the issue of population control. The different viewpoints may be derived from certain economic, religious, or political perspectives. Paul states that the student should be assessed on his or her flexibility, fairness, and breadth in representing all sides of an issue.

Reasoning dimensions include both empirical and conceptual reasoning skills. Another term for empirical dimensions is *scientific reasoning* based on the scientific method. Empirical dimensions are demonstrated when the student bases his or her assertions in the essay on appropriate data or evidence. Conceptual aspects focus on articulating the key ideas and concepts in the essay. In assessing a student in this area, he or she should be able to distinguish between appropriate data and inappropriate data, and should be able to discriminate between key concepts and irrelevant concepts.

Assumptions and implications respectively describe the background and the consequences of the central problem. Assumptions include the underlying presuppositions used in addressing the central problem. For instance, the student may make the assumption that the data, used as evidence, are methodologically sound. Or the student may make the assumption that there are no underlying factors such as gender or age that might influence the data. Implications address the likelihood of outcomes related to the central issue. In effect, it is a series of "what if" statements given a specific situation. For example, what if greenhouse gases are radically increasing global warming? In assessing assumptions and implications, the assessment should be based on the logic and consistency of the student's assumptions and on the realism and precision of his or her implications.

Conclusions involve a rational, logical, and relevant solution to the central problem. In addressing the solution, the student should detail the next step or the future direction of dealing with the problem. In assessing conclusions, Paul suggests that reasonableness, clarity, and documented support be among the criteria used.

Different assessment formats can be used to evaluate critical thinking skills. The accompanying essay item is one of these formats.

Managing interpersonal conflict is one of the more difficult skills to master. In our classroom discussions and textbook, Thomas and Kilman take the position that there are different ways of handling conflict. Using their model and their criteria for managing conflict, provide a detailed critical analysis of how best to handle the following conflict situation.

Another teacher in your school has repeatedly complained to the principal about the behavior and amount of noise that your class makes. The complaints center mainly on how your class acts in the hallway as it goes to the cafeteria and how your class conducts itself in the cafeteria. As a new teacher, you want to get along with everyone but you do not believe that your class actually causes such a problem. How do you manage this conflict?

Paul (1995) also provides some recommendations for how to assess critical thinking tasks. The following score rubric is based on some of his suggestions.

Teacher Application

Critical Reasoning Rubric

Rate each category on a four-point scale with a 4 being Outstanding, a 3 being Proficient, a 2 being Satisfactory, and a 1 being Unsatisfactory. Add the categories together for the total score.

Purpose/Goal
_____ Clarity of purpose
_____ Significant purpose
_____ Achievable goal

Question/Problem
_____ Clearly articulated question
_____ Appropriate problem
_____ Distinctiveness of central problem

Point of View
_____ Fairness of perspective
_____ Depth of perspective
_____ Flexibility of perspective

Reasoning Dimensions
_____ Logical ideas
_____ Relevant concepts
_____ Plausible ideas
_____ Appropriate use of data and evidence

Assumptions/Implications
_____ Rational assumptions
_____ Consistent assumptions
_____ Realistic implications
_____ Precision of implications

Conclusion
_____ Support for conclusion
_____ Significant conclusion
_____ Appropriate future direction
_____ Rational conclusion

_____ **Total Score**

There are a couple of additional points to make about scoring rubrics. Most experts recommend that you use quantitative scoring systems for grading essays. These scoring systems should be integrated into an overall grading policy (see Chapter 9). Generally speaking, I avoid using letter grades until the final grade is calculated in the grade book. I recommend that you keep everything on a numerical point scale. It is easier for everyone to understand, it is easier for you in keeping your class records, and it is less likely to cause any misunderstandings about grades. For example, in the previous rubric for critical reasoning, there are 21 separate categories. The maximum score is 21 multiplied by 4, which equals 84. The numerical point system should be based on this maximum score and should be integrated into your grading policy.

There are other alternatives for scoring these rubrics. For instance, grade each component of the essay on a satisfactory/unsatisfactory basis. Using a point system with this scoring technique would involve giving the student one point for satisfactory and zero points for unsatisfactory. You would then add up the total number of points for a maximum of 21 points on the scoring rubric. Again, this point system needs to be a part of an overall grading policy (as described in Chapter 9).

Communicating Teacher Expectations

All of this information about essays and rubrics is only as good as your ability to communicate your grading expectations and practices. As mentioned earlier, your students need to have an understanding of how they are going to be graded on essays. Supplying students with the rubrics and explaining the grading policies will go a long way toward helping them meet your expectations.

As with multiple-choice exams, students can be your best assessment editors for reviewing essay items. An open classroom meeting, as suggested by Glasser (1969), is a good idea for reviewing essay items. Glasser suggests that such a meeting works best when students are allowed to freely express their viewpoints without fear about grades or ridicule. The teacher avoids negative judgments and encourages interaction. Glasser also states that, given your comfort level, you may want to ask your students the question: "What would you do if you were the teacher?"

Other Constructed-Response Assessments

There are additional types of constructed-response assessments to consider: sentence completion, cloze, short-answer items, and oral examinations. These assessments may somewhat overlap with either objective assessments or performance-based assessments.

Sentence-completion items actually involve several different types of items. **Fill-in-the-blank items** ask the student to complete a sentence by filling in a missing word (or, in the case of first-grade students, it may be a missing letter or letters). A **cloze test item** leaves out words or a series of words from a paragraph or a phrase. The student must then fill in the missing words in the paragraph or phrase. The **short-answer question** asks the student to supply one word or a couple of words in response to a question. The following question is an example of a short-answer item:

What is the name of an arboreal marsupial that is native to North America?

These constructed-response items share some of the advantages and disadvantages of objective questions. Usually, these items have only one right answer. As with objective items, this may limit any subjective bias and may make it easier for you to grade. On the other hand, sentence-completion and short-answer items generally do not measure higher-level thinking skills. Whereas multiple-choice items usually measure simple recognition tasks, sentence-completion items involve recall tasks. Although recall tasks are slightly more complex than recognition tasks, both recall and recognition are still in the *knowledge* level of Bloom's Taxonomy (the *remember* level of the revised taxonomy).

Oral examinations are an often neglected aspect of constructed-response assessments. The typical format for offering oral exams is in a one-to-one interview situation with one teacher asking multiple questions of one student. However, other formats can be used, such as multiple teachers taking turns asking questions of one student. One teacher also may exam more than one student with this type of format, although the teacher would probably have to ask different questions for different students.

One of the best formats that I have seen for oral exams is to start out the exam with a few introductory questions and then progressively move to more difficult and more elaborate items. I start out with what I call "a lightning round." This is a rapid series of short-answer items, similar to what was discussed in the previous section. Then I move to the more complex questions that require more higher-level thinking skills. I use a checklist to check off the correct responses to each question.

Oral exams have a number of positive features about them, including the fact that it is almost impossible to cheat on them. They can force the student to think critically and to take a position on an issue. Follow-up, in-depth questions may be used to check student answers and verify statements. Also, skills used in speaking can be enhanced by repeated oral exams. On the downside, oral exams are affected somewhat by these very speaking skills. Those who are more facile in speaking may obtain better scores on oral exams. Individuals who are not so comfortable with public speaking or ESL students may not receive as good an evaluation. There is another downside to oral exams: They can be very time consuming for teachers and students.

Challenges to Constructed-Response Assessments

The biggest challenge to constructed-response assessments is clearly one of grading the items. Quite frankly, I still have trouble trusting myself when I grade students that I have known over the course of the semester. I wonder if I am somehow unconsciously biased for or against them when I grade their essays or portfolios. If there were some way to ensure that I could never know whose paper I was grading, I would feel more comfortable. Since that is usually not feasible, I am left trying to police myself against my own potential biases.

A number of factors produce biases about students. As a parent, school counselor, instructor, and teacher educator, I have seen and heard a number of different situations. I believe that teachers always take a number of expectations with them into the classroom. Some of those expectations may be based on demographic factors such as gender, age, and ethnicity, but some are also based on family background. Generally, teachers quickly size up their students and their parents. This can create a set of expectations about student performance. Expectations can also be based on previous assessment history. All teachers must be very careful that these expectations do not become self-fulfilling prophecies.

Given all of the above, I am a firm believer in minimizing one's own potential bias with constructed-response items. By using scoring rubrics that appropriately define what will be graded and by effectively communicating what will be expected, you can minimize potential bias. Don't forget—being upfront about your grading policies sends a signal to your students that you want to be fair and consistent. Discussing the essay items with them after the assessment can provide you with valuable information on ways to make better items.

Chapter Summary

This chapter examined the various types of constructed-response assessments. A number of different categories were reviewed, including essays, sentence-completion, cloze, short-answer, and oral examinations.

One of the crucial distinctions about essay items is the difference between extended-response assessments and restricted-response assessments. Extended-response essays appear to offer more room for creativity on the part of the student, but they tend to be more difficult to grade. When all factors are considered, most experts in the field endorse the use of restricted-response essay items. Generally, this endorsement is based on the reliability involved in grading such items.

A number of grading alternatives for constructed-response assessments were offered in this chapter. Essays are often graded on stylistic concerns, particularly writing style. They also are graded on content. Teachers may want to use a combination of both. A scoring system for critical thinking skills was presented in this chapter and can be useful in some academic subjects.

The biggest challenge in using constructed-response assessments is in developing and communicating reliable grading methods. Devising a fair and consistent grading policy for your essays will enable you to effectively assess the higher-order thinking skills that can be tapped by using these items. If you do not have a good policy, you may be asking for unnecessary headaches.

CASE STUDY EPILOGUE

Mrs. Whitmore has now developed a list of reasons to include essays on the statewide standardized assessment. She also has developed what she believes is an appropriate format for the questions. In addition, she has created the basis for an effective method to score the essays.

Mrs. Whitmore states that her reasons for including essays are (1) they address higher-order cognitive abilities in a more effective way than objective items, (2) they provide a clear-cut method for addressing writing skills, and (3) they offer a better way to assess critical thinking and communication skills. In terms of an item format, Mrs. Whitmore thinks that clearly defined, restricted-response essays are the best type of format for using essays on standardized assessments.

To grade essays, Mrs. Whitmore believes that the best approach is to train a large number of essay graders. The graders will be trained on a common rubric that all graders will use to score the essays. Each grader will have to reach a common level of interscorer reliability or agreement. When the actual essays are graded, two graders will evaluate each essay. If there is a discrepancy in their scoring of the essay, a third grader will grade and score the essay.

CHAPTER ACTIVITIES

Websites

http://www.middleweb.com   The site appeals not only to middle school teachers and parents but also to students. There is a good section about introducing rubrics in the middle school, including samples of different types of assessments.

http://www.eduhound.com   Eduhound is an all-encompassing search engine. The motto "We tracked it down so you don't have to" really says it all. One pertinent feature is the "State Standards." The site offers a link to each state's standards page. Here, parents and teachers can find out what the state requires its students to learn at each level. The site also links to state assessment results.

http://www.nea.org/helpfrom/growing/works4me/library.html   From teaching tips to classroom content, this site brings ideas and discussions to the teacher by other teachers. Check out the "Top Ten Tips" as a starting point of the site.

Portfolio Activities

1. Review Mrs. Whitmore's situation in the Case Study. Write an essay for your portfolio that provides a rationale for using essays in standardized assessments. Address the issues of critical thinking and writing skills. In addition, address the following:
    - What are the best types of essay items to use?
    - Can essay items be used with large groups of students?
    - How should essay items be scored?
    - What types of procedures can be used to reliably score the test?
    Make a conclusion that indicates your own viewpoint on using essays in standardized assessments.

2. Based on your own academic major, design an interpretive essay using maps, graphs, or paragraphs. Provide your own scoring rubric for this essay.

KEY CONCEPTS

Cloze test item
Constructed-response assessments
Critical thinking skills
Extended-response essay questions
Fill-in-the-blank items

Interpretive essay
Interscorer reliability
Restricted-response essay questions
Short-answer question

REVIEW QUESTIONS

1. Explain the differences between extended-response and restricted-response essay items.

2. What are the features of an interpretive essay?

3. What is meant by interscorer reliability?

4. Describe the differences between holistic and analytical scoring.

5. What are the differences between a rubric that scores based on style and one that is based on content?

6. Describe Paul's critical reasoning model and how it can be applied to essays.

7. List and explain the strengths of constructed-response items.

8. Describe the challenges to constructed-response items.

SELF-ASSESSMENT

1. A type of essay item that allows the student maximum flexibility in answering the question is called:
   a. Restricted response
   b. Short answer
   c. Cloze
   d. Extended response
   e. Fill in the blank

2. Which of the following would be most appropriately assessed by an essay item?
   a. Stating a major formula in chemistry
   b. Interpreting the results of an experiment
   c. Recall the Newtonian laws of thermodynamics
   d. Locating a given element in the periodical table

3. One advantage of the essay item over the multiple-choice item is:
   a. Essays are easier to grade
   b. Essays provide a more extensive sampling of course content
   c. Essays better assess basic skills
   d. Essays better assess critical thinking

Answers to Self-Assessment: 1. d, 2. b, 3. d, 4. c, 5. e

4. A cloze item is most like:
   a. True/false item
   b. Extended-response item
   c. Fill-in-the-blank item
   d. Oral exam

5. In Paul's model of critical thinking, a rational, logical, and relevant solution to the central problem is termed:
   a. Assumptions
   b. Implications
   c. Introduction
   d. Purpose
   e. Conclusion

REFERENCES

Anderson, L.W., & Krathwohl, D.R. (Eds.). (2001). *A taxonomy for learning, teaching, and assessing: A revision of Bloom's Taxonomy.* New York: Longman.

Glasser, W. (1969). *Schools without failure.* New York: Harper and Row.

Graduate Management Admissions Council. (2003). *Understanding and using the analytical writing assessment.* Retrieved October 30, 2003, from http://www.gmac.com/gmac/default.htm.

Matthews, J. (2003, September 30). Concise, cogent, contentious. *The Washington Post*, p. A08.

Paul, R.W. (1995). *Critical thinking: How to prepare students for a rapidly changing world.* Santa Rosa, CA: Foundation for Critical Thinking.

Salvia, J., & Ysseldyke, J.E. (1998). *Assessment.* Boston: Houghton Mifflin.

8 Performance Assessment

JANE McKEE
Marshall University

KAREN LUCAS
West Virginia Department of Education

CASE STUDY

Mr. Smith teaches senior English at a local high school. For the Christmas season, he decided to have his English literature students research and present an Old English Christmas. Each student has a topic to research, groups of students plan the activities, and Mr. Smith gets permission from the principal of the school to have food for the occasion. The local district does not allow parties and/or food in the classrooms of the schools. However, Mr. Smith is able to convince the principal that this will be an educational experience that will enhance student understanding of the period of literature and history they are studying.

The students are very excited and plan a special program. Some of the young men have found a stuffed boar's head. They plan to place an apple in its mouth and parade the head around the room to start the festivities. Other students have researched music and carols that originated in the early centuries. Some will bring food of the time; others will present poems, readings, and skits. The excitement of the students has permeated the school building.

The day before the planned program, Mr. Smith is in the school office where he encounters another teacher. The teacher says, "I heard about the goings-on in your room tomorrow. Don't ask for any of my students to come to those shenanigans; my students will be learning!"

Mr. Smith believes that his students will be learning also. In fact, he is certain that he can hold his own with almost any other teacher in motivating his students to want to learn. But an angry Mr. Smith is left with a number of questions:

Does all learning have to be measured with a paper-and-pencil test?

How can any teacher actually meet every single objective and standard of the district and still have enjoyable activities for the students?

Are the students really learning?

How does the teacher know they are learning?

What are the current issues and problems with this type of assessment?

Introduction

The teacher in the Case Study, Mr. Smith, is engaged in a type of assessment known as *performance-based assessment*. This type of evaluation is intertwined with **authentic assessment** in which student responses are rated while the student is involved in a type of assessment situation that mirrors a real-life state of affairs. This authentic learning will motivate students to be more involved in their learning and will enhance their recall of the information. By pretending to be citizens of ninth-century England and engaging in the practices of that time, students will find three distinct advantages to the activity: (1) learning becomes more meaningful, (2) learning becomes more related to others, and (3) learning becomes fun.

Mr. Smith's colleague—let's call her Mrs. Doubtfire—wants to cast aspersions on the activity for several reasons. She may be unable to plan such a creative activity, she may be unwilling to allow students the freedom that an authentic assessment demands, and she may be jealous of the excitement generated by Mr. Smith's assignment itself. Whatever Mrs. Doubtfire's motivation, she has indeed created a small twinge of unease in Mr. Smith's mind.

Mr. Smith need not worry. His students are indeed learning—learning far more than if they read the chapter, answered the questions, and took a quiz. The learning in which they are engaged connects with knowledge about how humans learn. The more an assignment is one with which students identify, the more learning takes place (Wiggins & McTighe, 2002). Experience is a great teacher, and connecting the lives of ninth-century Englishmen to our lives today makes facts become alive and take on new identities as students assume the roles of their ancestors. The students begin to think critically about the lives of these Englishmen and engage in a number of activities that demonstrate their knowledge of life in England at this time. Suddenly, the students are in possession of much knowledge that will meet the content standards for English literature and the testing standards.

Given (2002) suggests that with regard to tactual and kinesthetic input, teachers can transform any concept or idea into manipulative materials or experiential activities. No doubt the denizens of ninth-century England on a December day in Mr. Smith's classroom find a multifaceted lesson awaiting them as they explore the culture, the arts, the music, and the traditions of the English people. According to Given, "The list [of activities] is limited only by a teacher's lack of imagination and unwillingness to explore and experiment with active alternatives to traditional paper-and-pencil tasks....We must accept the fact that the majority of children need physical activity and hands-on experiences to develop academic skills" (p. 102).

Teachers often find performance assessment a difficult type of evaluation due to several reasons. First, objective assessments with quantifiable numbers are much easier

Point/Counterpoint: Using Performance-Based Assessments

Point

Supporters of performance assessments state that these assessments effectively motivate students as they inquire, problem solve, and learn. Performance assessments appear to create more intrinsic motivation than traditional assessments. The flexibility of performance assessments allows students to better develop their own areas of interest. The involvement of students in performance activities enables teachers to better evaluate how knowledge is applied to authentic situations. Performance assessment encourages students to develop critical thinking skills, problem-solving skills, and creative thinking skills. Performance assessment can be directly linked to hands-on learning activities, which appear to be more likely to remain as part of students' long-term learning.

Counterpoint

Opponents of performance assessment point out that performance assessments usually are less reliable and valid in terms of their measurement than are objective assessments. The room for teacher bias in scoring performance assessments is much the same as with essay assessments. Some opponents also dislike the student-centered nature of these assessments. They believe that performance assessments create unfocused, disorganized instruction and assessments. This lack of focus on content may create serious problems in today's content-driven educational system. Opponents also state that the extensive time needed for preparation and evaluation for performance assessments can be better spent on other activities. Finally, opponents question whether performance assessments help students on standardized assessments.

to defend or explain to parents and students. Second, performance assessments take time and planning. Finally, performance-based assessments are not easy to implement in the beginning.

Pathway to Performance Assessment

Mr. Smith may have less uneasiness if he measures his activity by the three criteria for responsible assessment practices that emerge from assessment literature. Responsible assessment practices are evaluative, reflective, and supported (Strong, Silver, & Perini, 2001). In Figure 8.1, these practices are defined according to their relationship with students.

Performance assessments fit all three categories of responsible assessment practices. The Old English Christmas allowed Mr. Smith to evaluate the participation and level of accomplishment of each of his students. He could easily see their progress through the planning and implementation of the assignment. As he facilitated the project and met with each of his student groups, Mr. Smith could easily match the style of learning with the activities in which students were engaged. He could also determine if their understanding grew and deepened regarding Old English life.

The final responsible practice of support was integrated into the project from the planning stage. Mr. Smith assisted students in locating information that explained each area of study of the Old English Christmas. Particularly gratifying to Mr. Smith was the information that students gained through their own individual research in the library and in the community. Before beginning the project, Mr. Smith took a concentrated look at his district and state standards for English literature. He was able to incorporate each one into the activities planned for the project.

Although some parents and teachers still believe that standardized testing with multiple-choice questions remains the only way to determine learning, teachers with a greater vision of assessment realize that standardized testing is only one of many ways

FIGURE 8.1 Some Characteristics of Responsible Assessment Practices

Relevant to Content	Higher-Order Thinking skills	Collaborative in Nature
An assessment practice that is relevant to the content found in the curriculum will both add to the student knowledge and act as a motivating factor.	A responsible performance assessment task contains higher-order thinking skills such as application, evaluation, and synthesis.	When other content areas can be integrated into the assessment, it becomes richer and more meaningful to students.

to assess and evaluate the learning of children. In fact, performance assessment, also known as authentic assessment, can be a better way to assess learning in certain respects because the students must perform tasks that show their understanding of the content. If they can transfer, apply, and synthesize, the teacher can be sure that learning has taken place. These tasks may be more closely related to standards-based education because the students must display their knowledge of the concept through a piece of work that is uniquely tied to a specific standard for learning. Not only is the piece of work tied to a standard, but it is tied to an idea, an experience, or a situation known by the students. Real-world problems get some attention.

Several types of performance assessment assignments—such as a product, a performance, an exhibition, or a demonstration—may assist students in making responses. Manning and Bucher (2001) list the following characteristics of effective authentic assessment:

Effective Tasks
- Are essential, "big ideas" rather than trivial micro-facts or specialized skills
- Are in-depth in that they lead to other problems and questions
- Are feasible and can be done easily and safely within a school and classroom
- Typically include interactions between the teacher and the student and between students
- Provide multiple ways in which students can demonstrate they have met the criteria, allowing multiple points of view and multiple interpretations
- Allow for individual learning styles, aptitudes, and interest
- Involve cooperation, self-evaluation, and peer evaluation
- Require scoring that focuses on the essence of the task and not what is easiest to score
- Call on the professional judgment of the assessor (usually the teacher)
- May involve an audience of some kind in addition to the teacher
- Call for different measurement techniques
- Identify strengths as well as weaknesses
- Minimize needless and unfair comparisons

Inquiry, investigation, and research are three types of assignments that will allow students to plan and implement a solution to an authentic problem.

Inquiry

Inquiry is an instructional strategy that outlines a process for problem solving. This process uses data to discover answers to the problems and to create solutions for those problems. Students study a concept or topic, and through that study, they learn both content and problem solving. Students may create a hypothesis, and through data collection or manipulation of existing data, they analyze the situation and draw conclusions based on their study. Following is an example of such a task.

Teacher Application

The Election

Mr. McGovern's class in civics has followed the local election for the Board of Education in their district. Students have gathered campaign rhetoric and newspaper articles that indicate the thinking of the candidates who are running. Prior to the election Mr. McGovern has students identify topics of importance to the voters. Then students study the residential areas of the district that voters live in and make predictions about the winners of the election. On the day following the election, students take the voting results and begin an in-depth study of their previous predictions. Based on this study, the students in the civics class structure some important ideas that a candidate for a public office should take into consideration during the campaign.

This example shows how students gain a better understanding of the election process. They will be able to understand text terms and standardized test questions related to civics and the electoral process. Inquiry leads students to learning and understanding content that will transfer to other situations, including test situations. Inquiry can be used to strengthen student learning in any content area. By allowing students to hypothesize, analyze, predict, and study data, they begin to gain a comprehension of content concepts not found in vocabulary tests or other paper-and-pencil tests. Most public attention these days is riveted on the results of large-scale testing programs, but everyday classroom assessments that teachers use day in and day out can provide a powerful tool in improving student achievement.

The motivational aspect of problem solving is critical to engaging students in learning about anything from elections to mathematical concepts. Again, the central focus is on the transfer of knowledge as the student learns not only the content but also ways to solve problems in the future. Steps in an inquiry lesson include (1) identification of a problem, (2) formation of a hypothesis, (3) collection of data, (4) analysis of data, and (5) decisions on the meaning of the data (Jacobsen, Eggen, & Kauchak, 2002). Students will more easily complete any type of problem if they engage in these five steps of the inquiry lesson.

Benefits resulting from the inquiry method of performance assessment are varied. Certainly, both the teacher and the students benefit from a motivating exercise related to real-world activities. Interest enhances planning, and implementing the lessons and completing the required assignments meet the needs of the students' diverse learning styles. Engaging in exercises of this type strengthens the systematic inquiry skills that students are developing. The practice of critical thinking skills within the inquiry method will assist in the development of better decision makers, and a deeper discernment of content will improve student achievement in many different areas, including standardized test areas.

Investigation

Investigations of problems on TV programs focus on investigative processes that conclude all questions in one to three hours. This may give wrong ideas about investigation to some students. True investigation is not that tidy, but it does present motivational opportunities and learning conditions that will enhance student achievement. An **investigation** embodies several steps for successful work: (1) identification of the problem, (2) statement of the problem, (3) plans for investigation, and (4) evaluation of the results of the investigation with a future plan of action. Again, the practice of critical thinking skills, such as identifying a real problem, will enhance future thinking and decision making. Following is an example of science investigation projects.

Teacher Application

Science Projects

Water and air quality projects are always excellent learning experiences for students. Through content preparation and laboratory experiments, students can investigate the quality of the air and water in various vicinities of their own community. These assignments are of high interest due to the location and use of the elements by students and families. The assignments are often a way to bring in outside agencies to collaborate with students to enhance the student perceptions of government and state offices that monitor and oversee the safety of residents with regard to environmental issues.

Investigations can range over a vast territory from environmental to criminal to literary to mathematical investigations. Benefits include the motivation of working with authentic problems and actively choosing strategies to try to resolve the problems. While problem solving, students gain insight into concepts, skills, and strategies that improve future performance in ways that traditional testing do not. An example of a forensic investigation project is provided next.

Teacher Application

Forensic Projects

An increased awareness of forensic science has been supported by movies and television shows during recent years. Because of the new and increasingly sophisticated techniques of identification and because of national catastrophes such as airplane crashes, students have begun to be very interested in the process that can identify people by using a small amount of evidence. DNA progress has been a major factor in recognizing criminals and victims. Science classes can draw on experts in the field from local law enforcement agencies and on science resources from many different publishers that will allow students a rudimentary study of forensic science concepts. Investigation projects will assist students in understanding science topics, and increased motivation generally leads to increased achievement.

Research

Investigative projects lead to research. The world has many issues and problems that need decisions to be made by responsible, informed citizens. **Research** projects will allow students to gain this information that will guide their beliefs on complex issues and challenge their critical thinking skills. Knowledge, sophisticated thinking, and language abilities are needed to analyze a range of complex issues (Chaffee, 2000). The local newspaper is often a rich source of research projects. By identifying questions raised in particular stories, students' research may become more meaningful.

Research projects can also give students a strong background for current study. By looking at past practices and happenings, modern-day events take on a much more relevant perspective. Students might study and compare happenings in the global community at the time of speeches made at Normandy by Presidents Reagan, Clinton, and Bush. Students might study and compare Old English practices to see how current law, custom, and culture have been influenced by the people of that time.

The pathways of inquiry, investigation, and research allow students to create products, performances, and projects that display the results of their critical thinking into important and current issues. Through the application of knowledge, students reach the highest levels of Bloom's Taxonomy (Shurr, Thomason, & Thompson, 1995). By applying, synthesizing, and evaluating what has been learned, they can compose ways that clearly display their conclusions.

Types of Performance Assessment

Portfolio

Portfolios have been a popular form of assessment over the years for many professions. The portfolio concept allows demonstration of talent, as in the profession of modeling; demonstration of accomplishments, as in the profession of acting and architecture; and demonstration of financial stability, as in the professions of the world of business. These examples are only a few uses of a very popular assessment tool.

What Are Portfolios?   The word *portfolio* means the container in which artifacts are stored—artifacts that display the abilities and successes of the creator of the portfolio. One of the compelling characteristics of the portfolio is the ability to show growth and accomplishment over time. The artist could show periods and changes in style. The actress could show growth in roles from the ingénue to the leading lady. The stock portfolio could show the path of financial growth or loss. The architect could display all types of designs that would highlight his many talents. Recently, educational portfolios have been quite popular because of these attributes. Principals, teachers, and students are able to demonstrate growth and success over a period of time for their work or for the accomplishment of school goals. This chapter focuses on student portfolios, but the concept can be implemented in many ways in the education profession, as shown in this example.

Teacher Application

Learning about Portfolios

Miss Jones is attending a summer institute to learn about performance assessment. One of the sessions deals with a portfolio as a means of assessment. Miss Jones decides that this might be a welcome addition to her teaching strategies.

In the fall, Miss Jones returns to her biology classroom ready to use the portfolio as a means of assessing her students' learning. She has the students design covers for their portfolio and instructs them as to the material that will be placed in them. Miss Jones explains in detail how this will add to the students' science experience and how it will impact their grade.

A week after the opening of school, a colleague stops Miss Jones in the hall to find out about her summer and to hear details about the summer institute. Upon hearing about the portfolio idea, Ms. Tryeverything is skeptical about students keeping a portfolio rather than a notebook for a science class. She makes the idea of the portfolio seem as if it is a waste of time and certainly does not reflect the learning of the students.

Miss Jones, a little disheartened, returns to her classroom to reflect on this conversation. Miss Jones knows that she will impact her students' learning through the portfolio. She wants this to be the best experience that will allow students to showcase their work, but she also wants her students to learn factual information about the world of biology. Regardless of Ms. Tryeverything's attitude of this being a foolhardy way to teach biology, Miss Jones decides to forge ahead.

Miss Jones reviewed her notes and handouts from the workshop and began to devise the way in which the portfolio would become an integral part of her teaching strategies. She started to ask many questions of herself: How will I make the students realize the importance of the portfolio? How will parents be informed? Will they see the value of the portfolio? How will I grade these? Will this means of assessment show that my students are learning? Will students understand the concept of reflection?

For Miss Jones, **portfolios** are systematic collections of student work. Compiled over time, these collections, chosen by the the student and the teacher, provide illustrations of what students know and can do. These collections illustrate in-depth knowledge—how well students know content. In the portfolio are examples of a student's ability to use a variety of scientific tools. There are examples of how students personalize and internalize content (e.g., through in-depth study, music and art interpretations, writing fiction and nonfiction, mathematical modeling). A portfolio includes examples of how students communicate content using a variety of mediums (e.g., art, music, writing, mathematics, models, sculptures, and inventions). Students can display in their portfolio work samples that show both self-assessment and teacher assessment. A portfolio can contain student work samples that allow for planning for continuous growth by student and teacher.

Why Use Portfolios? Portfolios can be used to demonstrate accomplishments, understanding, and growth of students. It is a tool to assess student progress. The teacher can use the portfolio to monitor student progress and inform instruction so that appropriate decisions can be made about what to teach and how to teach. Teachers can become more aware of student learning difficulties and uncover problems needing attention in many areas, such as skill development, written expressions, collaboration with others, and growth in ability level. In addition, portfolios provide another means for dialog between teacher and students, thus allowing the teacher to become a better supporter of students' needs in both the affective and cognitive realms.

Portfolios can be used to communicate student achievement to parents and others. They also allow students to examine and critically assess their own learning. Portfolios can provide the recognition students need, which helps to foster self-esteem. Bringing together students and family members to review portfolios provides the family-school connection, and this connection is vital to student success.

How to Involve Parents?   Parents are very curious about their children's progress, and portfolios allow them the opportunity to see progress over time. There are a variety of ways to invite family members to review their children's portfolios. Here are a few ideas that Miss Jones might use:

- In a formal setting arranged by the teacher in the classroom
- At home with the aid of formatted response sheets
- During parent conferences in which the student leads the conference using the portfolio as the focal point
- At a "Back to School Night" when parents have a chance to look over the contents
- During a specially scheduled "Portfolio Presentation Night"

How Will the Portfolio Be Graded?   Because the portfolio is a different way of assessing student work, it is best suited to being graded by using a rubric. A rubric provided by the teacher can help students assess their own portfolios and provide a reflective look at their work. Reflection becomes a vital part of the work accomplished with the portfolio. Figure 8.2 is a sample of a rubric that Miss Jones might use.

If Miss Jones uses the portfolio rubric, it will certainly provide her with the information that her students are learning. She may find that only positive things can come from portfolios. As her students create portfolios that include serious self-reflection, it might be a good idea for her to undergo a similar experience. She could begin a review of what is going on in her classroom and continue to reflect so she can perfect it next year. Miss Jones also may want to keep a journal about the portfolios. This year can certainly be a challenge for her, but a challenge to look forward to having, so that her students have the best learning experiences possible.

Product

Another effective type of performance assessment is the product. The **product** takes all the steps of Bloom's Taxonomy as students learn facts, and comprehend, analyze, apply, synthesize, and evaluate their knowledge to create an artifact. The product represents as nearly as possible a real-world application of specific learning.

FIGURE 8.2   Portfolio Rubric

Indicator	1 Poor	2 Acceptable	3 Good	4 Very Good
Is complete				
Is organized				
Contains varied samples of written work				
Shows evidence of using many resources				
Shows evidence of problem solving				
Shows evidence of decision making				
Shows evidence of higher-level thinking skills				
Includes examples of both individual and group work				
Includes self-reflective comments				
Reflects enthusiasm for learning				
Contains many pieces that were not required or assigned				
Shows evidence of what student has learned				
Displays the pride student has in his or her work				
Shows maximum effort to reach my educational goals				
Is presented in a neat and orderly manner				

Products include but are not limited to the following (Shurr, Thomason, & Thompson (1995):

Essays	Designs	Dances
Stories	Notebooks	Scrapbooks
Novels	Study Cards	Newspapers
Artwork	Flash Cards	Diaries
Displays	Photographs	Transparencies
Lectures	Pictures	Collections
Sketches	Videotapes	Letters
Plans	Charts	Interview
Articles	Graphs	Surveys
Books	Maps	Field Trips
Compositions	Diagrams	Filmstrips
Experiments	Exhibits	Mobiles
Models	Audiotapes	Artifacts
Games	Plays	Blueprints

Several planning steps will assist the product creation to be a smooth, relevant, well-thought out assignment. First, study the curriculum topics, themes, or concepts to determine which could best be measured by a product. Second, provide the students with a list of product choices that could be selected for the assignment. Always allow students to brainstorm or to plan a product of their own. Sometimes these ideas surpass what textbooks or teachers have in mind for assessment. Third, have students organize their thinking and come up with a plan for accomplishing the product. Adding timelines will enhance the organizational procedure and give the students a clear path to finishing their production. The fourth step is to give students all requirements and all categories of assessment of the product. A rubric or checklist should be given that will openly state the requirements for evaluation. Now that students know the criteria for assessing the product and the timeline for completion of the product, they can aim toward producing the best possible example of their knowledge. If the students prepared the product via PowerPoint, they can do a PowerPoint presentation for their classmates. The presentation will require explanation of each slide, thereby combining product and presentation.

Shurr, Thomason, and Thompson (1995) provide 10 reasons why student products make good assessment tools:

1. They can demonstrate originality.
2. They can demonstrate knowledge effectively and attractively.
3. They can reflect growth in social and academic skills and attitudes that are not reflected in paper-and-pencil tests.
4. They can engage students who are otherwise unenthusiastic about school.
5. They can bring education to life, making it memorable for students.
6. They can demonstrate to the community in concrete terms what students are achieving.

7. They allow for the integration of reading/writing/speaking skills with other subject areas.
8. They can give students flexible time to do thoughtful work.
9. They can permit students to work cooperatively with others.
10. They can encourage creativity.

Presentation

Students should constantly be involved in *presentations*. They should be comfortable expressing their opinions to various groups that include peers, teachers, parents, and others. This skill will enable them to be excellent learners and to make an impact on audiences about important questions and issues.

Students can present any of the types of performance assessment mentioned in this chapter. If the students create a portfolio or a product, they can present that assignment orally before a panel, a class, a teacher, and others for experience in learning to think on their feet and in using clear and concise terms for discussion. The performance itself can also be an assessment of learning. Certain tasks—such as role-play, skits, television shows, movies, advertisements, and other audiovisual tasks—will present as performance the knowledge, comprehension, analysis, and application that takes place in creating such an assignment.

Miss Jones combines the portfolio and performance when she asks her students to display and comment on their portfolios to parents at a special portfolio evening event. She could also ask students to present a topic from the portfolio. Since this is a biology class, students will use charts and graphs to show what has been learned. The idea of performance, such as the subsequent application, is applicable in some way to all content classes. It can be integrated into the assignments to allow students to learn performance skills and to work through a dread of speaking to groups.

Teacher Application

Winter Doldrums

Ms. Ashe knew that January and February were long months for her eighth-grade English students so she devised a plan called "Winter Doldrums—Chase Them Away." Students were given the opportunity to teach the class. Certain guidelines were in place: The topic had to be one in which the student was expert; the lesson plan had to be created and approved; the students had to be actively involved in the activities; and the day and time had to be selected carefully so that other work was not interrupted. Students had great ideas and taught classmates such diverse subjects as rock climbing, skiing, baking, and knitting. These lessons served several purposes for Ms. Ashe's class. The students learned presentation skills, speaking skills, and organization skills—all important in English class! In addition, their classmates took active roles in the learning, found out about new subjects, and were motivated during some cold, winter days to read, write, and discuss. Winter doldrums really were chased away!

Performance should be authentic and meaningful, and the context of the problems should be rich, realistic, and enticing—within the inevitable constraints on time and resources. The use of creative presentation in the elementary classroom allows students to use their critical thinking skills to process information that has been given to them. Examples of elementary creative performances/presentations include role-playing, simulations, and skits. Elementary students react well to creating characters and situations in their minds. An example of one such activity is provided here.

Teacher Application

The Fire Fighter
Elementary children, grades kindergarten through 5, received information about fire fighting, how to prevent fire problems in their homes, and the importance of the job of the fire fighters. Through a creative performance, the older students acted out the duties of a fire fighter from the time a call came to the station until the fire was extinguished at the site. A performance test checked the understanding of all of the children to stop, drop, and roll if their clothing caught on fire.

Perhaps the most widely practiced performance is the speech. Students are asked to create various types of speeches and deliver them to audiences. Students must decide the type of speech, the type of audience, the time allotted for their talk, and the points they wish to make during the talk. A generic checklist (see Figure 8.3) can assist children in planning for this assignment and will allow them to be familiar with the categories of evaluation.

Measuring Performance

Rubrics

Rubrics display scoring standards for authentic assessments to assist students in planning their projects to meet the highest standards. Students should always have a copy of the rubric before beginning the assessment. As noted in Chapter 7, there are two popular types of rubrics: holistic and analytic. *Holistic rubrics* assess student work as a whole and give only one single grade. *Analytic rubrics* identify and assess components of a finished product. With analytic rubrics, students receive separate scores for each component of the performance or product. Each type of rubric can be used effectively depending on the assignment, the grade level of the students, and the amount of detail that the teacher would like to include in the assessment rubric.

Rubrics are different from checklists in that a written description accompanies each evaluation statement. When teachers use checklists or rating scales, students often understand through listening and participating what the differences between the categories may be, but they do not always know how to put that difference into words. A

FIGURE 8.3   Checklist for Speech

	Excellent 5	4	Fair 3	2	Poor 1
Name _____					
Grade _____ Speech Topic _____					
Topic organized for particular purpose					
Higher-level thinking involved					
Speech clearly delivered					
Eye contact					
Voice tone					
Total impression					

rubric, shared with students as they begin projects, will be a guide to excellence by understanding more fully what is expected for each evaluative point. Examples of rubrics and how to use them with portfolios are shown in Figure 8.4 and 8.5.

In this chapter's Case Study, Mr. Smith planned extensively for his Old English Christmas project. He provided resources for his students and guided them in preparing an authentic experience. Mr. Smith, however, worried about the learning aspect of the project. How would he be able to grade such an experience? He knew that the students had worked diligently and enthusiastically on the project. He knew that their

FIGURE 8.4   Holistic Rubric for Fiction Writing Content

The authentic assessment assignment will receive an overall scoring number.

- 5—The plot, setting, and characters are developed fully and organized well. The who, what, where, when, and why are explained using interesting language and sufficient detail.
- 4—Most parts of the story mentioned in a score of 5 are developed and organized well. A couple of aspects may need to be more fully or more interestingly developed.
- 3—Some aspects of the story are developed and organized well, but not as much detail or organization is expressed as in a score of 4.
- 2—A few parts of the story are developed somewhat. Organization and language usage need improvement.
- 1—Parts of the story are addressed without attention to detail or organization.

Source: Adapted from www.teachervision.com/lesson-plans/lesson-4524.html

FIGURE 8.5 Analytic Rubric for Level I

The student will receive a number for each component of the performance assignment.

- **Task Completion**
1—Minimal completion of the task and/or responses frequently inappropriate
2—Practical completion of the task, responses mostly appropriate yet undeveloped
3—Completion of the task, responses appropriate and adequately developed
4—Superior completion of the task, responses appropriate and with elaboration

- **Comprehensibility**
1—Responses barely comprehensible
2—Responses mostly comprehensible, requiring interpretation on the part of the listener
3—Responses comprehensible, requiring minimal interpretation on the part of the listener
4—Responses readily comprehensible, requiring no interpretation on the part of the listener

- **Fluency**
1—Speech halting and uneven with long pauses and/or incomplete thoughts
2—Speech choppy and/or slow with frequent pauses, few or no incomplete thoughts
3—Some hesitation but manages to continue and complete thoughts
4—Speech continuous with few pauses or stumbling

- **Pronunciation**
1—Frequently interferes with communication
2—Occasionally interferes with communication
3—Does not interfere with communication
4—Enhances communication

- **Vocabulary**
1—Inadequate and/or inaccurate use of vocabulary
2—Somewhat inadequate and/or inaccurate use of vocabulary
3—Adequate and accurate use of vocabulary
4—Rich use of vocabulary

- **Grammar**
1—Inadequate and/or inaccurate use of basic language structures
2—Emerging use of basic language structures
3—Emerging control of basic language structure
4—Control of basic language structures

Source: Adapted from http://www.fcps.edu/DIS/OHSICS/forlng?PALS/rubrics/1spk_an.htm

knowledge about England in the early years had grown and deepened, but he was not satisfied with his grading method. Generally, Mr. Smith told students that they had done a good job and they received an A or B. Some students who had been absent or who had not met deadlines received a C or D with the admonishment that their work was not "up to par." Surely, Mr. Smith thought, there must be an alternative way to evaluate each student's work.

Actually, what Mr. Smith needed was his own particular rubric, or set of standards, that described the vision he held in his mind for excellent, good, and fair work on the Old English Christmas. He could have created a rubric that viewed each group's contribution as a whole, or created a rubric that viewed each individual's contribution, or created a detailed rubric for each person's job within the group. An example of a rubric for a group is found in Figure 8.6.

FIGURE 8.6   Group Rubric for Evaluation of Old English Christmas Project

Rubric Category	Excellent (90–95)	Good (80–89)	Fair (70–79)
Content Knowledge	Group went beyond requirements in project; gave extra material that was accurate and relevant to their assignment for the project; and presented the content in an engaging way.	Project material was presented in an accurate way according to the assignment requirement; there were no added materials; presentation did not hold the entire group's attention.	Group presented some content material, but several pieces of the material were missing, raising questions about the meaning of the group's project.
Presentation	Group presented project in many learning styles that appealed to various students; creative ideas enhanced the knowledge; held together by the theme of the group's assignment.	Group presented the project using several different ways of presentation. The group thought critically about the presentation and was able to discern a theme. Some creativity was evidenced.	Group presented the project in very few ways. Creativity was lacking. The presentation was a series of events unrelated by any theme.
Group Dynamics	Group worked together each day and was able to solve problems by group consensus. Each member participated in the assignment in each area: writing, visual presentation, and oral presentation.	Group met often. Some ideas were discarded because the group could not agree on the ideas. Each member participated in each area: writing, visual presentation, and oral presentation.	Group met a few times. Mostly, members worked individually and then put work together. Not all students participated in each area: writing, visual presentation, and oral presentation.

A more detailed rubric is provided in the Figure 8.7. With this rubric, Mr. Smith is able to assess group, individual, and group manager performance on the assignment. The rubric is especially helpful in reporting progress to parents and guardians of the students. They are able to understand the missing pieces in a critically thoughtful

FIGURE 8.7   General Rubric for Old English Christmas Project

Group Rubric Category	Excellent (3)	Good (2)	Fair (1)
Content Knowledge	Group went beyond requirements in project; gave extra material that was accurate and relevant to their assignment for the project.	Project material was presented in an accurate way according to the assignment requirement.	Group presented some content material, but several pieces of the material were missing, raising questions about the group's project.
Presentation	Group presented project in many learning styles that appealed to various students; creative ideas enhanced the knowledge; held together by the theme of the group's assignment.	Group presented the project using several different ways of presentation. The group thought critically about the presentation and was able to discern a theme.	Group presented the project in very few ways. Creativity was lacking. The presentation was a series of events unrelated by any theme.
Group Dynamics	Group worked together each day and was able to solve problems by group consensus. Each member participated in the assignment in each area: writing, visual presentation, and oral presentation.	Group met often. Some ideas were discarded because the group could not agree on the ideas. Each member participated in each area: writing, visual presentation, and oral presentation.	Group met a few times. Mostly, members worked individually and then put work together. Not all students participated in each area: writing, visual presentation, and oral presentation.
Individual Member Rubric Category	**Excellent (3)**	**Good (2)**	**Fair (1)**
Individual Assignment	Student presented accurate content knowledge that covered the topic assigned. The assignment was relevant to the group project and added to the overall effectiveness of the group.	Student presented accurate content knowledge that met the assignment requirement. The knowledge was basic and added to the understanding of the project but did not assist in creating an overall effectiveness.	Student presented some content knowledge that was correct. However, the knowledge did not answer all questions regarding the student's portion of the assignment and detracted from the overall effectiveness of the project.

FIGURE 8.7 Continued

Group Rubric Category	Excellent (3)	Good (2)	Fair (1)
Presentation	Student participated in every area of the presentation, bringing clarity, expression, and relevance to the assignment.	Student participated in some areas of the presentation. The student spoke hesitantly and did not add to the overall effectiveness of the project in every area.	Student participated in the presentation but did not speak extensively about the subject, leaving the audience without an understanding of that portion of the project.
Group Dynamics	Student worked well with group by presenting ideas, listening to others, suggesting compromise, and volunteering to assist in various ways	Student worked well with group by presenting ideas and listening to others. Assisted the group in several ways but needed to help in other ways.	Student did not work well with group due to various reasons, such as absence, failure to meet deadlines, and argumentativeness. The group lost effectiveness due to the student's poor group dynamics.

Rubric for Group Manager	Excellent (3)	Good (2)	Fair (1)
Leadership	Student leader was able to lead students to make decisions based on the work itself and not on individual preferences. Student also led group to respect opinions of each member and to work for consensus.	Student leader was able to get group respect but was not able to get group into a cohesive oneness that made decisions that were acceptable for each member.	The group never came together for the assignment. The students did work individually and gave it to the manager.
Performance	Student leader organized the performance with the assistance of each member. Was able to encourage decisions based on strengths of participants, not what the student leader wanted to do.	Student leader allowed others to make decisions without giving an opinion regarding the organization. The results were not connected throughout the presentation.	Student leader was unable to get all students to participate, and the talents of the participants were not used wisely.
Group Dynamics	Student leader interacted with each individual, making each member feel like an important part of the group and a part of the whole assignment.	Student leader interacted with each individual, making each member feel his or her part was important. The group did not display a sense of togetherness.	Student leader interacted on an individual basis but could not create a group state of mind.

assignment. They, along with their children, have a stronger knowledge of what would have improved the project.

Rubrics appeal to both teachers and students. There is no question of what is wanted; the answer is found in the indicators of the rubric. By making teachers' expectations clear, student achievement often rises. The visual learning style is met by demonstrating how a good performance looks. Manning and Bucher (2001) recommend that to be effective, a rubric should be organized around a skill, focus on a small number of evaluative criteria, and be sufficiently brief that a teacher will want to use it. The teacher can change the scoring numbers to create a snapshot of what might be missing in the student's performance.

Evaluation Checklists

As mentioned in the section on rubrics, **evaluation checklists** generally have a scale for evaluation but do not describe the behaviors in detail. The use of checklists varies from just an overall evaluation to measuring progress through the performance project. Figures 8.8 and 8.9 illustrate two types of checklists that show how Mr. Smith could have evaluated the music aspect of his Old English Christmas project.

FIGURE 8.8 Overall Evaluation Checklist for Music in the Old English Project

The rubic uses a four-point scale for the measurement of music:

4 Excellent—Went beyond the class assignment with work and performance.

3 Good—Did a good job of fulfilling the requirements of the class assignment.

2 Fair—Attempted to fulfill the requirements of the class assignment, but failed to complete all elements of the assignment. Errors were evident.

1 Poor—Attempted to complete some of the requirements of the assignment. Most elements were not completed, and major errors were evident.

Topic	Excellent (4)	Good (3)	Fair (2)	Poor (1)
Research on songs of the period		×		
Plan for playing and/or singing songs by the group	×			
History for songs presented to the group in interesting ways			×	
Songs were integrated into the project to create a holistic picture of Old England.		×		
Total Evaluation		×		

FIGURE 8.9   Evaluation Checklist for Progress through Performance Project in Music

Topic	Deadline	Project Complete	More Data Needed	Deadline
Research on songs of the period	November 28	No	Yes	December 1
Plan for playing and/or singing songs by the group	November 28	Yes		
History for songs presented to the group in interesting ways	November 26	No	Yes	December 4
Songs will be integrated into the project to create a holistic picture of Old England.	December 5	No		

An advantage of the checklist is its inclination for self-evaluation. Students will become more sophisticated in their ability to make decisions for self-improvement as they continue to use checklists. These items can be easily compared to past items. Thus, the student can see a pattern of growth and development. A checklist that supports this self-evaluation is one that has open-ended questions and an opportunity for comment. An example is provided in Figure 8.10.

Common Evaluation Instruments

The evaluation instruments seen in Figures 8.11 and 8.12 are common to a specific type of assignment. A common evaluation instrument can be created for a speech, a group assignment, a research paper, and so on. Certain characteristics must be present in order to ensure an above-average authentic assessment. The evaluation instrument is then used each time the specific assignment is made.

The disadvantage of the common evaluation instrument with a number scale is its lack of rubric indicators that give a "snapshot" of what is desired in the assignment itself. Parents often wonder what is missing from the work. The common instruments shown in Figures 8.11 and 8.12 leave a space for comments on content and tend to assist both student and parent in a better awareness of the grading process.

Rubrics, checklists, and common evaluation instruments can keep students focused if the instruments are administered at different times throughout the authentic assessment plan. Students will have knowledge of where they stand in relation to the final grade, and they will have an opportunity to improve their work. Rather than just a right or wrong answer, students gain the opportunity to grow and develop as learners, to self-evaluate their own abilities, to apply their knowledge to a product, and to gain insight into real-world situations.

FIGURE 8.10   Checklist: Old English Christmas Project

| Student _____ |
| Teacher _____ |

The student	Yes	No	Comments/Evidence
1. Made good musical choices	___	___	_____
2. Found enough information	___	___	_____
3. Engaged other students in learning the songs	___	___	_____
4. Created an activity that was fun	___	___	_____
5. Added to the overall understanding of life in the Old English days	___	___	_____

FIGURE 8.11   Evaluation Checklist for Small Group Assignment

Group Skills	Comments
Exhibited leadership	
Listened to others	
Used group consensus to solve problems	
Met deadlines	
Supported group members	
Reported progress to the group in a timely manner	
Shared with others	
Helped create a reflective environment that made self-evaluation possible	

FIGURE 8.12   Evaluation Checklist for Portfolio Assignment

Topic	Comments
All subjects included in the portfolio	
Evidence of good work provided	
Critical thinking about entries is displayed	
Organization creates a logical product that is understood by any reader	
Evidence of self-evaluation is present	
Evidence of impact on learning is evident	

Comparison and Contrast of Assessment Types

The classroom teacher will have a repertoire of assessment strategies that will serve different purposes at different times. Often, students need a body of knowledge before attempting assignments that require certain facts and skills. As noted in Chapter 3, Bloom's Taxonomy builds on the higher-order thinking skills to produce high-quality thinking. Students begin with the facts and comprehension of them before they apply, analyze, synthesize, and evaluate within the assignments. In choosing a teaching and assessing strategy, the teacher will study the content, the students, and the expected results. Figure 8.13 shows various types of assessment and uses for each.

FIGURE 8.13   Types of Assessment and Uses

Type of Assessment	Uses
True/False	Assesses factual knowledge
Multiple Choice	Thinks about the question, analyzes, and comprehends the correct answer
Short Answer	Assesses facts; skills
Essay	Encourages reflection, analysis, and comprehension of knowledge; clarity in writing
Performance	Takes knowledge and demonstrates understanding by applying the knowledge to a practical situation

Many researchers have added important pieces to the authentic assessment theme. Education researchers have shown the role of constructing knowledge in deeper understanding of topics to be critical for learning. Grant Wiggins and Jay McTighe are two of the leading proponents of performance assessment. They have spent time and effort in supporting this type of assessment by refining processes for designing and scoring tasks. Their focus has been on assessment, but their interest in teaching and learning resulted in the book, *Understanding by Design* (Wiggins & McTighe, 1998). These authors emphasize the point that performance-based or authentic assessment is only one of a repertoire of assessments necessary to evaluate student learning. Performance assessment is, however, one that is critical to meeting the learning needs of students and studying their understanding of content knowledge.

John Dewey is the pioneer in performance assessment. Dewey believed that learning took place when students were involved in authentic experiences that allowed them to apply facts to demonstrate understanding. Constructing learning, according to Dewey, leads to understanding. The focus in teaching should be on facilitating the learner's gain through his or her application of learning in situations that would assist in constructing a new perspective about life and about the appropriate behaviors necessary (Kellough & Kellough, 2003). Dewey's emphasis on learning through doing has influenced classroom strategies, including hands-on strategies, problem-solving strategies, and authentic assessment. Dewey believed that children learn by exploring their environments and that learning involved in solving real-world problems was useful and alive learning (Jacobsen, Eggen, & Kauchak, 2002).

Howard Gardner and his work with multiple intelligences have made authentic assessment an important part of meeting the needs of diverse children. When Gardner demonstrated the different ways in which people learn, he gave **performance** a major role among his intelligences. Students complete projects if they are linguistic, musical, spatial, bodily-kinesthetic, or naturalist learners. With logical-mathematical intelligence, individuals deal with problem solving and create products to explain their viewpoints and to demonstrate their understanding. Reflection is the major activity in the interpersonal and intrapersonal learning intelligences, but the reflection allows time to consider future behaviors and performances.

These noted researchers are but a few of those who find authentic assessment a worthwhile type of assessment in that it allows students to demonstrate what they know and are able to do with the knowledge received in the classroom.

A recent assessment strategy is called *backward design.* The instructor plans the assessment first and then plans lessons based on what is to be learned. If Mr. Smith found his Old English Christmas to be a motivating exercise for his students, he might want to engage in backward design for his next unit of study. The Middle Ages in English literature is a very popular period among students and adults because of the staging of Renaissance fairs. The unique features of the Middle Ages intrigue people of all ages as they study and learn about the Knights of the Round Table, the Canterbury Tales, the food and eating habits of the period, and the other traditions of the English people. Not only does a Renaissance fair teach this knowledge but it is also fun! Mr. Smith could decide on a Renaissance fair and then plan the pieces of knowledge to be learned by surveying his state content standards and objectives. His integrated unit would draw participation from faculty in social studies, music, art, mathematics, science, and drama. Depending on the resources available, Mr. Smith might even consider opening the event to parents and other community members. As students planned their activities, dress, and performances, they would also incorporate critical thinking, long-range planning, and time management into the project. Mr. Smith will need assistance from school faculty and personnel, parents, and community members to stage the type of fair that would be most educational. Sometimes the central district office will offer financial assistance to create learning situations that motivate students to apply their learning. Backward design is an excellent way to identify early in the planning process those resources that must be gathered in order to create an effective learning experience.

Teachers often avoid authentic assessment for various reasons, but the most common reason is fear of failure on the standardized tests used by the state to judge the quality of the school. Teachers are afraid that the use of this type of teaching and assessment will take time that could be used to go over factual knowledge that may appear on the test. Although students may remember selected items for the all-important test, teachers must remember that the deepest learning occurs in four ways: (1) reading, (2) listening, (3) manipulating/using hands-on activities, and (4) viewing/observing (Lewin & Shoemaker, 1998). When students have the opportunity to engage in all four ways of knowing, the learning is deep and will be evident on the day of the test. The students who engaged in the Old English Christmas will be able to define vocabulary words, interpret reading passages, and answer specific knowledge questions that have been part of the authentic assessment enjoyed by the students. Problem-solving skills will be honed by research projects and performance design. These skills will enable students to improve test performance. Aligning state P–12 standards and objectives to the authentic assessment activities will allay the fears of teachers that students are not obtaining the necessary knowledge for the test.

Further applications of the authentic assessment strategy found in classrooms include most subjects and consist of various types of assessments. Often, the foreign language classes hold a festival day that teaches vocabulary, customs, traditions, and cultural information. Social studies classes conduct a trial that may have local origins, such as designating all restaurants in a city as nonsmoking, or replaying an important past event, such as the Scopes trial. Mathematics students can remodel their rooms at home using mathematical formulas. English students can produce a literary magazine for the school. Science students can conduct an important experiment that will inform the town about its water or air quality. Drama students can assume the persona of past figures in order to teach others about a certain time, period, or event. Teachers find that authentic assessments bring excitement and interest to classroom content.

True success of the authentic assessment strategy is measured by student behaviors. The success of any lesson can be summarized by the following statements:

1. Students controlled the study.
2. All students participated in meaningful ways.
3. Students evaluated the quality of the assessment.
4. Students were eager to present their projects to other interested students and adults.

5. Students gave suggestions for future authentic assessment projects that were part of their class content.
6. Student learning was well documented and presented according to rubric requirements.
7. Students scored well on related content assessments.

Chapter Summary

Performance or authentic assessment presents students with the opportunity to apply knowledge in order to gain a greater and deeper understanding of that knowledge. This type of assessment, while measuring an understanding of knowledge, presents an array of assignments that mirror life problems that students may be facing. Performance assessment becomes a way to measure exactly where a student is situated in understanding through that student's performance and allows assessment to assist in future study plans for that student.

According to Wiggins (1990), assessment should primarily support the needs of learners. Therefore, having a grading scale that informs students of standards for evaluation allows the students to rehearse until they are ready to present their perspectives. Nothing is a secret. Students use knowledge in a higher-order thinking arena to present the best example of their understanding of the subject matter. Wiggins also notes that authentic tasks and assessments provide greater clarity and meaning to the student. Because of these factors, they should be useful in improving both learning and instruction.

CASE STUDY EPILOGUE

Mr. Smith's Old English Christmas was a great success. The students talked about the activities for weeks. Word spread throughout the school about the entertainment, the food, and the games. Mr. Smith noticed a definite interest in his class after this activity; in fact, one student told him that she came to school "just for this class!" Another by-product of the authentic assessment displayed itself on the final unit test of the Old English period. Students answered essay questions with enthusiasm and a much greater understanding of life in the British Isles at this particular time in history. Questions continued to come about a repeat type of assessment from students in every one of Mr. Smith's English classes.

Two teachers asked Mr. Smith to make time to talk to them about how he had constructed the assessment and the activities leading up to the actual event. One of the teachers was a mathematics teacher and one was a social studies teacher. Both of the teachers were impressed by the motivational qualities of the activity. When they heard about the test results, they were even more interested in authentic assessment. After talking about the possibilities of doing a type of authentic assessment together, the teachers decided to visit a local middle school and talk with teachers who had created a day called Pioneer Day for their students. On this day local artisans came and demonstrated ways of living in the early 1800s in the part of the state in which they lived. Students participated as artisan assistants and organizers of other events for Pioneer Day.

After the visit to the middle school, the teachers made the decision to try a smaller collaborative project among the three of them that would culminate with an authentic assessment event in the spring and then try to convince other teachers to take part in a total school activity in the fall. This activity would relate to the national election for president that would occur in November.

Working together, the mathematics teacher, the social studies teacher, and the English teacher chose the topic—the three branches of government—and planned activities that involved reading and writing, mathematical concepts plus charts and graphs, and a final activity in which students would challenge a law passed by Congress and present their case before the Supreme Court. Students would assume all roles in the activities, and teachers found written materials that would guide the court case.

Mr. Smith's anxiety about the benefits of authentic assessment faded, as he was again involved in an activity that brought motivational learning. In fact, the very information contained in the authentic assessment appeared on the standardized test that students were required to take in the spring. Whether or not all teachers participated in a fall authentic assessment activity, Mr. Smith felt sure that this type of activity would continue to be part of his assessment.

CHAPTER ACTIVITIES

Websites

http://carla.acad.umn.edu/MLPA-miniguide/performance.html This website provides information on performance-based assessments for foreign language instructors. The site provides a variety of ideas and models for student-centered, real-life assessments of second language learning.

http://jonathan.mueller.faculty.noctrl.edu/toolbox/ This well-made website offers an excellent contrast and comparison of traditional and performance assessments. It provides a number of good examples for developing your own authentic assessments.

http://www.funderstanding.com/authentic_assessment.cfm This website gives a description of authentic assessments, provides some useful examples, and gives links to related subjects.

http://www.uni.edu/profdev/assess.html This website provides numerous links to sites about performance-based assessments and scoring rubrics.

Portfolio Activities

1. 1. Review the Chapter Case Study. Can you find the answers to Mr. Smith's questions? List the answers to each question in your portfolio:
   - Does all learning have to be measured with a paper-and-pencil test?
   - How can any teacher actually meet every single objective and standard of the district and still have enjoyable activities for the students?
   - Are the students really learning?

- How does the teacher know they are learning?
- What are the current issues and problems with this type of assessment?

2. Keeping in touch with parents regarding student progress is essential for learning. However, it is not always an easy task when only a number or letter is involved. Authentic assessments offer an excellent snapshot of knowledge, skills, and ability to use them on the part of the student. The rubric is the way to demonstrate to parents the weak areas in a student's subject that will need extra time and effort. Design and score a rubric and write a cover letter for parents that explains the rubric.

3. Using the guidelines from this chapter, design your own performance-based activity, assessment, and rubric.

4. Using a backward design, plan an authentic assessment activity that would be appropriate for a content unit that is part of your field of expertise. Make sure that two or three other subject areas are included in the planning of the assessment. Provide standards and objectives that would be met by the activity and thus serve as rationale for including authentic assessment of the students in your classroom.

KEY CONCEPTS

Authentic assessment
Evaluation checklists
Inquiry
Investigation
Performance

Portfolio
Product
Research
Rubrics

REVIEW QUESTIONS

1. List and describe the major differences between performance assessments and traditional assessments.

2. Compare Mr. Smith's Old English Christmas instruction and the type of teaching on this topic with traditional direct instruction.

3. Describe the scoring and grading procedures for performance assessments.

4. What are the benefits of using performance assessments?

5. What are the factors that constitute an effective rubric for performance assessments?

6. Describe the ways that parents can be involved in performance assessments.

7. What is meant by a "backward design" and how does it work?

8. Describe the characteristics of an appropriate performance assessment.

9. How do student portfolios enhance classroom learning?

10. Explain the different aspects of inquiry and investigation.

SELF-ASSESSMENT

1. Which of the following is a type of performance-based assessment?
   a. Final exam
   b. Creative science project
   c. Standardized achievement test
   d. Pop quiz

2. Which of the following is one of three responsible assessment practices as indicated by Strong, Silver, and Perini?
   a. Reactive
   b. Regurgitative
   c. Reflective
   d. Renounced

3. The type of rubric that supplies only one single score or grade for the entire assessment is called:
   a. Analytical
   b. Reflective
   c. General
   d. Holistic

4. A process for answering questions and solving problems based on the logical examination of facts and observations is termed:
   a. Observation
   b. Checklist
   c. Inquiry
   d. Product

5. A type of performance assessment that is based on the use of stories, novels, or artwork is called:
   a. Portfolio
   b. Product
   c. Presentation
   d. Investigation

REFERENCES

Chaffee, J. (2000). *Thinking critically*. New York: Houghton Mifflin.

Forte, I., & Shurr, S. (1993). *The definitive middle school guide*. Nashville, TN: D. C. Heath.

Given, B.K. (2002). *Teaching to the brain's natural learning systems*. Alexandria, VA: ASCD.

How to assess student work. (1997). Columbus, OH: Merrill/Prentice Hall Professional Educator's Library.

Jacobsen, D.A., Eggen, P., & Kauchak, D. (2002) *Methods for teaching: Promoting student learning*. Columbus, OH: Merrill/Prentice Hall.

Joyce, B., Weil, M., & Showers, B. (1992). *Models of teaching*. Boston: Allyn and Bacon.

Kellough, R.D., & Kellough, N.G. (2003). *Secondary school teaching: A guide to methods and resources*. Columbus, OH: Merrill/Prentice Hall.

Answers to Self-Assessment: 1. b, 2. c, 3. d, 4. c, 5. b

Lewin, L., & Shoemaker, B.J. (1998). *Great performances: Creating classroom-based assessment tasks.* Alexandria, VA: Association for Supervision and Curriculum Development.

Manning, M.L., & Bucher, K.T. (2001). *Teaching in the middle school.* Columbus, OH: Merrill/Prentice Hall.

Project SUMIT. *The theory of multiple intelligences.* http://www.pz.harvard.edu/sumit/MISUMIT. HTM.

Science assessment resource. (2000). Madison, WI: Wisconsin Center for Education Research.

Shurr, S.L., Thomason, J., & Thompson, M. (1995) *Teaching at the middle level.* Lexington, MA: D. C. Heath.

Strong, R.W., Silver, H.F., & Perini, M.J. (2001). *Teaching what matters most: Standards and strategies for raising student achievement.* Alexandria, VA: Association for Supervision and Curriculum Development. (ERIC Document Reproduction Service No. ED 455 219).

Wiggins, G. (1990). *The case for authentic assessment.* (ERIC Digest: ED 328 611). http://www.askeric.org/plweb-cgi/obtain.pl.

Wiggins, G., & McTighe, J. (1998). *Understanding by design.* Alexandria, VA: ASCD.

CHAPTER

9   Assessments and Grades

CASE STUDY

Mrs. Williamson teaches third grade at a large, diverse elementary school in a midwestern city. One of her students, Alex, is popular with his classmates and kind of a class clown. Alex is having some trouble completing his class work and homework. His classroom assessment scores reflect this trouble in nearly every subject area.

During the middle of the fall semester, Mrs. Williamson started mailing home Alex's class papers, test scores, and homework assignments. Attached to them were letters explaining that his work was not what was expected for a third-grade student and that she would like a parent-teacher conference. Mrs. Williamson never received any reply.

At the end of the fall term, Mrs. Williamson made a number of telephone calls to the parents of Alex. On two occasions, she talked on the phone to Alex's mother. Both times the mother agreed to appointments with Mrs. Williamson but failed to appear at either appointment.

In the spring term, Mrs. Williamson finally sent a certified letter to the family. The letter stated that she was considering a recommendation of retention for Alex. The next day, Alex's parents came to the principal's office demanding an explanation. The principal asked Mrs. Williamson to meet with them in his presence.

When Mrs. Williamson entered the room, Alex's father exclaimed, "I have never seen such a crummy piece of business as this letter!"

Mrs. Williamson quietly replied that this was not the first letter that she sent home. In fact, she sent numerous letters and test papers home indicating that Alex's work was not acceptable. She also scheduled two meetings with Alex's mother about the situation.

The father replied, "I have never heard a word or seen a paper about any of this stuff. The only thing I know is that I will not allow Alex to fail third grade under any circumstances."

Mrs. Williamson is left with the following questions:

What else should she do about this parent-teacher conference?

What other approaches could she have taken?

Is there any way to handle irate parents under these circumstances?

What role should her principal play in this situation?

What are her professional alternatives?

Introduction

It is difficult for parents to set aside their egos and emotions when it comes to their own children. Nearly all parents believe that they know what is best for their children, even in the classroom. Thus, many parents think that they are the experts, not the teacher.

As a classroom teacher, you need to be aware of these biases and to consider these underlying factors. You are dealing with a very complex emotional situation. Many parents see their children as an extension of themselves, as well as an extension of their hopes and dreams. Classroom assessments, and particularly classroom grades, call for clearheaded thinking about situations often filled with intense feelings.

Determining grades are among the more difficult areas you will face in your teaching career. The egos of parents and students are only one factor that produces difficulties. Almost by its very nature the process of assigning grades often involves some sort of comparative standard. No matter how much you avoid making personal comparisons, it is almost inevitable that parents and students will still make such comparisons. In addition to all the other emotions, you also may have to face the problems produced by envy and jealousy.

To compound these problems, there is little general agreement among educators about current grading practices. Some educators believe that academic standards must be increased and stricter grading policies need to be employed. Other educators reject the idea of grading practices that lead to academic failure or grade-level retention. Some call for a "Schools without Failure" approach (Glasser, 1969); others indicate that such policies may be lower academic standards and cause grade inflation (Honan, 1998).

The research on grading practices does not provide any clear-cut answers. Even the question as to whether giving tests and grades will increase achievement is debated in the research. For example, Moos and Moos (1978) conducted a study on classroom climate and found that high academic standards, competitive classroom environments, and a large number of low grades were related to increased absenteeism and dropouts. On the other hand, Williams and Ware (1976) found that students who expected to receive a test after viewing a videotaped instructional module scored higher on the test than a control group of students who did not expect to be tested immediately after viewing the videotape.

The purpose of this chapter is to examine the issues and practices involved in making decisions about grades. As part of these issues and practices, various types of grading systems will be reviewed. The ways that assessments are transformed into grades will be examined, as well as the methods for preparing grades. Dealing with grade challenges and communicating grades to parents will also be discussed.

Why Have Grades?

Grading practices have strengths and challenges that are similar to other assessment areas. The traditional system of grading based on classroom achievement is subject to considerable criticism. However, there are also disagreements about alternatives to traditional grading practices. A series of polls demonstrate widespread disagreements among teachers, education professors, and the public over the issue of the state assessments, grading practices, and student retention policies (Sengupta, 1997). Sponsored by Public Agenda, a nonpartisan research group, these polls found that fewer than 50 percent of education professors believe that standardized tests should be a factor in promotion/retention decisions for students in elementary school and junior high school. Nevertheless, 70 percent of the public believe that these test scores should be used for this purpose.

More than 75 percent of education professors reject the use of multiple-choice exams in determining grades. However, more than 50 percent of public school teachers endorse the use of multiple-choice exams (Sengupta, 1997). In general, education professors and teachers also differ in their academic failure policies. Most professors of education reject policies that include the retention of students, but the majority of teachers were in favor of retention policies.

As indicated in Chapter 1, the public's call for accountability in education is one major reason for current grading policies. Parents, school boards, and employers want grades that give a concrete measure of student performance. The public's attitude is that a demonstrable level of achievement should be associated with an eighth-grade education, a high school diploma, or a college degree. Therefore, the public's expectation is that a passing grade for a given educational level should indicate a certain level of knowledge. The call for national tests and minimum competency testing are examples of the increasing demands by politicians and the public for educational accountability. Requiring beginning teachers to pass a professional skills test in order to be certified is another example.

Another reason for the present system of grading is communication. Each subsequent level of education requires an appropriately communicated standard from the previous level. As a teacher, you need to answer two questions as part of this communication process: Where does an individual student perform on some generally accepted criterion of achievement? And where does an individual student perform in relation to his or her peers? A third-grade teacher wants that type of information from a student's second-grade teacher. High school teachers need that information from middle school teachers.

Beginning teachers should be aware that assigning grades is almost as much a measure of the teacher as of the student. Teachers are quickly judged by students, parents, and colleagues as to whether they are fair, easy, hard, honest, consistent, or considerate (or any number of adjectives both mentionable and unmentionable). The essential professional (and legal) question remains: Are you able to judge student performance in a manner that is fair, appropriate, and without discriminatory intent? When grades have been challenged, these are among the considerations made by grade appeal committees and school lawyers.

Grading Policies

In most school systems, it is essential that you develop a written policy detailed in your unit plan or syllabus to show the procedures for transforming formal assessments into grades. Just as most school systems require written lesson plans, most school systems require some type of written plan for determining grades. In creating a policy for transforming assessments into grades, there are certain decisions to consider. The three major decisions are:

> ### Three Decisions about Grading Policies
> 1. What type of grading practices do you want to use?
> 2. What type of grades do you want to give?
> 3. What is the relationship between formal assessments and final grades?

Most of this chapter is devoted to examining these three decisions. As with anything else, the first step is the most difficult: What type of grading practices do you want to use?

Choosing the Type of Grading Practice

The traditional view of grading practices is that grades should be based on student achievement. For example, grades in a geometry class should be based on how well students achieve an understanding of the principles of Euclidean geometry. This traditional view has been challenged in recent years (Thorndike, 1997). Some educators emphasize the need to individualize grades based on each student's ability or potential. For other educators, such as Bruner, the emphasis is on evaluating the degree of discovery learning.

As with performance-based procedures, a number of alternative grading systems have been proposed to encourage more realistic and appropriate grading methods. In contrast to the essentially summative assessments used in traditional grading practices, alternative grading practices involve a number of other options. Some researchers encourage a process approach to grading; others propose a progress approach to grades. There are educators who propose grading based on effort, and there are others who emphasize self-esteem and affective considerations in making decisions about grades. This section examines these alternative methods for grading students.

Grading on the Basis of Process

Some educators stress the importance of grading the learning process rather than the end product. **Grading on the basis of process** often emphasizes the use of performance-based assessment procedures. For instance, in using portfolios, the focus of process grading may be on the conceptual shifts that students make in dealing with a given subject or issue. With these conceptual changes, the teacher wants to see increases in applying, understanding, and transforming the information. Over the course of a semester, the teacher then judges the quantity and quality of these changes in determining final grades.

Some Constructivist approaches also emphasize the use of process grading. Not only is the focus on conceptual shifts, but Constructivist procedures also may concentrate on the ability to construct a solution to a problem. Some Constructivists state that the ability to construct a solution on one's own can be the most important aspect of grading decisions. In some cases, the ability to construct a solution may be more important than the correctness of the solution.

With grading based on process, the heart of the issue is the development of a common standard for assigning grades to students. Developing a common standard in a given classroom *is* possible. Scoring rubrics are available, such as Figure 9.1 for a physical education class. With physical education and motor activities, it is relatively easy to observe and document skill changes. The sample rubric asks the teacher to assess the student on various performance activities and to rate the student on a scale ranging from 0 to 5. The scale also provides the student with an opportunity to self-assess. This rubric typically is administered at the beginning of the term and at designated times throughout the term. Therefore, by the end of the term, student changes in skill performance can be evaluated.

Nevertheless, it is altogether different when assessing internal cognitive changes. Even with a scoring rubric, grading cognitive abilities based on process raises the following questions: How does one evaluate and judge an essentially subjective event such as a conceptual shift or a paradigm change? How does one compare different students' changes in process or shifts in conceptualizing? Is one student's process change of greater weight, value, or importance than another student's change?

FIGURE 9.1   Fitness Rubric for Basketball

Name _____ Date _____					
Fitness Benefits	0 **Low**	1	2	3	4	5 **High**
Muscular Strength						
Muscular Endurance						
Flexibility						
Caloric Consumption						
Cardiovascular						
Fitness Requirements	0	1	2	3	4	5
Muscular Strength						
Muscular Endurance						
Flexibility						
Body Composition						
Cardiovascular						
Self-Rating	0	1	2	3	4	5
Muscular Strength						
Muscular Endurance						
Flexibility						
Body Composition						
Cardiovascular						

There also appears to be little commonality among teachers about their scoring rubrics. Thus, teachers often end up reinventing the wheel in creating their own grading standards. This is obviously a very time-consuming practice. In fact, one recent survey of teachers and their portfolio assessments found that the two biggest barriers to portfolio use in the classroom were the amount of time required and the problems with scoring the portfolios (Wolfe & Miller, 1997).

In the area of mathematics, a critique of process grading states that such procedures create "fuzzy math" (Steinberg, 1997). For example, some Constructivist procedures emphasize processing and constructing solutions as more important than finding the correct answer. Critics of this approach claim that there are "right" answers and "wrong" answers in basic mathematics. A fundamental aspect of mathematics is the degree of precision and consistency that it provides in understanding phenomena. Some opponents of process grading claim that reinforcing the idea that the process is more important than a correct solution is to deprive children of a fundamental principle in mathematical understanding.

Grading on the Basis of Progress

When **grading on the basis of progress,** the teacher initially determines the individual level of each student and establishes a baseline level of achievement or performance. Instruction is then tailor-made to meet the individual level and needs of the child. The key to the grading is the amount of progress made from this baseline level. A final grade reflects the amount of academic progress from the baseline to the end of the instructional unit. Supporters of this approach state that it offers individualized instruction and grading practices based on the individual level of each child. Critics of this approach contend that it produces a separate grading system for each child.

The question of uniform grading standards appears to have produced the most controversy. If grades are based on progress from the baseline level, there could be widespread grading disparities. For example, let's say you have two third-grade students. One child starts the year reading on a second-grade level but advances to a fourth-grade level. The second child starts out at a third-grade level but also advances to the same fourth-grade level. Should the two students receive different grades? One student has made more progress but both students have ended up at the same level of achievement.

The issue of fair and consistent grading standards has obvious classroom implications. In addition, the legal difficulties posed by grading different students with different standards have raised serious concerns about such policies.

Grading on the Basis of Effort

Given that students enter the classroom with widely different ability levels, some educators have proposed that students be graded on the amount of effort. With **grading on the basis of effort,** students with lower initial ability levels will still be able to have "good" grades because they can demonstrate a greater amount of effort. Such a practice would appear to help individuals who are at risk in the classroom because of their socio-economic background. In effect, effort may be able to compensate for background. Many teachers admit that they take into account student effort in moving a grade slightly upward at the end of the term. For instance, the borderline C+ student is given a B because of her effort on the classroom project and her participation in classroom discussions.

The problems with grading based on effort are similar to what we have seen with grading on the basis of progress. What if one student makes a heroic effort on the out-of-class assignments but scores lower than the other students on the classroom exams? Does the student with the heroic effort receive as good as or even better grade than the students who actually performed at a higher overall level? It is difficult to define effort and certainly difficult to quantify effort in a way that is fair and consistent for all students. Because of the fairness and consistency issues, grading based on effort remains a problem.

Diversity and Grades

Other alternatives to traditional grading practices stress cultural, attitudinal, and affective considerations. These concerns often emphasize the role of student self-esteem. These considerations may occur most frequently with the following students: children who speak English as a second language (ESL), children from low-income families, and children from ethnic minority backgrounds. These cultural and affective concerns may be amplified when retention policies are reviewed, since these children tend to be retained at higher rates when compared to mainstream students.

As noted in Chapter 4, ESL students, low-income students, and children from ethnic minority backgrounds frequently appear to be alienated from or stereotyped by the mainstream culture. Mass media portrayals may increase detrimental images of these groups. If internalized, these negative stereotypes can adversely affect children's self-esteem. Graham (1989) states, "Far too many minority children perform poorly in school not because they lack basic intellectual capacities or specific learning skills but because they have low expectations, feel hopeless, lack interest, or give up in the face of potential failure" (p. 40).

The argument is made that these students are devalued because of cultural factors and that they may internalize this devaluation with negative effects to their self-esteem. By affecting self-esteem in this manner, these factors also threaten the students' ability to achieve in school. Therefore, some argue that special grading considerations should be made for students from different cultural backgrounds.

Should your students receive special grading consideration because of family background? Should self-esteem be considered in reviewing your students' classroom performance? Can you devise a fair grading system that factors into account income, language, and ethnic background?

Special academic considerations may be needed to address these problems. However, the question of what type of accommodations is a matter of debate. Should special assessment considerations be made when using standardized test scores? For instance, with college placements or high school academic tracks, should a certain percentage of placements be guaranteed for minority students regardless of test scores? Should a special type of weighted formula for test scores and grades be used in considering minority students for such placements?

Children with Disabilities and Grades

Similar issues and questions occur when considering children with disabilities. In particular, the concern that some children with disabilities may exhibit learned helplessness and essentially give up on academic tasks has been noted (Woolfolk, 2001). As mentioned in Chapter 1, reasonable accommodations are mandated for children with disabilities, in part to compensate for these problems.

The Regular Education Initiative and other special education inclusion policies attempt to deal with the social difficulties of children with disabilities. One of the assumptions about inclusion practices is that they can promote social interactions and can create peer friendships. However, there has been considerable debate about the effectiveness of these inclusion practices. In particular, the issues of grading and evaluation have been of increasing concern (Wagner, Newman, D'Amico, Jap, Butler-Dailin, Marder, & Cox, 1991).

In practice, inclusion policies may vary from full inclusion to different types of part-time inclusion. In either case, children with disabilities may be assessed and graded with other children in regular education classrooms. In terms of grades, the question often asked is: Should a separate set of assessment and grading procedures be used with children with disabilities?

Much of the present discussion about assessments and grades focuses on children with mild or moderate retardation. The issue of grades becomes particularly acute when such children are placed in regular education classrooms. Should the same grading and assessment procedures be used with these children that are used with children without the special education diagnosis?

Wagner and colleagues (1991) claim that children with mild to moderate disabilities tend to receive inflated grades in regular education. They also tend to drop out at a higher rate than children placed in special education classes. Patton and Polloway (1994) state that inclusion of children with mild to moderate retardation can occur. However, they point out that regular education classes may present an overwhelming challenge. Patton and Polloway indicate that nonacademic classes (e.g., art and drafting) and extracurricular activities may provide more viable forums for inclusion.

Full-inclusion practices for children with disabilities still have not adequately addressed the issue of assessments and grades for many students. As with children from diverse backgrounds, the same question occurs: Can a fair and consistent grading policy be established that appropriately evaluates all children?

Grading on the Basis of Achievement

In the end, we are right back where we started from on the issue of grading practices. The traditional practice of **grading on the basis of achievement** remains the choice of many educators. Using teacher-made, formal, classroom assessments to grade students on a common standard of achievement wins out.

Why is this the case? There are several reasons. No other system of grading practices appears to be as fair to all students as grading based on achievement. In part, this is because achievement grading tends to be more objective than alternative practices. Because of the objectivity, achievement grading tends to be a little easier for everyone to understand and it tends to be a lot easier to document. This is true whether it is documenting that a student learned five new vocabulary words for the week, correctly applied the formula for calculating the area of a rectangle, or demonstrated mastery of the periodical table. In any case, achievement grading appears to be the most objective grading practice. Objectivity can be an important factor in responding to parents and grade challenges.

Related to objectivity and documentation is the issue of reliability. In this sense, reliability is the consistency of the grading procedures. The reliability of using achievement as the basis for grading also appears to be greater than with other methods. Because it is easier to score and document many types of achievement, this type of grading procedure tends to be more reliable than alternative methods.

With the No Child Left Behind Act, current trends at the federal level appear to concentrate on objective achievement levels. In addition, the increasing use of standards-based performance in many states also seems to endorse using achievement as the basis for grades. In fact, at both the federal and state levels even school systems are actually being graded and ranked. For instance, the No Child Left Behind Act mandates the use of state report cards and school district report cards that detail how well schools are performing.

In summary, it is not that traditional grading practices are without fault. In fact, grading based on achievement has its problems. Yet the problems appear to be less than those found in other grading practices. Given some of the administrative, legislative, and legal issues, the traditional grading practice also wins out because it presents fewer areas of legal challenge to school systems.

Point/Counterpoint: State Report Cards—
Comparing School Performance

Point

Supporters of state-by-state, school district and school comparisons point out that the public has a right to know exactly where certain schools stand when compared to other schools in other states. Using school report cards involves disseminating a variety of information about schools. In addition to achievement test scores, the information can be grade-point averages, attendance rates, dropout rates, special education placements, minority enrollment, and advanced placement enrollment. Supporters state that this information provides parents, school board members, and legislators with a viable overview of how each school performs. Informed decisions can be made about schools, teachers, and administrators. Proponents claim that school report cards can be an effective way to achieve educational accountability. Schools that have poor report cards can be held accountable for their problems and schools that have good report cards can be recognized.

Counterpoint

Opponents of school report cards and comparisons point out that these report cards rarely provide more than a one-time snapshot of a school or school district. While some states and school districts do provide considerable information on their school report cards, the essential focus is still on standardized test scores. Since standardized test scores are the prime focus, opponents state that such comparisons are inherently biased because of three factors: socioeconomic, diversity, and ESL issues. The prime predictor of a school's test scores are socioeconomic. Wealthy states, school districts, and schools tend to do better on test scores. Less well off states, school districts, and schools tend to do worse. The socioeconomic bias with test scores is amplified in schools with large numbers of minority or ESL students. These students tend to come from less well off economic backgrounds. Their test scores tend to be lower because of this fact. Opponents of state and school report cards claim that the outcome of this practice is simply to reinforce a situation that is already inherently biased.

Types of Grades

This section examines how you go about assigning overall grades in the classroom. Three types of grades typically are used: traditional letter grades, skill checklist grades, and pass/fail grades. Usually, your school or school system will require a particular type of grading system. You then transform your formal assessments into one of these types of grades and write them on a report card.

Letter grades are the most common type of grading system. An advantage of the A, B, C, D, F system is that everyone is familiar with it and everyone understands it. Letter grades are also easy to communicate with other educators. Therefore, the ease of communication and the ease of comprehension are major pluses for letter grades.

Challenges to letter grades often revolve around the limited range of measurement with letter grades. With letter grades, the overall evaluation of student performance in a course is being summarized by one single value. For instance, a student's achievement in English literature for a whole semester is reduced to one single grade. In addition, this grade may have a relatively arbitrary range. If the range for a C is 70 to 79, the student who makes a 79 gets the same grade as the one who makes a 70. Another criticism is that letter grades may encourage competition between students rather than cooperation. A final criticism is that letter grades may not be appropriate for younger children.

For younger children, a **checklist of skills** often is used. This is especially true in kindergarten and in some primary grades. A checklist provides an assessment of a wide range of skills and performance levels. Part of an adapted kindergarten checklist is shown in Figure 9.2. This particular checklist is graded on a three-point scale with either Proficient, Satisfactory, or Needs Improvement. Checklists also may be graded

FIGURE 9.2 Kindergarten Developmental Checklist

Name_____   Date _____

School _____   Teacher _____

Key
P = Proficient
S = Satisfactory
N = Needs Improvement

Academic Skills	**Motor Skills**	**Social Skills**
_____ Oral Language	_____ Fine Motor	_____ Peers
_____ Reading Readiness	_____ Large Motor	_____ Classroom
_____ Drawing Skills	_____ Hand Dominance	_____ Playground
_____ Writing Skills		_____ Adults
_____ Math Readiness		
_____ Music Skills		

using pass/fail or numeric grades. For example, with a pass/fail system, the teacher would simply write "pass" or "fail" beside each of the separate areas. With numeric grades, the teacher may use a scale from 1 to 5 or may use percentages ranging from 0 to 100 percent. The advantages of checklist grades is that they may offer a wider range of skills to document. If using the typical Proficient, Satisfactory, Needs Improvement scale, they also may avoid some of the stigma associated with failing grades.

Challenges to checklists tend to center on the communication question. In effect, to what extent do checklists provide information that can be used by the child's next teacher? Is there really a common standard with checklists? Do most teachers rate motor skills in the same way with the same children? How can checklist scores from first grade fit with letter grades in the other grades? Despite these questions, many school systems use checklists in kindergarten and some use them in first and second grades.

Pass/fail grading systems also are available for teachers. Pass/fail grades tend to be used more in areas such as an internship, practicum, or independent study, and are sometimes used in the primary grades. Pass/fail grades narrow the spectrum of choices that a teacher has to make about a grade. That is both the good news and the bad news about pass/fail grades. A teacher does not have to make the sometimes difficult distinction between a B or a C letter grade. On the other hand, a student who barely passes gets the same grade as someone who does exemplary work.

Terwilliger (1989) makes the following recommendations about grading systems:

1. Data collected for purposes of grading student achievement should be expressed in quantitative form.
2. Such data should be collected over time and should be formulated within an explicit set of guidelines available to each student.
3. Assignment of a failing grade should reflect a judgment that the student does not possess a minimum level of competency.
4. A minimum level of competency should be independent of other students' levels of performance.
5. The minimum level of competency should represent the essential course objectives that all students must achieve to certify a minimum level of mastery of the course material.

Terwilliger (1989) presented the argument that failing a student in a course should be a decision based strictly on a pass/fail judgment. Assessments used to measure the attainment of minimal competency also should be based on pass/fail measures. Terwilliger also believes that failure rates should be low and that failure should reflect serious deficiencies in achieving minimal competence.

Terwilliger's (1989) comment about the quantification of grades is very important to consider. In general, it appears that using numeric grades may be the best approach to take during the course of the semester. Many educators urge that transforming formal assessments into grades be completed with numerical values. Each formal assessment used in your classroom can carry a numerical weight or value. At the end of the term, these numerical values can be converted into final letter grades for your report card. During the term, the numerical values can provide a quick indicator to the students about their overall classroom progress. The next section further discusses how to transform assessments into final grades.

The Relationship between Assessments and Final Grades

When considering the relationship between formal assessments and final grades, there are a number of factors to consider. First of all, there is a relationship among assessments, instruction, and grades to take into account. Teachers need to have some sort of rational relationship between how much instruction they provide and how much numerical weight or value each assessment is given in their grading policy. For example, in an American history class the objectives and lesson plans for a two-week period concentrate on the American Revolution. The formal assessment reflects these objectives and plans. To encourage students to analyze the underlying factors in this time period, the teacher designs a constructed-response assessment that focuses on higher-level thinking skills for just this unit. The assessment then carries a type of grading value that reflects a two-week period in the nine-week term. Although it need not be exactly the fraction of 2/9, this fraction should provide a ballpark figure for how to weight the value of this assessment. In effect, assessments need to reflect how much instruction has been given on a topic. The weight or value for an assessment should have a relationship with the final grade in the course. In this case, around 20 percent of the final grade in the term should be accounted for by the one assessment on the American Revolution.

Documenting how each formal assessment relates to other formal assessments can help students plan accordingly for the term or semester. This also lets students know exactly what is expected of them with each formal assessment. Using these guidelines will provide students and parents with an ongoing knowledge of what their overall grade is at any time. Establishing explicit connections between assessments and grades can go a long way in avoiding potential problems. An example of these connections is provided in the following teacher application.

Teacher Application

Sixth-Grade Math Class

Ms. Donato wants to develop a grading policy for her students based on a number of features. First of all, she feels that it is important that students have short, weekly quizzes that determine a significant part of their grade. These weekly quizzes examine each separate area of her instruction for the nine-week term. Second, she also requires a midterm and final exam in her course. In addition, she has her students keep a portfolio of their major in-class and out-of-class work assignments.

Ms. Donato also wants to keep her grading policy short and sweet so that all students can understand it. In doing so, she develops the following grading policy and hands it out on the first day of the fall term.

Assessments and Grades. There will be nine weekly quizzes. Each quiz will be worth 5 points. There will be one midterm and one final exam. Each of those exams will be worth 15 points. The portfolio assignment will be worth 25 points.

Total Quiz Points	45 points
Exam 1	15 points
Exam 2	15 points
Portfolio	25 points
Total Points	100 points

A = 90–100 points
B = 80–89 points
C = 70–79 points
D = 60–69 points
F = Below 60 points

In reviewing this teacher application, note that each weekly math quiz accounts for 5 percent of the total grade received for mathematics on the nine-week report card. There are nine such math quizzes, which accounts for 45 percent of the total grade in the class. The remaining assessments involve a midterm exam (15 percent of total grade), a final exam (15 percent of total grade), and the portfolio assignments (25 percent of total grade). Ms. Donato uses a a criterion-referenced grading system with 90 out of a possible 100 points needed for an A.

Teachers need to communicate in writing the grading policies at the beginning of each grading period. Students and parents need to know where each formal assessment fits into the overall grading policy. A written policy also sends a message to students and parents that the teacher wants to be fair and consistent with everyone in the class.

Frequent feedback about formal assessments, completed in a nonthreatening manner, can help students correct their mistakes. Offering students an opportunity to discuss in private any questions about their grades can go a long way in avoiding disagreements and problems. Also, providing regular feedback to the parents may avoid potential questions about why their child is having problems in school. It is imperative that parents be notified about problems as soon as possible. This may help reduce an overly emotional reaction of some parents when informed their child is having academic difficulty.

Preparing Final Grades

In preparing grades, most teachers use some type of formal **grade book** or grading document to record grades. From this grade book the grades are transferred to report cards and permanent records. A grade book may contain a number of different types of assessment activities. Typically, it contains only those formal assessments that the teacher uses to calculate the final grade for the course or unit. An example of a grade book for Ms. Donato's math class is provided in Figure 9.3.

FIGURE 9.3 Math Grade Book

Nine Weekly Quizzes														
Name	**Quizzes**									**Midterm**	**Final**	**Portfolio**	**Total**	**Grade**
	1	**2**	**3**	**4**	**5**	**6**	**7**	**8**	**9**					
Archer, W.	5	5	5	5	5	5	5	5	5	14	12	22	93	A
Bishop, C.	5	5	3	4	5	3	3	4	3	13	12	20	85	B
Davis, B.	5	4	4	3	4	4	5	4	3	15	13	18	82	B
Downs, E.	4	5	5	5	5	3	5	5	4	14	13	23	91	A
Ferris, D.	2	5	3	4	3	2	4	3	3	12	10	22	73	C
Martin, S.	4	4	5	5	5	5	4	4	4	15	13	23	91	A
Matthews, E.	4	4	2	3	3	3	2	4	3	12	14	22	76	C
Sherrill, D.	5	5	3	4	4	5	3	4	4	14	15	24	82	B

In examining Ms. Donato's grade book, it is evident that she carefully documents each separate area and grade. As Terwilliger (1989) recommends, she uses numerical grades during the term and totals up all the points at the end. Only at the end of the term does Ms. Donato actually report and use letter grades.

When preparing your final grades, you have to make some choices about grading standards and policies. In the end, grading often involves lonely and difficult decisions. Even after many years of teaching, most teachers still agonize over individual grades. Basically, you have two ways of setting up final grades. Just as assessments can be criterion referenced or norm referenced, final grades also can be criterion referenced or norm referenced.

Ms. Donato used a criterion-referenced grading system. That is, she set a standard, such as 90 or more out of 100 points is the criteria for receiving an A in a semester. For a B, the student must have between 80 to 89 points, and so on. No matter how many students reach the criteria, they all receive the same grade.

Norm-referenced grades are based on a comparative ranking procedure. After ranking the students on the total scores from their formal assessments, the grading procedure is that the top-ranked students get the top grades and the lowest-ranked students get the lowest overall grades. Student scores are ranked by either points or percentages. For instance, the top 25 percent of the students in a class receive an A. The choice of the system is up to the teacher. Some teachers use the following system:

A = Top 25%
B = Next 25%
C = Next 25%
D = Next 15%
F = Next 10%

Norm-referenced approaches may cause a certain amount of problems for students. Students may not be motivated to help each other because the standard for grades is comparative. This can increase competition in the classroom. There can also be a question of fairness with students. What happens if a large number of students score very well on all of their assessments? A majority of students might have scored 90 percent or better overall on all their assessments and therefore be clustered together at the top of the scale. Some students will have to receive lower grades even though they did quite well on every assessment. In general, most educators recommend some type of criterion-referenced approach because it appears to reduce unwanted competition and comparisons between students.

Quality Control Issues with Grades

Quality control with grading practices presents a number of disparate issues. Not only must a teacher's assessments meet certain standards, but additional criteria must be met with his or her grading procedures. These criteria range from school district policies about assessments and grades to statewide standards that address legal issues. School-based guidelines and school district regulations may include the following policies: proper documentation of how student assessments are transformed into grades, procedures for notifying parents of student grades, retention and social promotion policies, and appeal procedures for student grades.

In practice, many school principals review grading procedures and grade reports with teachers. As with other assessment practices, principals may cross-check grades with standardized test scores. By completing such comparisons, some measure of quality control in grading practices may be achieved. For example, by comparing standardized test scores for a particular teacher, the principal may find that a significant number of students are not achieving in mathematics at the typical test norms established for their grade. The principal might then review these test scores with the teacher and find ways to appropriately change the curriculum in this area for this grade.

Grades and Retention

Another issue involving grades and educational standards is retention of students because of low academic performance. A frequently debated question concerning grades and retention concerns whether they are a positive educational tool. A number of studies have measured the effects of grades and student retention on achievement. Clark (1969) states that students perform at a higher level on research papers when they expect to be graded, than a control group of students who do not expect to receive a grade. While it is often assumed by educators that grades are a positive motivation tool (appropriate learning = good grade), Stipek (1996) notes that the context and language used by the teacher can influence whether the grades are viewed by the student as positive or negative.

In terms of retention, Holmes and Matthews (1984) find problems with failing or retaining students for a full academic year. They state that retained students tend to have lower academic, social, and behavioral performance levels than comparable students who are promoted. It does not appear that retention increased later classroom achievement. In fact, it may have further decreased student achievement. This finding was replicated by Roderick (1994). Paris and Cunningham (1998) note in their research review on this subject: "When children are retained on the basis of specific academic achievement, it is hoped that the extra year provides compensatory experiences that will foster future development. Unfortunately, the research does not support this prediction" (p. 128).

Thus, the research appears to show that the expectation of being graded increases achievement. Grade-level retention does not appear to help students. This is the paradox that many elementary teachers face: Grades are given on the assumptions that they both reflect achievement and increase achievement. But if a student does not reach a given performance level, then he or she is retained, which probably decreases the student's overall achievement. Because of this paradox about retention, many school systems are now requiring summer school sessions and special tutoring programs for academically deficient students. These policies hopefully will correct the student's academic problems and allow the student to be promoted to the next grade level in the fall semester.

Avoiding Grade Challenges

In general, the legal system in the United States has sided with teachers and schools in legal challenges to grades and related issues such as educational malpractice. Zirkel and Richardson (1988) state, "A long line of court decisions concur that academic evaluations of students are not amendable to the fact finding process of judicial and administrative decision making" (p. 46).

The burden of proving that a grade is incorrect is on the student. Potential legal issues for teachers involve two basic aspects: (1) discriminatory intent on the part of the teacher and (2) the lack of a rational or appropriate relationship between the classroom instruction, the assessment measures, and the grades given to the student.

If the teacher applies the same, uniform standards to all students in the instructional and grading process, then discriminatory intent would not be a viable argument. If there is a clear relationship between the assessments and the instruction, it would be very difficult to prove a lack of an appropriate or rational relationship.

Other ways to avoid grade challenges are to be open about grading policies, exhibit fairness about grading practices, and show consistency in administering these policies and practices. If a teacher has a written grading policy that everyone understands, then the openness question should be satisfied. If a teacher follows his or her written policy, then the consistency issue should be satisfied. If formal assessments are administered and graded in a fair manner, then this criterion should be satisfied.

Difficulties may occur in this area when some students are treated in a differential fashion. By avoiding differential assignments or grading practices, a teacher can limit the chances that he or she will have a grade appeal. Extra credit assignments to make up grades or other special treatment for individual students may appear discriminatory and may result in grade appeals.

Communicating with Parents

The first thing that most veteran teachers or principals will tell you about communicating with parents is: documentation, documentation, documentation. Make sure you have a paper trail by documenting your activities and assessments with students. Keep copies of all relevant formal assessments about students and keep all appropriate grading policy guidelines where you can readily present them to parents. When there is a request for a parent-teacher conference, make sure that you have all these documents in order and that they are ready for viewing by the parents.

The second thing that veteran teachers will tell you almost seems like a contradiction with the first thing: As much as possible, avoid listing any personal comments or judgments in grade books, permanent records, report cards, or assessments. Written personal interpretations about students, even though well intentioned, may be misconstrued. If there are problems with parents about grades or retentions, any statement that might be construed as unfair, biased, or discriminatory may come back to haunt you. Most veteran teachers will caution you to let the student's performance on the formal assessments tell the story to the parents, not you.

A federal privacy law (Buckley Amendment) governs all communications with parents of children who are under the age of 18. Therefore, all communications with parents should be private, whether they are by telephone, letters, or face-to-face conferences. Private conferences also may diminish the possibility of any outside interference in the communication process and may reduce the possibility of amplifying the problems.

Finally, these communications should be completed in a formative rather than summative manner. Assessments and grades should be viewed as a way of making improvements. A plan should be developed with the parents for helping the student to improve. After all, this is one area in which parents and teachers have a common goal: They both want to help the student. Some questions that a teacher might ask in such a situation are:

1. Where can we go from here to provide more help for the student?
2. How can we change or improve what we are doing with the student?
3. What is our specific plan for improvement?
4. What is a win/win situation for everyone?

Chapter Summary

This chapter reviewed a number of policies concerning grading practices. A considerable amount of disagreement exists over grading policies and practices. Although there is criticism over the traditional practice of assigning letter grades based on classroom achievement, no alternative grading practice has emerged to replace the traditional approach. Among the alternatives considered are grading on the basis of process, grading on the basis of progress, and grading on the basis of effort. Because of the issues of fairness and consistency, these alternative policies are still not widely accepted.

The question of alternative grading practices with academically at-risk children and children with disabilities was also reviewed. As with other alternative grading policies, the issues of fairness and consistency are also raised with these children. No consensus has yet emerged as to whether special grading policies should be used in these areas.

A number of guidelines were proposed for grading policies. Included among these suggestions were quantify formal assessments so that each assessment has a numerical value, provide your grading policy to all students and parents at the beginning of the school term, use criterion-referenced grading practices, provide feedback on a regular basis to students and parents, and carefully document all formal assessments.

CASE STUDY EPILOGUE

Mrs. Williamson has decided to change her policies somewhat. She has decided to take even greater care in documenting and disseminating information to parents in the future. She will notify all parents by certified letter in early December of any potential problems with students and the posssibility of retention. She will send a copy of the letters to her principal and to the assistant superintendent of instruction. Mrs. Williamson will also keep a portfolio of all major activities of each student. This will include homework, class work, assigned papers, classroom assessments, and standardized assessment scores. She will use these items to validate her own grading policies.

Mrs. Williamson will also try to bring parents to her classroom by having special activities such as plays and projects that increase parental involvement. She will emphasize to parents that they are an important part of the educational process. In addition, Mrs. Williamson will encourage parents to monitor and discuss classroom assignments with their children.

CHAPTER ACTIVITIES

Websites

www.principals.org   This website, created by the National Association of Secondary School Principals, offers a number of articles, position papers, court cases, and legislative actions on grades and policy issues.

http://uga.berkeley.edu/sled/bgd/grading.html   Developed by Barbara Davis at Berkeley, this site offers a number of ideas on grading practices and policies as well as some tips on handling irate students.

www.middleweb.com   Designed by middle school educators, this website offers a number of articles and tips on developing grading practices and on working with parents. Go to the site index and check out either Assessment/Evaluation or Parents and Public.

Portfolio Activities

1. Review the Case Study in this chapter. Answers the questions concerning Mrs. Williamson's parent-teacher conference. List the answers to these questions in your portfolio:
   - What would you do about a parent-teacher conference like the one in the Case Study?
   - Is there any other approach that you would take?
   - How would you handle irate parents under these circumstances?
   - What role do you feel the principal should play in this situation?
   - What would be the next step to take about dealing with Alex and his parents?

2. Develop your own assessment and grading policy. Make sure that you list the following aspects in your policy:
   - The role of each formal assessment in your grading policy
   - The numerical value of each formal assessment
   - How each formal assessment contributes toward a specific grade (e.g., "The student needs 200 points for an A").
   - How to calculate final grades—by criterion referenced or norm referenced
   - Your policy on retention or academic failure

KEY CONCEPTS

Checklist of skills
Grade book
Grading on the basis of achievement
Grading on the basis of effort

Grading on the basis of process
Grading on the basis of progress
Letter grades

REVIEW QUESTIONS

1. Describe what is meant by *grading based on progress*.

2. Explain the concept of *rational relationship*.

3. List and describe the three major decisions that teachers must make about grades.

4. What are the five recommendations that Terwilliger (1989) makes about grading practices?

5. What does the research indicate about full grade-level retention?

6. Explain what the research indicates about the relationship between grading practices and inclusion policies.

7. Would you support a state or school report card? List your reasons for or against this proposal.

8. List and describe appropriate practices during parent conferences about grades.

SELF-ASSESSMENT

1. What are the two main reasons that the public wants traditional grading practices to remain in place?
   a. Progress and self-esteem
   b. Self-esteem and self-awareness
   c. Communication and self-esteem
   d. Communication and accountability
   e. Self-esteem and the legal issues involved in *Brown* vs. *Board of Education*

2. Constructivists often prefer to use the following type of grading practice:
   a. Grading on the basis of progress
   b. Grading on the basis of process
   c. Grading on the basis of effort
   d. Grading on the basis of achievement
   e. Grading on the basis of analysis

3. The research on retention appear to indicate that:
   a. Full grade-level retention is positive for all students
   b. Full grade-level retention is positive for male students
   c. Full grade-level retention does not increase subsequent achievement
   d. Full grade-level retention does increase later achievement
   e. Social and behavioral levels are never affected by full grade-level retention

4. Mrs. Merritt's grading system is based on the idea that students should be compared with each other. Therefore, Mrs. Merritt uses a system that ensures a given number of As, Bs, Cs, Ds, and Fs. Her system is most likely:
   a. Criterion referenced
   b. Norm referenced
   c. Mastery based
   d. Accountability based
   e. Cooperatively referenced

5. Mr. Hayes's method of grading is based on the idea that student improvement from the first day of class is the most important factor. So Mr. Hayes gives a pretest at the beginning of the term and a posttest at the end. What type of grading policy is he using?
   a. Grading on the basis of progress
   b. Grading on the basis of process
   c. Grading on the basis of effort
   d. Grading on the basis of achievement
   e. Grading on the basis of analysis

6. What are the two factors on which students may successfully challenge grades?
   a. Tough standards and charter schools
   b. Discriminatory practice and lack of rational relationship
   c. Grading on the basis of progress and grading on the basis of process
   d. Analytical scoring systems

Answers to Self-Assessment: 1. d, 2. b, 3. c, 4. b , 5. a, 6. b, 7. d

7. Veteran teachers generally advise one major thing to do in preparing for a parent conference. This is:
   a. Homogeneous grouping
   b. Grading on the basis of process
   c. Grade analysis
   d. Documentation

REFERENCES

Carey, L.M. (1988). *Measuring and evaluating school learning.* Boston: Allyn and Bacon.

Clark, D.C. (1969). Competition for grades and graduate school performance. *Journal of Educational Research, 62,* 351–354.

Glasser, W. (1969). *Schools without failure.* New York: Harper and Row.

Graham, S. (1989). Motivation in Afro-Americans. In G.L. Berry & J.K. Asamen (Eds.), *Black students: Psychosocial issues and academic achievement* (pp. 40–68). Newbury Park, CA: Sage.

Holmes, C.T., & Matthews, K.M. (1984). The effects of nonpromotion on elementary and junior high school pupils: A meta-analysis. *Review of Educational Research, 54,* 225–236.

Honan, W.H. (1998, September 2). SAT scores declines even as grades rise. *The New York Times,* p. A26.

Hopkins, K.D., Stanley, J.C., & Hopkins B.R. (1990). *Educational and psychological measurement and evaluation* (7th ed.). Englewood Cliffs, NJ: Prentice Hall.

Moos, R.H., & Moos, B.S. (1978). Classroom social climate and student absences and grades. *Journal of Educational Psychology, 70,* 263–269.

Mosenthal, J.H., & Ball, D.L. (1992). Constructing new forms of teaching: Subject matter knowledge in inservice teacher education. *Journal of Teacher Education, 43*(5), 347–356.

Paris, S.G., & Cunningham A.E. (1998). Children becoming students. In D.C. Berliner & R.C. Calfee (Eds.), *Handbook of educational psychology* (pp. 117–147). New York: Simon and Schuster.

Patton, J.R., & Polloway, E.A. (1994). Mild mental retardation. In N.G. Haring, L. McCormick, & T.G. Haring (Eds.), *Exceptional children and youth* (6th ed., pp. 215–260). New York: Macmillan.

Popham, W.J. (1990). *Modern educational measurement: A practitioner's perspective.* Englewood Cliffs, NJ: Prentice Hall.

Roderick, M. (1994). Grade retention and school dropout: Investigating an association. *American Educational Research Journal, 31,* 729–760.

Sengupta, S. (1997, October 22). Are teachers of teachers out of touch? *The New York Times,* p. A20.

Steinberg, J. (1997, December 14). In math standards California stresses skills over analysis. *The New York Times,* p. A14.

Stipek, D.J. (1996). Motivation and instruction. In D. Berliner & R. Calfee (Eds.), *Handbook of educational psychology* (pp. 85–109). New York: Macmillan.

Terwilliger, J.S. (1989). Classroom standard setting and grading practices. *Educational Measurement: Issues and Practices, 8*(2), 15–19.

Thorndike, R.M. (1997). *Measurement and evaluation in psychology and education* (6th ed.). Columbus, OH: Merrill.

Wagner, M., Newman, L., D'Amico, R., Jap, E.D., Butler-Dailin, P., Marder, C., & Cox, R. (1991). *Youth with disabilities: How are they doing?* Menlo Park, CA: SRI International.

Wiggins, G. (1989). Teaching to the (authentic) test. *Educational Leadership, 46*(7), 41–47.

Williams, R.G., & Ware, J.E. (1976). Validity of student ratings of instruction under different incentive conditions. *Journal of Educational Psychology, 68,* 48–56.

Wolfe, E., & Miller, T.R. (1997). Barriers to implementation of portfolio assessment in secondary education. *Applied Measurement in Education, 10,* 235–251.

Woolfolk, A. (2001). *Educational psychology* (8th ed.). Boston: Allyn and Bacon.

Zirkel, P.A., & Richardson, S.N. (1988). *A digest of Supreme Court decisions affecting education.* Bloomington, IN: Phi Delta Kappa Foundation.

CASE STUDY

Mrs. Campbell is the principal of a small elementary school in rural Appalachia. Her state has a policy of placing schools and school systems under direct state control if their achievement test scores fall 25 percent below the state-mandated standard. If the entire school system falls below the state standard, administrative personnel such as superintendents and assistant superintendents will be replaced. If it is an individual school, it means that the principal and assistant principals will be replaced.

Recently, Mrs. Campbell was notified that her school's test scores were 30 percent below the state-mandated standard. Her school superintendent called her to his office and explained that she has two years to reach the state standards. Mrs. Campbell replied that her school has the lowest average socioeconomic level of any school in the district. Her school also has the highest number of special education placements. The superintendent listened sympathetically and then stated, "It is not my decision. The state department of education makes the rules. I have to do what I am ordered to do."

What should Mrs. Campbell do about raising her school's test scores?

Should schools and school systems be required to have a certain level of test scores?

Should socioeconomic level and special education placements be considered in this kind of situation?

Should Mrs. Campbell lose her job because of her school's test scores?

Introduction

My first thought about standardized assessments is that you had better understand them in order to deal with them. In today's schools there seems to be no escaping these tests. You either effectively use these tests or you will be used by them. Like it or not, standardized assessments are part of the big stick wielded to make teachers accountable.

The big stick got a little bigger in 2002, when President Bush signed the **No Child Left Behind Act**. This law mandates an increasing amount of standardized testing of all school children in every state. For instance, every child in grades 3 through 8 must be tested annually in every state. Specific consequences are threatened, such as loss of federal funding for school systems that do not meet the required standards on these state tests.

Many teachers wonder how the field of education has reached this position with standardized assessments. It almost seems like the tail (testing) wags the dog (instruction). To understand how the United States has reached these present circumstances, a brief review of the background of standardized testing is needed.

Background of Standardized Assessments

Types of Standardized Assessments

The term **standardized assessment** means that all students answer the same items, take the test under the same conditions, and are scored the same way. All test scores are compared with a uniform reference group. This reference group provides the test norms. Generally, there is extensive pretesting and preselection of test items prior to the publication of standardized assessments. It is important to remember that these extensive pretesting and preselection procedures distinguish standardized assessments from other types of formal assessments. Test publishing companies spend a great deal of effort and money on establishing norms and pretesting questions.

There are three major categories of standardized assessments commonly used in public schools: achievement tests, aptitude tests, and intelligence tests. **Achievement tests** attempt to measure the present knowledge base of students in specific academic areas. Achievement tests are the dominant form of standardized assessments administered in schools. Academic **aptitude tests** attempt to measure the potential for learning in a given educational setting. Usually given in high school, aptitude tests typically are used for college admissions. **Intelligence tests** attempt to measure general mental ability. Currently, intelligence tests are primarily administered as part of the psychoeducational battery required by federal law for possible special education referral and placement.

Binet's Test

Standardized tests are not unique to twenty-first–century America. Standardized civil service tests were developed in China over 2,500 years ago. Standardized curriculum and testing practices also were developed in France and in the Soviet Union during the twentieth century.

The modern era of standardized testing began in 1904 with Alfred Binet, a French psychologist. Binet is credited with developing the first modern test of intelligence. It is from his original test that all other intelligence tests were derived. In fact, Binet's work was the catalyst for much of the standardized assessment field.

Looking back at Binet, you may want to condemn his work in light of the current emphasis on standardized testing. Yet you need to understand the context of his original contribution. Prior to Binet, mental retardation was diagnosed by medical doctors who looked for "degenerative physical signs" (Gould, 1981). Due to the influence of Darwin, these "degenerative signs" were considered "evolutionary throwbacks" (Gould, 1981). In effect, the mentally retarded were considered a return to an earlier stage of human evolution. Doctors examined children by looking for small skull sizes or certain facial features, such as large overhanging foreheads with large protruding eyes (Neanderthal features). There was no actual objective measurement of the children's intellectual abilities.

These practices began to change in 1904, when Binet received an appointment from the French government to help develop a program to diagnose and place children with mental retardation in special schools. As part of his appointment, Binet began work on a test to distinguish between children of normal intelligence and children of subnormal intelligence.

The impact of Binet and his test is significant. Binet changed the assessment of the mentally retarded from subjective observation to objective testing. The number of individuals incorrectly labeled as mentally retarded was reduced. This is probably the main reason why the Stanford-Binet Test of Mental Ability (the fourth edition of

Binet's original test) remains one of the two most commonly used measures of intelligence in public schools. In Binet's day, this test was given in an individual situation with one psychologist administering the test to one student.

American Hereditarians

When Binet's test was translated into English and transformed from an individual test to a group test, a number of problems occurred. First and foremost, the group of Americans who translated and transformed the test believed that intelligence was almost completely an inherited trait. They also believed that Binet's test (and their revision of it) fully measured this inborn ability. Their belief that intelligence was inherited led to their name, the **American Hereditarians.**

Think of it this way: The American Hereditarians believed their test measured an innate physical attribute in much the same way as a vision test given by an optometrist. When an optometrist says that a person has 20/40 vision, the individual takes it to mean that this measures a physical property of his or her eyes. The American Hereditarians believed that an IQ score measured a physical property of a person's brain. Since they believed that an IQ score also was due almost completely to genetic factors, environment was not believed to play any discernable role in IQ scores.

All of this would not have been so bad except that the American Hereditarians claimed that any group differences in IQ scores would have to be due to genetics rather than environment. Not only did they make claims that inborn differences occurred between racial groups, but the American Hereditarians also stated that certain ethnic groups—such as Russians, Italians, Hungarians, and Jews—were generally below normal in intelligence (Goddard, 1917).

These viewpoints led to a number of abuses of intelligence testing. Intelligence test scores sometimes were used to support racist policies in the United States. Immigration quotas were enacted in the 1920s to limit certain ethnic and racial groups believed to have below normal test scores (Gould, 1981). Involuntary sterilization of individuals with below normal intelligence test scores was conducted from the 1920s to the 1960s.

Transition to Achievement Tests

In the 1950s and 1960s, group intelligence tests were the dominant form of group testing in U.S. public schools. However, because of the history of being associated with discriminatory practices, IQ tests generally ceased to be used in a group form by the early 1970s. At that time, group IQ tests were replaced by group achievement tests.

Besides avoiding the association with discriminatory policies, achievement tests offered a more direct method for measuring actual classroom learning. Initially, achievement tests were used to review how individual students in a classroom compared with their classmates. Gradually, these tests assumed a larger and larger policy role in the 1980s and 1990s when tenure, funding, and merit pay decisions were increasingly based on student scores. Today, they have assumed the somewhat dubious title of "high-stakes tests."

The No Child Left Behind Act and Standardized Assessments

One of the major changes brought about by the No Child Left Behind Act is in the area of standardized assessments. In a historical sense, this federal legislation is the culmination of national trends in using standardized tests that go back to the late 1970s and early 1980s. It reflects the belief that increased standardized testing will result in increased accountability.

The No Child Left Behind Act requires specific performance standards and standardized test performance that proves these standards were met. These standards are to be developed by each individual state and are then to be approved by the federal Department of Education. These standards require annual standardized testing for all students in grades 3 through 8. Annual statewide progress goals must be documented to ensure that all groups of students reach proficiency on these standards within 12 years. Assessment results and state progress objectives must be broken down by poverty, race, ethnicity, disability, and limited English proficiency.

The emphasis in No Child Left Behind is on standards and assessments created by each individual state. Therefore, each state is granted the freedom to make choices about their own standards and assessments. Many states have developed, or are in the process of developing, their own statewide standardized assessments. States also can set their own assessment standards and criteria for improvement. One outcome is an apparent increase in the use of statewide assessments for individual states rather than increases in any type of national test.

Standardized Achievement Tests

Like swallows returning to Capistrano, every spring the achievement tests return to the classroom. The tests return each year for a week full of anxiety and concern. Then they are gone until next year. But like the question of global warming, the issue of standardized testing seems to heat up and become more intense each year. As mentioned at the beginning of this chapter, the role of standardized achievement tests has become a national policy issue. Achievement tests have moved from just "high-stakes testing" to "high-stakes politics."

Types of Standardized Achievement Tests

Different types of standardized achievement tests range from the springtime tests that nearly everyone takes to specialized tests for individuals with learning disabilities. All these categories are designed to measure knowledge acquired through classroom learning and to provide an estimate of the overall knowledge base of students. There are three main types of standardized achievement tests:

Categories of Standardized Achievement Tests
1. **Group achievement tests** assess general and basic skills of large groups of students across the different states. They are based on national norms and developed by national test publishing companies.
2. **Statewide assessment tests** assess a variety of skills of students within one state and are aligned with state standards and instructional objectives. These tests are usually developed by one state and often in consultation with major test publishing companies.
3. **Diagnostic achievement tests** assess specific skills of students in areas such as reading or mathematics. Developed by major test publishing companies, these tests most often are used to diagnose specific learning problems or learning disabilities.

Standardized Group Achievement Tests

Group achievement tests are designed to measure the learning of general and basic skills by large groups of students. They determine such things as grade-level norms, school-level norms, and school district norms. These tests provide classroom teachers with a printout of the scores of each individual student. The results also provide comparative information about each student with the normative group for the test. Most tests also provide a printout of how each school compares with school district scores, state scores, and national norms.

Group achievement tests are made by commercial testing and publishing companies. Until recently, these tests dominated the achievement test market and tended to dominate the standardized testing market. They are geared toward a national market and provide national norms. A number of such achievement tests are on the market today.

Available Group Achievement Tests

I have contacted every state department of education testing administration bureau about their use of standardized assessments and have found that 29 states continue to use group achievement tests. This number has decreased in the last decade. In the 2001–2002 school year, the following three tests accounted for most of the group achievement tests used in public schools:

1. Stanford Achievement Test (9th edition)
2. Iowa Tests of Basic Skills
3. Terra Nova/Comprehensive Tests of Basic Skills

The question is always asked as to which of these assessments is most appropriate to use. Perhaps the best response is that given by Thorndike (1997):

The tests are similar in terms of the time and effort that have gone into their development and the time it takes to administer them. Their overall quality is high, and they cover the same range of students and have similar content areas. . . . The test development and norming procedures are generally exemplary. (p. 267)

Making a distinction among the different types of general achievement tests is difficult. In deciding which test to use, the best advice is to *choose the most recently revised test*. The most recently revised assessment will generally have more accurate norms and will include the latest advances in test item development.

Group Achievement Test Content

The content of achievement tests is geared toward specific knowledge levels believed appropriate for a certain age or grade. Although there are some minor variations among tests, all of the achievement batteries attempt to cover a broad range of academic knowledge expected of most students. The areas that are measured include reading comprehension, vocabulary, spelling, science, social science, listening skills, mathematical computation, and mathematical concepts. Some of the upper-level forms, developed for middle and high school students, also cover study skills and more advanced math areas. An example of the type of content available in achievement tests follows.

Sample Achievement Test Questions

A blacksmith is someone who:
a. makes horseshoes
b. fixes pipes
c. builds houses
d. chops wood

33 is 50% of:
a. 16.7
b. 60
c. 66
d. 96

Which volume of the encyclopedia should be examined for information about Kit Carson?
a. Volume C
b. Volume F
c. Volume K
d. Volume S

As can be seen with these questions, the type of item used is multiple choice. All of the general achievement test batteries are oriented toward multiple-choice items that measure basic skills in specific academic areas. As previously noted in earlier chapters, this type of test item is widely used and is widely criticized. Multiple-choice tests appear to best measure specific basic skills but not necessarily the application of these skills to new situations.

Administering Group Achievement Tests

Group achievement tests present a series of academic subtests that must be completed in a particular time frame. For example, a reading subtest may have a 30-minute time limit, whereas a math subtest may have a 45-minute time limit. The tests are administered in group situations and must be monitored by appropriate school personnel to ensure the integrity of the test and to maintain the time limits and protocols for the tests.

There has been a great deal of concern that the integrity of achievement tests may have been compromised. Several problems can occur if the tests are not properly administered. One major problem is that the test norms become invalid if the integrity of the test is compromised. If the norms are invalid, comparisons between schools or school systems become invalid. In responding to these problems, the American Psychological Association, in conjunction with the American Educational Research Association and the National Council on Measurements in Education, developed a series of standards for test administration, scoring, interpretation, and evaluation (American Psychological Association, 1985). The APA guidelines have strict instructions for those who administer the tests:

1. The test administrator is responsible for strictly following the procedures given in the test manual.
2. The test administrator is responsible for eliminating the possibility of cheating by using special seating arrangements, proctors, or identification methods for examinees.
3. The test administrator is responsible for ensuring the security and integrity of the tests by keeping them in a locked storage area.

Another area of concern in test administration is when teachers attempt to teach the test. It is unethical for teachers to examine the content of standardized tests to determine what will be taught in their classrooms. (Further information on test preparation polices are provided in the final chapter of this textbook.)

An additional area of concern in standardized test administration is in providing special testing conditions for students with disabilities. Students with disabilities have the right to special testing conditions. Reasonable assessment accommodations are guaranteed not only to those with physical or sensory disabilities, such as visual impairments, but also to those with diagnosed learning disabilities.

Statewide Assessments

Statewide assessments share a great deal of similarity with group achievement tests. In fact, the two terms are often used synonymously. This can cause a good deal of confusion, since there are some important differences between the two types of assessments. The major distinction between the two is that statewide assessment tests are designed to assess the standards and objectives of just one particular state, whereas group achievement tests are designed for a national population. This usually means that local and state educators are involved in the construction of statewide assessments, typically in consultation with a major testing company. This also means that the assessment is valid only in the state for which it was designed. This limits state-by-state comparisons.

Statewide assessments are called by many different terms (some of which cannot be repeated in a textbook). Among the terms used are *proficiency test, competency test, minimum skills test,* and *graduation test.* Generally, statewide assessments are criterion-referenced assessments, which evaluate students on the basis of a specific performance standard. For example, a statewide assessment standard might use cut-off scores of 50, 70, or 100 as the performance criteria on certain subtests. Regardless of how many students reach these criteria, those students meeting or surpassing the performance standard on the statewide assessment will pass the test. Group achievement tests are generally norm referenced in their scoring procedures.

Point/Counterpoint: Standardized Testing Leads to Standardized Teaching

Point

Critics of high-stakes, standardized testing state that it simply leads to standardized teaching. In effect, enacting performance standards that are linked to test outcomes has a direct effect on teachers and instruction. Standardized testing simply turns teaching into a robot-like activity. Teachers become concerned with what it takes to enable students to pass the tests. If teaching to the test is what it takes, that is what teachers will do. Ultimately, teaching may become a situation where all teachers will be teaching on the same page of the same book on the same day. Meeting performance standards as determined by standardized tests are already resulting in some schools being in this situation.

Counterpoint

Supporters of high-stakes testing reject the link between standardized testing and standardized teaching. Supporters claim that performance standards, with appropriately measured outcomes, are simply another way to do what teachers have always done in the classroom. Using standardized tests is just a more reliable method of measuring these outcomes than are teacher-constructed assessments. If the standards are appropriately linked with the curriculum, then it does not matter if the teacher teaches to the test or not. Good standards, linked to the curriculum and instruction, are the key to student learning. As long as the teacher meets the standards, then the method of instruction is not important. The students have demonstrated that they have obtained the desired knowledge. Having a certain knowledge base and being able to demonstrate it on a test are the two important factors in the classroom.

As mentioned earlier, I contacted each state department of education about its testing policies. In the 2001–2002 school year, 39 states used their own statewide assessments. This number has increased in the last decade. There does seem to be a tendency toward developing and using statewide assessments as an alternative to the group achievement tests. Some states continue to use both standardized group achievement tests and statewide assessment tests.

Diagnostic Achievement Tests

Diagnostic achievement tests generally are used in two ways: (1) as a screening test to pinpoint specific academic problems, usually in math or reading; and (2) as part of a psychoeducational battery to determine special education placements.

Most diagnostic achievement tests are given in an individual situation and are either reading tests, writing tests, or mathematics tests. As reported by Salvia and Ysseldyke (1998), reading difficulties are the single-most frequent reason for referring a student for any type of psychoeducational assessment.

There are many different types of diagnostic achievement tests. Included among the more common ones are:

1. The Woodcock-Johnson Psycho-Educational Battery-Revised
2. The Key Math-Revised Inventory
3. The Peabody Individual Achievement Test-Revised
4. Stanford Diagnostic Reading and Mathematics Tests
5. The Wide Range Achievement Test-Revised,
6. The Metropolitan Diagnostic Reading, Mathematics, and Language Tests

Content of Diagnostic Achievement Tests

Since diagnostic tests usually focus on a specific subject area, the content of diagnostic achievement tests tends to be much more subject specific than group achievement tests. Therefore, the amount of assessed skills per subject tend to be greater than in group achievement tests. For example, some diagnostic reading tests cover such skills as visual and auditory discrimination, phonetic analysis, reading comprehension, vocabulary, word-attack skills, and reading rates. Math diagnostic tests cover such areas as time measurement, word problems, fractions, numeration, numerical reasoning, and geometry, as well as the traditional areas of addition, subtraction, multiplication, and division.

Administering and Interpreting Diagnostic Achievement Tests

There is some question in the educational and psychological communities about who is qualified to administer and interpret tests that lead to a psychoeducational diagnosis.

Group achievement tests are available for teachers to administer and interpret. Individual intelligence tests, such as the Stanford-Binet and Wechsler Battery, are available only to qualified school psychologists. Diagnostic achievement tests fall somewhere in between.

In regard to whether classroom teachers are qualified to administer and interpret diagnostic achievement tests, McLoughlin and Lewis (1990) address the problem in their review of the Key Math-R, a diagnostic achievement test for mathematics: "No special training is required to administer the Key Math-R.... Test interpretation, however, is best accomplished by professionals with training in psychometrics and experience in teaching mathematics" (p. 342). Thus, McLoughlin and Lewis claim that classroom teachers are quite capable of administering such tests. Their background and training for appropriate interpretation, however, may be lacking. Many classroom teachers may not have the basic training in testing and measurement necessary to appropriately interpret certain tests.

On the other hand, present practices in public schools often require teachers to administer and interpret a series of screening tests, which may include a diagnostic achievement test. These screening tests are completed prior to a referral for a complete psychoeducational evaluation. (The psychoeducational evaluation is administered by a school psychologist prior to special education placement.) Such practices force the classroom teacher to play an important initial role in administering and interpreting tests. These tests often become a factor in determining special education placements.

Aptitude Tests

There are two major aptitude tests used today: the American College Test (ACT) and the Scholastic Assessment Test (SAT). In general, these tests are used for college admissions and placement purposes. They typically are administered during the junior or senior year of high school.

American College Test (ACT)

The American College Test, first used in 1959, is designed as an aptitude test to predict college success. A number of colleges base part of their admission requirements on ACT scores. The test contains four subtests and a composite score. The four subtests are English Usage, Social Studies Reading, Natural Science Reading, and Mathematics Usage. The average composite score for the ACT was 20.8 in 2002 (American College Test, 2002).

Officials administering the ACT program note that students who completed at least 4 years of English, 3 years of math, 3 years of social studies, and 3 years of natural sciences in high school had an average composite score that was almost 2 points higher than the national average (Wilson, 1991). This finding would seem to indicate that scores on the ACT can be affected by academic preparation, especially with math scores.

Scholastic Assessment Test (SAT)

The Scholastic Aptitude Test, developed in 1926, is the oldest and most frequently used academic aptitude test. The SAT consists of two separate subtests, Verbal and Mathematical, which are then combined to give a composite score. The Verbal component is largely based on reading comprehension. The Mathematical component consists of basic mathematics with some elementary algebra and geometry. The average SAT scores in 2002 were 504 Verbal and 516 Mathematical (College Board, 2002).

Controversy swirls around college aptitude tests. High school grades are a better predictor of college grades than ACT or SAT scores. Nevertheless, using a formula that combines high school grades with aptitude scores results in a better prediction of college grades than using just high school grades. Part of the reason for this seeming contradiction is that there is such a variation between high schools in their grading policies. An A at one high school may be equivalent to a C at another school. Proponents of aptitude tests claim that the tests evaluate students on a common standard, whereas high school grades often do not.

However, as pointed out in previous chapters, the SAT and ACT have problems with ethnic differences, gender differences, or both. Critics have suggested changes in these tests to limit possible test bias. Because of these problems, a number of colleges and universities have scaled back their use of these two tests. In response to these controversies, the SAT has announced its intention to include an essay question as part of the test.

Intelligence Tests

A number of intelligence tests (or mental ability tests) are used in public schools, but the two most frequently used contemporary individual intelligence test batteries are the Stanford-Binet Intelligence Scale (4th ed.; 1986) and the Wechsler Intelligence Scale for Children-III (1992). Different school psychologists may use either of these tests, usually as a standard part of the psychoeducational assessment for possible special education placement.

Stanford-Binet Intelligence Scale (4th Edition)

The Stanford-Binet Intelligence Scale (1986) has undergone a number of transformations from the original English-language version developed by Terman (1916). The latest revision of the Stanford-Binet is the fourth edition, which addresses some of the criticisms that have been leveled at the Stanford-Binet test and at intelligence tests in general.

In responding to these criticisms, the Stanford-Binet Intelligence Scale (1986) generally has avoided using the term *intelligence quotient* or *IQ score*. The *IQ score* has been replaced with the *standard age score* (SAS). This change in terminology came after the term *IQ score* was removed from a number of group intelligence tests. Now, the only major individual intelligence test to consistently use the term is the Wechsler Battery.

The Stanford-Binet was criticized for being too heavily weighted toward vocabulary and reasoning skills. The new version attempts to correct for such biases by increasing the variety of subtests included in the battery. There are now 15 subtests in the latest Stanford-Binet scale. These are grouped into four ability scales: Verbal Reasoning, Abstract/Visual Reasoning, Quantitative Reasoning, and Short Term Memory.

Wechsler Test Battery

The Wechsler Battery of Intelligence tests is divided into three separate versions. The Wechsler Preschool Primary Scale of Intelligence-Revised (WPPSI-R) (1989) is for ages 3 to 7; the Wechsler Intelligence Scale for Children-III (WISC-III; 1992) is for ages 6 to 16; and the Wechsler Adult Intelligence Scale-Revised (WAIS-III; 1997) is for ages 16 years and older.

The WISC-III test is one of the most commonly used tests in public schools. With a few exceptions, the WPPSI-R and the WAIS-III follow the same general format. The WISC-III is divided into two basic sections: verbal and performance. The verbal section examines reasoning and vocabulary skills and the performance section examines visual-spatial skills. The combined score from these two sections yields a full-scale IQ score. Thus, the examiner can obtain three IQ scores from this test.

Statistical Measures in Testing

A number of statistical techniques were created in conjunction with the development of standardized assessments. Many of these techniques are important for you to understand in order to interpret the test scores. As a teacher , it is essential that you are able to understand and interpret the test scores of your students in order to explain these results to both the students and parents. Besides interpreting the tests, you also have to make academic decisions based on student test scores. Included among them are decisions about whether a child needs special education and what types of individualized educational programs are needed for students.

This section will explain the test score information using several statistical terms: *mean, median, mode, range, percentile rank, standard deviation*, and *stanine scores*. Besides these statistical elements, there are several other concepts that teachers need to understand for scoring, administering, and interpreting tests: these are *raw scores, standard scores, age equivalent scores, grade equivalent scores, basals*, and *ceilings*.

Measures of Central Tendency

Measures of central tendency provide a description of the middle or central points of a particular distribution. The three basic measures of central tendency are the mean, the median, and the mode. Among the various measures of central tendency, the best known and most commonly used measure is the **mean,** or arithmetic average. To refresh your memory for computing the mean, the formula is the sum of the scores in the distribution divided by the number of scores in the distribution. For example, if the distribution is 12, 14, 29, 33, 45, 51, the mean is 30.667.

The **median** is the middle most case in a distribution. In effect, the median is the number that splits the distribution into two equal halves. Think of the median on the interstate, it separates the cars into two equal groups (at least we hope so). When the distribution contains an odd number of cases, the median will be the middle value in the distribution. The median is the middle-most case in a distribution without regard to the values of the cases. For example, in the distribution 190, 100, 75, 50, 45, the median is 75.

The **mode** is the most frequently occurring number in a distribution. For example, in the distribution 120, 100, 100, 85, 72, 40, the mode is 100. There can be more than one mode in the distribution. When there are two modes, the distribution is termed *bimodal* (though some of my students call it a *co-mode*).

Because of the way standardized tests are constructed, the mean, median, and mode on such tests nearly always have the same value. The mean, median, and mode on both the Stanford-Binet and the WISC-III is 100. A number of other standardized tests, such as the Wide Range Achievement Test-Revised, also have 100 as their mean, median, and mode.

Measures of Variability

Measures of variability are used to reflect the variation of scores. Like measures of central tendency, they provide a method for summarizing one part of a distribution of scores into a single number. There are two commonly used measures of variability in the educational assessment field: range and standard deviation. The **range** is simply the highest number in the distribution minus the lowest number.

Standard deviation represents a standard method of determining how scores deviate from the mean. The standard deviation also has an important relationship in describing the normal curve. The formula for deriving a standard deviation involves the following four steps:

Calculating the Standard Deviation

1. Subtract the mean from each raw score. The remainder will be the difference score; for example X (the number) – M (the mean) = d (the difference score).

   X M d
   18 – 14 =   4
   16 – 14 =   2
   14 – 14 =   0
   12 – 14 = –2
   10 – 14 = –4

2. Square each difference score and sum the squares.

    4 squared = 16
    2 squared = 4
    0 squared = 0
    −2 squared = 4
    −4 squared = 16
    16 + 4 + 0 + 4 + 16 = 40

3. Divide the sum of the squares by the number of scores: 40 divided by 5 = 8.

4. Take the square root of this dividend: The square root of 8 is 2.828.

5. The standard deviation is 2.828.

As indicated in this example, the standard deviation represents a standard method for determining how scores deviate from the mean. The relationship of standard deviation is represented by the normal curve, which has considerable use in educational practices. Figure 10.1 shows the relationship between the normal curve and standard deviation.

As indicated in the normal curve, the percentage of scores between the mean and one standard deviation above the mean is approximately 34 percent. The percentage of scores between one standard deviation above the mean and two standard deviations above the mean is approximately 13.5 percent. The percentages in the graph will always remain constant as long as the distribution is normal, and the percentages will always be symmetrical as long as the distribution forms a normal curve.

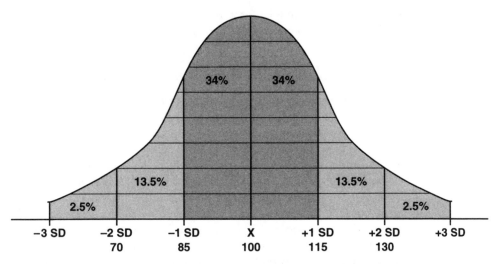

FIGURE 10.1 Relationship between the Normal Curve and Standard Deviation

In counting the percentage of scores between one end of the distribution and the mean, the result is 2.5 percent + 13.5 percent + 34 percent = 50 percent. In effect, 50 percent of the scores are below the mean and 50 percent of the scores are above the mean. The percentage of scores falling between the end of the distribution and two standard deviations from the mean is approximately 2.5 percent.

Along with the mean, the standard deviation is reported in manuals for standardized assessments. For the WISC-III, the overall mean is 100 with a standard deviation of 15. This information provides a gauge for determining if a sample of students taking the test is like the population for whom the test was normed. If the sample is normally distributed, then approximately 34 percent of the students should fall between the mean and one standard deviation below the mean. Thus, 34 percent of the students should fall between 85 (–1 SD) and 100. Most of the students (68 percent) should fall between 85 and 115.

Standard deviation often is used as part of a system for diagnosing children with disabilities. This is particularly true with learning disabilities and mental retardation. The next chapter presents specific information on how standard deviation is used with special education.

Stanine scores are a scoring system based on the normal curve. **Stanines** have a mean of 5 and a standard deviation of 2. On the WISC-III, an IQ score of 115 would produce a stanine score of 7. Stanines have limited use and generally can be used only with scores that fall within 2 SDs from the mean. On the WISC-III, an IQ score of 100 would result in a stanine score of 5.

Although not generally included as a measure of variability, percentile ranks are a frequently reported measure of student ability. They do provide a measure of how a student scores in relationship to other students. The **percentile rank** is a point in a distribution of scores, indicating the percentage of people who scored below that point. For instance, scoring at the 50th percentile rank means the student scored better than 50 percent of the people taking the test. A student who scored at the tenth percentile rank did better than 10 percent of the people taking the test.

Scoring Procedures for Standardized Assessments

Raw scores are the actual responses of the student to the test items. In effect, they are the number of items on a given scale or subscale for which the student obtained a correct response. For example, on the WISC-III, the raw score on the vocabulary subtest is the number of words the student correctly defined, multiplied by two. (The WISC-III gives two points for each correct definition of the stimulus word.)

Standard scores are raw scores transformed to some type of common scale, standard scale, or normal curve equivalent. For example, on the WISC-III, a raw score of 50 on the vocabulary test means that the student correctly answered 25 of the items on that subtest. This raw score of 50 is then transformed to a standard score of 10 based on a standard score procedure used by the test publishers.

Age equivalent scores are scores normed for a given age group. For example, if a 5-year-old student correctly answers an appropriate number of items designed for the average 5-year-old, the student will receive an age equivalent score of 5 years old. However, that's about as far as one can go with these scores. Age equivalent and grade equivalent scores are frequently misinterpreted. They pretty much relate only to a specific age or grade. For example, the reading score for a 7-year-old student indicates that he is reading on 9.5 age level. It doesn't mean that he has mastered the reading skills of a 9½-year-old. What it means is that the 7-year-old is reading above average for his age group. That's it and that's all. Most experts recommend staying away from age and grade equivalent scores because parents misunderstand them. Stick with percentiles.

Grade equivalent scores are scores normed for a given grade level. For example, if a student answers an appropriate number of items for the average third-grader, the student receives a third-grade equivalent score. But what was just said about age equivalent scores applies to these scores as well. A child who is in fourth grade but whose math scores are at a 7.3 grade level has not mastered the math skills for seventh grade. All it means is that the child is well above the rest of the fourth-graders. It does not mean that the child is equivalent to the children actually in seventh grade. Conversely, a below-level grade equivalent score simply means that the child has scored lower than her grade-level peers. It does not mean that she is actually reading at that low a grade level.

Basals are the baseline or initial testing level of the child. It is any point on a test where the subject successfully passes enough items to establish a reasonable starting point for the test administration. For example, a basal may be the most advanced point on the test where the child obtained three or five correct responses in a row.

Ceilings are the upper limit of the test administration. The ceiling is the point where the subject obtained the last correct response before missing the designated number of items that ended the testing on that particular scale.

Conducting Conferences about Test Scores

One of the many roles of teachers is to interpret test scores to students and parents in a conference. A few simple guidelines apply. Conferences about test scores, as well as about grades, must be held in private. Besides the previously mentioned Buckley Amendment, there are sound ethical reasons to protect the confidentiality of academic records. Ethically, it creates serious classroom problems if test scores become commonly known. Students and parents will make unfavorable comparisons about classmates, which may engender a great deal of unnecessary and unwanted competition in and out of the classroom.

Conferences about test scores should be viewed in a formative rather than summative manner. Test scores generally should be seen as a way of making improvements. Among the goals of the conference should be a plan or a contract with the student for necessary improvements. Conferences should also help teachers and parents examine differences between various subtests of the assessments or discrepancies between classroom assessment performance and standardized assessment performance. Such discrepancies may indicate a lack of motivation or some type of specific learning problem. In either case, these types of discrepancies need to be explored until a satisfactory explanation can be found.

When interpreting standardized assessment scores, I find that both teachers and parents have the easiest time with understanding percentiles. Percentile scores are not subject to the same statistical problems as are grade equivalent or age equivalent scores. Unless there is a good reason to do otherwise, I would generally recommend that percentiles be the score provided to the parents.

Chapter Summary

This chapter examined a number of different categories and aspects of standardized assessments. The three major categories of standardized assessments used in U.S. schools are achievement tests, aptitude tests, and intelligence tests. Achievement tests are the most commonly used category. In the last three decades, group achievement tests and statewide assessments have increasingly been used to make major educational funding and policy decisions. These decisions have included such areas as funding formulas, personnel and tenure decisions, and merit pay decisions.

The second part of this chapter reviewed a number of statistical and scoring methods used with standardized assessments. Measures of central tendency and measures of variability were presented. In addition, a number of different scoring systems—such as stanines, percentiles, age equivalent scores, and grade equivalent scores—were also presented. The last part of the chapter included some suggestions on conducting parent conferences about standardized assessments.

CASE STUDY EPILOGUE

Mrs. Campbell has decided to undertake a series of steps to improve her school's test scores. Her first step is to call a series of faculty meetings to generate ideas for developing instruction, transforming assessments practices, and preparing for standardized assessments. The faculty divide into work groups to plan for these areas.

Mrs. Campbell also announces a policy where instruction and assessment will be more closely linked together at the school. She brings in two assessment experts who help teachers to increase their use of informal assessments in the classroom. The experts also help teachers to better develop their formal classroom assessments.

A program for test preparation is initiated by Mrs. Campbell. This program focuses on a number of different areas: time management, using different test formats, and reading to identify important information. All students practice this program one time a week during the spring term.

And last, Mrs. Campbell begins a parental involvement program at the school. Parents become involved in both instruction and assessment practices. They tutor students in reading and math and they help in training students about test-taking strategies.

CHAPTER ACTIVITIES

Websites

http://www.nochildleftbehind.gov. The No Child Left Behind site is graphically pleasing and offers the basics and specifics of the federal program. Parents can learn what they can do to help their child succeed. Teachers can get tips, news, and recent legislation, as well as find their state contact person.

http://www.edexcellence.net The Thomas B. Fordham foundation offers ideas and tips for educational reform. The standards and assessment section contains numerous links to current research on state and national assessments.

www.achieve.org The goal of this website is "to provide high-quality information and advice as states work to raise standards, improve accountability and increase student achievement." In the resource section, viewers may choose their state to be directly linked to those resources. Also, the site contains a list of educational organizations links.

Portfolio Activities

1. Review Mrs. Campbell's situation in the Chapter Case Study. What should Mrs. Campbell do about her school's test scores? Write an essay in your portfolio that addresses Mrs. Campbell's circumstances. Take a position for and then against each of the following issues raised in the Case Study:
   - Schools and school systems should be required to have a certain level of test scores.
   - Principals, teachers, and superintendents should lose their jobs when test scores are below a certain level.
   - Socioeconomic level and special education placements should be considered in making decisions about test scores.
   - Schools should devote a major part of their academic year in preparing for the state tests.

2. Write a second essay for your portfolio that compares and contrasts the use of group achievement tests versus the use of statewide assessment tests. Describe two positive and two negative features concerning each of these two types of assessment procedures. Which one of these assessments would you choose? Provide a detailed rationale about your choice.

KEY CONCEPTS

Achievement tests	Median
Age equivalent scores	Mode
American Hereditarians	No Child Left Behind Act
Aptitude tests	Percentile rank
Basals	Range
Ceilings	Raw score
Diagnostic achievement tests	Standard deviation
Grade equivalent scores	Standard scores
Group achievement tests	Standardized assessment
Intelligence tests	Stanines
Mean	Statewide assessment tests

REVIEW QUESTIONS

1. List and describe the three major types of standardized assessments used in public schools.

2. Explain the history of IQ tests and why group IQ tests are no longer used in public schools.

3. List and describe the differences between group achievement tests, statewide assessment tests, and diagnostic achievement tests.

4. What is the difference between a basal and a ceiling in testing children?

5. Explain the differences between grade equivalent scores and age equivalent scores.

6. Describe the different types of measures of variability.

7. What are some of the major controversies about college aptitude tests?

8. Review and explain the history of achievement tests in public schools.

SELF-ASSESSMENT

1. The sum of the scores divided by the number of scores is the equation for:
   a. Standard deviation
   b. Mean
   c. Variance
   d. Correlation
   e. Range

2. In the normal curve, the percentage of scores between the mean and one standard deviation above the mean is:
   a. 38%

Answers to Self-Assessment: 1. b, 2. d, 3. b, 4. c, 5. b, 6. e, 7. d, 8. d

    b. 22%
    c. 16.5%
    d. 34%
    e. 50%

3. The most common type of standardized test given to elementary school students is:
    a. Aptitude test
    b. Achievement test
    c. Intelligence test
    d. Personality test
    e. Attitude test

4. Terra Nova is listed as the following type of test:
    a. Intelligence
    b. Aptitude
    c. Achievement
    d. Creativity
    e. Personality

5. Standardized academic tests that measure the potential for academic ability are termed:
    a. Intelligence
    b. Aptitude
    c. Achievement
    d. Creativity
    e. Personality

6. The average score on an IQ test is:
    a. 85
    b. 90
    c. 70
    d. 115
    e. 100

7. The two most commonly used intelligence tests are:
    a. Wechsler and the GRE
    b. SAT and Stanford-Binet
    c. CTBS and the Stanford-9
    d. Wechsler and the Stanford-Binet
    e. DAT and the CTBS

8. When raw scores are transformed to some type of common scale, standard scale, or normal curve equivalent, they are called:
    a. IQ scores
    b. Median scores
    c. Standard deviation scores
    d. Standard scores
    e. Aptitude scores

REFERENCES

American College Test. (2002). *2002 National Score Report.* Iowa City, IA: ACT Inc.

American Psychological Association. (1985). *Standards for educational and psychological tests.* Washington, DC: Author.

Binet, A., & Simon, T. (1973). *The development of intelligence in children.* Reprint of the 1916 edition by Classics in Psychology. (Elizabeth S. Kite, Translator). New York: Arno Press.

College Board. (2002). *College board seniors' national report, 2002.* Princeton, NJ: Author.

Goddard, H.H. (1917). Mental tests and the immigrant. *Journal of Delinquency, 2,* 243–277.

Gould, S.J. (1981). *The mismeasure of man.* New York: W. W. Norton.

McLoughlin, J.A., & Lewis, R.B. (1990). *Assessing special students.* Columbus, OH: Merrill.

Salvia, J., & Ysseldyke, J.E. (1998). *Assessment* (7th ed.). Boston: Houghton Mifflin.

Stanford-Binet Intelligence Scale, 4th ed. (1986). Chicago: Riverside Publishing.

Terman, L.M. (1916). *The measurement of intelligence.* Boston: Houghton Mifflin.

Thorndike, R.M. (1997). *Measurement and evaluation in psychology and education* (6th ed.). Columbus, OH: Merrill.

Wechsler, D. (1989). *Manual for the Wechsler Preschool Primary Scale of Intelligence-Revised.* New York: The Psychological Corporation.

Wechsler, D. (1992*). Manual for the Wechsler Intelligence Scale for Children-III.* New York: The Psychological Corporation.

Wilson, R. (1991). Average score on ACT held steady. *The Chronicle of Higher Education, 38,* 2, 42.

11 Assessments, At-Risk Students, and Special Education

CASE STUDY

Mrs. Maynard has taught second grade for three years in a wealthy, suburban school district in the northeast. Her teacher education major was exclusively in kindergarten through sixth-grade regular classrooms. She had one survey class in special education.

The school district in which Mrs. Maynard teaches is noted for its innovative programs. There are a number of very active parents' groups. Among them is a local parents' advocacy group for children with disabilities. This advocacy group recently announced its overwhelming support for a full-inclusion policy.

During the spring term, a new school superintendent was appointed by the school district. The new superintendent announced that he will implement the new full-inclusion policy. This means that all special education children, regardless of their disability, will be placed in regular education settings. Children with disabilities will include the full range of impairments, such as visually impaired, mentally retarded, and those with physical disabilities.

Many of the teachers in the district have questioned their own training and ability to handle children with disabilities. Some principals have stated that their classrooms do not have the appropriate physical facilities to accommodate some of the children with disabilities. Nevertheless, the local school board has agreed to implement this new policy. Mrs. Maynard is left with the following questions:

What impact will this policy have on a second-grade teacher?

How will this policy change her assessment methods?

What type of reasonable accommodations could be made for these children?

What type of changes might be needed about playground activities or physical education?

What type of additional training or extra educational support would be needed?

How would you feel about teaching a classroom of 25 children, which included some children with severe disabilities?

Introduction

There is an increasing emphasis on inclusion policies for children with disabilities, but exactly what inclusion policies are we talking about? Inclusion policies range from a policy of varying placements based on the degree of disability to a policy of full inclusion mandating that all children with disabilities be placed in the mainstream classroom (Garigulo, 2003). Full-inclusion practices can radically affect the regular classroom and transform how teachers assess their students.

Current special education policies place primary-grade teachers on the frontline for assessing, diagnosing, and referring children with disabilities. If full-inclusion policies are mandated, you will need to instruct and assess children with a variety of different disabilities. One goal of this chapter is to provide you with the information to understand assessment practices and special education. This chapter also will examine the different types of assessments used to determine and classify children with disabilities.

The first section examines the area of children at risk, as well as the relationship between at-risk factors and disabilities. The second section reviews the categories of special education with an emphasis on the four most common types of special education placements: learning disabilities, speech impairments, emotional disorders, and mental retardation. The chapter ends with a discussion of assessment accommodations for children with disabilities.

Children at Risk

Children at risk for educational problems include children who have certain predisposing factors that may cause them to be low educational achievers, to be placed in special education, to drop out, or to be retained. There are two major categories of at-risk factors: biological risk factors and environmental risk factors (Overton, 2003). Biological risk factors include prenatal problems, maternal drug/alcohol use during pregnancy, toxin exposure, or birthing problems. Environmental risk factors usually are family and social interaction problems during early childhood, such as abuse or neglect, and often stem from adverse socioeconomic conditions. Both types of risk factors can produce a variety of physical, developmental, or psychological disabilities.

The effects of these at-risk factors on mental and physical functioning are only now becoming fully documented. It is clear that the degree of problems produced by these conditions range from the relatively mild to the very severe. Thus, the mental abilities for at-risk children range from near normal intelligence to severe mental retardation (Stevens & Price, 1992). Their physical problems have a similar variability. Assessing and evaluating these children in a regular classroom may require the teacher to develop unique and special accommodations. Two biological at-risk factors currently undergoing considerable scrutiny for producing disabilities are fetal alcohol syndrome and lead exposure.

Fetal Alcohol Syndrome

Fetal alcohol syndrome (FAS) is the single leading cause of mental retardation in the world (Burgess & Streissguth, 1992). FAS is a medical diagnosis that is based on three distinct characteristics in the child (Burgess & Streissguth, 1992):

1. Growth deficiency, such as low birth weight
2. Certain specific facial and physical abnormalities
3. Central nervous system dysfunctions

Burgess and Streissguth (1992) point out that a new term is being used in this area: *fetal alcohol effect (FAE).* This syndrome also involves women who drink alcohol during pregnancy. However, the physical effects of the drinking on the child are not nearly as pronounced as with FAS. For instance, the facial and physical abnormalities are much less present or even absent. However, the cognitive deficits are as severe in FAE as they are in FAS.

In terms of distinctive behavioral effects, Burgess and Streissguth (1992) indicate some common characteristics of children with fetal alcohol syndrome and fetal alcohol effect. The major behavioral characteristics are high levels of activity, impulsivity, distractibility, and poor communication skills.

In terms of mental and educational functioning, the average IQ scores for this population are between 65 and 70 (Burgess & Streissguth, 1992). Researchers stress the need for early assessments and intervention in this area. The most important areas of educational intervention are in teaching communication skills and in improving adaptive living skills.

Many inclusion policies currently place these children in regular classrooms. In terms of assessment practices, children with FAS or FAE usually will need assessments similar to the mildly mentally retarded or to the borderline mentally retarded. As mentioned in an earlier chapter, regular classroom teachers are faced with a difficult paradox with these children. A reasonable assessment accommodation for these children is providing extra time on their assessments.

Childhood Exposure to Lead

The controversy concerning **childhood exposure to lead** has had a long history. Research has linked childhood exposure to lead with neurobehavioral problems since the 1890s (Needleman, 1992). The basic transmittal mechanism of lead toxins is thought to be lead-based paints in homes. As paint deteriorates, it flakes or chips. Children who then touch the deteriorating paint may ingest lead particles through nail biting or thumb sucking. In addition, lead in gasoline, soil, or construction materials has contributed to the problem.

The Agency for Toxic Substances and Disease Registry estimated that 16 percent of all American children have blood lead levels in the neurotoxic range (Needleman, 1992). The behavioral and cognitive factors that are most affected by lead exposure are in the areas of language functioning, distractibility, and attention span (Needleman, 1992). The association of lead exposure with both learning disabilities and attention deficit disorders now seems warranted. Lead exposure may be a major factor in causing learning disabilities and ADHD problems. Therefore, the type of assessment practices for these students will be similar to what is seen with ADHD or LD children.

Environmental Risk Factors

A number of environmental factors may be associated with causing children to be at risk for school failure and for special education placement. Dysfunctional families, low maternal educational level, or poor maternal-infant interactions seem most associated with at-risk problems (Overton, 2003). In many cases, these factors are related to the educational and socioeconomic status of the parents.

In fact, being from lower socioeconomic levels can be considered a factor in and of itself for being an at-risk child. Parents from lower socioeconomic levels tend to participate less in prenatal education programs, have poorer nutrition, and have less adequate health care. The prenatal nutritional and health care standards seem to be particularly associated with at-risk problems.

These factors produce problems for both genders. However, low socioeconomic status also seems to be associated with producing a subgroup of males who have low academic achievement, low academic aspirations, and low vocational aspirations (Mckee & Banks, 1994). In terms of its effect on academic and vocational aspirations, a low socioeconomic background appears to have a more pronounced, adverse impact on males than females (Mckee & Banks, 1994). There are some indications that these males will become increasingly alienated from school during the latter part of their secondary education. They also appear to be more likely to drop out from school.

Early Assessment and Education for At-Risk Children

The Individuals with Disabilities Education Act (IDEA; 1997), along with its amendments, is the current federal law that governs the field of special education, as well as infants and young children who are at risk or disabled. IDEA and its amendments provide specific criteria about assessments for children who are under the age of 3 years old:

> The state shall provide, at a minimum, for each infant or toddler with a disability, and the infant's or toddler's family to receive—
> a multidisciplinary assessment of the unique strengths and needs of the infant or toddler and the identification of services appropriate to meet such needs;
> a family-directed assessment of the resources, priorities, and concerns of the family. (IDEA, 1997, p. 62)

The assessment of the infant or toddler involves a number of areas. These include an infant health history, medical evaluation, sensory assessments, cognitive tests (e.g., the Wechsler Battery), language tests, developmental behavior scales, and motor assessments. A global, multifaceted approach to early childhood assessment is the goal. One noted problem with infant and toddler assessments is the test quality. In general, young children do not test very well because language and concentration are not fully developed. This reduces the reliability and validity of some of the assessment instruments to levels that are barely adequate to below acceptable (Overton, 2003).

The family-directed assessment examines a variety of resources and priorities relating to the development of the young child. These might include such areas as income and family support of the child. Along with the infant assessment, this assessment also leads to the establishment of an **individual family services plan.** This plan specifies interventions, outcomes, and timelines for the young child. It also details the types of placement and services to be provided the child.

Early childhood assessment, diagnosis, and placement in special compensatory education programs appear to offer the best hope for helping children at risk and disabled. Among the best known of these programs is Head Start, a federally funded compensatory program for low income preschool children that began in 1965. Head Start programs have generated a number of research reviews (McKey et al., 1985; Guralnick & Bennet, 1987). A careful analysis of this research indicates that most Head Start children do achieve some short-term standardized and classroom assessment gains over matched controls. However, in many instances, these assessment gains "fade out" by the end of the third grade. In effect, the early academic gains are not maintained after the primary grades.

Nevertheless, other types of positive outcomes, particularly in the social sphere, seem to be maintained. One of the best-known examples of these gains was in the Perry

Preschool Project (Schweinhart & Weilart, 1983). The Perry Preschool Project followed Head Start children and matched controls well into adolescence. Significant positive effects were found for Head Start participants over a control group in such areas as employment, arrest records, dropout rates, and years in special education (Schweinhart & Weikart, 1983).

A number of other highly intensive, experimental programs, formed by consortiums of public schools, early childhood agencies, and universities have consistently been able to demonstrate short-term positive outcomes with at-risk children. These programs maintained frequent, concentrated amounts of instructional time with a very favorable ratio of teachers to children. They also relied on a large cadre of educational specialists, social workers, and health providers.

Breitmayer and Ramey (1986) studied the effects of one such early childhood program specifically designed to help children at risk. Their study determined at-risk criteria based on factors such as family income, Apgar scores (measures of neonatal responsiveness and physical appearance that are determined immediately after birth), maternal IQ scores, and parental educational level. The researchers randomly assigned subjects either to a special compensatory program or to a control group immediately after birth. The children in the special compensatory education program performed significantly better on a variety of assessments of cognitive ability when tested at 54 months after birth. An associated finding was that the early intervention program seemed to produce the greatest differences in those children who were most at risk. In effect, the children who had the greatest positive increases on the assessments were those children who were initially in the highest risk categories.

In summary, being at risk for school failure should not be viewed as an "all-or-nothing" state. There is a considerable variation among children who have at-risk conditions. A number of research studies indicate that early childhood education programs may help children with at-risk conditions.

Children with Disabilities and Assessment Issues

The Defining Aspects of Special Education

Special education involves providing a free and appropriate education for every child with disabilities between the ages of 3 and 21, regardless of how serious the disability may be (Public Law 101-476). Public Law 101-476, now commonly called the *Individuals with Disabilities Education Act (IDEA)*, along with its amendments, is the culmination of many years of federal legislation that began with Public Law 94-142, passed by Congress in 1975. This series of legislation established one of the most comprehensive special education programs in the world.

Along with racial integration in the 1960s, the integration of children with disabilities into the public education system in the 1970s may be viewed as one of the triumphs of twentieth-century American education. As mentioned earlier in this chapter, many people now want to take this integration of special education children a step further. They want to mandate full inclusion for all children with disabilities.

Special Education Regulations and Procedures

Policies for special education testing and referral are determined by federal and state laws. Because of the degree of litigation in this area, teachers need to be particularly aware of the different special education laws and regulations.

The following requirements are mandated by the IDEA (Public Law 101-476) and its amendments.

Individuals with Disabilities Education Act
1. All children with disabilities, ages 3 through 21, have the right to free and appropriate education.
2. All children with disabilities have the right to the least restrictive environment. This means that children with disabilities should be placed in as normal a setting as possible. They should be mainstreamed or placed in the regular classroom whenever possible.
3. Each child with disabilities should have an individualized educational plan (IEP) written by a multidisciplinary team composed of the classroom teacher, the special education teacher, the school psychologist, and the child's parents.
4. All assessments used to measure, diagnose, or place children with disabilities must be free from racial or cultural bias. Testing should be completed in the child's native language. Assessments must not be biased because of the child's disability.
5. Children with disabilities will be identified through a psychoeducational evaluation composed of a series of appropriate assessments.
6. The final decision for placement in a special education program will not be made until after a thorough evaluation. The decision for placement will be made by a multidisciplinary team composed of teachers, administrators, school psychologists, and the parents.

In a practical sense, many special education referrals by classroom teachers follow a particular sequence. Initially, the regular classroom teacher in a primary grade will notice that a child has a problem. The teacher then will observe, complete informal assessments, and complete screening tests. At this point, the teacher will contact the parents and discuss the situation. If the parents agree in writing, a referral for a full psychoeducational evaluation will be undertaken.

After the full evaluation by the school psychologist, the multidisciplinary team will meet and make a decision to place or not to place the child in a special education program. Providing special education placements and bearing the costs of the placements are the responsibility of the local school system. It also should be noted that the parents' agreement with any special education placement decision is generally mandated.

Special Education Categories

The different categories of children with disabilities have changed since the inception of Public Law 94-142. In particular, the growth of the category of children with learn-

Point/Counterpoint: Mandating Full Inclusion

Point

Supporters of full-inclusion practices state that the regular classroom is the optimum environment for children with disabilities. By placing children with disabilities in the regular classroom, their academic and socialization skills will develop in a way that is similar to mainstream children. Supporters state that past policies of placing children with disabilities in special education classes was just like segregation. Segregating children with disabilities, by placing them in special education classes, produced the same social and educational problems as segregation based on race and ethnicity.

Proponents of full inclusion acknowledge that some changes will have to be made in the regular classroom in order to accommodate children with disabilities. These changes will involve curriculum, teaching, and assessment practices. Nevertheless, supporters of full inclusion state that a new system of instruction is needed that fully integrates all students into the same general education classroom. They claim that students with disabilities will achieve at a higher rate when they are placed in regular classrooms. To deprive them of this opportunity is to deny them a full and equal education.

Counterpoint

Opponents of full inclusion state that inclusion should be based on the needs of each individual child with disabilities. Many children with disabilities do profit from inclusion but some children do not. The decision must be on a case-by-case basis with a full involvement of the multidisciplinary team, including parents. To make a blanket policy of full inclusion for all children is not in the best interests of all children.

Critics of full inclusion note that the research on student achievement with full inclusion does not necessarily support this practice. At best, the research is mixed. As noted before by opponents of full inclusion, it appears that some children's achievement is increased by this practice. On the other hand, some children's achievement is not.

According to opponents, many school districts support full inclusion because it saves money. It is less expensive to educate children with disabilities in the general education classroom than it is in special education classrooms. Unfortunately, this means that financial considerations tend to drive policy rather than what is in the best interest of all children.

---

ing disabilities is frequently noted. Learning disabilities now account for over half of all special education placements. Speech impairments account for nearly 20 percent of all placements. The mentally retarded (11 percent) and the emotionally disturbed (8 percent) are the third and fourth largest categories of special education placements. These four categories account for nearly 90 percent of the 5.5 million children who receive special education in U.S. schools (U.S. Department of Education, 2000). Table 11.1 provides a further breakdown of the percentage of children placed in the different special education categories.

Assessments, At-Risk Students, and Special Education

TABLE 11.1   Disability Categories and Percentage of Special Education Enrollment

Disability Category	Percent of Special Education Enrollment
1. Mentally retarded	11.02
2. Hearing impaired	1.27
3. Speech impaired	19.39
4. Visually impaired	0.47
5. Emotionally disturbed	8.36
6. Orthopedically impaired	1.25
7. Other health impaired	3.98
8. Deaf-blind	0.02
9. Multiple disabilities	1.94
10. Learning disabled	50.84
11. Traumatic brain injury	0.23
12. Autism	0.96
13. Developmentally delayed	0.21

Source: U.S. Department of Education (2000).

Certain categories of children with disabilities tend to be assessed and diagnosed by specific personnel. Physicians typically diagnose those with sensory or physically challenged conditions. These may include the hearing impaired, visually impaired, orthopedically impaired, other health impaired, multiple disabilities, autistic, and traumatic brain injured. Speech pathologists diagnose the speech impaired.

Other disabilities tend to be diagnosed by psychologists after a referral from teachers or school personnel. These categories include the mentally retarded, the emotionally disturbed, attention deficit/hyperactivity disorder (ADHD), and the learning disabled. As noted earlier, teachers in the primary grades often initiate referrals for these categories, as well as for speech impairments.

Assessment and Diagnosis of Children with Disabilities

In the previous chapter, there was some discussion of the diagnostic aspects of the different standardized assessments that measure intelligence and achievement. In particular, the use of the concept of standard deviation and the normal curve are used to determine some categories of special education. This next section provides more detail about how these assessments are used to diagnose and place children with disabilities.

It is important for regular classroom teachers to understand the different assessment criteria used to diagnose students. It is perhaps even more important for teachers to be able to detect any signs of disabilities, particularly in the areas of learning disabilities, emotional disorders, and ADHD. Regular classroom teachers often initiate the process for detecting, assessing, and referring these categories of children with disabilities.

Standard Deviation and Special Education

Many state regulations for determining who receives special education are based solely on standard deviation scores. Generally, IQ scores that are two standard deviations below the mean or lower are a diagnostic sign of mental retardation. On the Wechsler test battery, this would be an IQ score of 70 or lower. Based on the normal curve, the percentage of the population that will score 70 or less is approximately 2.5 percent. On the Stanford-Binet, the cutoff score is 68 or two standard deviations below the mean.

In determining if a child has a learning disability, a frequently used diagnostic sign is a one standard deviation or greater difference between the Verbal and Performance parts of the WISC-III. For example, if a child's Verbal score is 84 and his Performance score is 107, it could be indicative of a language-related learning disability such as dyslexia. Another diagnostic sign for a reading disability is a one standard deviation or greater difference between the total or full scale IQ score and the child's score on a diagnostic achievement test for reading. For example, the child has a full scale IQ score on the WISC-III of 105. On the Wide Range Achievement Test-Revised (WRAT), the child's reading score is 80. This is a 25-point difference on the deviation score scale. It is well beyond the 15-point standard deviation difference.

Diagnostic Characteristics of Major Special Education Categories

A more detailed discussion of the characteristics associated with the four most frequently occurring categories of special education are included in this section. These categories are: speech impairments, mental retardation, learning disabilities, and the emotionally disturbed. A discussion of attention-deficit/hyperactivity disorder also is presented in this section. The focus of the discussion is on understanding the characteristics of each category, as well as the assessment aspects associated with each category.

Speech Impairments

Speech impairments are the second-most common reason for referral to special education. Speech impairments can be caused by factors ranging from detectable neurological/physical abnormalities to purely psychological/emotional problems. The two major types of speech disorders that occur in school-age children are articulation disorders and stuttering.

Articulation disorders (also called *phonological disorders*) are defined as a consistent failure to correctly express proper speech sounds or phonemes. Children may mispronounce the sounds, substitute other sounds, or omit the proper sounds altogether.

What classroom teachers need to watch for with students are how they express certain consonant sounds. Articulation disorders almost always involve consonant sounds, particularly *r, s, z, sh, th, f, l,* and *ch.* Articulation disorders are more common in males.

Stuttering is a marked impairment of speech fluency characterized by repetitions or perseverations of sounds. Stuttering is viewed as having a genetic basis (American Psychiatric Association, 2000). The likelihood of stuttering is increased by social conditions, especially where there is pressure to talk. Conversely, stuttering is decreased or even absent in singing, talking to pets, or talking to inanimate objects. The onset of this speech impairment is concurrent with the development of speech between the ages of 2 and 7.

With the initial onset of stuttering, the child is often unaware of the problem behavior. However, as the awareness increases, the child will often demonstrate certain accompanying behaviors, such as eye blinks, tics, jerking of the head, or fist clinching. Stuttering is three times more common in males (American Psychiatric Association, 2000).

With either articulation or stuttering problems, early referral and assessments for speech therapy by teachers can be critical. If treated at an early age, articulation problems can be completely eliminated. With stuttering, as many as 80 percent of students will recover with proper treatment (American Psychiatric Association, 2000).

Mental Retardation

Mental retardation is defined by having significantly below-average intellectual performance and accompanying difficulties in adaptive functioning in one's social environment. The onset must be prior to age 18. IQ scores that are two standard deviations below the mean or lower are one diagnostic sign for mental retardation. In effect, IQ scores of 70 or lower on the Wechsler Intelligence Scale for Children-III (WISC-III) signify mental retardation. To be diagnosed as mentally retarded, the individual also must have a deficit in the level of adaptive functioning. **Adaptive functioning** is the ability to complete the important tasks of daily living or of the classroom. This type of functioning means a significant deficit in performance on certain assessments. The assessments include tests of adaptive functioning, observational and behavioral measures, teacher-constructed classroom tests, or standardized achievement tests.

For instance, one indication of problems in adaptive functioning is when a student has scores on a group achievement test that are two standard deviations below the mean. Some regulations specify two grade levels below the norm as another diagnostic sign of mental retardation. The same degree of discrepancy between present age or grade level and the child's classroom performance also would be a possible sign for retardation.

You, as the teacher, need to keep an important point in mind: If a child can make it academically in your classroom, then the child usually is considered to have adapted. If a student is successful on your classroom assessments and can socially function in your classroom, then most educators will agree that he or she should not be placed in a special education classroom. Going beyond that, by successfully adapting to your classroom, the child is, by definition, not considered mentally retarded.

Categories of Mental Retardation.   The American Association on Mental Deficiency (AAMD) has provided the most widely used classification system for the different categories of mental retardation (Grossman, 1983). Its subgroup classifications of the mentally retarded include four commonly accepted grouping based on WISC-III IQ scores:

> Mild retardation: 55 to 70 IQ
> Moderate retardation: 40 to 55 IQ
> Severe retardation: 25 to 40 IQ
> Profound retardation: Below 25 IQ

The incidence of mental retardation in the general population appears to be between 1 and 3 percent, depending on the stringency of the various classification procedures (Haring, McCormick, & Haring, 1994). The vast majority of the mentally retarded are in the mildly retarded range. The gender ratio indicates that there are three males to every two females in the mentally retarded population (American Psychiatric Association, 2000).

The greater the degree of mental impairment, the more likely it is that there is a detectable physical or neurological cause for the mental retardation. For instance, McLaren and Bryson (1987) report that in the mildly mentally retarded population, a detectable physical/neurological cause could not be found for 60 to 75 percent of the cases. However, when IQ scores were below 50, the results were reversed. Between 60 and 75 percent of this latter population did have a specific physical or neurological cause for their impairment.

Learning Disabilities

One of the most widely used definitions of *learning disabilities* was devised by the National Joint Committee on Learning Disabilities (1987): "Learning disabilities is a generic term that refers to a heterogeneous group of disorders manifested by significant difficulties in the acquisition and use of listening, speaking, reading, writing, reasoning, or mathematical abilities. These disorders are intrinsic to the individual and presumed to be due to central nervous system dysfunction" (p. 107).

Learning disabilities appear to affect between 5 and 10 percent of children in the primary grades (Lerner, 1989). There is considerable controversy about how to diagnose, assess, and treat learning disabilities. Part of the controversy centers on establishing an accurate and widely accepted standard for defining the various types of learning disabilities. Another related problem is the differing assessment methods used for determining whether a child has a learning disability. Because of these two problems, there have been considerable differences among states and school systems in the frequency of children diagnosed with learning disabilities.

In determining whether a child has a learning disability (LD), a generally used diagnostic sign is a significant discrepancy between ability and achievement. As previously mentioned, a significant discrepancy is a one standard deviation or greater difference between ability (IQ score) and achievement (as measured by an achievement test). However, this standard is not universally accepted.

Causes of Learning Disabilities.

There is a great deal of debate over what causes learning disabilities. One important point must be stressed about the possible causes of learning disabilities: There is no one single cause. The etiology and progression of a learning disability are unique to each individual.

A growing body of research indicates that some LD children have a genetic cause for their learning disability (Defries & Decker, 1982). However, the exact nature of the genetic transmission is still undetermined. Some research points to a sex-linked trait (Vellutino, 1987). Estimates of the gender ratios for learning disabilities indicate that they are considerably more common in males. Different estimates of the male-to-female ratio for learning disabilities show that LD problems are anywhere from two to four times more common in males.

Yet, there also appears to be a number of environmental causes for learning disabilities. As noted in the Children at Risk section, there is a relationship between childhood exposure to lead and the development of some learning disabilities. Brain accidents and brain trauma during birth or early childhood also appear to have a relationship with the onset of some learning disabilities.

Neurological Problems, Degree of Impairment, and Successful Remediation.

Generally speaking, there appears to be a relationship between the frequency of detectable neurological problems and the pervasiveness of the learning disability. Thus, the more organic or "hard" neurological assessment signs that an LD child has, the more pervasive will be her or his impairment. For example, those children with abnormal electroencephalograms (EEGs) or CAT scans may have a greater impairment.

Therefore, in addition to physical and psychological assessments, it is important to complete neurological assessments on children with possible LD indications. Those with distinct neurological signs also may have greater difficulty in successful treatment and intervention. As with other types of exceptionalities, the more pervasive the impairment, the more difficult the treatment. However, successful remediation of learning disabilities of all types may be accomplished.

If diagnosed and treated at an early age, the likelihood for successful remediation from such a disability appears to be better than at later age periods. Thus, the likelihood for successful treatment appears to be dependent on both the initial severity of the problem and the age at which intervention is initiated. Even so, significant remediation has been found to occur as late as the college-age years (Guyer & Sabatino, 1989; Guyer, Banks, & Guyer, 1993).

Whatever the causes, learning disabilities are seen as a significant difficulty in the acquisition of a specific academic ability in children who are average or above average in intelligence. A learning disability diagnosis is given only when all other possible causes have been eliminated. For instance, physical, visual, or auditory impairments have been eliminated as possible causes for the learning disability by medical assessments. Mental retardation also must be eliminated as a possible cause, as well as emotional disturbance or cultural deprivation.

Language-Related Learning Disabilities.   The most common type of learning disability is a language-related learning disability. This disability occurs when a student demonstrates average or better intelligence but exhibits a specific impairment in reading, spelling, or writing. This type of disorder is sometimes referred to as *dyslexia*. (In contrast, math disorders are termed *dyscalculia*.) Language-related learning disabilities are at least three times more common in males (Defries, 1989).

Some of the characteristics of language-related learning disabilities are indicated by how children process their reading or writing. For example, a child with a language-related learning disability improperly rotates, inverts, or reverses letters or words when writing. Improper rotations involve writing a letter horizontally when it should be written vertically. For instance, a child writes a *W* for an *E*. Inverting a letter is done when a *u* is written for an *n*. Reversals are writing a *b* for a *d* or a *p* for a *q*.

Learning disabilities are now the most frequently occurring type of disability in public schools. Since classroom teachers are largely responsible for originating referrals for this category, additional possible assessment signs are provided in the accompanying teacher application.

Teacher Application

Assessment Signs of a Possible Learning Disability
Classroom teachers should note the following signs of a possible learning disability when completing informal or formal classroom assessments:

1. Difficulty in distinguishing left from right is significantly delayed for the child's age/grade level.
   Examples: The child inconsistently shifts from right to left in the use of his hands or legs in classroom or physical activities. The child frequently is unable to follow directions in physical education activities that require her to use the left foot then the right foot or to use the right hand then the left hand.
2. Motor-coordination difficulties are significantly delayed for the child's age level.
   Examples: The child has a frequent inability to successfully participate in physical education or activities such as dance. The child is unable to throw and catch a ball or to perform coordinated motor activities such as constructing crafts or models.
3. Language-processing difficulties in speech, reading, or writing are significantly delayed for the child's age level.
   Examples: When children first begin to read, they finger point to the words or they move their lips. They are unable to read silently as well. When a child consistently continues these three activities for a significant time after other children have stopped, this may be a sign of a reading disability.
4. Mathematical-processing difficulties are significantly delayed for the child's age level.
   Examples: The child is consistently unable to grasp the concept of set or group. The child is presented with a group of three apples, then asked to add a group of four oranges to the first group. He must go back and count each item in each group rather than add the two groups together. He has consistent difficulty in working through a series of mathe-

matical steps in the appropriate sequence. However, he has no trouble with each individual step.

5. Visual/perceptual-processing difficulties are significantly delayed for the child's age level.
   Examples: The child has trouble in constructing puzzles and block designs. She has difficulty in tracing patterns or in recalling geometric designs and then tracing them correctly.

6. Attention span and concentration difficulties are significantly delayed for the child's age level.
   Examples: The child is easily and consistently distracted by extraneous stimuli. The child is unable to remain in one place long enough to finish a task.

None of the above problems should be taken as a sign in and of itself of a learning disability. These difficulties should be used only in conjunction with other assessment difficulties and used with students who are consistently behind in a specific academic area. The key words are *consistently behind,* since these difficulties also are stages that all children go through on the way to developing appropriate academic skills.

Extreme caution should be used in labeling a child with a learning disabilities designation. Only the school psychologist in consultation with the multidisciplinary team can actually make this determination.

Emotionally Disturbed

The **emotionally disturbed** (also commonly called *emotional disorders/behavior disorders*) include a range of responses that are characterized by a child's degree of departure from socially appropriate norms. These responses adversely affect the child's educational performance. They persist over a long period of time and they are exhibited to a marked degree (Haring, McCormick, & Haring, 1994). The prevalence of emotional disorders in children is listed at approximately 1 percent of the school-age population. However, this estimate does not count those children who may have a learning disability or ADHD with an accompanying emotional disorder.

To some extent, the younger a child is, the more a mental disorder is manifested in behavioral terms, such as withdrawal behaviors or acting-out behaviors. This is one reason for the semantic distinction between mental disorders in adults and emotionally disturbed or emotional/behavior disorders in children. Other manifestations of emotional disorders are:

1. A general, pervasive mood of unhappiness or depression
2. An inability to build and maintain interpersonal relationships with peers or teachers
3. Overly aggressive behavior, including antisocial acts
4. Frequent displays of anxiety or inferiority

These manifestations can be associated with disorders such as depression, antisocial activity, or eating disorders. As with mental disorders in adults, the etiology and treatment regimens for emotionally disturbed children are varied. There is no general agreement in the psychological community on the causes for these disorders. There is also considerable debate on how to treat these problems. Yet, as with other disorders listed in this chapter, the earlier the intervention, the better the outcome.

Attention-Deficit/Hyperactivity Disorder

Attention-deficit/hyperactivity disorder (ADHD) is characterized by frequent displays of developmentally inappropriate levels of inattention, impulsiveness, and hyperactivity (American Psychiatric Association, 2000). There has been some question as to the classification of ADHD in the overall categories of special education: Is it a learning disability or is it a separate disorder?

Part of the problem with independently categorizing attention-deficit/hyperactivity disorder is that at least 20 percent of learning disabled students also have ADHD (Silver, 1990). Another problem is that children with ADHD also are frequently classified as having an emotional/behavior disorder. In fact, according to much of the current literature, ADHD appears at times to be almost three separate disorders: an *attention deficit disorder*, a *hyperactivity-impulsivity disorder*, and a *combined type*. The last type combines both of these aspects into an attention-deficit/hyperactivity disorder. The attention deficit sometimes appears to be similar to certain types of learning disabilities. The hyperactivity-impulsivity disorder is often manifested in terms of behavior problems. While each aspect can appear together for a combined ADHD disorder, these two distinct aspects also can appear separately. The latest classification of ADHD by the American Psychiatric Association (2000) reflects this division into three separate subsets of ADHD. Following are some of the diagnostic signs that may indicate an ADHD disorder (adapted from the American Psychiatric Association, 2000).

Signs of Attention-Deficit/Hyperactivity Disorder
1. Persistent failure to attend to details; exhibits carelessness and slipshod work in classroom activities
2. Poor attention span in classroom or play activities
3. Trouble following teacher instructions or directions
4. Problems in organizing classroom work and meeting deadlines
5. Distracted and forgetful about classroom assignments
6. Constantly fidgets and squirms during classroom activities
7. Inappropriate classroom behavior, such as leaving seat, running, or talking out of turn
8. Problems playing with peers and following rules for game activities

Attention-deficit/hyperactivity disorder appears to be successfully treated by stimulant medications in approximately 60 to 75 percent of the cases (Lerner, 1989). Ritalin remains the drug of choice in treating ADHD, although a number of new medications have recently been added to the market, as well as time-release forms of Ritalin.

Nevertheless, careful monitoring of these stimulant medications, particularly at the outset, is warranted. Adverse reactions to the medication can occur (Lerner, 1989).

Other Assessment Issues

Two other assessment practices in the special education field are examined in this section. These practices are functional assessment and assessment accommodations. A **functional assessment** is a type of assessment that examines a student's classroom behaviors to determine what is the purpose or function of certain behaviors. **Assessment accommodations** are the special assessment conditions that may be reasonably required for some children with disabilities.

Functional Assessments

A functional assessment typically requires classroom observations of the student's behavior, teacher interviews, parental interviews, school record reviews, and behavior ratings scales. For example, a child with ADHD frequently disrupts the class with acting-out behaviors. A functional assessment would first involve observing the child's behavior in the classroom. Then, interviews of significant adults would be conducted in order to find out if the same acting-out behaviors occur in other settings, such as at home or at play. A functional assessment is particularly useful in determining the antecedent conditions that may trigger the acting-out behavior. For example, transitions from one classroom activity or subject to another may trigger acting-out behavior in the ADHD student.

Assessment Accommodations

Assessment accommodations are mandated by the Individual with Disabilities Act (1997). These accommodations include a variety of reasonable changes in assessment situations in order to facilitate the assessment of children with disabilities as shown in the following teacher application. There are two basic types of assessment accommodations for children with disabilities: assistive technology and conventional accommodations.

Teacher Application

Assessment Accommodations for Children with Disabilities
The following list of suggested accommodations for assessments is provided by Elliott, Kratochwill, and Schulte (1998):

1. *Motivational.* Extrinsic reinforcement, such as verbal praise, may work best for some students with disabilities.

2. *Assistance Prior to Assessment.* Assessment training in test-taking skills, such as preparing for multiple-choice formats or other testing procedures.
3. *Schedule Accommodations.* Extra time or different schedules for assessments.
4. *Setting.* Any specialized setting needs, such as a special testing room or specialized lighting or acoustical systems.
5. *Assistance during Assessment.* Tests may be administered by special education personnel who can assist in such ways as reading questions out loud, turning pages, or recording responses.
6. *Use of Assessment Aids.* The use of assistive technology of other equipment to help in taking the assessment.
7. *Test Format.* Alternative ways of presenting the assessment format such as the use of audiotapes or Braille.

Assistive Technology

Assistive technology is any type of technological device that can aid children with disabilities in the learning or assessment process. There has been a dramatic increase in the numbers of assistive devices in the last decade. This section will discuss some of the more recent assistive technology devices.

For students with severe speech impairments, Dyna Vox is a communication aid that makes it easy for learners to create messages and to send them electronically with a simple touch. Dyna Vox is available with personalized voice output (DECtalk) that provides different voices ranging from young children to adult to fit the age of the student (Duhaney & Duhaney, 2000).

Students who are hearing impaired can benefit from captioned programming systems (e.g., RAPIDTEXT) that provide subtitles for television and other video presentations. When this type of captioning is used in education settings, a stenographer enters the teacher's words, which are displayed to the student on a computer monitor. There also is a frequency modulated (FM) system for students with hearing impairments. The teacher wears a microphone that is connected to a small transmitter. The student wears a lightweight FM radio receiver, which picks up the signal, converts it, amplifies it, and shapes it to the child's needs (Duhaney & Duhaney, 2000).

Text- and graphics-based software that supports the writing process may be best suited for students with learning disabilities. Computers and word-processing software make revision of writing and reorganization of ideas much easier. Grammar, spellchecker, dictionaries, and thesaurus programs assist in the mechanics of writing. One program for a reading learning disability is Omni 3000 (Ochoa, Vasquez, & Gerber, 1999). This program is an optical recognition reading program that scans text and then reads it aloud. The Kurzwell Reading Machine scans printed documents and converts text into electronic speech. There also are some screen magnification programs. They enlarge printed text, adjust the size and graphics, and control the number of lines and words per page. A software program, Math Word Problems, helps students with difficulties in solving math word problems. It sorts out relevant problem information, chooses correct operations, and completes computations accurately.

For students with physical disabilities who have difficulty using traditional input devices, there are a variety of switches, optical pointers, voice-controlled devices, and word prediction software. For example, HeadMaster, a mouse emulator, allows a student who is unable to operate the computer with his or her own hands to use the head to do so. There are also different software programs that project an image of a keyboard on the display to help students fulfill keyboard operation.

For students with visual impairments, there is a wide range of assistive technology devices. DigiVox is an output device that helps students with print-reading difficulties. It can record a quantity of spoken messages for all occasions and replay them with a simple touch whenever they are needed.

In certain cases, these assistive technologies will be necessary to appropriately assess students with disabilities. The type of assistive devices needed for assessments should be listed in the IEP developed by the multidisciplinary team. It is clear that more assistive technology is on the way and will supplement the use of computers in this area.

Conventional Accommodations

Conventional accommodations include a variety of nontechnological accommodations that serve to facilitate the assessment of children with disabilities.

As noted earlier, extra time on assessments is one of the most frequently used type of conventional accommodation. This accommodation is used with children who have learning disabilities, are mentally retarded, or have ADHD. Another accommodation, using tutors to read text aloud, has been used with a variety of disabilities. Yet another assessment accommodation is administering tests in shortened segments spaced with breaks. This helps students with physically challenged conditions who may fatigue easily. It also may facilitate ADHD students who are easily distracted. Another frequently used accommodation is an isolated assessment situation. This involves administering an exam to a single student in a separate facility.

The key factor is that assessments measure content knowledge, not the degree of disability. This is why reasonable accommodations are so important. With inclusion policies on the increase, it is clear that regular classroom teachers need to be familiar with assessment accommodations.

Chapter Summary

This chapter examined the relationships between at-risk factors, children with disabilities, and assessments. A number of different factors can cause disabilities. These range from genetic factors, to maternal alcohol and drug use, to environmental toxins. These factors also may produce considerable variation in the level of cognitive skills and adaptive functioning in your students.

Regular classroom teachers play an increasingly important role in assessing and referring students for special education diagnoses. It is essential that you understand the different categories and diagnostic signs of children with disabilities. Early assessment and intervention can be an important aspect of successful treatment. With inclusion policies, it also is critical that regular classroom teachers have a better understanding of the backgrounds and needs of children with disabilities.

Assessment accommodations are another important part of inclusion policies. These types of accommodations are necessary in order that children with disabilities be assessed on their knowledge and not on their level of disability. Assistive technologies are being used more and more in the regular classroom. Awareness of these technologies and how to integrate them in the classroom is another area of need for regular classroom teachers.

CASE STUDY EPILOGUE

Mrs. Maynard has developed a number of methods to transform her class to meet the requirements of a full-inclusion policy. These transformations include changes in her instruction and assessment procedures. In terms of instruction, Mrs. Maynard has decided to focus more on small group instruction that will offer some children with disabilities more direct and explicit instruction. She also has decided to increase the number of hands-on tasks, use of manipulatives, and scaffolding procedures as needed in her inclusive classroom. Mrs. Maynard also establishes a "buddy system" of student tutors for students have special classroom needs.

In terms of assessments, Mrs. Maynard has altered her assessment practices to have classroom tests administered in shortened segments spaced with breaks. She has also screened off one area of her classroom to be used as a special instructional or assessment area for students who need tutoring or testing in a more stimulus-free situation. Mrs. Maynard has ensured that each type of assistive device and computer program is available for students with disabilities. She has also has altered the types of assessments given in her classroom. She has stopped using strictly timed assessments and, as much as possible, offers untimed assessments.

CHAPTER ACTIVITIES

Websites

http://www.abledata.com   This website is part of a federally funded project to provide information about assistive technologies. Its database has information on 19,000 assistive technology devices and includes information on prices and descriptions of the devices.

www.kurzweiledu.com   This is the website for Kurzweil Educational Systems. This company provides software products and other assistive technologies for the visually impaired and the learning disabled.

www.reedmartin.com   This site is for parents and teachers who want specifics about laws concerning educating children with special needs. Teachers can find out everything they need to know about IEPs and other state requirements. The site contains information about specific disabilities and state assessment policies.

http://www.ed.gov/offices/OSERS/Policy/IDEA/   IDEA offers the teacher, student, and parent vast information about this important law. The site shares IDEAs that work, most recent legislation, and assessment information.

Portfolio Activities

1. Review Mrs. Maynard's situation in the Chapter Case Study. Write an essay for your portfolio that addresses the following questions:
   - What impact would this policy have on you as a teacher?
   - How would this policy change your assessment methods?
   - What type of reasonable accommodations would be made for these children?
   - What type of changes might be needed about playground activities or physical education at your school?
   - What type of additional training or extra educational support would you need in your classroom?
   - How would you feel about teaching a classroom of 25 children, 4 of whom have severe disabilities?

2. Write an essay that describes the use of assessment accommodations for a child in your present or future classroom. List and describe one type of assistive technology device and one type of conventional accommodation that you would use. Provide a rationale for the use of each of these accommodations.

KEY CONCEPTS

Adaptive functioning
Articulation disorders
Assessment accommodations
Assistive technology
Attention-deficit/hyperactivity disorder
  (ADHD)
Biological risk factors
Childhood exposure to lead
Children at risk

Conventional accommodations
Emotionally disturbed
Environmental risk factors
Fetal alcohol syndrome
Functional assessment
Individual Family Services Plan
Mental retardation
Special education
Stuttering

REVIEW QUESTIONS

1. What are the major causes for biological risk factors and environmental risk factors?

2. List and describe the three major characteristics of fetal alcohol syndrome.

3. Explain the cognitive and behavioral effects of lead poisoning on young children.

4. Describe the major characteristics of IDEA.

5. Analyze the relationship between neurological problems, degree of impairment, and successful remediation with children who have learning disabilities.

6. Describe the concept of adaptive functioning and explain how it relates to diagnosing children with disabilities.

7. Explain the relationship between the concept of standard deviation and diagnosing learning disabilites.

8. Describe what is meant by assistive technology. How are the various technologies used to help different types of disabilities?

SELF-ASSESSMENT

1. The IQ cutoff score for mental retardation/mental impairment is:
   a. 100
   b. 15
   c. 130
   d. 50
   e. 70

2. The more "hard" neurological or physical signs that a learning disabled child displays:
   a. The less pervasive the problem
   b. The more pervasive the problem
   c. The easier it is to treat the disorder
   d. The more likely the child will be to overcome the disorder

3. The incidence of learning disabilities is:
   a. Greater in females
   b. Greater in males
   c. No actual gender difference

4. "Hard" neurological signs or physical signs would be most common among which group of the mentally retarded/impaired?
   a. Mildly impaired
   b. Moderately impaired
   c. Severely impaired

5. The incidence of mental retardation is greater in which group?
   a. Males
   b. Females
   c. No gender differences

6. Failure to appropriately pronounce certain consonant sounds is:
   a. Stuttering disorder
   b. Tourette's syndrome
   c. Articulation disorder
   d. Down's syndrome

7. The single-most common type of disability is:
   a. Speech disability
   b. Mental retardation

Answers to Self-Assessment: 1. e, 2. b, 3. b, 4. c, 5. a, 6. c, 7. c, 8. c

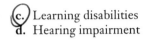
c. Learning disabilities
d. Hearing impairment

8. A child whose IQ score was between 55 and 70 would most likely be diagnosed as:
  a. Moderately retarded
  b. Learning disabled
  c. Mildly retarded
  d. Severely retarded

REFERENCES

American Psychiatric Association. (2000). *Diagnostic and statistical manual of mental disorders—Text revision*. Washington, DC: Author.

Birsch, H.G., & Gussow, J.D. (1970). *Disadvantaged children: Health, nutrition and school failure*. New York: Harcourt Brace.

Breitmayer, B.J., & Ramey, C.T. (1986). Biological nonoptimality and quality of postnatal environment as codeterminants of intellectual development. *Child Development, 57*, 1151–1165.

Burgess, D.M., & Steissguth, A.P. (1992). Fetal alcohol syndrome and fetal alcohol effects: Principles for educators. *Phi Delta Kappan, 74* (1), 24–34.

Defries, J.C. (1989). Gender ratios in children with reading disability and their affected relatives: A commentary. *Journal of Learning Disabilities, 22*, 9, 544–545.

Defries, J.C., & Decker, S. (1982). Genetic aspects of reading disability: A family study. In R.N. Malatesha & P.G. Aaron (Eds.), *Reading disorders: Varieties and treatments* (pp. 255–279). New York: Academic Press.

Duhaney, L.M.G., & Duhaney, D.C. (2000). Assistive technology: Meeting the needs of learners with disabilities. *International Journal of Instructional Media, 27*(4), 393–402.

Elliott, S.N., Kratochwill, T.R., & Schulte, A.G. (1998). The assessment accommodation checklist: Who, what, where when, why, and how? *Teaching Exceptional Children, 31*, 10–14.

Garigulo, R.M. (2003). *Special education in contemporary society*. Belmont, CA: Wadsworth.

Grossman, H.J. (1983). *Classification of mental retardation*. Washington, DC: American Association on Mental Deficiency.

Guralnick, M., & Bennett, C. (1987). *Effectiveness of early intervention*. New York: Academic Press.

Guyer, B.P., Banks, S.R., & Guyer, K.E. (1993). Spelling improvement for college students who are dyslexic. *Annals of Dyslexia, 43*, 186–193.

Guyer, B.P., & Sabatino, D. (1989). The effectiveness of a multisensory alphabetic phonetic approach with college students who are learning disabled. *Journal of Learning Disabilities, 22*(7), 430–434.

Haring, N.G., McCormick, L., & Haring, T.G. (Eds.). (1994). *Exceptional children and youth* (6th ed.) New York: Merrill.

Individuals with Disabilities Education Act, Public Law No. 105–117 (1997).

Lerner, J. (1989). *Learning disabilities: Theories, diagnoses, and teaching strategies* (5th ed.). Boston: Houghton Mifflin.

Mckee, J., & Banks, S.R. (1994, February 14). *Educating rural youth—What teacher education should know: A replication of the Maine study*. A presentation at the Association for Teacher Education, National Conference, Atlanta, GA.

McKey, R.H., Condelli, L., Granson, H., Barrett, B., McConsky, C., & Plantz, M. (1985). *The impact of Head Start on children, families, and communities* (Final report of the Head Start Evaluation, Synthesis, and Utilization Project). Washington, DC: CSR.

McLaren, J., & Bryson, S.E. (1987). Review of recent epidemiological studies of mental retardation: Prevalence, associated disorders, and etiology. *American Journal of Mental Retardation, 92*, 243–254.

National Joint Committee on Learning Disabilities. (1987). Learning disabilities: Issues on definition. *Journal of Learning Disabilities*, 10(2), 107–108.

Needleman, H.L. (1992). Childhood exposure to lead: A common cause of school failure. *Phi Delta Kappan*, 74(1), 35–37.

Ochoa, T.A., Vasquez, L.R., & Gerber, M.M. (1999). New generation of computer-assisted learning tools for students with disabilities. *Intervention in School and Clinic*, 34(4), 251–255.

Overton, T. (2003). *Assessing learners with special needs* (4th ed.). Upper Saddle River, NJ: Merrill Prentice Hall.

Schweinhart, L.J., & Weilart, D.P. (1983). The effects of the Perry Preschool Project on youths through age 15. In *As the Twig is Bent: Lasting effects of preschool programs*. Consortium for Longitudinal Studies (pp. 71–101). Hillsdale, NJ: Erlbaum.

Silver, L.B. (1990). Attention deficit hyperactivity disorder: Is it a learning disability or a related disorder? *Journal of Learning Disabilities*, 23, 394–397.

Stevens, L.J., & Price, M. (1992). Meeting the challenge of educating children at risk. *Phi Delta Kappan*, 74(1), 18–23.

U.S. Department of Education. (2000). *Twenty-second annual report to Congress on the implementation of the Individuals with Disabilities Act*. Washington, DC: U.S. Government Printing Office.

Vellutino, F.R. (1987). Dyslexia. *Scientific American*, 256(3), 34–41.

CHAPTER

12 Motivation and Assessment

C A S E   S T U D Y

Mr. Foster teaches general mathematics in a middle school. Intrinsic interest and motivation are difficult commodities to find in his classes. Mr. Foster has tried a number of approaches. For example, he tried the "never smile until Christmas" approach and attempted to motivate students from the outset of class with scare tactics, and he tried a behavioral approach, using tokens and other types of positive reinforcement including free time at the end of the class.

Unfortunately, nothing seems to work. A few students are intrinsically motivated by the subject area. But most students' expressions appear more glazed over than the doughnuts at a Krispy Kreme store. On his assessments some students perform quite well, some become filled with anxiety, but most of them simply appear to go through the motions.

Mr. Foster wants to know about how to motivate his students in a subject that many students either fear or dislike. He specifically wants to know the answers to the following questions:

What are the factors that serve to motivate students?

Is intrinsic motivation or extrinsic motivation more important?

Does fear of failure motivate students?

Does curiosity motivate students?

Is there one magic method that will motivate all students?

Do assessments really motivate students?

Introduction

What motivates students is a constant source of fascination for teachers. This is particularly true on those never-ending Friday afternoons in May. In fact, along with classroom management issues, motivation perennially is listed by teachers as one of their most difficult classroom problems. As teachers, we all want to know how to motivate students to do their best during our instruction and our assessments. But we often make one fatal mistake about motivation: *We assume that what motivates us will also motivate our students.*

What motivates people also has been the subject of interest and controversy for well over a century. In the United States, for a good part of the twentieth century, many psychologists and educators subscribed to a behavioral view of motivation. Most behaviorists believed that human motivation was solely determined by external reinforcement or reward. A behavior was retained only when some type of payoff followed it. Unrewarded behaviors were quickly extinguished. Appropriate performance on assessments was awarded with gold stars, smiley faces, or tokens. This was believed to increase student performance.

Beginning in the 1960s and certainly influential by the 1970s, cognitive models came to dominate motivation research. While not completely discarding the role of external or extrinsic reinforcement, cognitive views focused on a variety of cognitive factors that motivate behavior, learning, and achievement. In particular, cognitive models more closely examined the issue of internal motivation or intrinsic motivation. In education, cognitive models were interested in the cognitive and emotional factors that resulted in an intrinsic motivation to achieve.

A number of different approaches to motivation are reviewed in this chapter. Included among these approaches are purely cognitive approaches, such as Kagan and Lang's viewpoint on motivational factors in school; Weiner's attribution theory; Rotter's locus of control model; and McClelland's achievement motivation model. In addition to these approaches, Bandura's social cognitive theory is reviewed.

This chapter also examines ideas about motivation and how these ideas can be applied to assessments. Some of the ideas about motivation and assessment presented in this chapter are student motives in schools, negative motivation, self-efficacy, learned helplessness, and achievement motivation. The issue of extrinsic versus intrinsic motivation is also reviewed, as is a discussion of development and motivation.

Cognitive Views of Motivation

One the distinguishing features of human beings is the ability to generate a cognitive representation of a future event (Kagan & Lang, 1978). These ideas, or cognitive representations, about what a person wants to experience are what is defined as motives. More specifically, a motive is a state of mind "created by the tension between the unsatisfactory reality of the present and the presumably more satisfying state later" (Kagan & Lang, 1978, p. 246).

Motives are more than mere ideas. For example, a student realizes that a research paper is not finished. The image or mental representation of placing the completed assignment on the teacher's desk is a motive or anticipated state. This motive may prompt the student to strive toward achieving this desired state. The student may be unsure about the ability to complete the task but still knows what to do to accomplish the goal. The student also knows the consequences associated with not completing the task.

Motives and Actions

Teachers know that strong motives do not always lead to action. Sometimes students do not have the ability to do what they want to do. They do not act because they expect to fail despite their effort. How a motive results in success on an assessment is a complicated process. A student may have many motives that coexist at one time. Which motive will activate a student's behavior? Most educators agree with Abraham Maslow and say that these motives exist in some sort of hierarchy. The strongest motive produces the behavior.

Students may exhibit the same behavior in similar assessment situations but with different motives. For example, on Monday, a student may work hard on a formal classroom assessment because she wants the social status among her peers that comes with success on the test. On another day, the student may work hard on a portfolio assessment because she wants the approval of the teacher.

Kagan and Lang (1978) contend that children and adolescents have six basic motives that operate in schools: (1) desire for approval; (2) desire to model or imitate; (3) desire for mastery; (4) desire to resolve uncertainty; (5) desire for control, power, and status; and (6) desire to vent hostility. A description follows as to how these basic motives relate to assessments:

Negative Motivation and Assessments

Ames and Ames (1991) reviewed the conditions that produced negative student motivation and the ways to reduce those conditions in the classroom. In regard to assessments, negative motivation is defined as the student having the mental image that the assigned assessment task cannot be successfully finished. In effect, a student has no viable strategy for getting from the beginning to the end of the assessment task. Often, the outcome is that the student does not persist in adequately completing the assessment.

Six Basic Motives

1. *The Desire for Approval.* A dominant motive for children is to have the approval of parents, teachers, peers, and significant adults. Those students who have clear parental approval and involvement in their schooling tend to have better assessment performance. As mentioned in Chapter 4, minority students who see schools as controlled by a dominant culture may become increasingly oppositional toward assessments. These students tend to seek out peers for approval rather than teachers. Many students also turn more to their peers for approval when they reach adolescence. Despite all of this, teacher approval still remains a major motive for most elementary school children.

2. *The Desire to Be Similar to the Teacher.* Young children, especially in elementary school, often identify with a significant adult and try to imitate that person's behaviors. Modeling may be stronger if the child sees the adult as being like the child in some way and as being successful and positive with his or her life. A positive teacher is going to be a positive role model. Fairness, emotional sensitivity, and consideration are all factors a teacher can model to set the tone for your classroom climate. Students will then have a positive attitude about the class, which should result in a positive attitude about the classroom assessments.

3. *The Desire for Mastery.* Mastery is the desire to increase one's knowledge, skill, or talent. It is one aspect of intrinsic motivation. Or as Maslow stated, it can be the desire to self-actualize: to be the best person that one can be. Mastery on assessments is a student's attempt to match his behavior to a standard he has set. Too often, teachers are oriented toward students mastering the test rather than mastering the subject area. Ideally, students would develop an internalized sense of mastering material on their own that results in an intrinsic motivation to learn. Realistically, intrinsic motivation for many students is only in certain subject areas. For instance, some students have a desire for mastery in Spanish but not mathematics. Other students have a desire for mastery in biology but not English. Mastery orientation can be contrasted with what is called a *performance goal orientation*. A student with a performance goal orientation wants to succeed in order to show others that he or she can do better. In effect, the reason for school success is to compete and win out over other students (Wolters, Yu, & Pintrich, 1996). Mastery orientation is to compete against a standard one has set for oneself.

4. *The Desire to Resolve Uncertainty.* Children are curious about new and different events that happen in their lives. Novelty and uncertainty can intrigue students. Instruction and assessments that tap into the need to resolve ambiguity and uncertainty can stimulate this inherent sense of curiosity. By stimulating curiosity, teachers can increase another aspect that results in an intrinsic motivation to learn.

5. *The Desire for Control, Power, and Status.* Children of all ages have power struggles with their parents. These power struggles often appear to reach their maximum during early adolescence. To some extent, power struggles between students and teachers also reach their greatest intensity at this time. In terms of socialization, there does seem to be a turning away from parents and teachers during this time and an orientation toward peers. Peer relationships, particularly, play a vital role in status development in adolescence. Because of this influence, peers may have a considerable effect on other students' achievement motivations and educational aspirations.

6. *The Desire to Vent Hostility.* Hostility and revenge are strong motives that, according to theorists, become priorities whenever other motives are not gratified. Students often attempt to satisfy this motive by overt and aggressive acts of rebellion. Other actions may be less obvious, such as the desire to punish parents by failing to achieve in school. Hostility is a negative emotion and usually has a negative impact on the teaching-learning process, except when a student demonstrates ability to show that a teacher is wrong ("I'll show Mrs. Campbell, who I think hates me, that I'm OK. I'll ace her test just to show her she is wrong about me"). Negative motivations are seldom used for positive purposes; therefore, most educators try to get rid of them in classroom situations. The next section further examines the area of negative motivation and assessments.

"What type of thinking evokes negative motivation?" is a question Ames and Ames (1991) ask. The following is a summary of their answers:

Thoughts about Self-Worth. Beliefs, thoughts, or perceptions about self-worth relate to how a student makes attributions about assessments and grades. (**Attributions** are the rationales that people devise for their failures and successes.) One thought pattern, often leading to failure, involves avoiding the appearance of "trying hard" to make good grades. Students sometimes want success without showing effort. The attribution is: "I can succeed on this test without any apparent effort." Some students will do extensive studying at home but then "goof off" during school hours in an attempt to look like they are not "trying hard."

Covington (1984) also examined the self-worth motive. He made a distinction between private and public images of self-worth. Covington suggested that students attempt to develop these images so they are consistent with each other. "Doing nothing" might be a motivated behavior if it is intended to keep a person from seeing himself or herself as failing.

Covington and Omelich (1979) demonstrated through their research how excuses help students maintain more positive self-perceptions under conditions of failure. These authors believe that students are faced with a double-edged sword. Either students use little or no effort on a task, which increases the likelihood of failure but gives them the excuse that they did not really try, or they exhibit a high level of effort, which indicates low ability if they fail but does not provide a good excuse for failure. Students attempt to find excuses that work as a shield against outcomes that diminish their sense of self-worth. Students can maintain positive self-images if they can come up with good excuses.

Academic Self-Efficacy.   Academic self-efficacy is a type of estimate that students make about their ability to accomplish an academic task, such as solving a mathematics problem. Students think to themselves, "Will I be good at doing this task?" There is considerable evidence that these personal expectations influence achievement behaviors. Students identify with their abilities in each of the academic areas, such as writing, reading, and mathematics. The thought pattern of "I do not have the ability in chemistry" results in low self-efficacy and negative motivation about assessments in that subject area.

Attributions about Success and Failure.   Students also think about why they do or do not accomplish what they attempt. Weiner (1984) suggests that there are four reasons students use to explain their successes and failures: ability, effort, task difficulty, and luck. When students rationalize about the causes for their academic failures, their attributions can evoke negative motivation. The next section provides a detailed examination of this area.

Attribution Theory

Weiner (1984) developed a model about attributions and students' academic performance. **Causal attributions** (ideas about why students succeed or fail) are produced when there has been either an unexpected outcome or an aversive outcome. Students generate a variety of explanations for these unexpected outcomes. As mentioned above, the major ways students explain their success or failure are:

1. High or low ability or aptitude
2. Good or poor effort
3. Task ease or difficulty
4. Good or bad luck

Students do not try to explain why all outcomes were obtained. However, when confronted with the bad news of failure, or even the good news of an unexpected success, students will seek an answer as to why they failed or succeeded. The student, according to Weiner's (1984) attribution theory, will base the cause on either internal or external factors. The **internal factors** are their ability (aptitude or skill) or their effort (amount of work or study). In effect, the student sees success or failure as related to ability, to effort, or to both. The **external factors** are when attributions are made based on luck or task difficulty.

The internal versus external dimensions appear related to how students feel about their performance. A success attributed to internal factors usually leads to pride and satisfaction. Failure, though, when attributed to internal factors, produces feelings of shame, incompetence, or guilt. Guilt especially occurs if the attribution was lack of effort.

Teachers want to know: What are the desirable attributions to promote among students? Forsterling (1985) suggests how to promote positive attributions in his review of attribution research. The following teacher application summarizes his suggestions.

Teacher Application

Using Attributions

Desirable Attributions

1. When a student succeeds on an assessment, the teacher should reinforce the student so that the achievement is attributed to the child's ability to perform the assessment.
   "Zoe, you really showed everyone today how smart you are. You have a real skill at mathematics."
   Attributing success to the student's own internal ability results in increased self-esteem and self-efficacy. This will further motivate achievement on the next assessment.
2. When a student fails, the teacher should reinforce the attribution that it was due to a lack of effort.
   "Ed, you have the ability to make an A in chemistry but you did not study for the midterm."
   Hopefully, this should result in optimism about the student's ability and lead to persistence on future assessments.

Undesirable Attributions

1. When a student succeeds, the teacher should *not* reinforce attributing the success to luck.
   "Maria, wow, you made an A. Guess it was just your lucky day."
   Such attributions can result in indifference and low motivation.
2. When a student fails, the teacher should *not* reinforce the attribution that it was due to a lack of ability.
   "Joe, I just don't think you have what it takes to do calculus. Stick with general math."
   This may result in feelings of inferiority and further low achievement.

It *is* possible to do something to influence the attributions that students make for successes and failures. Forsterling (1985) reviewed 15 attributional training studies and concluded that these training programs generally produce both cognitive and behavioral changes. Usually, those in the training program increase attributions for failures to a lack of effort (the desired direction) and improved in both performance and persistence.

Locus of Control

Rotter (1966) originally developed the conceptual framework for the locus of control. **Locus of control** is a personality dimension concerned with an individual's sense of personal responsibility for successes and failures. People with an **internal locus of control** attribute their behavior to forces inside them. They see themselves as responsible for their own successes and failures. People with an **external locus of control** attribute their behavior to external forces, such as luck, fate, divine intervention, or parents. They tend to see their success and failures as outside their own control.

Most experts in this area acknowledge at least some sort of positive relationship between an internal locus of control and academic achievement (Stipek, 1996). Reinforcing students for the attitude that they are in charge of their lives and their assessment performance appears to increase such performance. For instance, deCharms (1984) reports on one 10-week training unit designed to emphasize four major concepts: self-concept, achievement motivation, realistic goal setting, and the origin-pawn concept.

The last goal was important in that students and teachers were taught to see themselves as "origins" (people who can take responsibility and control outcome) as opposed to "pawns" (people who cannot take responsibility and whose outcome is controlled by others). The trained students were compared with a control group who did not receive any training. Results significantly favored the trained group on a standardized group achievement test. The trained students also had fewer absences and fewer tardy reports.

Learned Helplessness

Learned helplessness is another area that relates to the motive of achievement and the motive to avoid failure. The original theory of **learned helplessness** was that constant, uncontrollable negative events caused the individual to give up and become helpless in terms of behavior, achievement, and motivation. This idea has somewhat been changed to the view that the attributions made about these constant, negative events cause this state of giving up. In effect, learned helplessness may be an outcome that can lead to low motivation and a negative emotional state (such as depression) but it is dependent on individual differences in how attributions are made about the events.

How does this concept relate to assessment and instruction? Dweck (1986) reports that learned helplessness is related to students developing an internal and stable explanation for failure on assessments. Therefore, failures (and even successes) are seen as beyond the students' control. This promotes feelings of giving up and helplessness. In effect, students develop the belief from their assessment experiences in the classroom that they cannot control the outcome. They no longer make an effort. The lack of effort increases their amount of failures. The situation becomes a vicious cycle that reinforces the students' self-perceptions of learned helplessness.

Achievement Motivation

McClelland, Atkinson, Clark, and Lowell (1953) originally defined much of the work on the construct of achievement motivation. They viewed **achievement motivation** as a high need for achievement, high goal setting, and attempts to obtain a high level of excellence. They also viewed parenting styles, especially the emphasis by the mother on the child's independence and self-reliance at an early age, as influencing the development of a high need to achieve.

Atkinson (1957) made an additional contribution to the work on achievement motivation by distinguishing the need for achievement from the need to avoid failure. Some students put forth effort on assessments because they desire to succeed; others exert themselves to avoid failure. Atkinson believed that both needs exist in all students but at different levels. Coexisting within each student is an interest in success and an anxiety about failure.

If the motive to succeed is stronger than the motive to avoid failure, then students will set goals of moderate difficulty. However, when students follow a motive to avoid failure, they have the tendency to choose either very easy or very difficult objectives. The rationale for the behavior of those who want to avoid failure is that they will be off the hook either way. The easy task is a sure thing, and if they fail at the more difficult task, they can explain it away because the task was too hard to accomplish (Atkinson, 1964).

Instructional and assessment strategies should be varied for students who appear to have a high achievement need. Students with a high need for achievement can benefit from setting their own learning goals, at least some of the time, and being asked to demonstrate on assessments works of high quality. Conversely, students with a motive to avoid failure can benefit from sequentially paced learning exercises with frequent assessments and considerable reinforcement for goal attainment.

Social Cognitive View of Motivation

Bandura (1986) developed the social cognitive theory, which replaced his earlier work on social learning. *Social cognitive theory* is a "perspective in which people function as anticipative, purposive and self-evaluating proactive regulators of their motivation and actions" (Bandura & Locke, 2003, p. 87). The factors that form the core of this theory are "intentionality, forethought, self-reactiveness, and self-reflectiveness" (p. 95).

In this model, motivation involves planning, setting goals, anticipating likely outcomes, setting personal standards, and a variety of self-regulating mechanisms (Bandura & Locke, 2003). The focus of these self-regulating mechanisms are on monitoring and reflecting about what actions increase a sense of self-worth and personal satisfaction and avoiding actions that decrease these factors. Thus, there is continuous feedback loop among the goal-setting and anticipation aspects that occur before an activity and the self-examination and self-adjustment aspects that occur after an activity.

A key link between the goal setting and self-regulatory features is personal self-efficacy. As noted in Chapter 4, **self-efficacy** is a prediction about how successful one will be on a particular task. Bandura and Locke (2003) note that self-efficacy is based partly on previous performance and partly on anticipated goals, beliefs, and expectations. Therefore, self-efficacy is composed of both previous experiences and anticipated future outcomes. The relationship between past experiences and future outcomes may be in a state of continual transformation. For instance, as students set goals and work to achieve them, they undergo a continuous self-evaluation. If they perceive that they have achieved their goals, their sense of positive self-efficacy may increase. If they perceive that they did not meet their goals, this self-efficacy may decrease.

Recurrent failures can lead to a significantly lowered sense of self-efficacy. A lower sense of self-efficacy tends to affect whether or not a student will undertake a task, invest the time needed to complete the task, and have anxiety about the task. Perhaps even more important, students who are low in self-efficacy tend to avoid seeking assistance from teachers or peers.

Some of the research indicates that teachers can effectively intervene when students have a lower sense of self-efficacy. Among the interventions that teachers can undertake are helping students set realistic and attainable goals, helping students develop metacognitive strategies, providing appropriate models, and giving constructive feedback (Schunk, 1991). For example, a student has a history of poor performance in mathematics. The student's teacher, however, provides a supportive classroom environment, helps in setting goals, and gives specific strategies to effectively learn math.

The student may be able to overcome a negative sense of self-efficacy about math by these interventions.

Another aspect of social cognitive theory is that vicarious learning (or observational learning) can be an effective strategy to motivate students. If a student is successful on a given task and receives a positive outcome, other students who observed the successful student can be motivated on the same task by observing this success. In fact, social cognitive theory states that using peer models in a variety of educational situations may be an effective strategy for enhancing motivation in students. Successful peers will motivate other students to emulate their performance.

Another area in this model deals with the role of reinforcement in motivation. Earlier work by Bandura indicated support for a somewhat traditional behavioral view on the use of extrinsic reinforcement. This earlier position was that the likelihood of a behavior being emitted is increased by the use of reinforcement. The individual may receive the reinforcement either directly or vicariously. Bandura currently views reinforcement as providing information about the previous behavior. In effect, a student who receives a reward for a behavior filters this consequence through a set of expectations, beliefs, and anticipations about similar future behaviors. It is this set of perceptions about the reinforcement that is critical to keeping the behavior, not the reinforcement itself. The next section further examines the issue of extrinsic reinforcement and its relationship to motivation.

Intrinsic Motivation versus Extrinsic Motivation

As noted at the beginning of this chapter, viewpoints about motivation are split into two camps: extrinsic motivation and intrinsic motivation. Extrinsic motivation is the label given for the idea that all behavior is the result of some type of external reinforcement. Intrinsic motivation is related to the view that behaviors are chosen as a goal by the student. Intrinsic motivation is based on the idea that students can be motivated by an interest in mastering a task and by a sense of curiosity.

Csikszentmihalyi and Nakamura (1989) originated the concept of the "flow experience," which is frequently connected with intrinsic motivation. Flow experience is what people feel when they actively enjoy what they are doing. The experience of "flow" is its own reward. People would not choose to do any other activity at that time. They are completely involved in what they are doing and their concentration is intense. Time passes quickly and there is no concern about failing or succeeding.

However, one person's flow experience can be another person's nightmare. For example, a friend of mine spends nearly all weekend restoring old cars. For him it is a perfect flow experience, even to the point that his wife has to remind him to come eat dinner. But for me, restoring old cars is equivalent to a visit to the dentist for a root canal.

According to Csikszentmihalyi and Nakamura (1989), the flow experience is rare. Fewer than 10 percent report it to happen daily. The theory of flow experience suggests that both the challenge and the skill of a task must be high to evoke flow. The researchers compared the amount of flow experience exhibited by teenagers in Italy and the United States. Students in Italy experienced flow more often than a comparable sample in the United States. Talented, higher-achieving students reported flow more often than equally talented but lower-achieving students.

Point/Counterpoint: Does Extrinsic Reinforcement Work?

Point

Supporters of extrinsic reinforcement point to the long history of using reward systems in schools and in business. They ask: Will students or employees work without having some type of tangible reward for their appropriate performance? Supporters point to the research work of Skinner and other behaviorists who find that token economies (organized formal reinforcement systems) are successful in a variety of settings. Proponents also note that teachers use a variety of reinforcement systems such as verbal praise, recognition, and grades, to increase student learning and performance. In a perfect world, students would be intrinsically motivated; however, in our world some students need external rewards to maintain their level of motivation. And even though this may not be optimum, these students are still learning something when they are rewarded.

Counterpoint

Opponents of using extrinsic reinforcement state that the issue is control, not learning. Using rewards is a method of asserting control over students or employees. For instance, a teacher who uses a reward system is saying, "If you do what I want, I will then give you what you want." This is simply a covert, though perhaps effective, method of forcing students to submit to external control. What this method does not bring about is a sense of internalized self-control. It simply weds the student to the rewards. When the rewards cease, the rewarded behaviors cease. There is no increase in internal motivation. In fact, a number of educators claim that extrinsic motivation and continuous reinforcement decrease any sense of intrinsic motivation. In effect, students come to expect payoffs and do not work without the expectation of a payoff.

Although we teachers wish that our classrooms could evoke "flow experiences" every day in our students, it does not seem very likely. The variation in what intrinsically motivates students does not make it possible. But there is a similar problem with extrinsic reinforcement: Gold stars and stickers do not work with everyone.

Regardless of where you stand on the issue of extrinsic reinforcement, all teachers are faced with a difficult problem about motivating students. The dilemma is that no one type of motivational procedure, be it extrinsic or intrinsic, is going to motivate all students all the time. In the end, teachers need to use a variety of motivational procedures for their students. As much as possible, teachers need to know what motivates individual students and then tailor classroom instruction and assessment to those individual needs and motives.

Development, Motivation, and Assessments

Little research data support a clear distinction between what motivates children on assessments in one grade level versus those in the next grade. Nevertheless, there is evidence that motivation is significantly affected by maturation. Children's ideas about a number of variables associated with motivation change as they become older and as they progress through school.

Stipek (1996) contends that young children in the primary grades tend to have more positive self-ratings of ability, more positive expectations, and a lower incidence of learned helplessness than children in later grades. Stipek indicates that part of the reason for more negative motivation later in school has to do with cognitive changes in regard to ability and effort. Children increasingly view ability as a type of inherent capacity and one that is separate from effort. By the time the child is age 12, higher effort often can imply lower ability.

Children also become more realistic as they become older. They are aware that some students are doing better than other students. There is some research that as early as fifth grade, students separate into two tracks: the academic achievers and the under-achievers. The underachievers increasingly give up in terms of motivation and achievement as they progress through middle school and high school.

Developmentally appropriate practices also involve the relationships among development, motivation, and assessments. **Developmentally appropriate practices** are instructional and assessment practices designed to meet the appropriate developmental level of each individual student. Developmentally appropriate practices are based on the idea that biological and experiential maturity (readiness rather than age) should determine the level of instructional and assessment practices (Elkind, 1987).

The issue of developmentally appropriate practices is particularly important in the primary grades. At this level, there can be a wide variety of maturity levels. For instance, a first-grade classroom will have children whose birthdays are spaced from January to August. At this age, an eight-month difference may produce a considerable variation in developmental maturity levels.

To compensate for these differing maturational levels, teachers need to use a variety of informal and formal assessments to find the developmental level of each student. After determining the developmental level of each student, appropriate instructional materials can be provided. For example, learning centers that focus on reading, math, and science can be placed throughout the classroom. Children can move from center to center as they complete assignments at their developmental levels. Assessments also may be specific to the appropriate developmental levels. Using informal assessments, checklists, observations, self-assessments, parent interviews, and student portfolios tend to be favored as the type of assessment methods for developmentally appropriate practices.

Chapter Summary

This chapter reviewed a number of motivational aspects involved with assessments. The first section provided some guidance about the types of motives that might enhance assessment performance. Possible positive motives include the desire for approval from either teachers, parents, or peers; the sense to model or imitate successful adults; a sense of mastery of a subject; and a sense of curiosity.

The second section examined a number of other motivation areas. Negative motivation about assessments is one such area—that is, why some students do not make the necessary effort on assessments that result in successful outcomes. The role of attributions and locus of control were included as possible contributing factors with negative motivation.

Social cognitive theory was then reviewed. This model presents the viewpoint that both past experience and anticipatory goal setting are involved in motivating students in their classroom performance. Self-efficacy is a crucial link between past performance on assessments and the goals and expectations about future assessments. A number of suggestions on how to increase student self-efficacy were presented.

The final section considered two areas: extrinsic versus intrinsic motivation and the effect of development on motivation and assessments. The differences between extrinsic and intrinsic motivation were presented. The role of development and of developmentally appropriate practices were then reviewed.

CASE STUDY EPILOGUE

Mr. Foster has now changed his instruction and assessments in a number of ways. Because of students' attitudes toward math, he now works on increasing student self-efficacy. He begins his course by using informal assessments to determine the level of math understanding in his students. He then assists each student to set realistic goals and develop strategies to help study for the course. He also brings in role models from local businesses who explain how math is used at their work.

In terms of formal assessments, Mr. Foster gives an objective formal assessment every other week to his classes. He finds that this tends to lower overall math anxiety in his students. He also requires that they meet in small cooperative learning groups during each class. Each group keeps a group portfolio that details their work on different math problems. Mr. Foster moves from group to group during cooperative learning to ensure on task behavior and to answer questions. With this grade level, Mr. Foster finds that allowing for cooperative learning increases student attention and motivation.

CHAPTER ACTIVITIES

Websites

http://www.emory.edu/EDUCATION/mfp/effpage.html   This site provides a wealth of resources on social cognitive theory, self-efficacy, and Albert Bandura. Everything you need to know and more about this model can be found here.

http://seamonkey.ed.asu.edu/~jimbo/RIBARY_Folder/motivati.htm   This site provides an excellent review of the differences between intrinsic and extrinsic motivation. It also provides some resources for classroom motivation.

http://home.earthlink.net/~bmgei/educate/docs/motivate/motconts.htm This website, designed by a presently practicing teacher, provides a variety of suggestions about classroom activities to increase student motivation.

Portfolio Activities

1. Review Mr. Foster's situation in the Chapter Case Study. Write an essay based on what you have found out about motivation in this chapter. Answer each of the following questions and list them in your portfolio:
   - What are the factors that serve to motivate students?
   - Is intrinsic motivation or extrinsic motivation more important? Why?
   - Does fear of failure motivate students? Why or why not?
   - Does curiosity motivate students? Why or why not?
   - Is there one magic method that will motivate all students? Support your answer.
   - Do assessments really motivate students? Explain your answer.

2. Go to this website: http://seamonkey.ed.asu.edu/~jimbo/RIBARY_Folder/motivati. htm. Use the material from it to write an essay in your portfolio examining intrinsic and extrinsic motivation. Compare and contrast intrinsic and extrinsic motivation and answer the following:
   - Explain why intrinsic motivation is essential in the classroom.
   - Reflect on a time in your life when you were extrinsically motivated and and a time when you were intrinsically motivated.
   - What were the rewards, reasons, or outcomes in each case?
   - What can you do as a teacher to increase intrinsic motivation?

KEY CONCEPTS

Achievement motivation
Attributions
Causal attributions
Developmentally appropriate practices
External factors
External locus of control
Internal factors

Internal locus of control
Learned helplessness
Locus of control
Motive
Negative motivation
Self-efficacy

REVIEW QUESTIONS

1. Describe what is meant by a *motive* and give an example of motives and assessments.

2. Describe Kagan and Lang's six basic motives that operate in schools.

3. According to Ames and Ames, what are the three types of thinking that evoke negative motivation?

4. Explain the differences between attributions made due to *internal factors* and attributions made due to *external factors*.

5. Compare and contrast the terms *internal locus of control* and *external locus of control*. List one example of each type of locus of control.

6. According to social cognitive theory, what are the basic mechanisms of motivation?

7. Describe some of the major factors in the relationship between development, assessment, and motivation.

8. What are some methods that a teacher can use to increase self-efficacy?

SELF-ASSESSMENT

1. Kagan and Lang suggest six motives that operate in schools. Which is one of these motives?
   a. Desire for disapproval
   b. Desire to resolve uncertainty
   c. Desire to gratify individual wishes
   d. Desire for monetary rewards

2. Negative motivation could be described as:
   a. Peer pressure to fail
   b. A mental image that the task cannot be successfully finished
   c. Success without effort in academics but not in athletics
   d. Self-perception that allows students to do their best and excel

3. Ideas about why students succeed or fail are known as:
   a. Causal attributions
   b. Desirable inhibitions
   c. Intrinsic motivational causations
   d. Extrinsic motivation

4. A student with an external locus of control who scores an A on an exam may attribute the grade to:
   a. Fate or luck
   b. Study habits
   c. Self-confidence
   d. A great memory

5. Csikszentmihalyi and Nakamura describe what people feel when they actively enjoy what they are doing which contains its own reward as:
   a. Flow experience
   b. Personal achievement
   c. Extrinsic ability
   d. Free will motivation

6. Social cognitive theory emphasizes the role of:
   a. Fate or luck
   b. Self-awareness
   c. Negative motivation and learned helplessness
   d. Self-efficacy

Answers to Self-Assessment: 1. b, 2. b, 3. a, 4. a, 5. a, 6. d, 7. c, 8. d

7. Another term that is used for external reinforcement is:
  a. Self-efficacy
  b. Self-worth
  c. Extrinsic reinforcement
  d. Intrinsic reinforcement

8. Which theorist is most closely associated with social cognitive theory?
  a. Kagan
  b. Piaget
  c. Ames
  d. Bandura

REFERENCES

Ames, R., & Ames, C. (1991). Motivation and effective teaching. In L. Idol & V.F. Jones (Eds.), *Educational values and cognitive instruction: Implications for reform* (pp. 247–269). Hillsdale, NJ: Lawrence Erlbaum.

Atkinson, J. (1957). Motivational determinants of risk-taking behavior. *Psychological Review*, 64, 359–372.

Atkinson, J. (1964). *An introduction to motivation.* Princeton, NJ: Van Nostrand.

Bandura, A. (1986). *Social foundations of thought and action.* Englewood Cliffs, NJ: Prentice Hall.

Bandura, A., & Locke, E.A. (2003). Negative self-efficacy and goal effects revisited. *Journal of Applied Psychology*, 88(1), 87–99.

Covington, M. (1984). The motive for self-worth. In C. Ames & R. Ames (Eds.), *Research on motivation in education: Student motivation* (Vol. 1, pp. 78–108). Orlando, FL: Academic Press.

Covington, M., & Omelich, C. (1979). Effort: The double-edged sword in school achievement. *Journal of Educational Psychology*, 71, 688–700.

Csikszentmihalyi, M., & Nakamura, J. (1989). The dynamics of intrinsic motivation: A study of adolescents. In C. Ames & R. Ames (Eds.), *Research on motivation in education: Goals and Cognition* (Vol. 3, pp. 45–71). San Diego: Academic Press.

deCharms, R. (1984). Motivation enhancement in educational settings. In C. Ames & R. Ames (Eds.), *Research on motivation in education: Goals in cognition* (Vol. 3, pp. 45–71). San Diego: Academic Press.

Dweck, C. (1986). Motivational processes affecting learning. *American Psychologist*, 41, 1040–1048.

Elkind, D. (1987). *Miseducation: Preschoolers at risk.* New York: Knopf.

Forsterling, F. (1985). Attributional retraining: A review. *Psychological Bulletin*, 98(3), 453–512.

Kagan, J., & Lang, C. (1978). *Psychology and education: An introduction.* New York: Harcourt, Brace, & Jovanovich.

McClelland, D., Atkinson, J., Clark, R., & Lowell E. (1953). *The achievement motive.* New York: Appleton-Century-Crofts.

Rotter, J. (1966). Generalized expectancies for internal versus external control of reinforcement. *Psychological Monographs*, 80, 1–28.

Schunk, D.H. (1991). Self-efficacy and academic motivation. *Educational Psychologist*, 26, 207–231.

Stipek, D.J. (1996). Motivation and instruction. In D.C.Berliner & R.C. Calfee (Eds.), *Handbook of educational psychology.* New York: Simon & Schuster.

Weiner, B. (1984). Principles for a theory of student motivation and their application within an attributional framework. In C. Ames & R. Ames (Eds.), *Research on motivation in education: Student motivation* (Vol.1, pp. 15–36). Orlando, FL: Academic Press.

Wolters, C.A., Yu, S.L., & Pintrich, P.R. (1996). The relation between goal orientation and students' motivational beliefs and self-regulated learning. *Learning and Individual Differences*, 8, 211–238.

13 Special Considerations with Assessments

CASE STUDY

Mr. Thompson is in his second year of teaching physical sciences at a new high school in an urban school district in the southeast. Due to increased science standards and course requirements for graduation in his state, Mr. Thompson's science courses are flooded with students. However, many of his students have little or no background in chemistry and physics or even general science.

Mr. Thompson has discovered that this situation is causing a number of different problems. Many of his students complain that his classroom is not supportive for students with little science experience. They also complain that the math needed for his classes was not available to them. Some of them have complained that Mr. Thompson is not as helpful about the situation as he should be. Other students have asked for special test review and test preparation classes. Right before the first test, Mr. Thompson also had a number of students tell him that they had more test anxiety about his classroom tests than in any other course.

During and after the first test, Mr. Thompson became aware of a potentially even bigger problem. A number of students appeared to be copying each other's answers on the exam. When he checks some of their scores, he finds that there are many similar answers.

These problems leave Mr. Thompson with a number of questions. Among them are the following:

What can he do to provide a more positive classroom environment?

What can he do to be a more helpful teacher?

What can he do to make the test situations more positive?

How can he more effectively help students prepare for exams?

What are some ways to decrease test anxiety in students?

What should he do about academic cheating?

Introduction

This chapter analyzes a number of special issues and concerns about assessment administration and assessment practices. A good part of these issues and concerns deal with the relationship between the classroom environment and assessments. For example, the first section of this chapter examines the factors involved in creating a positive classroom assessment environment. Included among these aspects are supportive teacher behaviors, assessment practices, classroom physical conditions, and classroom seating arrangements.

The second section of this chapter reviews a number of different problem areas with classroom assessment practices. This section begins with an examination of the different methods of test preparation. Ethical and unethical test preparation practices are detailed. The next part contains the problem of test anxiety. This section reviews the research on test anxiety and presents recommendations for dealing with test anxiety. The end of this chapter provides a critical analysis on the problems of academic cheating. This section examines ways that teachers may combat cheating.

Classroom Environment and Assessments

Classroom environment is the overall setting and context in which all classroom activities occur. It includes the social climate of the classroom, the physical features of the room, the assessment situation and context, and instructional activities of the teacher. Therefore, classroom environment ranges from the educational to the social to the physical features of a classroom.

Classroom climate is a subcategory of classroom environment that focuses on the emotional and social interactions in the classroom. Every organization has its own climate. In the classroom, the climate is largely determined by the social and psychological relationships between the teacher and the students (Rosenfeld, 1983). This relationship gives each individual classroom its own atmosphere or personality. The leading factor in developing these relationships is the teacher.

Classroom assessment environment also is a subcategory of classroom environment. Classroom assessment environment focuses on the background and context created for students during different assessment procedures (Stiggins & Conklin, 1992). As with classroom climate, the central factor is the teacher. There are a number of aspects to consider about classroom environment and classroom assessment environment. The next section examines these various aspects.

Creating a Positive Environment

The research on classroom environment and climate indicates that teacher immediacy and responsiveness behaviors are important factors in students' perceptions of a supportive classroom (Jordan & Merkel, 1994). **Teacher immediacy and responsiveness behaviors** indicate that the teacher wants positive communications. These actions include eye contact, smiling, physical proximity, encouraging questions, and praising students' work. These teacher behaviors indicate an interest in immediate and active responding to student needs. The more a teacher demonstrates these behaviors, the more positive the students' views about the classroom will be.

Other teacher behaviors that may help produce a supportive classroom environment are:

1. Teachers who are sensitive as to when students need help and when they do not
2. Teachers who allow some individual freedom and choice by students
3. Teachers who actively strive to create a positive feeling between students

The ability to create a harmonious working atmosphere among students appears to be especially important. Group activities, group projects, and informal group assessments may help in nurturing a supportive climate. Students who are used to working in teams seem more likely to be supportive of each other. The research indicates a number of teacher behaviors that can enhance a supportive classroom environment. The following is a list of some of these activities:

Factors Contributing to a Supportive Environment
1. A teacher who uses a relaxed and open manner in student interactions
2. A teacher who promotes cooperation among students
3. A teacher who encourages a free exchange of ideas
4. A teacher who clearly defines what is expected of students
5. A teacher who consistently demonstrates a desire for students to succeed in class
6. A teacher who provides useful feedback to students
7. A teacher who moves around the classroom, interacting positively with students
8. A teacher who has positive expectations for student performance

Unfortunately, research indicates that the environment in many classrooms tends to be negative rather than supportive (Myers & Rocca, 2001). A negative environment can cause a number of problems with classroom assessments. In particular, test anxiety, inappropriate behavior, and negative self-efficacy can be increased in a negative classroom environment. There are a number of classroom environment factors that can adversely affect your students:

Factors Contributing to a Negative Environment
1. A teacher who embarrasses students when they miss questions on a test or during class discussion
2. A teacher who makes disparaging remarks about students' performance on assessments
3. A teacher who encourages competition among students on assessments
4. A teacher who is overly intrusive or overly controlling in every aspect of student behavior
5. A teacher who inappropriately responds to students' requests.

Classroom Assessment Environment

Clearly, certain aspects—positive or negative—can have an effect on the quality of assessments in your classroom environment. As previously stated, the way that each individual classroom teacher interacts with students is the prime variable. Some educators have focused more specifically on the factors that contribute to the classroom assessment environment. Recall that Stiggins and Conklin (1992) defined the *classroom assessment environment* as the context created for students during different assessment procedures. There are a number of aspects Siggins and Conklin discuss in developing a positive classroom assessment environment. Among these factors are the following:

1. A variety of appropriate assessment methods closely linked to instruction
2. Selecting assessments that have established quality
3. Clearly defined expectations and positive perceptions of students
4. Fair and consistent assessment policies in grading students
5. Effective feedback after assessments

Research on classroom assessment environments indicates that the environment has an impact on student achievement in the classroom (Brookhart, 1997). Not surprisingly, classrooms with a positive assessment environment tend to have better student achievement (Brookhart, 1997). The research also demonstrates that there is a reciprocal relationship between classroom assessment environment and the factors of assessment perceptions, appropriate expectations, effective feedback, and self-efficacy (Brookhart & DeVoge, 1999). In positive assessment environments, students appear to perceive assessments in a more favorable light. Teachers who provide appropriate expectations and effective feedback generally bring about an increase in achievement in their students. Student self-efficacy also should be influenced in a positive manner with a positive assessment environment.

On the other hand, there are certain areas of the classroom assessment environment that may be beyond the teacher's control. Class size can be a factor in this environment. There is a tendency for larger classes to have a somewhat less positive and supportive environment. Schoolwide or systemwide policies may have an effect on the assessment environment. For example, increasing academic standards may have an impact on the assessment environment. The actual physical layout of buildings or classrooms can also have an impact. The next section further examines the physical structure factors involved in the classroom assessment environment.

Classroom Structure and Conditions

The physical features and conditions of the classroom are an important part of the assessment environment. Room temperature, lighting, classroom design, and seating arrangements can all have an impact on student achievement and the quality of assessment practices. The following teacher application specifically addresses the physical comfort and conditions of the classroom.

Teacher Application

Classroom Structure and Conditions for Assessments
- Is the classroom temperature comfortable during assessments?
- Is the lighting appropriate for students?
- Is the room well ventilated?
- Are there any unnecessary distractions, such as too much noise during assessments?
- Are the seating arrangements comfortable?
- Are computers, lab equipment, and other instructional devices arranged in an appropriate manner to match the students' needs during assessments?
- Does the design and upkeep of the classroom make it an inviting place for students to take assessments?

A physically uncomfortable environment can be a distraction to students during assessments. Loud noise levels, high temperatures, and poor ventilation almost certainly reduce performance. An uncomfortable environment can result in incorrect or unreliable levels of achievement among students. In addition to these factors, there are a number of issues concerning seating arrangements. The next section reviews these issues.

Seating Arrangements

Many studies have indicated that when students are allowed to choose their own seats in a classroom, there is a noticeable effect on achievement during formal and informal assessments (Levine, O'Neal, & McDonald, 1980; Wulf, 1976). Students who choose to sit nearest to the teacher tend to have higher rates of achievement; students who choose to sit far from the teacher tend to have lower rates of achievement. However, when students are assigned seats, this effect essentially disappears, with no significant relationship between seat assignment and achievement. A similar pattern can be seen with class participation on informal assessments. If allowed to choose their own seats, students who sit near the teacher will participate more in class discussions and on informal assessments requiring student participation.

Another aspect about seating arrangements is the issue of organizing classroom seating during assessments. There are three standard patterns:

1. **Row seating** refers to the traditional seating of four or five rows with desks one behind another.
2. **Circular seating** (or *semicircular seating*) consists of some type of circular arrangement with all desks having a clear view of the teacher.
3. **Cluster seating** refers to groups of students seated at large tables.

One recent survey of K–5 classroom seating arrangements found that approximately 75 percent of elementary school classrooms use some form of cluster seating (Patton, Snell, Knight, & Gerken, 2001). The primary grades are more likely than later grades to use cluster seating. According to the researchers, these findings are in marked contrast to previous surveys in this area that indicated that row seating was the predominant pattern in elementary classrooms through the 1980s.

The major reason for the change is the idea that cooperative learning and group assessment activities are fostered by cluster seating arrangements. Patton and colleagues (2001) state that many teachers believe that cluster seating helps foster cooperative learning and that cooperative learning helps foster student achievement. However, the authors note that previous research does not clearly indicate that these beliefs are supported.

Achievement levels on classroom assessments do not appear to be any greater with cluster seating than with other forms of seating. As previously indicated, assigned seating arrangements do not appear to have any effect on student achievement. The research is more straightforward about the issue of off-task behaviors. A number of studies of K–12 students indicate that row seating, not cluster seating, decreases off-task behaviors and increases on-task behaviors (Axelrod, Hall, & Tams, 1979; Wheldall, Morris, Vaughan, & Ng, 1981; Wheldall & Lam, 1987). In these studies, seating in rows markedly reduced off-task behavior when compared with cluster seating. Seating in rows, versus clusters, produced noticeable increases in on-task behaviors.

There may be an increase in student participation when a circular/horseshoe seating arrangement is used rather than row seating (Rosenfeld, Lambert, & Black, 1985). Circular seating arrangements may enhance instruction and informal assessments that focus on group discussion and student participation. Again, participation with this seating arrangement appears to be primarily influenced by whether students choose their seats or are assigned seats.

So what's a teacher to do about choosing seating arrangements? Papalia (1976) makes an important point about classroom seating: No one seating arrangement is going to work all the time. For some activities row seating may be better, whereas with other activities it may be better to use either cluster or circular seating. Papalia's review states that the following activities may be best performed with the three major seating arrangements:

Instruction, Assessments, and Seating Arrangements

1. **Cluster Seating.** Tutoring, peer teaching, peer assessments, use of self-instructional materials, and cooperative grouping according to interests and activities

2. **Row Seating.** Introduction of new material, formal assessments, independent work, and audiovisual presentations
3. **Circular Seating.** Teacher mobility, eye contact, interpersonal communication, and game playing

Perhaps the best advice is to change seating arrangements based on the preceding activities. Rather than rely on only one type of seating, altering your seating arrangements based on your assessment and instructional activities may enhance the classroom environment.

Test Preparation and Assessments

Popham (1987) coined the term high-stakes testing to refer to school districts where major educational decisions are based on standardized test scores. As noted before, there is considerable controversy about the use of high-stakes testing. Many educators believe that such testing may improve test scores but without a corresponding gain in learning (Cannell, 1988; Shepard, 1990; Shepard & Dougherty, 1991).

High-stakes testing has produced some other troubling educational problems. One such problem is the extensive time spent in preparation for taking the tests. Weeks and even months in some cases may be devoted to test preparation. One elementary school that I am familiar with spent an entire year preparing for the standardized assessments. The school was on a state watch list for low test scores and had one year to bring up its scores to the mandated level or be placed under direct state control. Although the school succeeded in meeting the mandated score, it devoted the entire year to test-taking skills and test preparation for this standardized test. It is perhaps the most extreme form of "teaching to the content of the test" about which I personally know.

Smith (1991) studied various types of state test preparation programs. These programs included test-taking skills, exhortations by the faculty, teaching content known to be covered by the test, teaching to the test, stress inoculation, practicing parallel tests items, and cheating.

Teaching test-taking skills, such as limiting guessing and answering the easy questions first, is clearly ethical. However, some of the other test preparation aspects are clearly not ethical. For instance, it is clearly unethical to teach the test items directly, either through teaching to a previous or a current version of the test. Parallel forms, provided by the publisher for actual practice by students, is an ethical practice, although a somewhat questionable teaching practice. In effect, practice tests and practice test exercises are acceptable, but they are not really what teaching and learning are all about. Cheating by teachers or administrators is clearly unethical.

In their survey of high-stakes testing, Shepard and Dougherty (1991) found that 6 percent of teachers believed that changing incorrect answers to correct ones on answer documents occurred in their school. The study reported that 8 percent of teachers indicated that students who might have trouble on the test were encouraged to be absent on the day of testing. Additional findings indicated that 23 percent of teachers believed that hints to correct answers were given and that 18 percent believed that questions were rephrased to help students in their school.

These types of teacher behaviors are considered unethical by the major professional educational and psychological associations. Such practices compromise the integrity of the tests and call into question the entire assessment and educational process.

Formal Preparatory Programs and Assessments

A number of companies claim that they can produce a significant increase in students' scores with formal preparatory classes and programs. Messick (1982) presented evidence that coaching and preparatory programs were able to substantially improve SAT scores. On the other hand, in his review of the effects of preparatory programs, Cunningham (1986) stated that short-term courses result in only modest improvements in assessment scores. Cunningham did acknowledge, however, that intensive training may produce greater increases in scores. Cunningham also pointed out that the scores on mathematics tests were more likely to be improved than other areas. This finding appears to be consistent with other research.

In the teacher application section that follows, a number of veteran teachers were asked to provide their views on test preparation programs and how they use standardized assessment scores.

Teacher Application

Views on Test Preparation and on Using Test Scores
I use a testing and instructional program called Scoring High to prepare students for the Comprehensive Test of Basic Skills (CTBS). I use it so children can test in a format like the CTBS. I also use this program as a review. I check the results of the CTBS to see if modifications are needed for students who are having trouble. But I do not use them to put [the students] into levels. I teach whole-class instruction; I do not track. I think that these types of tests are only one indicator. Some children cannot test well but do well otherwise. I think tracking and labeling can have a real negative impact if [a child is] placed in a low group.—*Linda Parker, third-grade teacher*

I do not do any special preparation for the Comprehensive Test of Basic Skills. Unless everyone does it, it would be unfair.—*Nancy Thompson, third-grade teacher*

As a school, we do a test item analysis of our standardized achievement scores. Our whole faculty senate looks at strengths and weaknesses. We go to work on the weaknesses.—*Nancy Goheen, first-grade teacher*

I use a standardized achievement scores only when another indicator, such as classroom performance, observations, verbal or nonverbal ability, would indicate a need to use them. Very high or very low achievers would be checked. I think my own classroom measures are more helpful. The standardized tests take up too much time. I would rather use the time for classroom instruction.—*Rebecca Queen, second-grade teacher*

On some of these tests I think that students are tested on materials that have never been covered in class. Keep in mind that learning outcomes vary from school system to school system, from county to county, and from state to state. It is unfair to assume that a standardized test or a national exam can take all this into account.—*Sheila Leach, sixth-grade teacher*

We use these types of tests to chart student progress and the weaknesses of each child. We pass the information along to the next teacher to see what skills are weak. That way she will know what needs to be worked on. It cuts wasted time for the next teacher.—*Mary Russell, first-grade teacher*

As indicated in these statements, individual teachers have a number of different ideas about test preparation programs and how to use test results. Some teachers and schools use formal test preparation programs; others believe that such programs are either inherently unfair to certain students or an inappropriate instructional practice.

Test Preparation Activities

Teaching test-taking skills and teaching how to deal with the stress or anxiety about tests are appropriate activities for teachers. Test-taking skills include three separate areas: time management, practicing with different test formats, and identifying the important information in items.

Time management on tests helps students plan how much they can devote to each part of the test. One recommendation is that students read through the test and answer the items that they are sure about during this first read. During the second read, they should then deal with the items that they are uncertain about on the first read. This helps students manage the remaining time on the test and allows them to focus on the questions that pose problems for them.

Practicing with different item formats allows students to understand some of the differences between different types of assessments. For example, practicing with certain item formats, such as multiple-choice items, may enable students to select the correct answer by the process of elimination. Another important aspect of using different formats help students with completing computerized answer sheets. Many students have problems with following directions and responding on "bubble sheets." Practicing how to actually answer items from a test booklet with a bubble sheet may help students achieve at a higher rate.

Identifying important information in items involves ensuring that students can select the essential parts of the test questions and can effectively respond to the questions. For example, in responding to an essay question, the students are able to identify what is the central underlying theme to the question. Students can eliminate certain parts of their responses and focus on just the essentials. Figure 13.1 shows some recommendations from one state department of education on how to prepare for standardized assessments.

Numerous programs and state websites now exist for preparing students for standardized formal assessments. This proliferation shows the effects of high-stakes testing

Point/Counterpoint: Extensive Test Preparation

Point

Supporters of extensive test preparation point out that standardized assessments in public schools appear to be here to stay. The issue is how best to deal with them. School systems are forced by the public and government agencies to administer these tests; therefore, school systems must do their best in providing students with an equal opportunity in taking the tests. For example, supporters of test preparation programs claim that intensive programs can level the playing field for children from low-income, minority, or second-language backgrounds. These children often are not provided with the type of educational support offered to mainstream children. By training students in test-taking strategies, in different testing formats, and in using practice tests, school districts are providing a service rather than a disservice to these students. They are offering a way to cope with an otherwise difficult situation. Some supporters of test preparation believe that these practices should be integrated into the regular curriculum. By using test preparation as part of regular instruction, school systems can maximize the support that they provide to students. Therefore, all students will have an equal opportunity to do well on these tests.

Counterpoint

Opponents of extensive test preparation state that the practice simply puts the cart before the horse. The goal of assessment is to support instruction. Extensive test preparation does just the opposite: Instruction ends up supporting assessment. The time spent on test preparation is far better spent on direct instruction. Opponents claim that test preparation programs are simply teaching to whatever is the current version of standardized tests. No real teaching and no real learning is completed in this situation. As soon as the test is over, the test preparation skills are forgotten. Critics of standardized assessment also state that extensive test preparation can be very expensive as well as time consuming. Wealthier school systems and students may be able to afford the courses, whereas the less well off cannot afford the programs. The end result may be that the wealthier school systems will do even better, while poorer school systems will be even more worse off. Extensive test preparation simply may reinforce already existing disparities between school systems.

---

on U.S. education. One result of the increase in high-stakes testing appears to be a corresponding increase in test anxiety.

Test Anxiety

Test anxiety consists of a continuum of responses ranging from a queasy feeling at the start of the test to an incapacitating phobia. Some models more specifically refer to it as *evaluation anxiety*. Early work by Liebert and Morris (1967) indicates that incapacitating test anxiety has two components: worry and emotionality. Worry is the cognitive component that focuses on failure, whereas emotionality is the affective component that

FIGURE 13.1   Test Strategies for Students, Parents, and Teachers: Tennessee Department of Education

General Test Taking Skills

Time-Using Strategies

- Work as rapidly as possible with reasonable accuracy.
- Don't spend too much time on any one question.
- On scrap paper, keep a record of the unanswered items which you may go back to if time permits.
- Use time remaining after completion of the test to go back and check your answers.

Error-Avoidance Strategies

- Pay careful attention to directions.
- Decide exactly what the question is asking; one response is clearly best.
- Ask the examiner for clarification of directions before the test begins.
- If you are using a separate answer sheet, make sure to record the answer in the correct position on the sheet.
- Be sure to completely erase incorrect answers.

Miscellaneous Tips

- Don't make wild guesses. Many times you can get the correct answer by reasoning and eliminating wrong answers.
- Only change an answer if you are sure the first one you picked was wrong.
- Tackle items one at a time rather than thinking about the whole test.
- Do not expect to find a pattern in the positions of the correct choices.

Students: Test Taking Strategies

Before the Test

- Do your class work.
- Have a clear understanding of homework assignments before leaving class.
- Keep a record of assignments received and completed.
- Make a study schedule and follow it.
- Tell your parents about schoolwork and homework.
- Follow directions.
- Return homework when it is due.
- Get make-up assignments when returning from an absence.
- See teachers for additional help.
- Find out when tests will be given.
- Become familiar with a multiple-choice format.
- Get a good night's rest and eat a normal breakfast before testing.

During the Test

- Read all directions carefully.
- Completely read each passage and accompanying questions.
- Read every possible answer—the best one could be last.
- Reread, when necessary, the parts of a passage needed for selecting the correct answer.
- Eliminate answer choices that are clearly wrong.

(continued)

FIGURE 13.1 Continued

- Skip very difficult questions until all other questions have been answered.
- Keep a good attitude. Think positively!

After the Test
- Ask the teacher to explain your test scores.
- Ask your teacher to suggest areas of study that will help you do even better on the next test.

Parents: Test Support Strategies

Before Testing
- Encourage your child to take responsibility for homework.
- Set aside a specific time for study each day.
- Provide a well lighted, quiet setting for study.
- Ask to see homework assignments every day.
- Help your child learn to find information independently.
- Use homework to keep up with what your child is learning in school.
- Praise your child for work done well.
- Ask your child to read aloud.
- Encourage your child to ask questions at home and in class.
- Know how long your child watches TV.
- Know what your child watches on TV. Discuss programs together.
- Show interest in your child's daily activities. Ask what happened at school today.
- Talk with and listen to your child. Ask each other questions and share experiences.
- Get to know your child's teachers.
- Attend parent-teacher conferences.
- Confer with teachers on a regular basis.
- Let your child know that you think a good education is important.
- Note test dates on your home calendar.

On the Day of Testing
- See that your child is rested and has time for breakfast.
- See that your child arrives at school on time and is relaxed.
- Encourage your child to do the best work possible.
- Don't send your child to school if illness is apparent.

After Testing
- Examine all test reports sent home.
- See your child's principal, counselor, or teacher if additional information is required.

Teachers: Administration Strategies

Before Test Administration
- Inform students in advance of test dates.
- Explain the reasons for testing.
- Create a comfortable testing environment.
- Use a variety of test formats during the school year.
- Become familiar with the materials and procedures to be used with machine scored tests.

FIGURE 13.1 Continued

- Read the Examiner's Manual well in advance of the test.
- Encourage all students to be present on test dates.

During Test Administration
- Adhere to time limits specified for tests.
- Read directions to students and answer questions about directions before starting the test.
- Expect every student to read all test content material without assistance unless otherwise noted in the Examiner's Manual.
- Monitor to ensure that students begin marking answers in the proper area of the answer sheet.
- Make sure students work independently.

Source: Tennessee Department of Education (2003).

produces some of the adverse physiological responses (cold sweats, elevated heart rate, and upset stomach, etc.) associated with test anxiety. In either case, test anxiety does appear to have a significant negative effect on student achievement.

Other models show that test anxiety may have some additional factors. For example, Wine (1971) proposes that the effect of test anxiety on performance is due to cognitive interference. According to this model, during an assessment the student divides his or her attention between the test materials and a negative preoccupation about the test. This interferes with the student's recall of material and reduces his or her performance. A second model (Wittmaier, 1972) states that test anxiety has a cumulative effect that begins with the studying of the material and the prior fear of the testing situation. According to this model, students are fearful of the test beforehand and therefore they do not fully learn the material. This fear snowballs as the test approaches and the students realize that they are not fully prepared for the test. When the time comes to take the test, they have poor performance because of the cumulative fear and the correspondingly poor study habits.

Some research indicates that, to some degree, people who have a high level of general anxiety or trait anxiety tend to also have a high level of test anxiety (Zohar, 1998). Thus, general anxiety and test anxiety may be somewhat related. In effect, one predictor of test anxiety is a higher than normal level of general anxiety. But a number of other factors also appear to be related to test anxiety, including self-efficacy about the specific course or subject, the type of test situation, and gender.

When students have negative self-efficacy about a course, they tend to have more test anxiety (Bandalos, Yeates, & Thorndike-Christ, 1995). The complexity of the relationship between self-efficacy and test anxiety indicates that other variables, such as self-esteem and type of attributions, play some role as well. Low academic self-esteem and external attributions about success may predict test anxiety. The type of test situation that is most likely to trigger test anxiety is a timed test (Hill & Eaton, 1977); untimed test situations tend to reduce test anxiety. Women tend to have higher levels of test anxiety than do men (AAUW, 1992).

Many of these variables may interact with each other and compound the effects of test anxiety. For example, there may be a cumulative effect of prior experience compounded by generally high anxiety levels coupled with negative self-efficacy about a class. Figure 13.2 shows a survey instrument used to informally assess test anxiety.

FIGURE 13.2   Test Anxiety Questionnaire

The items in the questionnaire refer to experiences that may cause fear or apprehension. For each item, place a check in the box under the column that describes how much you are *frightened by it*. Work quickly, but be sure to consider each item individually. For each box you check, write down the corresponding number of points:

Not At All = 1; A Little = 2; A Fair Amount = 3; Much = 4; Very Much = 5.

Situation	Not at All	A Little	A Fair Amount	Much	Very Much
1. Going into a regularly scheduled class period in which the teacher asks students to participate.					
2. Rereading the answers I gave on the test before turning it in.					
3. Sitting down to study before a regularly scheduled class.					
4. Turning my completed test paper in.					
5. Hearing the announcement of a coming test.					
6. Having a test returned.					
7. Reading the first question on a final exam.					
8. Studying for a class in which I am scared of the teacher.					
9. Being in class waiting for my corrected test to be returned.					
10. Seeing a test question and not being sure of the answer.					
11. Studying for a test the night before.					

FIGURE 13.2   Continued

Situation	Not at All	A Little	A Fair Amount	Much	Very Much
12. Waiting to enter the room where a test is to be given.					
13. Waiting for a test to be handed out.					
14. Being called on to answer a question in class by a teacher who scares me.					
15. Waiting for the day my corrected test will be returned.					
16. Seeing my standing on the exam relative to other people's standing.					
17. Discussing with the teacher an answer I believed to be right, but that was marked wrong.					
18. Waiting to see my letter grade on the test.					
19. Studying for a quiz.					
20. Studying for a midterm.					
21. Studying for a final.					
22. Discussing my approaching test with friends a few weeks before the test.					
23. After the test, listening to the answers that my friends selected.					
24. Looking at the clock to see how much time remains during the exam.					
25. Seeing the number of questions that need to be answered on the test.					
26. On an essay exam, seeing a question I cannot answer.					

(continued)

FIGURE 13.2 Continued

Situation	Not at All	A Little	A Fair Amount	Much	Very Much
27. On a multiple-choice test, seeing a question I cannot answer.					
28. Being asked by someone if I am ready for a forthcoming exam.					
29. Being the first one to finish an exam and turn it in.					
30. Being asked by a friend where I stand in the class.					
31. Being asked by a friend the results of a test on which I did poorly.					
32. Discovering I need an A or B on the next test to pass the course.					
33. Discovering I need an A or B on the final to maintain the grade-point average necessary to remain in school.					
34. Remembering my past reactions while preparing for another test.					
35. Seeking out the teacher for advice or help.					
36. Being told to see the teacher concerning some aspects of my class work.					
37. Asking for a make-up exam after missing the scheduled exam.					
38. Being the last one to finish an exam and turn it in.					
39. Discussing the course content with fellow students before entering the classroom the day of the exam.					

FIGURE 13.2   Continued

Situation	Not at All	A Little	A Fair Amount	Much	Very Much
40. Reviewing study materials the night before an exam.					
41. On the first day of the course hearing the teacher announce dates of the midterm and final exams.					
42. Having the teacher ask a question of the class that deals with the course material and then look in my direction.					
43. Making an appointment to see the teacher regarding some course problem.					
44. Thinking about a coming exam *3 weeks before* it is scheduled.					
45. Thinking about a coming exam *1 week before* it is scheduled.					
46. Thinking about a coming exam *the weekend* before it is scheduled.					
47. Thinking about a coming exam *the night before* it is scheduled.					
48. Thinking about an upcoming exam *the hour before* it is scheduled.					
Totals for Each Column					
TOTAL SCORE :					

Note: To analyze your Test Anxiety Questionnaire, add up the totals from each column. A score of 145 or higher indicates that you may have a problem with test anxiety.

Source: Student Learning Assistance Center, Southwest Texas State University (2003).

A number of different programs have been developed to reduce test anxiety. Some of the methods used in these programs are readily available to teachers. Following is a summary of some of the methods used in these programs.

1. **Legitimize Anxiety.** Tell students that it is OK to be anxious. Everyone has anxiety. It is only when people allow it to overwhelm them that it becomes a problem. Have students express and reflect on their own test anxiety.

2. **Deal with Expectations.** Tell students exactly what is expected of them in class and on the test. Students with test anxiety allow their fear of the unknown aspects of the test to overwhelm their resources. By knowing exactly what is expected of them, you remove the fear of the unknown.

3. **Relaxation Training Paired with Imagery Techniques.** As with phobias, systematic desensitization techniques appear to have considerable success in reducing test anxiety. These techniques teach the student to relax while imagining the test situation. Pairing the relaxed state with the imagined test situation appears to be effective.

4. **Rational Cognitive Scripts.** Many test-anxious students develop irrational fears, beliefs, and attitudes about their own test performance. Have students articulate these irrational thoughts. Help students to replace them with positive scripts.

5. **Time Management.** Many test-anxious students do not appropriately budget their study time. Develop student contracts about study time. Using buddy systems in which students study together also may help with time management.

6. **Exam Sessions.** A number of techniques in administering the test may help test-anxious students. Extra time on tests or untimed tests can help. Also, practice exams may desensitize students to test anxiety. Suggest to students that they wait until they reach a relaxed state before they turn the exam over and begin. Allowing test-anxious students to take an exam in a separate room from other students is another possible technique.

Test anxiety is something that teachers can help students effectively overcome. Avoiding situations where overall grades are determined by one single exam can diminish test anxiety. Minimizing time limitations on assessments can also help, as will building self-esteem and self-efficacy about a particular academic subject.

Academic Dishonesty and Classroom Assessments

Media reports of academic dishonesty in high schools and colleges suggest that classroom cheating has reached massive proportions (Deutsch, 1988; McLoughlin, 1987). The Carnegie Commission on Education (Singhal & Johnson, 1979) report that 30 to 50 percent of college students admitted to cheating. This problem is not only an educational issue but clearly a social issue that affects the integrity of the assessment process.

Evans and Craig (1990) state that research findings indicate that the incidence of cheating among students from elementary grades to graduate school is 40 percent or more. They also state that results of their own study on cheating in middle schools and high schools point to an increase in cheating with each successive grade level.

Students appear to cheat more in classes when they perceive the teacher to be incompetent or when the teacher does not take active steps to prevent cheating (Evans, Craig, & Mietzel, 1991). Evans, Craig, and Mietzel also indicate that students who have the following characteristics are more likely to cheat: low self-esteem, a defiance of authority, and an external locus of control.

Certain measures may curb cheating incidences. Evans and Craig (1990) claim that cheating is decreased by avoiding assessments "where grading is on a curve and where grades are based on just one or two exams or other products" (p. 50). In effect, using criterion-referenced assessments (where students are not directly competing with each other) will reduce academic cheating. Using a variety of assessments, so that the final grade does not rely on just one or two assessments, also will reduce cheating.

Other factors also may decrease cheating on exams, including appropriate test security, use of in-class term paper assignments, use of essay items, changing assessment items each school term, and administering multiple forms of the same classroom assessment. As with other aspects involved with assessments, consistent policies are of prime importance. Differential treatment of students in the assessment process can only result in a loss of the teacher's personal credibility and integrity.

As with other aspects of effective assessments, this area can help the teacher maintain the academic integrity of the classroom. Failure to prevent academic dishonesty will, in turn, contribute to a poor public perception of the present educational system. Any public perception of failure in maintaining the integrity of grades may lend credence to those who want to increase teacher accountability by further employing external standardized assessments to measure student outcomes.

Chapter Summary

This chapter reviewed issues and problems related to the administration of classroom assessments. An analysis of the relationship of classroom environment to assessment was presented and a number of conclusions were made. First of all, the social and emotional relationship between teacher and students is the critical factor in classroom environment and assessments. Positive teacher immediacy and responsiveness behaviors determine if a classroom environment is supportive. Promoting cooperation among students, providing appropriate expectations and feedback, and encouraging a free exchange of ideas are other teacher behaviors that can create a supportive environment.

In terms of creating a supportive classroom assessment environment, many of the same factors are involved. In addition, using a variety of assessments that are linked to instruction, using assessments of established quality, and using fair and consistent grading policies are other factors that create a positive assessment environment. Physical conditions and seating arrangements also are factors in creating a positive assessment environment. A number of different conditions—such as lighting, ventilation, and noise reduction—are necessary for effective assessments. Different guidelines for seating arrangements with different activities were also detailed.

Test preparation activities also were included in this chapter. The extensive use of test preparation in schools was noted. The increasing use of test preparation appears to detract from regular instructional activities. The ability of test preparation programs to increase test scores was reviewed.

The last parts of this chapter discussed the issues of academic misconduct and test anxiety. Some researchers believe that cheating on tests is increasing in schools and colleges. Teacher behaviors that can decrease the possibility of cheating were proposed. Test anxiety problems were also examined. The background of test anxiety and its relationship to other forms of anxiety were described and methods that teachers can use to lower test anxiety were detailed.

CASE STUDY EPILOGUE

Mr. Thompson has decided to transform his classroom environment and assessment practices in a number of ways. His first goal is to be more responsive to student needs and requests. As part of this goal, he implements a series of open class discussions about science topics. He also uses a number of informal self-assessments and peer assessments prior to any formal assessments. Mr. Thompson uses these assessments to ensure that he is on target with what students need in his courses.

Along with these changes, Mr. Thompson also institutes a number of group projects designed to increase cooperation among students. Each group becomes a team working on projects in the science lab, in the computer lab, and on some writing assignments. Mr. Thompson also provides a clear and explicit set of guidelines for each formal assessment. During the class right before each assessment, he reviews the material and provides a series of practice questions. After each formal assessment, he goes over each item and provides feedback to students.

Mr. Thompson also tries to deal with test anxiety in his students. He uses a buddy system to help students study for the exam. He provides take-home study guides with clear directions for how to study for each exam. As much as possible, he provides extended time limits for all students. Mr. Thompson also provides extensive test preparations with a clear set of expectations for the students.

CHAPTER ACTIVITIES

Websites

http://www.inspiringteachers.com   "Inspiring teachers" is a site every new teacher should see. It has some great tips about reducing test anxiety, mentoring, and much more. Viewers also may want to join the National Association of Beginning Teachers.

http://www.ehhs.cmich.edu/~mspears/plagiarism.html   Plagiarism Q&A is an extremely informational site about combating cheating. The site gives tips on how the teacher can address the topic in the classroom and also serves as "Plagiarism 101." Teachers must be aware that thousands of sites exist online for students to download research papers. Some include Cheater.com at http://www.cheater.com/, Collegiate Care at http://www.papers-online.com/, and Thousands of Papers at http://www.termpapers-on-file.com/.

http://intranet.cps.k12.il.us/Assessments/Preparation/preparation.html   This website, developed by the Chicago Public School System, is devoted to various assessment methods and strategies. The site lists a number of different test preparation areas.

Portfolio Activities

1. Review Mr. Thompson's problems in the case study. Answer the following items:
   - What can you do to provide a positive classroom environment?
   - What can you do to be more supportive about your assessments?
   - What type of classroom structure and conditions would your use?
   - What types of seating arrangement would you use during assessments?
   - How can you help students prepare for exams?
   - What type of policy would you have about academic cheating?

2. Go this website: http://www.inspiringteachers.com. Write an essay on the different methods that you could use to decrease test anxiety in your students. Based on your own opinion and experience, rank these methods from most effective to least effective.

KEY CONCEPTS

Circular seating
Classroom assessment environment
Classroom climate
Classroom environment
Cluster seating

High-stakes testing
Row seating
Teacher immediacy and responsiveness
   behaviors
Test anxiety

REVIEW QUESTIONS

1. List and describe the major aspects of classroom environment.

2. Describe the different features of teacher responsiveness behaviors.

3. What are the methods used to create a supportive classroom environment?

4. What are the behaviors that can cause a negative classroom environment?

5. Describe the three major types of seating arrangements and list the type of instructional and assessment activities that are recommended for each type.

6. List and describe the major aspects of test preparation programs.

7. What are the methods that teachers can use to limit test anxiety?

8. List and describe the different ways that teachers can curb academic cheating.

SELF-ASSESSMENT

1. A correct description of text anxiety would include:
   a. Women suffer less test anxiety than men
   b. Test anxiety is related to general anxiety
   c. High self-esteem may lead to test anxiety
   d. High self-efficacy about the subject material can cause test anxiety

2. The type of seating arrangement most often used in the primary grades is:
   a. Row seating
   b. Circular seating
   c. Cluster seating
   d. Concert seating

3. The part of classroom environment that focuses on the emotional and social interactions in the classroom is called:
   a. Assessment support
   b. Classroom climate
   c. Instructional role placement
   d. Conflict management

4. Which of the following is listed as a way to reduce test anxiety?
   a. Providing make-up exams on request
   b. Cluster seating
   c. Untimed assessments
   d. Multiple-choice items

5. Which of the following is an appropriate method of standardized test preparation?
   a. Teaching test-taking skills
   b. Using old forms of the test
   c. Using items from previous tests
   d. Encouraging certain students to seek test exemptions

6. Which seating arrangement is recommended for formal classroom assessments?
   a. Cluster seating
   b. Circular seating
   c. Horseshoe seating
   d. Row seating

7. Evans and Craig (1990) estimate that the percentage of students engaged in academic cheating from elementary school through graduate school is:
   a. 10%
   b. 20%
   c. 40%
   d. 60%

Answers to Self-Assessment: 1. b, 2. c, 3. b, 4. c, 5. a, 6. d, 7. c

REFERENCES

American Association of University Women. (1992). *How schools shortchange girls.* Washington, DC: American Association of University Women Educational Foundation.

Axelrod, D., Hall, R.V., & Tams, A. (1979). Comparison of two common classroom seating arrangements. *Academic Therapy*, 15, 29–63.

Bandalos, D.L., Yates, K., & Thorndike-Christ, T. (1995). Effects of math self-concept, perceived self-efficacy, and attributions for failure and success on test anxiety. *Journal of Educational Psychology*, 87(4), 611–623.

Brookhart, S.M. (1997). Effects of the classroom assessment environment on mathematics and science achievement. *Journal of Educational Research*, 90(6), 323–331.

Brookhart, S.M., & DeVoge, J.G. (1999). Testing a theory about the role of classroom assessment in student motivation and achievement. *Applied Measurement in Education*, 12(3), 409–426.

Cannell, J.J. (1988). Nationally normed elementary achievement testing in America's public schools: How all 50 states are above the national average. *Educational Measurement: Issues and Practice*, 7(2), 5–9.

Cunningham, G.K. *(1986). Educational and psychological measurement.* New York: Macmillan.

Deutsch, C.H. (1988, April). Cheating: Alive and flourishing. *New York Times Educational Supplement*, 137, 25–29.

Evans, E.D., & Craig, D.C. (1990). Teacher and student perceptions of academic cheating in middle and senior high schools. *Journal of Educational Research*, 84(1), 44–52.

Evans, E.D., Craig, D.C., & Mietzel G. (1991). Adolescents' cognitions and attributions for academic cheating: A cross national study. (ERIC Document Reproduction Service No. ED 335 612).

Hill, K.T., & Eaton, W.O. (1977). The interaction of test-anxiety and success-failure experiences in determining children's arithmetic performance. *Developmental Psychology*, 13, 205–211.

Jordan, F.F., & Merkel, A. (1994, November). *The relationship of selected personal and communication climate variables to cognitive learning in the college classroom.* Paper presented at the annual meeting of the Speech Communication Association, New Orleans, LA.

Levine, D., O'Neal, E., & McDonald, P. (1980, September). Classroom ecology: The effects of seating position on grades and participation. *Personality and Social Psychology Bulletin*, 6(3), 409–412.

Liebert, R., & Morris, L. (1967). Cognitive and emotional components of test anxiety: A distinction and some initial data. *Psychological Reports*, 20, 975, 978.

McLoughlin, M. (1987, February 23). A nation of liars. *U.S. News and World Report*, 54–60.

Messick, S. (1982). Issues of effectiveness and equity in the coaching controversy: Implications for educational and testing practice. *Educational Psychologist*, 17, 67–91.

Myers, S., & Rocca, K. (2001). Perceived instructor argumentativeness and verbal aggression in the college classroom: Effects on student perceptions of climate, apprehension, and state motivation. *Western Journal of Communication*, 65(2), 113–138.

Papalia, A. (1976). *Learner-centered language teaching: Methods and materials.* Rowley, MA: Newbury House.

Patton, J., Snell, J., Knight, W., & Gerken K. (2001, April). *A survey study of elementary classroom seating designs.* Paper presented at the Annual Meeting of the National Association of School Psychologists. Washington, DC.

Popham, W.J. (1987). The merits of measurement-driven instruction. *Phi Delta Kappan*, 68, 979–682.

Rosenfeld, L.B. (1983). Communication climate and coping mechanisms in the college classroom. *Communication Education*, 32, 167–175.

Rosenfeld, P., Lambert, N.M., & Black, A. (1985). Desk arrangement effects on pupil classroom behavior. *Journal of Educational Psychology*, 77(1), 101–108.

Shepard, L.A. (1990). Inflated test score gains: Is the problem old norms or teaching the test? *Educational Measurement: Issues and Practice*, 9, 15–22.

Shepard, L.A., & Dougherty, K.C. (1991). *Effects of high-stakes testing on instruction.* Paper presented at the annual meeting of the American Educational Research Association, Chicago.

Singhal, A.C., & Johnson, P. (1979). How to halt student dishonesty. *College Student Journal*, 13, 13–19.

Smith, M.L. (1991). Meanings of test preparation. *American Educational Research Journal*, 28(3), 521–542.

Stiggins, R.J., & Conklin, N.E. (1992). *In teacher's hands: Investigating the practices of classroom assessment.* Albany, NY: SUNY Press.

Student Learning Assistance Center, Southwest Texas State University. (2003). *Test anxiety questionnaire.* Retrieved October, 25, 2003, from http://www.swt.edu/slac/StSkillsid/TstAnxty.htm.

Tennessee Department of Education. (2003). *Test strategies for students, parents, and teachers.* Retrieved October 28, 2003, from http://www.state.tn.us/education/tsteststrategies.htm.

Whedall, K., & Lam, Y. (1987). Rows versus tables. II. The effect of two classroom seating arrangements on classroom disruption rate, on-task behaviour and teacher behaviour in three special school classes. *Educational Psychology*, 7(1), 303–312.

Wheldall, K., Morris, M., Vaughan, P., & Ng, Y.Y. (1981). Rows versus tables: An example of the use of behavioural ecology in two classes of eleven-year-old children. *Educational Psychology*, 1, 171–189.

Wine, J.D. (1971). Test anxiety and direction of attention. *Psychological Bulletin*, 76, 92–104.

Wittmaier, B. (1972). Test anxiety and study habits. *Journal of Educational Research*, 65, 852–854.

Wulf, K.M. (1976, April). *Relationship of assigned classroom seating area to achievement variables.* Paper presented at the annual meeting of the American Educational Research Association, San Francisco.

Zohar, D. (1998). An additive model of test anxiety: Role of exam-specific expectations. *Journal of Educational Psychology*, 90, 330–340.

CHAPTER

14 Teacher Assessment and Teacher Development

CASE STUDY

Ms. Hatfield just started her first year as a fourth-grade teacher in a suburban elementary school on the West Coast. Like other school districts around the country, her school system is implementing the changes brought about by the No Child Left Behind Act. There is considerable discussion among the teachers about the types of changes involved in meeting this new federal legislation. For example, many of the primary-grade teachers are concerned that the emphasis on reading is taking away from other subject areas such as math and science. Another area of concern for all the teachers is the new federal mandates about teacher quality. These new mandates have produced a complete transformation in the teacher evaluation system used in Ms. Hatfield's school district and state.

Since this is her first teacher evaluation, Ms. Hatfield wants to fully understand all the different aspects of this process. The complex relationship among federal standards, state standards, and local school district performance-based evaluations are among the areas she wants to understand. She has the following questions about this process:

What are the school district's evaluation standards?

What are the school district's methods and procedures in evaluating new teachers?

What impact has No Child Left Behind had on local teacher evaluations?

What are the changes at the state level that may affect her evaluation?

What type of documentation does she need for a successful teacher evaluation?

What kind of expectations would a principal have about a new teacher?

What type of self-assessment should she conduct to prepare for her formal teacher evaluation?

Introduction

The professional growth and development of teachers is the fundamental purpose for teacher assessment. The goal is to enable teachers to receive appropriate feedback in order to improve their teaching and their students' learning. This is similar to the main purpose for the assessment of students: for feedback and self-improvement.

At times, this purpose for teacher assessment may be at odds with views on teacher assessment espoused by the general public or by educational stakeholders. This latter point of view on assessment tends to be more focused on accountability and on "weeding out bad teachers." As noted in Chapter 1, teacher accountability has become a major educational and social issue. Nevertheless, there is one commonality to the two perspectives: Both viewpoints genuinely want to improve classroom instruction and student learning.

The first section of this chapter reviews the basis for teacher assessment. It begins with an overview of standards-based teacher assessment policies. These policies contain federal, state, and local guidelines for teacher assessment. The next section examines formal teacher assessment procedures used by various states and school systems. The chapter concludes with a review of how teachers can prepare for their formal classroom assessments. There will be an analysis of the research on the problems and challenges of new teachers as well as an examination of the procedures for the completion of self-assessments by new teachers.

Standards-Based Teacher Assessment

As with student assessment, much of the overall structure for teacher assessment now stems from federal and state standards. Standards-based teacher assessment mandates exacting, specific standards that teachers must meet in order to be employed, retained, or tenured. As mentioned in Chapter 1, the **No Child Left Behind Act** mandates specific standards in the area of **teacher quality**. While individual states and school districts are given considerable latitude in enacting **teacher standards,** they still must meet certain federal guidelines or risk losing certain federal funds. In addition, school districts must implement these standards and link them with their formal assessment of

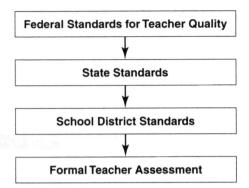

FIGURE 14.1   **Teacher Standards and Teacher Assessment**

individual teachers. This final step, the formal assessment of individual teachers, is conducted at the local school district and school level. Figure 14.1 shows the relationship between these different aspects.

No Child Left Behind and Teacher Quality Standards

A summary of the federal standards for teacher quality are provided in this section. The purpose of the teacher quality standards in No Child Left Behind legislation is "to ensure that all students have effective teachers; that is, teachers with the subject-matter knowledge and teaching skills necessary to help all children achieve high academic standards, regardless of individual learning styles or needs. In this regard, the program provides substantial funding to help States and districts recruit, train, reward, and retain effective teachers" (U.S. Department of Education, 2003).

As part of these standards, the federal legislation attempts to ensure that teachers in core academic subject areas meet certain minimum standards. These standards are included in the definition of a highly qualified teacher in the No Child Left Behind Act. A **highly qualified teacher** is defined as a teacher who:

1. Has obtained full State certification as a teacher or passed the State teacher licensing examination and holds a license to teach in the State, and does not have certification or licensure requirements waived on an emergency, temporary, or provisional basis;
2. Holds a minimum of a bachelor's degree; and
3. Has demonstrated subject matter competency in each of the academic subjects in which the teacher teaches, in a manner determined by the State (U.S. Department of Education, 2003).

Newly hired teachers are required to meet the highly qualified standard as of the 2002–2003 school year. The main part of these **federal teaching standards** require that all new teachers have full certification, a bachelor's degree, and subject matter competency in the courses that they are required to teach. Currently employed teachers must meet the highly qualified standard by the end of the 2005–2006 school year. They do this by passing a state academic subject test or a special state evaluation, or by completing appropriate college coursework in an academic major.

State Standards

In addition to meeting the federal standards, each state must develop its own additional standards for what constitutes a highly qualified teacher. Therefore, **state standards** for teachers focus on the individual requirements within a given state for teachers. For example, the Tennessee Department of Education's state standards are given on page 305.

Other states have similar policies for determining what a qualified teacher is in order to meet the federal guidelines of No Child Left Behind. Like Tennessee, a number of states and school districts now endorse the use of National Board Certification as part of or an alternative to their requirements for a "highly qualified teacher" under the No Child Left Behind Act. The standards for this certification are provided in the next section.

National Board Certification

National Board Certification is granted by the **National Board for Professional Teaching Standards.** This is an independent, nonprofit organization whose governing board has a number of educators, political leaders, and community leaders. The organization notes that a majority of the governing board is composed of classroom teachers. The National Board for Professional Teaching Standards has certain specific standards and includes performance-based assessments to determine if teachers meet these standards. A description of the five major core standards is on pages 306–307.

The process for National Board Certification involves performance-based assessments that measure a teacher's practice in regard to these previously listed standards. The **assessment procedures for National Board Certification** include:

- A portfolio of each teacher's classroom work and the work of their students
- Videotapes of teaching
- Analysis of classroom teaching and student learning from documented evidence
- A two-day written assessment at a certified assessment center that examines the teacher's subject matter knowledge and the teacher's understanding of how to teach these subjects to his or her students

To apply for National Board Certification, you must have a bachelor's degree and three years of classroom experience. The certification is valid for 10 years and the certification fee is $2,300. A number of states and school districts will partly or fully fund this fee. In addition, a number of states and school districts also offer salary increases or supplements to teachers who earn National Board Certification.

Highly Qualified Teachers in Tennessee

Highly Qualified Elementary Teachers

"A highly qualified elementary teacher (K–6) who is *new* to the profession is one who is fully licensed to teach in Tennessee (including the specified alternative routes) with no licensure requirements waived, holds at least a bachelor's degree, and has passed one of the Praxis teacher licensure tests designated on the test options list for the assigned teaching area.

A highly qualified *existing* elementary teacher (K–6) who is not new to the profession is one who is fully licensed to teach in Tennessee (including the specified alternative routes) with no licensure requirements waived, holds at least a bachelor's degree, and has:

passed one of the NTE or Praxis teacher licensure tests designated on the test options list or achieved National Board Certification at the elementary level, or demonstrated competence in reading, writing, mathematics and other areas of basic elementary school curriculum via a highly objective uniform state standard of evaluation.

Highly Qualified Middle (7–8) and Secondary Teachers (9–12)

A highly qualified middle or secondary teacher (7–12) who is *new* to the profession is one who is fully licensed to teach in Tennessee (including the specified alternative routes) with no licensure requirements waived, holds at least a bachelor's degree, and has demonstrated competency in each academic subject assigned to teach by having:

passed one of the Praxis teacher licensure tests designated on the test options list, or an academic major in the subject area, or the coursework equivalent of an academic major (24 semester hours), or a graduate degree in the subject area, or National Board Certification in the subject area.

A highly qualified *existing* middle or secondary teacher (7–12) who is not new to the profession is one who is fully licensed to teach in Tennessee (including the specified alternative routes) with no licensure requirements waived, holds at least a bachelor's degree, and has demonstrated competency in each academic subject assigned to teach by having:

passed one of the NTE or Praxis teacher licensure tests designated on the test options list, or an academic major in the subject area, or the coursework equivalent of an academic major (24 semester hours), or a graduate degree in the subject area, or National Board Certification in the subject area, or demonstrated competence in all academic subject areas via a highly objective uniform state standard of evaluation. (Tennessee State Department of Education, 2003)

National Board for Professional Teaching Standards: Core Propositions

1. *Teachers are committed to students and their learning.* Accomplished teachers are dedicated to making knowledge accessible to all students. They act on the belief that all students can learn. They treat students equitably, recognizing the individual differences that distinguish one student from another and taking account of these differences in their practice. They adjust their practice based on observation and knowledge of their students' interests, abilities, skills, knowledge, family circumstances and peer relationships.

Accomplished teachers understand how students develop and learn. They incorporate the prevailing theories of cognition and intelligence in their practice. They are aware of the influence of context and culture on behavior. They develop students' cognitive capacity and their respect for learning. Equally important, they foster students' self-esteem, motivation, character, civic responsibility and their respect for individual, cultural, religious and racial differences.

2. *Teachers know the subjects they teach and how to teach those subjects to students.* Accomplished teachers have a rich understanding of the subject(s) they teach and appreciate how knowledge in their subject is created, organized, linked to other disciplines and applied to real-world settings. While faithfully representing the collective wisdom of our culture and upholding the value of disciplinary knowledge, they also develop the critical and analytical capacities of their students.

Accomplished teachers command specialized knowledge of how to convey and reveal subject matter to students. They are aware of the preconceptions and background knowledge that students typically bring to each subject and of strategies and instructional materials that can be of assistance. They understand where difficulties are likely to arise and modify their practice accordingly. Their instructional repertoire allows them to create multiple paths to the subjects they teach, and they are adept at teaching students how to pose and solve their own problems.

3. *Teachers are responsible for managing and monitoring student learning.* Accomplished teachers create, enrich, maintain and alter instructional settings to capture and sustain the interest of their students and to make the most effective use of time. They also are adept at engaging students and adults to assist their teaching and at enlisting their colleagues' knowledge and expertise to complement their own. Accomplished teachers command a range of generic instructional techniques, know when each is appropriate and can implement them as needed. They are as aware of ineffectual or damaging practice as they are devoted to elegant practice.

They know how to engage groups of students to ensure a disciplined learning environment, and how to organize instruction to allow the schools' goals for students to be met. They are adept at setting norms for social interaction among students and between students and teachers. They understand how to motivate students to learn and how to maintain their interest even in the face of temporary failure.

Accomplished teachers can assess the progress of individual students as well as that of the class as a whole. They employ multiple methods for measuring student growth and understanding and can clearly explain student performance to parents.

4. *Teachers think systematically about their practice and learn from experience.* Accomplished teachers are models of educated persons, exemplifying the virtues they seek to inspire in students—curiosity, tolerance, honesty, fairness, respect for diversity and appreciation of cultural differences—and the capacities that are prerequisites for intellectual growth: the ability to reason and take multiple perspectives to be creative and take risks, and to adopt an experimental and problem-solving orientation.

Accomplished teachers draw on their knowledge of human development, subject matter and instruction, and their understanding of their students to make principled judgments about sound practice. Their decisions are not only grounded in the literature, but also in their experience. They engage in lifelong learning which they seek to encourage in their students.

Striving to strengthen their teaching, accomplished teachers critically examine their practice, seek to expand their repertoire, deepen their knowledge, sharpen their judgment and adapt their teaching to new findings, ideas and theories.

5. *Teachers are members of learning communities.* Accomplished teachers contribute to the effectiveness of the school by working collaboratively with other professionals on instructional policy, curriculum development and staff development. They can evaluate school progress and the allocation of school resources in light of their understanding of state and local educational objectives. They are knowledgeable about specialized school and community resources that can be engaged for their students' benefit, and are skilled at employing such resources as needed.

Accomplished teachers find ways to work collaboratively and creatively with parents, engaging them productively in the work of the school. (National Board for Professional Teaching Standards, 2003)

School District Standards

School district standards may be developed as part of state standards or to supplement state standards. This section reviews the six performance standards for the Montgomery County School System in Maryland. As noted by the school district, some of these standards are based on standards from the National Board for Professional Teaching Standards (see Figure 14.2).

Formal Assessment of Teachers

The actual formal assessment and evaluation of teachers is completed at the local school district and school level. **Teacher assessment** involves the overall process of information gathering about a teacher. **Teacher evaluation** is the process of interpretation and judgment of this information. Teacher evaluation includes decisions about rehiring a teacher, promoting a teacher on a career ladder, granting tenure, or giving merit pay.

At the school district level, the formal assessment and evaluation of teachers is generally derived from the performance standards and criteria developed by the state or the school district. For example, the Montgomery County, Maryland, school district

FIGURE 14.2   Montgomery County Public Schools: Performance Standards

Standard I:	Teachers are committed to students and their learning.
Standard II:	Teachers know the subjects they teach and how to teach them to students.
Standard III:	Teachers are responsible for establishing and managing student learning in a positive learning environment.
Standard IV:	Teachers continually assess student progress, analyze the results, and adapt instruction to improve student achievement.
Standard V:	Teachers are committed to continuous improvement and professional development.
Standard VI:	Teachers exhibit a high degree of professionalism.

Source: Montgomery County Public Schools (2003).

has created an assessment system of teachers that is aligned with the previously listed six performance standards. There is a specific system and process for assessing teachers for Montgomery County Schools. This assessment system includes the following components: "Direct observation of the teacher's work, reviews of the teacher's planning and self-assessment, reviews of the teacher's long term professional growth plans and efforts, and a review of student achievement data are all utilized in the formal performance evaluation of each teacher" (Montgomery County Public Schools, 2003).

In this school district's teacher evaluation policy, the six performance standards are further supported by specific performance criteria. In addition, teacher rubrics of what a teacher needs to do in order to meet a specific standard are provided. As noted by the school district, "The purpose of the examples in each rubric is to create a sample picture of what teaching looks like when it meets and when it does not meet the Montgomery County Public Schools performance standards. These examples are not provided to suggest that every teacher is expected to be doing all or everything that is described in either column. It is a template against which to compare a teacher's overall performance on the six performance standards" (Montgomery County Public Schools, 2003).

To summarize thus far, a teacher in the Montgomery County school system is evaluated on six performance standards. Each of these standards has certain performance criteria and an evaluation rubric assigned to it. A team of trained administrative and peer evaluators complete the assessment of each teacher. In using the rubric, the evaluators score the teacher performance as either meeting the standard or not meeting the standard. Figure 14.3 shows performance standard IV with the performance criteria and the rubric associated with it. This is one of the six performance standards in the school system.

As indicated in the rubric of Figure 14.3, Montgomery County Public Schools endorses certain assessment practices as part of meeting the standards listed in its teacher evaluations. Included among these practices are:

**FIGURE 14.3   Montgomery County Public Schools
Performance Evaluation: Standard IV**

Standard IV Description
Teachers continually assess student progress, analyze the results, and adapt instruction to improve student achievement.

Performance Criteria for Standard IV
A. Teachers use a variety of formal and informal assessment techniques.
B. Teachers analyze student results and plan instruction accordingly.

Rubric for Standard IV

Meets Standard	Below Standard
Uses a variety of formal and informal assessment formats (extended response, performance tasks, student journals, portfolios, checklists, observations of student work in class, etc.)	Assessment usually paper/pencil, based on short answer or recall questions
Assessment takes place before, during and after instruction; teacher adapts variety of assessments within and between topics	Assessments are infrequent and only summative
Makes accommodations to assessment to meet the needs of students with differing learning styles or special needs; continually seeks new methods to meet students' needs	Little or no accommodations made to assessments; all students assessed in the same way, regardless of student needs
Develops rubrics for students to evaluate their own and others' work; students apply these rubrics to self-evaluation and evaluation of others; students create rubrics for evaluating their own and others' work	Students not involved in self-evaluation or evaluation of others' work; limited or inappropriate use of rubrics for evaluation of student work
Expectations for student performance are clearly articulated; homework and long-term projects articulate to families important learning goals; students and families understand what is expected and how to improve performance	Expectations for student performance unclear or not specified
Maintains records of student performance that students and families can check regularly; informs students and families on a regular basis	Record-keeping not consistently maintained; students and families unsure of status
Regularly uses multiple sources of assessment data to plan and modify instruction; uses pre-assessments to plan instruction and regroup students; uses assessment data to ensure that all students, regardless of prior achievement or background characteristics, are progressing appropriately (proficiency, productivity, equity, and quality)	Little or no evidence of use of assessment results (proficiency, productivity, equity, and quality) in lessons or instructional plans

(continued)

FIGURE 14.3   Continued

Meets Standard	Below Standard
When planning instructional goals, considers articulation of instruction among prior, current and future grades or school levels	Little or no evidence of awareness of or consideration for prior or later instructional goals
Uses prior year's student performance data (proficiency, productivity, equity, and quality) and other relevant information in designing current year's instructional goals to improve student achievement	Limited or no acknowledgment of students' educational histories in planning current year's instructional goals (proficiency, productivity, equity, and quality)
Regularly monitors student performance and progress in later years to self-assess relevance of instructional goals to students' learning needs and achievement	Limited or no evidence of follow-up of student performance or progress
Convenes/participates in meetings to evaluate student needs; solicits and shares information with other school staff to maintain continuous academic and social/emotional development of each student	Limited or no participation in meetings to evaluate student needs; limited or no evidence of sharing information

Source: Montgomery County Public Schools (2003).

- Using a variety of formal and informal assessments
- Using assessments before, during, and after instruction
- Using assessment accommodations for students with special needs
- Using rubrics for self-assessments and peer assessments
- Using clearly articulated expectations for student performance
- Using appropriate record-keeping and feedback for students.

In evaluating teachers, Montgomery County Public Schools provides an extensive system of peer review and assessment with a separate rubric for each performance standard. Evaluators are trained by the school district. These evaluators then perform an assessment using the six rubrics aligned with the performance standard. The school district also provides a detailed improvement plan for teachers who fail to meet the appropriate standards on the teacher evaluation.

Other states and school districts may use different methods. An example of an assessment rubric for teacher evaluation in West Virginia is shown in Figure 14.4. As indicated in the West Virginia evaluation rubric, there are seven different performance areas: Programs of Study, Classroom Climate, Instructional Management Systems, Student Progress, Communication, Professional Work Habits, and Technology Standards. Teachers are assessed in each of these areas on a scale that has four levels: Exemplary, Exceeds Standards, Meets Standards, and Unsatisfactory. Many of these areas are similar to other teacher evaluation rubrics. However, the West Virginia teacher evalu-

FIGURE 14.4 West Virginia Board of Education Policy 5310: Teacher Evaluation

Teacher's Name _____   Years of Experience in County ⬚ 1–3
                                            (regular full-time only)   ⬚ 4–5

Grade Level/Subject _____

School _____   Evaluation Period _____

Directions: For each area of responsibility, mark the appropriate rating in the box provided.

Rating Scale:

Exemplary (EXEM) Performance is consistently exceptional in meeting performance criteria demonstrated by providing extraordinary opportunities for student success through instructional strategies that confirm the teacher's expertise and the ability to reach all students.

Exceeds Standards (EXS) Performance is consistently above average in meeting performance criteria demonstrated by going beyond established standards and instructional practices in reaching all students.

Meets Standards (MS) Performance is consistently adequate in meeting performance criteria.

Unsatisfactory (UNS) Performance is not consistently acceptable in meeting performance criteria.

I. Programs of Study   EXEM ⬚   EXS ⬚   MS ⬚   UNS ⬚

Comments

  A. Bases instruction on adopted curricula for the school.
  B. Demonstrates accurate and current knowledge in subject field.
  C. Develops appropriate lessons to teach instructional objectives.
  D. Employs a variety of instructional strategies to augment achievement.
  E. Utilizes content scope and sequence in planning.

II. Classroom Climate   EXEM ⬚   EXS ⬚   MS ⬚   UNS ⬚

Comments

  A. Follows established school discipline procedures which include the WV Student Code of Conduct.
  B. Establishes procedures and rules that enhance learning.
  C. Encourages students' attendance.
  D. Sets high positive expectations for student performance.
  E. Encourages and acknowledges individual students' accomplishments and appropriate behavior.
  F. Treats students in a fair and equitable manner.
  G. Accommodates individual learning differences.
  H. Creates and maintains an environment that supports learning.
  I. Communicates with parents.

(continued)

FIGURE 14.4 **Continued**

III. Instructional Management Systems	EXEM ☐	EXS ☐	MS ☐	UNS ☐

Comments

A. Prepares and implements lesson plans.

B. Begins lesson or instructional activity with a review of previous materials as appropriate.

C. Has materials, supplies, and equipment ready at the start of the lesson or instructional activity.

D. Introduces the instructional activity and specifies instructional objectives.

E. Directs and adequately supervises students to be on task quickly at the beginning of each instructional activity.

F. Presents reading, writing, speaking, and listening strategies using concepts and language which students understand.

G. Provides relevant examples and demonstrations to illustrate concepts and skills.

H. Assigns developmentally appropriate tasks.

I. Provides instructional pacing that ensures students' understanding.

J. Maximizes student time on task.

K. Makes effective transitions between instructional activities.

L. Summarizes the main point(s) of the instructional activity.

M. Encourages students to express ideas clearly and accurately.

N. Incorporates higher-level thinking skills.

O. Assists students to develop productive work habits and study skills.

P. Provides remediation activities for students.

Q. Designs, delivers, and assesses students' learning activities addressing the state-adopted instructional goals and objectives.

R. Integrates a variety of technology applications and learning tools to augment student achievement.

IV. Student Progress	EXEM ☐	EXS ☐	MS ☐	UNS ☐

Comments

A. Follows grading policies and regulations.

B. Maintains accurate and complete student records.

C. Monitors and evaluates student progress.

D. Provides feedback on student work.

E. Monitors student attendance.

FIGURE 14.4   Continued

V. Communication	EXEM ☐	EXS ☐	MS ☐	UNS ☐

Comments

  A. Communicates student progress according to established procedures and policies.

  B. Communicates regularly and effectively with students, co-workers, parents/guardians, and community and exhibits appropriate interactive skills.

  C. Follows confidentiality procedures regarding students, parents/guardians, and fellow staff members.

  D. Speaks and writes standard English clearly, correctly, and distinctly.

  E. Determines and utilizes appropriate community resources.

VI. Professional Work Habits	EXEM ☐	EXS ☐	MS ☐	UNS ☐

Comments

  A. Adheres to established laws, policies, rules, and regulations.

  B. Interacts appropriately with students, other educational personnel, and parents.

  C. Participates in activities which foster professional growth.

  D. Is punctual with reports, grades, records, and in reporting to work.

  E. Performs assigned duties.

  F. Strives to meet county/school goals.

  G. Commands respect by example in appearance, manners, behavior, and language.

VII. Technology Standards	EXEM ☐	EXS ☐	MS ☐	UNS ☐

Comments

  A. Demonstrates a sound understanding of technology operations and concepts.

  B. Plans and designs effective learning environments and plans experiences supported by technology.

  C. Implements curriculum plans that include methods and strategies for applying technology to maximize student learning.

  D. Applies technology to enhance productivity and professional practice.

  E. Uses technology to enhance productivity and professional practice.

  F. Understands the social, ethical, legal, and human issues surrounding the use of technology in PreK–12 schools and applies that understanding in practice.

(continued)

FIGURE 14.4   Continued

Commendations:

Suggestions:

Identified Deficiencies and Recommendations:

Signing this evaluation form indicates only that the employee has had an opportunity to confer with the evaluator regarding its contents. (The employee has the right to include a written statement as an addendum to the evaluation.)

_____	
Employee's Signature Date	Addendum Attached
	Yes____ No ____
_____	
Evaluator's Signature Date	

Source: West Virginia Board of Education (2003).

---

ation is different in one way from many rubrics: This evaluation includes a separate area for evaluating the use of technology. Whereas this evaluation form is standard in West Virginia schools, supplementary rubrics and evaluation measures may be included by local school districts.

Formal assessments of teachers involve a great deal of time, effort, and money on the part of school systems. This investment almost certainly has increased since the implementation of the No Child Left Behind Act. In terms of teacher assessment, the transformation of schools and teachers with this legislation is still to be fully realized. In particular, the role of standardized assessments in evaluating teachers, schools, school districts, and states is still controversial.

Preparing for Formal Teacher Assessments

What can new teachers do to prepare for their annual teacher assessments? This section will explore two separate areas in regard to teacher preparation. The first area examines

Point/Counterpoint: Should Students' Scores on Standardized Assessments Be Used to Evaluate Teachers?

Point

Supporters of using standardized assessments, such as standardized achievement tests or statewide tests, state that they provide an objective, direct measure of student performance. These tests are independently created and generally have acceptable levels of reliability and validity. Supporters claim that the level of potential bias due to gender, ethnicity, or teacher bias is relatively limited with these tests.

Given their independence, objectivity, and general lack of bias, these tests offer one of the better ways to measure classroom instruction. Even though they actually are measuring student performance, they can, by logical inference, assess the instructional qualities of teachers. If students do well on these tests, the logical assumption is that teachers are doing well in teaching them. Supporters also note that the general public, as well as educational stakeholders such as school boards and state officials, want an independent method of evaluating teachers.

Counterpoint

Opponents of using standardized tests as part of teacher evaluations state that the key issue is the validity of these standardized tests. These tests can be valid, in a limited way, as a measure of student performance. But only in this sense can they be valid. Standardized tests cannot be a valid measure of teacher performance. They are not designed to measure teacher performance and there are a number of problems with using them in this manner. For example, the socioeconomic status of students has a major impact on their standardized test performance. (Many researchers believe that socioeconomic status is the single-most important predictor of standardized test performance.) Teachers cannot control for the socioeconomic status of their students. Yet if standardized tests are used to measure instructional performance, teachers will be evaluated on this factor.

There are other problems with using standardized assessments for evaluating teachers. These problems include difficulties in reliably and validly assessing students with special needs and students with ESL backgrounds. Opponents state that it is unfair to use these tests to evaluate teachers, when students from diverse backgrounds may produce differential test results.

---

the research on the development of new teachers and the problems that they encounter. The second area reviews self-assessment practices for teachers.

This section emphasizes an understanding of the challenges of new teachers and how to effectively meet these challenges. As previously mentioned, the purpose of teacher assessment should be on feedback and self-improvement. Teacher assessment should assist teachers in their own professional development in order to improve their own classroom instruction and assessment. Self-assessment can be an important part of this professional development. By engaging in an ongoing self-assessment, a new teacher can be proactive. This is a far, far better thing to do than to sit and wait until it's time for your formal assessment.

Challenges for New Teachers

To understand the classroom problems, concerns, and challenges of new teachers, it is important to review the research on how new teachers develop in the early stages of their careers. This research can provide a framework for understanding some of the difficulties faced by new teachers. It can also enable new teachers to focus on potential problem areas when they complete their own self-assessments.

In looking at this research, a series of findings emerge about the career development of new teachers. It appears that novice teachers take a relatively complex path during their first years of career development. For example, many beginning teachers undergo considerable changes in how they view the issues of classroom control and student behavior. Fuller (1969) provides one view on the way that novice teachers start their careers. Fuller states that novice teachers undergo a development process with three sequential stages:

1. Concern with self
2. Concern with task management
3. Concern with impact on students

The first stage involves one's own personal self. In effect, new teachers are self-oriented and inward-turning. They are concerned with their personal ability to succeed in general and with their ability to be good teachers in particular. After moving beyond the first stage, the next concern of these teachers is with instructional tasks. The focus is on developing appropriate teaching strategies and managing instructional time. After these first two stages are resolved, teachers turn outward and become concerned with the impact of their teaching on their students. They want to ensure that students are academically prepared and can achieve both inside and outside the classroom.

Brophy (1988) indicates that new teachers often have two misconceptions about their initial classroom experiences that can dramatically affect their development as teachers. These two common misconceptions tend to be mutually exclusive. In effect, novice teachers have either one or the other of these incorrect ideas:

1. Novice teachers believe that effective classroom management must occur by instilling student obedience and controlling student behavior through intimidation or fear of punishment.
2. Novice teachers believe that warm, caring regard toward children will always lead to friendly, positive student-teacher interactions without any need to act as an authority figure.

These misconceptions must be worked through so that some sort of middle ground can be found between the overcontrol of the first misconception and the overidealism of the second one.

According to a study by Brock and Grady (1998), beginning teachers list the following problems as their biggest concerns (ranked in order of difficulty):

1. Classroom management
2. Working with mainstreamed students
3. Determining appropriate expectations for students
4. Dealing with job stress
5. Handling angry parents
6. Keeping up with paperwork
7. Grading/evaluating students

Besides these concerns, beginning teachers also report concerns about being isolated and overwhelmed (Leiberman & Miller, 1994). They express a need for support and structure in their initial teaching years. Without this support they may experience job burnout and leave the profession.

One of the most influential factors in providing support and structure for beginning teachers is their principal. There is a considerable body of research evidence indicating that principals play a key role in the careers of beginning teachers (Chester, 1992; Hughes, 1994; Lee, 1994). Principals also play a major, if not decisive, role in the evaluation of new teachers. In many school districts, principals make a major contribution to the tenure and retention decisions of new teachers.

Therefore, a supportive principal can make a decisive difference in the career of a beginning teacher. According to Brock and Grady (1998), the areas of assistance that beginning teachers want from a supportive principal are:

1. Communicating the standards for good teaching in the school
2. Defining what are the expectations for students in the school
3. Affirming classroom practices and providing feedback at regularly scheduled meetings
4. Assigning appropriate mentors

In Brock and Grady's study (1998), principals also were surveyed about the types of assistance that they offered to beginning teachers. The results, indicating the percentage of principals in the study offering each of the various types of assistance, were as follows:

Mentors	94%
Fall orientation	61%
Year-long induction program	22%
Occasional meetings during the year	11%

Most of the principals (60 percent) in the Brock and Grady study stated that they chose mentors based on the grade level of the beginning teacher. A smaller number (30 percent) stated that they based mentor selection on a match of personal attributes between beginning teacher and mentoring teacher. The remaining 10 percent of principals stated that they based their selection of mentors on random factors.

So, what can a beginning teacher learn from all this research? As previously mentioned, Brophy (1988) makes the point that new teachers often have problems with finding a middle ground in their classroom management style. This viewpoint has considerable support in previously cited research that indicates classroom management is the number one problem for beginning teachers. Once they begin teaching, new teachers move through a stage where they are either very control oriented or very permissive with students. However, novice teachers typically do not end up as authoritarian or laissez-faire teachers. In general, they appear to accept and implement the current standard of management in their school or school system. As Wilson and Cameron (1996) note, the common, institutional expectations of classroom management tend to win out with novice teachers. These management expectations usually emphasize classroom teaching procedures that maximize instructional outcomes over student emotional and interpersonal needs.

Other research findings about novice teachers indicate that working with special needs students, determining expectations, dealing with job stress and demands, dealing with parents, managing paperwork overload, and grading/evaluation are major problems. In order to deal with these problems, first-year teachers believe that they need a year-long professional assistance program. To overcome these previously listed problems, the types of assistance needed included the following: help in developing lesson plans, pacing instruction, paperwork demands, and creating assessments.

Brock and Grady (1998) quoted one first-year, beginning teacher about the need for a year-long assistance program: "Don't forget that at the end of the school year we're still beginning teachers. We have never ended a school year before" (p. 181). Brock and Grady's study found that only 22 percent of principals offered such a program.

Teacher Self-Assessment

There is no question that teachers face a number of challenges, many of which may be of special concern during the initial years of teaching. Therefore, you may need to pay particular attention to understanding these problems during your **teacher self-assessment**. The questions of greatest interest are:

1. What areas should you be most concerned about during your self-assessments?
2. What methods can help you to conduct effective self-assessments?

As previously stated, principals play one of the most important roles in developing and evaluating beginning teachers. Principals have certain expectations about beginning teachers. What these expectations are can be critical for beginning teachers. Brock and Grady (1998) surveyed these expectations. They found that principals expected the following six attitudes and skills from beginning teachers:

1. A professional attitude
2. Adequate knowledge of subject areas
3. Good classroom management skills
4. Excellent communication skills

5. A belief that every child can learn
6. A desire to help students succeed (p. 180)

These attitudes and skills appear to fall into three areas:

1. Displaying a positive attitude about teaching and about children
2. Displaying good communication and management skills
3. Displaying appropriate knowledge of the classroom subject

It is hard to overemphasize the importance of having a positive attitude about teaching and children. A colleague of mine used to be a job recruiter for Disney World. She hired somewhere in the neighborhood of 10,000 to 12,000 employees during her career. She stated that the defining aspect of a successful job interview was a really good attitude. Skills and education were far less important. As she said, "If you have a positive attitude, we can help you learn the necessary skills. If you do not have a positive attitude, we cannot help you learn a thing."

In reviewing some of the other areas mentioned in this chapter, there are some additional skills that should be noted:

1. Creating appropriate lesson plans
2. Establishing a supportive classroom environment
3. Developing effective classroom assessment practices
4. Completing grades, records, and paperwork in a timely and appropriate manner
5. Using developmentally appropriate practices
6. Meeting the needs of diverse and special needs students

A number of the standards and rubrics in this chapter evaluate these teacher skills in addition to those listed earlier by Brock and Grady (1998). In performing your own self-assessments, you need to keep these aspects in mind.

Various methods can be used to conduct an effective self-assessment. Remember that the goal of self-assessment is the same as the goal of overall teacher assessment: to improve your instruction and your students' learning. Listed next are ways to complete a self-assessment.

Videotaping Your Teaching. For self-discovery and understanding, hardly any thing is more revealing than watching yourself teach on a videotape. It can be a wrenching, embarrassing activity the first time, but make yourself watch it. You will pick up on a number of distracting gestures and expressions. Your body language will become more evident to you. You also will understand much more about how responsive you are to student questions and student needs.

Peers and Mentors. Having peers or mentors watch you teach and provide constructive feedback is another method to self-assess your teaching performance. Peers and mentors who give constructive feedback can be especially important when discussing classroom problems. The key with your colleagues is to find someone with whom you feel comfortable talking about your classroom situations. In certain cases, assigned mentors may be someone with whom you feel comfortable. Unfortunately, sometimes this is not going to be the case. It can also be helpful to have peers or mentors watch a videotape with you. They can help review your initial lesson plans and assessments. Perhaps peers or mentors can observe your class. You can ask them to complete a peer observation inventory like the one seen in Figure 14.5.

FIGURE 14.5 Sample Peer Observation Report

Teacher Evaluated: _____ Grade Level _____

Number of Students Present _____ Date _____ Observer _____

Purpose: The purpose of this classroom observation is (1) to provide a database for accurate and equitable decisions on tenure and professional advancement and (2) to improve teacher performance.

Instructions: Please consider each item carefully and assign the highest scores only for unusually effective performance. Other materials, such as course syllabus, should be provided to the evaluator prior to the classroom visit.

Highest		*Satisfactory*		*Lowest*	*Not Applicable*
5	4	3	2	1	N/A

_____ 1. Defines instructional objectives for class.

_____ 2. Effectively organizes learning situations to meet the objectives of the class.

_____ 3. Uses instructional methods that encourage student participation.

_____ 4. Uses class time effectively.

_____ 5. Demonstrates enthusiasm for the subject matter.

_____ 6. Communicates clearly and effectively to the level of the students.

_____ 7. Explains important ideas simply and clearly.

_____ 8. Demonstrates command of subject matter.

_____ 9. Responds appropriately to student questions and comments.

_____ 10. Encourages critical thinking and analysis.

_____ 11. Discussion and activity are relevant to the course.

_____ 12. Overall rating.

What specific suggestions would you make concerning how this particular class could be improved?

Did you have a previsit conference? _____ Postvisit? _____

Student Feedback. There are a number of informal and formal methods for acquiring student feedback. Among the informal methods are classroom group meetings (Glasser, 1969) during which teachers and students bring up discussion topics. One of the topics can be about how the class is progressing. Glasser states that including students in discussions of classroom instructional activities, rules, and procedures produces a sense of shared ownership and involvement in the classroom. If conducted appropriately, group meetings can provide invaluable feedback to the teacher. Glasser suggests a number of questions, such as What would you do if you were the teacher? What is our plan for the day? What was one thing that you learned today?

Formal student feedback in the form of standardized teacher evaluation questionnaires also may be an option in certain cases. In general, students in high school settings may have the maturity level to make the type of judgments needed to successfully complete formal teacher evaluations. Even so, there can be problems with such evaluations. They may be linked to grading policies of the teachers (easier teachers may get better evaluations) or to whether the class is required or an elective course. In addition, they may be linked to instructional area. For example, some courses tend to be better liked by most students than other courses. This may impact the evaluation of the teacher. The complexity of using student evaluations is a constant issue in higher education. Nevertheless, they are regularly used at the college level. They can be used with certain stipulations at the secondary level, but they may be best used as an informal gauge of the teacher rather than as a formal method of evaluation.

Student Classroom Assessments. Another area of feedback is, of course, the student assessments that you conduct in your own classroom. These formal and informal assessments provide a wealth of information about how your instruction is received by your students. As mentioned in Chapter 2, item analysis can be used to review the test responses of students. This can provide feedback to you about your instruction. For example, if large numbers of students miss a given item, then you may need to review your instruction in that area. Ongoing informal assessments can provide a continuous stream of feedback about student learning during instruction.

Standardized Assessments. Standardized assessments offer another possibility for deriving information for your own self-assessments. These assessments can provide a considerable amount of feedback on your teaching performance. By cross-checking students' scores on standardized assessments, you may be able to find areas that need further appropriate instruction. However, it should be noted that standardized assessments are *not* a "be all to end all" way of evaluating teachers. Standardized student assessments measure student achievement levels. They do not necessarily measure teacher competence in any kind of direct fashion. At best, they are an indirect measure of teacher performance that provide only one of many windows on teaching ability.

Teacher Portfolio. Keep a portfolio of your teaching, including samples of everything that you do: peer observations, informal assessments, formal assessments, lesson plans, meetings, community involvement, parent contacts, and student letters. If you are disciplined enough, keep a reflective journal of your daily or weekly activities. A portfolio can be a documentation record to help you reflect on where you have been and where you are going. It can also provide documentation of your activities when you have a formal assessment.

Self-assessments can be way to plan and practice for your formal teacher assessment and evaluation. In this sense, you can achieve two important goals: You can complete self-assessments on an ongoing basis to help you develop your instruction, and by documenting your self-assessment activities you can provide a record of your teaching that will enhance your formal teacher assessment.

Chapter Summary

This chapter reviewed the process of teacher assessment. The role of federal, state, and local standards for teachers was examined in the first section. Federal guidelines for teacher standards mandate that by 2005–2006, all teachers must have full certification, a bachelor's degree, and subject matter competency in the courses that they are required to teach. State and local standards may supplement or increase the required federal standards, but they cannot decrease the standards and still receive specified federal entitlement money.

Actual teacher evaluations are conducted at the local school district and school levels. There are a number of ways that teachers may be assessed by schools and school systems. Many school evaluations examine the following: knowledge of subject area, classroom management skills, communication skills, and student assessment outcomes. Nearly all school systems now use some form of evaluation standards and rubrics to formally assess teachers.

Teachers can perform a variety of self-assessments in preparation of their formal teacher assessments. A self-assessment may include such aspects as videotaping and observing your teaching, peer observations with feedback, group meetings with students, and reviewing student assessments. Keeping a teacher portfolio that is a record of your activities is strongly recommended.

CASE STUDY EPILOGUE

Ms. Hatfield now understands that teacher assessments are a complex, interwoven set of federal, state, and local standards and mandates. She also understands that increasing federal involvement in public education means that teacher assessment standards and teacher accountability are going to be increased.

In preparing for her own teacher evaluation, Ms. Hatfield has talked to her principal, her assigned mentor, and some of the teachers in her school. They told her that the classroom observations conducted by her principal and her peers are a critical aspect of her annual assessment. They also told her that careful documentation of lesson plans, student assessments, multicultural activities, and inclusion practices were an important part of the annual evaluation.

Given their advice, Ms. Hatfield has decided to keep a complete teacher portfolio. Therefore, in addition to her usual record-keeping of tests and grades, Ms. Hatfield keeps sample records of special lesson plans, student activities, and comments from students and parents. Ms. Hatfield now carefully records all her inclusion activities as well as her materials on multicultural education.

CHAPTER ACTIVITIES

Websites

http://www.nea.org-edstats-images-status.pdf.url   This site provides the latest version of the National Education Association Report on the Status of the American Public School Teacher. The report publishes some of the most complete information on demographics, attitudes, and experiences of practicing teachers.

http://www.edweek.org   This website for *Education Week*, a major journal for educators, provides a wealth of information on teacher evaluations and state standards.

http://www.nbpts.org   This is the site for the National Board for Professional Teaching Standards, the organization that administers National Board Certification. The site provides directions, standards, and ideas for teachers.

Portfolio Activities

1. Review the Chapter Case Study. Find and list the answers to each question in your portfolio:
   - What is the relationship between federal standards for teacher assessments, state standards, and local standards?
   - What are some typical school district methods and procedures in evaluating new teachers?
   - What impact has No Child Left Behind had on local teacher evaluations?
   - What type of documentation would you need for a successful teacher evaluation?
   - What kind of expectations would a principal have about a new teacher?
   - What type of self-assessment should you conduct to prepare for her formal teacher evaluation?

2. Go to http://www.nea.org-edstats-images-status.pdf.url. Use the areas listed as Highlights and Professional Development in the site index. Find the following information:
   - What percentage of teachers are beginning teachers?
   - Are there more beginning teachers now than there were 30 years ago?
   - What are the basic demographic characteristics of teachers now, such as age, experience, and type of college degree?
   - What are the different types of professional development avenues open to teachers?

3. Write an essay for your portfolio that addresses the following question: As a prospective teacher, what position would you take on the debate over the provisions listed in the No Child Left Behind Act?

KEY CONCEPTS

Assessment procedures for National Board
   Certification
Federal teaching standards
Highly qualified teacher
National Board Certification
National Board for Professional Teaching
   Standards
No Child Left Behind Act

School district standards
State standards
Teacher assessment
Teacher evaluation
Teacher quality
Teacher self-assessment
Teacher standards

REVIEW QUESTIONS

1. What are the basic provisions that define a *highly qualified teacher* in the No Child Left Behind Act?

2. What are the differences between *teacher assessment* and *teacher evaluation*?

3. What are the five core standards or propositions listed by the National Board for Professional Teaching Standards?

4. What are the stages of development that a beginning teacher goes through as listed by Fuller?

5. Describe the two misconceptions of beginning teachers as noted by Brophy.

6. List three major concerns of beginning teachers.

7. List and describe the major forms of self-assessment that a teacher can use.

SELF-ASSESSMENT

1. Which of the following is a defining aspect of a "highly qualified teacher" under the provisions of the No Child Left Behind Act?
    a. ACT scores of 21 or higher
    b. Fully implemented teacher portfolios
    c. Holds at least a bachelor's degree
    d. College GPA of 3.0 or higher

2. The type of assessments used for National Board Certification are:
    a. Multiple-choice standardized
    b. Essay
    c. True/false
    d. Performance-based

3. The overall process of gathering information about a teacher is called:
    a. Teacher assessment

Answers to Self-Assessment: 1. c, 2. d, 3. a, 4. b, 5. d, 6. c

    b. Teacher evaluation
    c. National Board Certification
    d. Praxis II

4. According to Fuller, how many stages are in the development of a beginning teacher?
    a. 2
    b. 3
    c. 4
    d. 5

5. The number one problem of beginning teachers is:
    a. Preparing lesson plans and materials
    b. Paperwork overload
    c. Angry parents
    d. Classroom management

6. The most common form of assistance offered by principals is:
    a. Fall orientation
    b. Year-long induction program
    c. Mentors
    d. Occasional meetings during the year

REFERENCES

Brock, B., & Grady, M. (1998). Beginning teacher induction programs: The role of the principal. *The Clearing House*, 71(3), 179–183.

Brophy, J. (1988). Educating teachers about managing classrooms and students. *Teaching and Teacher Education*, 4, 1–18.

Casey, J.C., & Mitchell, R. (1996). Small epiphanies: The discoveries of beginning teachers. *Baylor Educator*, 21(1), 1, 14–35.

Chester, M.D. (1992, April). *Alterable factors that mediate the induction-year experience of teachers in urban schools.* Paper presented to the annual meeting of the American Educational Research Association, San Francisco.

Fuller, F. (1969). Concerns of teachers: A developmental conceptualization. *American Educational Research Journal*, 6, 207–226.

Glasser, W. (1969). *Schools without failure.* New York: Harper & Row.

Hughes, L.E. (1994). *The principal as leader.* New York: Macmillan.

Lee, R. (1994, April). *Perceptions of a beginning teacher: Exploring subjective reality.* Paper presented to the annual meeting of the American Educational Research Association, New Orleans, LA.

Leiberman, A., & Miller, L. (1994). *Teachers, their world and their work.* Alexandria, VA: Association for Supervision, Curriculum, and Development.

Montgomery County Public Schools. (2003). *Teacher evaluation in Montgomery County Schools,* Retrieved October 11, 2003, from http://www.mcps.k12.md.us/departments/personnel/TE/.

National Board for Professional Teaching Standards. (2003.) *Five core propositions.* Retrieved October 9, 2003, from http://www.nbpts.org/about/coreprops.cfm.

Tennessee State Department of Education. (2003). *Tennessee plan for implementing the teacher and paraprofessional quality provisions of the No Child Left Behind Act of 2001.* Retrieved September 28, 2003, from http://www.state.tn.us/education/fpnclbtchqltyimplplan.pdf.

U.S. Department of Education. (2003). *Improving teacher quality.* Retrieved September 25, 2003, from http://www.ed.gov/programs/teacherqual/guidance.doc.

Veenman, S. (1984). Perceived problems of beginning teachers. *Review of Educational Research*, 54(2), 143–178.

West Virginia Board of Education. (2003). *Policy 5310 teacher evaluation.* Retrieved October 2, 2003, from http://boe.cabe.k12.wv.us/School%20Management/New%20Evaluation%20Forms/Te acher%20Evaluation%20and%20Observation%20Forms.pdf.

Wilson, S., & Cameron, R. (1996). Student teacher perceptions of effective teaching: A developmental perspective. *Journal of Education for Teaching*, 22(2), 181–196.

APPENDIX

No Child Left Behind Act

This appendix provides an abbreviated form of key provisions and U.S. Department of Education explanations of the No Child Left Behind Act of 2001. The complete form of these government documents may be found at http://www.ed.gov/nclb/.

Introduction

On January 8, 2002, President George W. Bush signed into law the *No Child Left Behind Act of 2001*. This new law redefines the federal government's role in kindergarten through grade 12 education. The act is based on four basic principles:

1. Stronger accountability for results
2. Increased flexibility and local control
3. Expanded options for parents
4. An emphasis on teaching methods that have been proven to work

Accountability

The first principle of accountability for results involves the creation of standards in each state for what a child should know and learn in reading and math in grades 3 through 8. With those standards in place, student progress and achievement will be measured according to state tests designed to match those state standards and given to every child, every year. The new law will empower parents, citizens, educators, administrators, and policymakers with data from those annual assessments.

The data will be available in annual report cards on school performance and on statewide progress. They will give parents information about the quality of their children's schools, the qualifications of their children's teachers, and their children's progress in key subjects. The tests will give teachers and principals information about how each child is performing and how to help them diagnose and meet the needs of each student. The tests will also give policymakers and leaders at the state and local levels critical information about which schools and school districts are succeeding and why, so that this success may be expanded and any failures addressed. The following will explain the role of these new state tests in improving student achievement and address some of the misunderstandings about the changes to come.

Measuring Student Progress

States are required to use a method of measuring student progress that teachers use in their classrooms every day—testing. We need to test children on their academic knowledge and skills for the same reason we take them to the dentist to see if they have cavities—because we need to know. As caring adults, we want the children in our lives to have healthy teeth because we know that their teeth have to last a long time. If the dentist finds that their teeth are not healthy, then we get the cavity filled, and we teach them how to brush correctly, use dental floss, and avoid too much sugar. Children don't like going to the dentist, and we don't like the expense, but we do it because it's the right thing to do.

The same is true of annual academic assessment. Because education lasts a lifetime, leads to financial security, and gives children a chance to pursue the American dream, we want to know which children are catching on and which ones are not. We then want to take the ones who are not catching on and teach them how to read, how to add, how to study, and how to learn. Under the No Child Left Behind Act, each state retains the responsibility to decide what its students should learn in each grade. States are to develop rigorous academic standards (most are already doing this), and those standards should drive the curriculum, which, in turn, must drive instruction. Annual statewide assessments will be aligned with the curriculum to provide an external, independent measure of what is going on in the classroom, as well as an early indicator showing when a student needs extra help. The results of these tests can be used to direct resources, such as after-school tutoring or summer school, toward those who are falling behind. Extra help is not a punishment. It is a responsibility that enables students to catch up and to increase their chances of success during the next school year.

Cheryl Krehbiel, a fourth-grade teacher at Broad Acres Elementary School in Silver Springs, Maryland, said, "Clearly, students can't learn what I don't teach them. Having the courage to learn about my own professional needs from the [testing] data is a lesson that I can't afford to miss." Aside from taking an honest look at their own skills, teachers can also use test results at the beginning of the year to find out where a new class of students stands. For example, teachers who find that many of their students are weak in math can arrange the classroom schedule to include extra time for math instruction. If a parent knows that his or her child's school has had trouble in the past teaching grammar to third-graders, the parent can pay extra attention to his or her third-grader's progress in this area. Teachers and principals can look at district performance data to see which schools have the highest scores in math and encourage other schools to replicate the successful teaching practices from those schools.

Successful public schools are not only in the best interest of students, parents, and teachers but they are also important to a strong economy and viable communities. Susan Traiman, director of education initiatives at the Business Roundtable, said, "The business community sees testing as one of the most important tools for improvement. . . . It's very important to find out how you're doing, face up to any problems, and then have a proactive approach to doing something about it. . . . There will be consequences, and most of the consequences are to get folks extra help, to give them tools to succeed."

Employers need to have confidence that a high school diploma means something, that a graduate has the knowledge and skills needed to succeed. Members of a community need to have confidence that with each high school graduation, a new group of educated, productive citizens is on its way to taking on important roles in society.

Myths and Realities about Testing

Testing students is nothing new. Good teachers have always tried to measure how well their students are learning and have used tests to recognize student achievement and uncover learning problems. Without measuring student achievement, the only criteria governing student grades and promotion would be behavior in class and attendance.

Testing has only recently emerged as an issue because taxpayers are asking more and tougher questions about the performance of their schools and students and seeking more and better information about school and student performance. The results of teacher-designed exams and a wide assortment of "off-the-shelf" tests are helpful, but they shed little light on school performance and academic program impact. A strong accountability system composed of annual testing keyed to rigorous academic standards and a challenging curriculum taught in the school provides the sort of information needed to determine what works, what doesn't, how well students are achieving, and what to do to help those who need help.

As the use of standardized tests increases and parents are better able to understand the dimensions of school and student performance, there will be greater pressure on low-performing schools to improve. This worries those who might feel that pressure and so they have attempted to undermine the accountability movement by challenging the usefulness of testing. The once commonsense assumption that testing is part of learning is being challenged by myths created to undermine the effort to improve America's schools. The following section is a list of testing myths and responses to those myths, according to the U.S. Department of Education.

Testing Myth: Testing suppresses teaching and learning.

The Reality: A teacher is effective when a student learns. It is impossible to determine teaching effectiveness without determining learning results. A teacher can present a great lesson, but if the students do not understand, then the lesson has no value. Testing students on what they are taught has always been a part of teaching. The process of testing students on what they are learning over a course of instruction is universally understood and appreciated. Testing helps teachers understand what their students need, helps students understand what they need to learn, and helps parents understand how they might help their children.

Testing Myth: Testing narrows the curriculum by rewarding test-taking skills.

The Reality: Surely a quality education reaches far beyond the confines of any specific test. But annual testing is important. It establishes benchmarks of student knowledge. Tests keyed to rigorous state academic standards provide a measure of student knowledge and skills. If the academic standards are truly rigorous, student learning will be as well.

Testing Myth: Testing promotes "teaching to the test."

The Reality: Those who say testing gets in the way of learning frame a false dichotomy. Testing is part of teaching and learning. Gifted and inspiring teachers use tests to motivate students as well as to assess to their learning. Effective teachers recognize the value of testing and know how to employ testing in instruction.

Testing Myth: Testing does not measure what a student should know.

The Reality: In a strong accountability system, the curriculum is driven by academic standards, and annual tests are tied to the standards. With this in place, tests not only measure what a student should know but also provide a good indication of whether or not the student has indeed learned the material covered by the curriculum.

Testing Myth: Annual testing places too much emphasis on a single exam.

The Reality: Most Americans see the importance of visiting a physician for an annual checkup. They also recognize the importance of maintaining a healthy lifestyle and monitoring their health throughout the year. Annual testing provides important information on student achievement, so teachers and parents may determine how best to improve student performance and diagnose problems that might be associated with poor performance. If a single annual test were the only device a teacher used to gauge student performance, it would indeed be inadequate. Effective teachers assess their students in various ways during the school year. As they do this, they not only monitor student achievement but they also help to ensure that their students will excel on annual tests.

Testing Myth: Testing discriminates against different styles of test takers.

The Reality: A well-designed evaluation system accommodates special needs. Evaluating the performance of all students is not easy. Some students do have trouble taking tests. Some students score poorly for reasons outside the classroom. A good evaluation system will reflect the diversity of student learning and achievement.

Testing Myth: Testing provides little helpful information and accomplishes nothing.

The Reality: A good evaluation system provides invaluable information that can inform instruction and curriculum, help diagnose achievement problems, and inform decision making in the classroom, the school, the district, and the home. Testing is about providing useful information and it can change the way schools operate.

Testing Myth: Testing hurts the poor and people of color.

The Reality: The fact is that millions of young people—many from low-income families, many people of color—are being left behind every day because of low expectations for their academic achievement and a lack of adequate measures to determine academic achievement. These are the students who stand to benefit the most from annual testing. A strong accountability system will make it impossible to ignore achievement gaps where they exist. Moreover, where testing systems are now in place, low-income and minority students are indeed excelling. A recent study reports that there are more than 4,500 high-poverty and high-minority schools nationwide that scored in the top one-third on the state tests.

Testing Myth: **Testing will increase dropout rates and create physical and emotional illness in children.**

The Reality: The overwhelming majority of students who drop out of school do so because they are frustrated. They cannot read or write or learn. Testing helps with the early identification of students who are having trouble learning so they may get the services they need to succeed. Testing, in any form, does sometimes cause anxiety. Effective teachers understand this and help students prepare for it. Testing is a part of life, and young people need to be equipped to deal with it.

Increased Flexibility and Local Control

Under the No Child Left Behind Act, states and school districts have unprecedented flexibility in how they use federal education funds in exchange for greater accountability for results. It is possible for most school districts to transfer up to 50 percent of the federal formula grant funds they receive under the Improving Teacher Quality State Grants, Educational Technology, Innovative Programs, and Safe and Drug-Free Schools programs to any one of these programs, or to their Title I program, without separate approval. This allows districts to use funds for their particular needs, such as hiring new teachers, increasing teacher pay, and improving teacher training and professional development. Similarly, the law's consolidation of bilingual education programs gives states and districts more control in planning programs to benefit all limited English proficient students.

A new demonstration program allows selected states and school districts to consolidate funds received under a variety of federal education programs so that they can be used for any educational purpose authorized under the Elementary and Secondary Education Act, as amended by the NCLB Act, in order to assist them in making adequate yearly progress and narrowing achievement gaps. In addition, the new Improving Teacher Quality State Grants program gives states and districts greater flexibility to choose the teacher professional development strategies that best meet their needs to help raise student achievement.

Expanded Options for Parents

Under the No Child Left Behind Act, each state must measure every public school student's progress in reading and math in each of grades 3 through 8 and at least once during grades 10 through 12. By school year 2007–2008, assessments (or testing) in science will be underway. These assessments must be aligned with state academic content and achievement standards. They will provide parents with objective data on where their child stands academically.

No Child Left Behind requires states and school districts to give parents easy-to-read, detailed report cards on schools and districts, telling them which ones are succeeding and why. Included in the report cards are student achievement data broken out by race, ethnicity, gender, English language proficiency, migrant status, disability status, and low-income status—as well as important information about the professional qualifications of teachers. With these provisions, No Child Left Behind ensures that parents have important, timely information about the schools their children attend—whether they are performing well or not for all children, regardless of their background.

In this new era of education, children will no longer be trapped in the deadend of low-performing schools. Under No Child Left Behind, such schools must use their federal funds to make needed improvements. In the event of a school's continued poor performance, parents have options to ensure that their children receive the high-quality education to which they are entitled. That might mean that children can transfer to higher-performing schools in the area or receive supplemental educational services in the community, such as tutoring, after-school programs, or remedial classes.

When are children eligible for school choice?   Children are eligible for school choice when the Title I school they attend has not made adequate yearly progress in improving student achievement—as defined by the state—for two consecutive years or longer and is therefore identified as needing improvement, corrective action, or restructuring. Any child attending such a school must be offered the option of transferring to a public school in the district—including a public charter school—not identified for school improvement, unless such an option is prohibited by state law. No Child Left Behind requires that priority in providing school choice be given to the lowest-achieving children from low-income families. As of the 2002–2003 school year, school choice is available to students enrolled in schools that have been identified as needing improvement under the ESEA, as the statute existed prior to the enactment of No Child Left Behind.

Children are also eligible for school choice when they attend any "persistently dangerous school," as defined by the individual state. Any child who has been the victim of a violent crime on the grounds of his or her school is also eligible for school choice.

How do parents know if their child is eligible for school choice?   Under No Child Left Behind, school districts are required to notify parents if their child is eligible for school choice because his or her school has been identified as needing improvement, corrective action, or restructuring. They must notify parents no later than the first day of the school year following the year for which their school has been identified for improvement. States are required to ensure that school choice is offered as an option to parents in the event their child is attending a school that is "persistently dangerous" or has been the victim of a violent crime while on school grounds.

What action can parents take if their school or district does not offer school choice to their child who is eligible?   Schools and districts receiving Title I funds must provide choice for eligible students as described above. If they do not, parents are encouraged to contact their state department of education.

Do public school options include only schools in the same district? There may be situations where children in Title I schools have school options outside their own district. For instance, a school district may choose to enter into a cooperative agreement with another district that would allow their students to transfer into the other district's schools. In fact, the law requires that a district try "to the extent practicable" to establish such an agreement in the event that all of its schools have been identified as needing improvement, corrective action, or restructuring.

Is transportation available for children who exercise their right to attend another school? Subject to a funding cap established in the statute, districts must provide transportation for all students who exercise their school choice option under Title I. They must give priority to the lowest-achieving children from low-income families.

What are supplemental educational services? Supplemental educational services are additional academic instruction designed to increase the academic achievement of students in schools that have not met state targets for increasing student achievement (adequate yearly progress) for three or more years. These services may include tutoring and after-school services. They may be offered through public- or private-sector providers that are approved by the state, such as public schools, public charter schools, local education agencies, educational service agencies, and faith-based organizations. Private-sector providers may be either nonprofit or for-profit entities. States must maintain a list of approved providers across the state, organized by the school district or districts they serve, from which parents may select. States must also promote maximum participation by supplemental educational services providers to ensure that parents have as many choices as possible.

When are children eligible to receive supplemental educational services? Students from low-income families who remain in Title I schools that fail to meet state standards for at least three years are eligible to receive supplemental educational services.

Are parents notified about supplemental educational services? Yes. Local education agencies are required to provide annual notice to parents of eligible children about the availability of services and information on the approved providers.Can parents choose providers for tutoring and other supplemental educational services? Yes, parents of eligible children can choose from the list of state-approved providers. Most states have approved a diverse list of providers, as mentioned above. Upon request, the local education agency will help parents determine which provider would best fit their child's needs. When parents have made their selection, the local education agency must then contract with that provider to deliver the services.

What action can parents take if their child is eligible for tutoring or other supplemental educational services, but their school or district does not offer them? Districts receiving Title I funds must offer free tutoring and other extra help to eligible students, as described above. If eligible students are not being offered these services, parents are encouraged to contact their state department of education.

How are providers of supplemental educational services held accountable?
States must develop and apply objective criteria for evaluating providers and monitor
the quality of services that they offer. In addition, supplemental services providers must
give to parents, as well as to the school, information on their children's progress.

Teaching Methods Proven to Work

Under the No Child Left Behind Act, the federal government will invest in educational
practices that work—that research evidence has shown to be effective in improving student performance. Scientific research finds the best way to help those kids who need it
most. By using solid research we can get the best ideas to kids who will fail without
them. For example, an experiment might involve teaching two groups of children to
read using different methods and comparing the results to see which method is most
successful. Some children will learn to read with a variety of methods. Children having
problems learning to read need the most effective methods. Effective teaching and curricula can challenge children and interest them in learning—preventing problems of
violence, hyperactivity, and misidentification of learning disabilities. Thanks to scientific research, we know better ways to teach our children to read. We can do the same
in other areas. No Child Left Behind will bring solid, research-based programs to
schools throughout the nation. The following is a question and answer section about
No Child Left Behind.

**Does No Child Left Behind do anything to prevent bad or untested programs
from being used in the classroom?** For too many years, too many schools have
experimented with lessons and materials that have proven to be ineffective—at the
expense of their students. Under No Child Left Behind, federal support is targeted to
those educational programs that have demonstrated to be effective through rigorous
scientific research. Reading First is such a program. Programs and practices grounded
in scientifically based research are not fads or untested ideas; they have proven track
records of success. By funding such programs, No Child Left Behind encourages their
use, as opposed to the use of untried programs that may later turn out to be fads. Fur-
thermore, No Child Left Behind's accountability requirements bring real consequences to those schools that continually fail to improve student achievement as a result
of using programs and practices for which there is no evidence of success. Such schools
would be identified as needing improvement and required to make changes, as outlined
in the section on Accountability, including using education programs that are grounded
in scientifically based research.

What is scientifically based research? To say that an instructional program or practice is grounded in scientifically based research means there is reliable evidence that the
program or practice works. For example, to obtain reliable evidence about a reading
strategy or instructional practice, an experimental study may be done that involves using
an experimental/control group design to see if the method is effective in teaching children to read.

No Child Left Behind sets forth rigorous requirements to ensure that research is scientifically based. It moves the testing of educational practices toward the medical model used by scientists to assess the effectiveness of medications, therapies, and the like. Studies that test random samples of the population and that involve a control group are scientifically controlled. To gain scientifically based research about a particular educational program or practice, it must be the subject of such a study. Going back to the example of reading: No Child Left Behind requires that Reading First support those programs that teach children five skills (phonemic awareness, phonics, fluency, vocabulary, and comprehension). These skills have been shown to be critical to early reading success through years of scientifically based research on the practice of reading instruction. In April 2000, these research findings were reported in the congressionally mandated National Reading Panel report mentioned earlier; they have now been written into the new law.

How can parents find out about scientifically based research that applies to federal education programs, aside from the research on reading? In 2002, the Department of Education's Institute of Education Sciences (IES) established the *What Works Clearinghouse* to provide a central, independent, and trusted source of scientific evidence on what works in education for parents, educators, policymakers, and anyone else who is interested. All of the research collected and conducted by the clearinghouse follows the same high scientific standards as those used for reading research and will be available via the Internet from the clearinghouse or through the Department of Education's website. Parents may be able to use this information to find out about program and curricula selection at their child's school. The seven topics chosen for systematic review in the first year of the What Works Clearinghouse's operation reflect a wide range of our nation's most pressing education issues:

1. Interventions for Beginning Reading
2. Curriculum-Based Interventions for Increasing K–12 Math Achievement
3. High School Dropout Prevention
4. Peer-Assisted Learning in Elementary Schools: Reading, Mathematics, and Science Gains
5. Programs for Increasing Adult Literacy
6. Interventions to Reduce Delinquent, Disorderly, and Violent Behavior, in and out of School
7. Interventions for Elementary English Language Learners: Increasing English Language Acquisition and Academic Achievement

Over time, as the clearinghouse begins to produce its reports on these issues, parents will be able to ask their principal, teachers, and school board members about the extent to which they select programs and curricula that the research has determined to be effective. Under No Child Left Behind, educators are expected to consider the results of relevant scientifically based research—whenever such information is available—before making instructional decisions.

Teachers

The No Child Left Behind Act gives states and school districts the flexibility to find innovative ways to improve teacher quality, such as:

- Alternative ways of becoming a teacher, so that experienced professionals can become teachers faster
- Merit pay authorization enabling states and districts to reward good teachers and encourage them to stay in the profession
- Authorization to states and districts to give bonuses to teachers in high-need subject areas such as math and science to ensure that the United States remains competitive with the rest of the world in the twenty-first century.

No Child Left Behind protects teachers, principals, and other school professionals from harmful litigation when they take reasonable actions to maintain order and discipline in the classroom. Supporting teachers means giving them the very best tools—the best research-based lessons and materials and the best training—to ensure that no child is left behind.

INDEX

Grading systems, recommendations about, 204
Graduate Management Admissions Test (GMAT), 153
Group achievement tests, 220–222
Group rubric for evaluation, example of, 179, 180–182
Guessing in multiple-choice items, 132
Guided practice in Hunter's model, 60, 61–62

Head Start children, 73, 241
Hidden curriculum 73
Higher-order thinking and multiple-choice items, 133–134, 137, 138
Highly qualified teacher, definition of, 303–304, 305
High-stakes testing, 95, 218–219, 283
History questions, 108–109
Holistic rubrics, 176, 177
    example of, 177
Holistic scoring of essay items, definition of, 150
Homework self-assessment, example of, 113
Hostility, desire to gratify, 265
How Question in assessment, 128
Hunter's Model of Planning, 59–62, 66

Inclusion policies and practices, 17–18, 65, 200–201, 242–243
Independent practice in Hunter's model, 60, 62
Individual differences in assessment, 14–17
Individuals with Disabilities Education Act (IDEA), 18, 242, 243
Infants, toddlers, assessment of, 241–242
Informal assessments, 4, 26, 30, 94–142
    challenges, 113–116
    construction of, 100
    definition of, 95–96, 114
    informal analysis of, 39
    journaling, 100–102
    nonjudgmental nature of, 95–96, 97
    observational checklists, 110–111
    performance profile, 109–110
    questioning, 104–109
    and reflective teaching, 96–97
    self-assessment, 111–113
    student-centered, 97–100
    writing samples, 102–104
Informal curriculum, 73
Inquiry assignment for authentic assessment, 167–168
Instruction:

aligned with standards, 7
level compatibility with student level, 46
linked with assessment, 4–10, 19, 59–62
Instructional decisions, 8
Instructional feedback, 3, 4, 321
Instructional input in Hunter's model, 60, 61
Instructional materials, definition of, 9
Instructional objectives, 7, 19
Intelligence tests, 226–227
    abuses of, 218
    definition of, 217
    and gender, 84
Interpretive essay items, 146–148
Interscorer reliability in essay items, definition of, 149
Intrinsic motivation vs. extrinsic motivation, 270–271
Investigation assignment for authentic assessment, 169
Involuntary minorities, 75
Item analysis, 36–37, 39
Item difficulty, 36–37
Item discrimination, 37, 38

Journaling, 100–104

Kindergarten developmental checklist, example of, 203
Knowledge dimension of revised taxonomy, 52–53
    examples of, 56–57
Knowledge level of Bloom's Taxonomy, 47, 48
KWL response chart, 104

Language immersion programs, 80, 81
Language usage and test bias, 115
Latino American learning styles, 77
Lead exposure, 240
Learned helplessness, 268
Learner-centered principles, 98–99
Learning disabilities, 248–251
    assessment signs, 250–251
    causes of, 249
    definition of, 248
    language-related, 250
Learning styles, 99–100
    differences in, 75, 77–78
Least restrictive environment, 17–18
Lesson plans, 8–10
    definition of, 7